Treacherous Women of Imperial Japan

Other titles in the series:

Treacherous Women of Imperial Japan

Patriarchal fictions, patricidal fantasies

Hélène Bowen Raddeker

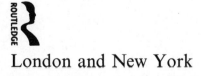

London and New York

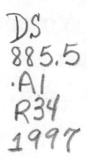

DS
885.5
·A1
R34
1997

First published 1997 by Routledge
11 New Fetter Lane, London EC4P 4EE

Simultaneously published in the USA and Canada
by Routledge
29 West 35th Street, New York, NY 10001

© 1997 Hélène Bowen Raddeker

Typeset in Times by BC Typesetting, Bristol
Printed and bound in Great Britain by
TJ International Ltd, Padstow, Cornwall

British Library Cataloguing in Publication Data
A catalogue record for this book is available from the British Library

Library of Congress Cataloging in Publication Data
Raddeker, Hélène Bowen, 1952–
    Treacherous women of imperial Japan: patriarchal fictions,
patricidal fantasies/Hélène Bowen Raddeker.
        p.   cm. – (Nissan Institute/Routledge Japanese studies
series)
    Includes bibliographical references and index.
    ISBN 0–415–17112–1 (alk. paper)
    1. Kanno, Sugako, 1881–1911. 2. Kaneko, Fumiko, 1902–1926.
3. Anarchists–Japan–Biography. 4. Socialist–Japan–Biography.
5. Japan–History–20th century–Biography. 6. Japan–Biography.
7. Meiji, Emperor of Japan, 1852–1912–Assassination attempt, 1910.
8. Taishō, Emperor of Japan, 1879–1926–Assassination attempt,
1923. 9. Hirohito, Emperor of Japan, 1901–1989–Assassination
attempt, 1923. I. Title. II. Series.
DS885.5.A1R34   1998
952.03′1′0922–dc21   97-23328
                                                                CIP

ISBN 0–415–17112–1

Contents

Acknowledgements

This book was over ten years in the making. In that total I would have to include three preparatory years in Japan as a Monbusho (Japanese Ministry of Education) research student as well as the few years it took to get the doctoral manuscript into book form. I have, therefore, 'lived with' and, I think, been on good terms with, Kanno Suga and Kaneko Fumiko for a good part of my life.

The individuals whose support I should acknowledge are innumerable, but I must first express my heartfelt thanks to Professor Gavan McCormack, my first supervisor in the History Department, La Trobe University, Melbourne. Without his faith in my abilities, I doubt I would have considered embarking even on Honours research.

My second supervisor, Dr Sandra Wilson, was also a constant source of encouragement and good advice. To her I extend my thanks for her sure grip on the editor's pen and patience in the face of my stubbornness. Inspiration and support has always been forthcoming also from Dr Vera Mackie of the Department of History, University of Melbourne.

During my first stay in Japan (1983–1986), I met many people who were kind and helpful. Apart from my supervisor, Professor Ōguchi Yūjirō, and Professor Tachi Kaoru, both of Ochanomizu Women's University, and also Professor Asukai Masamichi of Kyoto University, there were two who had already given me encouragement at La Trobe University in 1982: Professors Matsuzawa Tessei and Tsurumi Shunsuke. The latter acquainted me with the case of Kaneko Fumiko, and the respect with which he spoke of her led me to include her in my doctoral research. I could not fail to acknowledge also the inspiration and assistance provided by the anarchist publishers, Kokushoku Sensensha. Their bookshop and library – even their ancient photocopier – proved invaluable. To them I offer my gratitude, solidarity and best wishes for the future.

When I was finishing my doctoral thesis while teaching history at the University of Adelaide, I was also fortunate to receive the practical assistance of Dr Yoneyama Shōko in particular. She, Ms Aoki Naomi and Mrs Taguchi Kazuyo were all very patient in the face of persistent questioning on points of linguistic-cultural meaning. In this connection I must also thank a student, Mr Takabatake Ken, who once helped me to wade through some near-illegible handwritten documentation in Japanese.

There are others, too, to whom I would like to express my appreciation for the part they have played in my education, including, of course, my students, but I must acknowledge a huge debt to the History Department at La Trobe University. I was even more appreciative of the high level of discourse there on historiography and history theory when I began in 1990 to teach my own courses in modern and premodern Japanese history. That scholars there constituted a large part of my intellectual origins will be clear to some from the very beginning of this work.

Finally, my sincere thanks must also be extended to the solidarity offered by two comrades in the field, E. Patricia Tsurumi and John Crump, only one of whom I have been fortunate enough to meet as yet. To another 'comrade', distinguished Chinese historian, Dr Carney Fisher: 'Mata, ne!'

Hélène Bowen Raddeker
School of History
The University of New South Wales

Kanno Suga

Kaneko Fumiko

Part I
Preliminaries

1 Treason and treachery, documents and discourse

EULOGIES

Would anything at all remain for us of what they have been, in their violence or their singular misfortune, if they had not, at a given moment, collided with power and provoked its forces? After all, is it not one of the fundamental traits of our society that destiny takes the form of the relation to power, of the struggle along with or against it? The most intense point of lives, the one where their energy is concentrated, is precisely there where they clash with power, struggle with it, endeavour to utilise its forces or to escape its traps. The brief and strident words which come and go between power and the most unessential existences, are doubtless for the latter the sole monument that has ever been accorded to them; these words are what gives to them, in order to travel through time, the brief flash of sound and fury which carries them even to us.[1]

The 'in-famous' individuals spoken of here by Michel Foucault, in an essay entitled 'The Life of Infamous Men', were not so much notorious as obscure people whose 'crimes' were remarkable mostly for their ordinariness. Amongst these petty 'criminals' we find the 'scandalous monk', the 'battered woman', the 'inveterate and raging drunkard' and the 'quarrelsome merchant', but there are none accused of anything so grim as plotting regicide.[2] We find amongst them no allegedly treasonous subjects of the like of Kanno Suga (1881–1911) and Kaneko Fumiko (1903–1926). In another part of the world, Japan, at least a century and a half after Foucault's citizens collided with power, these two women achieved real 'infamy' when they were charged within fifteen years of each other, with conspiring to assassinate the reigning emperors. And, questions of their guilt or innocence of high treason aside, the conduct of both during the trials revealed them to be treacherous indeed. For Suga and Fumiko[3] were guilty of more than failing to honour the allegiance to the sovereign expected of modern Japanese citizens: each dared either to criticize or soundly condemn this 'godly father of the nation' or, rather, his creation and use as such for political ends in the name of the modern nation-state. In proudly taking up the name of 'traitor' – Suga as an anarchist, Fumiko as a nihilist – each of these undutiful daughters of the emperor set herself up in direct antagonism to the modern emperor-system.

The clashes with power that brought Kanno Suga and Kaneko Fumiko infamy were not as brief as those of Foucault's petty criminals – the brief 'monuments' to whose existences amount to no more than petitions (to the king), judgements and internment records. The first of the two Japanese legal cases lasted eight months, while the second extended over a period of two and a half years. Thus, the records of their exchanges with prosecutors and judges amount to rather more than a few 'brief and strident words'. In both cases, moreover, particularly Suga's, pre-imprisonment texts are extant. Yet despite the comparatively extensive documentation, we could still ask whether anything *would* have remained of them if not for their ultimate collisions with state power. Surely Kanno Suga would have been restored to history for other reasons: she was one of the first feminist-socialists in the early socialist movement in the Meiji era (1868–1912) and also one of the first female journalists in Japan. If the movement in recent decades to restore women to history had not occurred, her romance with Kōtoku Shūsui, the undisputed leader of the radical wing of the Meiji socialist movement, would have ensured her a place, albeit a small one, in the history books. Indeed, she was for a time treated as a romantic heroine largely by virtue of that relationship.[4]

In Kaneko Fumiko's case, on the other hand, it is doubtful that she would be known to history if she had not clashed with power. There was little amongst her activities before her imprisonment to suggest that even her name would be known to us today, if not for her subsequent notoriety. No doubt Fumiko would be amused by the irony of her accusers' securing her a place in history, something which few of them would be accorded. The mostly nameless police, prosecutors or judges involved in the case could not have foreseen that in one sense 'victims' like her would have the last say: power 'marked [her] with a blow of its claws', certainly, but it also 'instigated the few words which are left for us' of her life and her resistance.[5] Almost all of the available written and oral texts by Fumiko were produced in prison or the courtroom.

Yet there is another reason for the restoration to history of these two 'traitors': the manner of their deaths. For Suga and Fumiko not only collided with power, but died in the impact. The first was found guilty of *lèse majesté* and executed a week later on 25 January 1911; while the second was likewise sentenced to death in March 1926 but had her sentence commuted to life imprisonment soon after. This was a few months before her suicide, on 23 July 1926, was reported by prison authorities. It has been said that history is about dead people, and in one sense Suga and Fumiko could not be more dead to us – their deaths have *defined* them because scholars commonly associate them with political martyrdom. Their collision with power, therefore, is not in itself enough to account for the extent to which they are now known and respected in some circles in Japan as revolutionary heroes. And, of course, scholars have also contributed to the revolutionary immortality that is typically accorded someone who died at or in the hands of the state.[6]

TREACHERY RECONSIDERED

Whilst I shall discuss in detail in Chapter 2 the aims of this work, and its structural logic and methodology, I would make one further point both to effect a temporary closure to these preliminary reflections on 'eulogies' and open the way to later theoretical discussion. This is that the subjects' deaths have had a marked influence upon both the fact of their restoration to history and the ways in which they have been restored. Their deaths have been central to biographical reconstructions of their *lives* (and ascriptions of meaning to their lives), though this has not been acknowledged by those doing the restorations. When in prison each woman did *present* herself as either a self-sacrificing political 'martyr' only too happy to die for the Cause (Suga), or a self-assertive 'nihilistic' rebel who not only defied death but demanded the death penalty (Fumiko), but what we cannot forget is that this was resistance directed at an audience that included police, prosecutors, judges and other political opponents. Hence, my core question in Part II concerns not only the meanings that Suga and Fumiko themselves ascribed to their own deaths, but more the degree to which their participation in a public construction of their coming deaths was a *political* project.

What follows from this central focus is firstly the fact that, strictly speaking, while this book is about two women, it is not a work of gender analysis, even if social constructions of gender will often claim my attention. Furthermore, the book is about two individuals (women) whose political commitments were deemed by many contemporaries to be particularly 'treacherous', for a range of reasons that certainly included but also extended beyond their treasonous acts or ideas. Thus, it is not specifically about treason cases, even if I will be 'reading' texts, many of which (particularly in the case of Kaneko Fumiko) were produced within the context of trials for high treason. Nor, for that matter, is the focus of the work Japan's prewar and wartime emperor-system, though this too has an undeniable contextual importance. Broadly speaking, moreover, it might be about the lives and deaths of two individuals, yet it is not a developmental (narrative) work about the lives and ideas, the political careers of two individuals. It is not political biography. My structural inversion in Parts II and III of (engagements with) death followed by life (narratives) is the conscious opposite of linear, often teleological, life-narratives. Of more interest to me are the subject-positions constructed and claimed by Kanno Suga and Kaneko Fumiko in relation to the meanings they attributed to their own deaths and lives – and, further, how their self-presentations were weapons in an ideological war of words about social and political realities. More will be said subsequently about my theoretical inspirations and the 'structural' logic of the work. Firstly, however, some background detail about the two treason cases is called for in order to set the 'scene' for Part II.

THE HIGH TREASON INCIDENTS

The well-known Meiji High Treason Incident of 1910–1911 represented the culmination of a government policy of suppressing the young socialist movement. This policy was particularly severe during Katsura Tarō's second term as prime minister from July 1908 to August 1911. Therefore, of the well-known socialists who escaped the police drag-net in mid-1910, quite a few were already in prison and thus could not be accused of conspiracy. Ultimately, twelve out of twenty-six defendants were executed after being found guilty of contravening Article 73 of the Criminal Code, which read:

> Every person who has committed, or has attempted to commit, a dangerous (or injurious) act against [the person of] the Emperor, the Emperor's Grandmother, the Empress Dowager, the Empress, the Emperor's son, the Emperor's Grandson or the Heir to the throne shall be condemned to death.[7]

Twelve more of the accused first received the death sentence, but then had it commuted to life imprisonment through an imperial pardon, while the remaining two received lesser sentences. As F. G. Notehelfer points out, unfortunately for the defendants, the word translated here as 'attempted' (*kuwaen*) was ambiguous: it could be, and was, taken by the prosecution and judges to mean 'intended'; and this, in turn, meant that the trial would 'focus not on concrete acts, but on the question of "intent" . . . ideas, not facts.'[8]

Suga, the one woman amongst the twenty-six, had been involved in an anti-imperial plot unlike most of the defendants. On the grounds of intent, there is no doubt that she was guilty as charged. During the trial Suga not only spoke of receiving a letter from Miyashita Daikichi in January 1909 about his research into making bombs, but also about Uchiyama Gudō's visiting at about that time, saying he had managed to get hold of explosives from some miners.[9] According to Suga, Miyashita was one of the five defendants really involved in plans for an imperial assassination attempt; the others being Niimura Tadao, Furukawa Rikisaku and Kōtoku Shūsui.[10] Though she included Kōtoku in the number, she insisted that he had been sympathetic to the idea only at first.[11] Suga was actually referred to by defence lawyers then as the 'ringleader' of this 'conspiracy', even if prosecutors and judges had assumed the leader to be the well-known theorist of 'direct action', Kōtoku.

The defence lawyer, Hiraide Shū, believed that Suga and three others who had been involved in the plot *should* be sentenced to death, while Kōtoku and one other defendant should receive life imprisonment. There were five more defendants he thought deserving of five years' imprisonment, which leaves fifteen he apparently believed to be innocent.[12] It is easy to see why authors continue to refer to the case as a 'frame-up', or even suggest that Suga was one of those 'martyred': she had not, after all, actually *done* much at all. Still, the material evidence of 'anarchist chemistry', the trial testimonies of the co-conspirators, and also their personal testimonies (Suga's letters and prison diary, for example) make it clear that there was a conspiracy of sorts involving no more than a handful of people.

The less known and researched case of Kaneko Fumiko and Pak Yeol (J. Boku Retsu, legal Korean name Pak Choon Sik) is complicated by the issue of the atmosphere in which they were taken into 'protective custody' – each within a few days of the Great Kanto Earthquake of 1 September 1923.[13] Over a dozen members of their mainly *Korean* group of anarchists and nihilists, which they therefore ironically called the Futeisha (Malcontents' Society), were soon arrested as well. In the atmosphere of panic after the earthquake in which much of Tokyo and Yokohama was levelled, the infamous massacre of Koreans and other potential 'subversives' was already under way: several thousands were ultimately murdered by mobs of Japanese civilians, vigilantes, and civil or military police.[14] Unlike the Futeisha, many of the 'potential troublemakers' taken into protective custody did not survive it.

Fumiko and Pak Yeol were charged with vagrancy at first and detained for twenty-one days.[15] In the atmosphere of paranoid suspicion of '*futei senjin*' (malcontent Koreans), the authorities were taking no chances. Richard Mitchell observes that the 'vagrancy' charge was trumped up since police actually *created* Pak and Kaneko as vagrants to hold them while finding something else to charge them with. Police, it seems, urged their landlord to find new tenants and sell off their possessions because they wouldn't be back![16] Thus, on 20 October 1923, Kaneko, Pak, and the rest of the Futeisha[17] were charged with an infringement of the Public Peace Police Law (*Chian Keisatsu Hō*), to which a violation of the Explosives Control Law was added the following February. At this time all other members of the Futeisha but one were released. The one exception was Kim Choon Han who was charged with the explosives violation but not high treason. Kim Choon Han's lover, Niiyama Hatsuyo, first incriminated them, referring to Pak's attempts to procure bombs from Shanghai or Korea to use on the imperial family. Fumiko soon confessed to this in January 1924 (before Pak did).

Pak and Fumiko were specifically accused of trying to procure bombs from a Korean independence group based in Shanghai (K. *Ŭiyŏldan*, J. *Giretsudan*: 'Righteous Fighters Band'). This was through a comrade in Korea, apparently for the purpose of an attempt on the life of the emperor and crown prince. But in neither the Pak Yeol–Kaneko Fumiko treason case of 1925–1926 nor the Meiji High Treason Incident fifteen years earlier was material evidence (of acts or intent) deemed fundamental by investigators, prosecutors or judges. Certainly, Fumiko and Pak were sentenced mainly on the basis of their own confessions.[18] Fumiko had *not* been directly involved in the plans, it seems, so in effect she helped officials to 'frame' her. And therefore, finally on 17 July 1925 Fumiko and Pak were indicted for high treason (Article 73 of the Criminal Code) and the Supreme Court pretrial for this case began. According to the prewar Criminal Code, Article 295, the function of the preliminary hearing was to conduct an investigation to see whether there was enough evidence to warrant bringing the case to a public hearing.[19] One wonders, therefore, why the Meiji trial was closed, given that there was more material evidence than in the second case. Nevertheless, Fumiko's and Pak's public trial in the Supreme Court began on 26 February 1926 – at least it was public until the defendants' contemptuous attitude to the proceedings caused an uproar (largely of applause) which prompted the judge to close the court.

The two were sentenced to death on 25 March, but in ten days their death sentence was commuted to life imprisonment through a pardon issued by the emperor on the advice of the government. (The same had happened in the Meiji Treason Incident.) In part, the Cabinet headed by Wakatsuki Reijirō, prime minister from January 1926 to April 1927, had probably felt it inadvisable, in this case, to hang the defendants. On 27 December 1923, four months after Fumiko and Pak were arrested, there had been an actual attempt on the life of the then crown prince (Hirohito). This was the 'Toranomon [Sniper] Incident' involving a Japanese communist sympathizer, Nanba Daisuke, who was sentenced to death within one year, and hanged without delay. Also, only a few days after the Toranomon Incident there was an attempt on the life of the Taishō (1912–1926) emperor by a Korean named Kim Ji Sup. He was actually a member of the Ŭiyŏldan who had brought bombs with him from Shanghai.[20] Yet in this 'Nijūbashi Incident' at the imperial palace, Kim was sentenced only to life imprisonment. Perhaps in cases involving Koreans, whose homeland was under the 'paternal protection' of Japan, the Japanese authorities liked to make a show of benevolence, especially after widespread foreign censure over the post-earthquake massacre.

Morinaga Eisaburō remarks that Justice Ministry officials might have intended all along that Pak and Fumiko should receive life imprisonment.[21] The reason he gives for the commutation is the fact that their crime was an imperial assassination plan and not an actual attempt. This, however, had not stopped the Meiji judiciary from hanging twelve for a plot, and it does not entirely explain why the defendant in the Nijūbashi case only got life imprisonment. Hence, because of domestic and foreign censure of the Japanese government over the earlier massacre of Koreans, many commentators on the treason incident have expressed the view that, clearly, two scapegoats had been found. Pak and Fumiko were meant to be an illustration to the world that officials and police had been justified in their concerns over Korean subversives in Kanto early in September 1923.[22]

DOCUMENTS AND DISCOURSE

The texts that enable interpretation of Kanno Suga's and Kaneko Fumiko's constructions of death and life vary, both in their nature and in the difficulties they pose for the researcher. Contained in *Kanno Sugako Zenshū*[23] (her collected works) are journalistic writings and some poems from the period 1902 to 1909; personal letters, mostly from her last period of imprisonment from mid-1910; and the surviving portion of her prison diary entitled 'Shide no Michikusa' ('A Pause on the Way to Death').[24] Suga's journalistic texts will be utilized mainly in Part III of this book: 'Life-narratives'. The *Zenshū* also contains statements to the prosecution and testimonies from the preliminary proceedings. The actual Supreme Court records are not extant, and the pretrial documents only came to light at the end of the Second World War. The editor of the *Zenshū*, Shimizu Unosuke, notes that the diary was literally picked out from amongst the ashes of documents burnt by the Justice Ministry when the war ended. However, in Meiji, defence lawyer Hiraide Shū (and friends like the poet, Ishikawa Takuboku) had copied by hand some documents from the Supreme Court proceedings.[25] Finally, there are various collections of pretrial documents from the case that include the testimonies of all the defendants.[26]

From the Taishō legal case (1923–1926) an impressive number of records survive, copies of which have been produced by an anarchist publisher. These are the *Saiban Kiroku* (trial records) cited above, a magnificent volume of nearly 900 pages largely of testimonies of members of the Futeisha. It also contains records of witness interrogations pertaining to Fumiko's background from family and acquaintances. Copies of the magazines published by Pak, Fumiko and comrades (1922–1923) are also included in it. The same publisher, Kokushoku Sensensha, has produced a slim volume of Fumiko's prison poetry entitled *Akai Tsutsuji no Hana* (Red Azaleas), which also contains a few articles about her by contemporaries who knew her, as well as an interview with her mother conducted a few years after her death.[27]

Fumiko gave over 200 poems to a comrade, Kurihara Kazuo. He and other comrades managed to decipher some of those censored, and published a few in May 1926 while Fumiko was still alive. The few that were dated were written in the latter half of 1925. Apart from this, her prison memoirs, probably written before mid-1925 and first published not long after her death by comrades, have been reprinted in the postwar period more than once.[28] They are also now available in both partial and full English translation.[29] Fumiko did not give her manuscript any title, but in the postscript she wrote: '*What made me like this?* [my emphasis]. . . . Readers with compassion should understand . . . from my memoir.'[30] The original manuscript was ultimately given to Futeisha member Kurihara Kazuo by Preliminary Court Judge Tatematsu Kaisei and first published in 1931. Finally, there is also available the above-cited biography of Pak Yeol written by their lawyer, Fuse Tatsuji. It includes a lengthy section about Fumiko's ideas, and also some extracts from her prison testimonies.

As for the difficulties confronting the researcher who seeks to use trial records, the most important is the fact that, for a few reasons, confessions are of dubious reliability. That a defendant might admit to something does not necessarily make it true, even if, in the Japanese legal system, confession was (and is) regarded as the 'king of evidence' (*shokō no ō*).[31] The first problem to confront, however, is the possibility that records of confessions were invented or seriously distorted by interrogators. But if this were the case, surely surviving defendants, defence lawyers or others closely involved in the cases would have revealed it before now, given that the documents came to light at the end of the war. Pak Yeol survived the war in prison, as did his socialist lawyer, Fuse Tatsuji. At least four defendants in the earlier case also survived it and the defence-lawyer, Hiraide Shū, not only hand-copied trial records but wrote 'fictional' treatments of the trial that are consistent with preliminary trial records. Fuse Tatsuji, on the other hand, discussed Fumiko's ideas in such a way as to make it clear that in his view the records of her testimonies are accurate. Furthermore, one only has to compare her early testimonies, where she told the judge her life-story, with her actual memoirs to see that the latter is a repetition of the former, albeit in more detail. It is highly improbable that a significant part of this could have been invented.

It is also important to note that both Kaneko Fumiko and Pak Yeol consistently refused to talk to prosecutors, probably because of suspicions that they were more likely to distort their words. They refused to recognize the prosecutors' authority to interrogate them about any serious crime – with which, during the preliminaries, the two had not yet been charged.[32] Therefore, in their case the legal records available are of formal interrogations by judges, whether in court or in 'closed' pre-trial interrogation rooms. Of course, in prewar Japanese prisons various types of mental or physical pressure were applied, and torture practised. While the use of torture might have been proscribed (and trials based on evidence introduced in 1879), it was commonly used because of a preference for confessions as evidence.[33] Fumiko and Pak might not have been tortured, but their case does reveal how the authorities were able to trick or browbeat even intransigent defendants (like Pak) into confessions by reading the transcripts of confessions by other defendants to them.[34] None the less, the testimonies of different defendants in both treason cases can be checked against each other for verification, and against other writings like memoirs, diaries, poetry, personal letters and voluntary statements in court. Also included in the *Saiban Kiroku* from the second case are copies of written statements (really political treatises) by both Pak and Fumiko.

Despite the extensive documentation in the second treason case, however, it is still difficult to gauge with any certitude whether there was any *serious* plan afoot for imperial assassinations: perhaps Pak had already abandoned the idea by the time he was arrested. Perhaps both, not just Fumiko, exaggerated their practical guilt of conspiracy, and thus treason. Naturally, this would still make them guilty of being determined opponents of Japanese imperialism and the emperor-system: their refusal to play the game according to the rules of the Japanese state and legal system is in itself an indication of their 'treachery'. In fact, for the purposes of this study, Fumiko's eventual admission that she had pretended to be more guilty than she was – which was almost certainly not an attempt to evade the death penalty – renders her style of resistance even more interesting. The irony is that, by using prison documents *to interpret the meanings she ascribed to life and death*, we might come nearer to the facts of her case than those who simply dismiss the trial as the invention of paranoid police, prosecutors and judges. Inventive they might have been, even paranoid, but Fumiko did little to disabuse them of their delusions.

This leads me to comment on one further irony with which I will conclude: that perusal of Pak's and Fumiko's testimonies leaves one wondering why the authorities did not release such documents for publication. There was more public criticism of this second case so, if they had done, there would have been fewer public suspicions that it was *only* the government that had forged 'conspiracies'. After it was attacked by the opposition party in the Diet over its handling of the case, the government was eventually forced to admit that its case against the defendants was not strong because of the absence of material evidence.[35] The Rikken Seiyūkai had not raised the issue out of suspicions of a frame-up, but rather over a too 'lenient' treatment of the two defendants in prison and the courts.[36] Given the government's admission of a lack of evidence, public knowledge of the defendants' confessions would have lessened suspicions of a government conspiracy; and there might also have been less of a tendency to eulogize Fumiko as a revolutionary martyr or *victim* of the state after her death. To prefigure topics addressed in the next chapter,

I might observe that eulogies might then have involved a recognition of Fumiko's many-faceted refusal to play the game according to the rules of first confessing and then throwing oneself on the mercy of self-styled benevolent 'patriarchs'.

2 The work (structure, logic, method)

INTRODUCTION

This chapter is about the 'I' of the text. It concerns the theory, structural logic and methodology that has informed my writing of this book. Since the advent of the 'new history' in recent years and, more generally, self-reflexive scholarship, it now seems unnecessary to make any pretence at authorial invisibility. The influences upon both this self-reflexivity and what I have termed my 'structural' logic have been various: firstly, the 'Melbourne School' of ethnographic history,[1] whose synchronic style and critique of ('diachronic') linear narrative history was surely partly informed by structuralist critiques, for example Claude Lévi-Strauss' classic essay, 'History and Dialectic' in *The Savage Mind*. That essay brings to mind Hayden White's arguably equally 'classic' commentary on it in *Tropics of Discourse*.[2] I have also found inspirational various structuralist and poststructuralist, feminist and postfeminist works too numerous to cite at this point.

As to the specifics of this 'structuralist' logic, I have already called attention to the fact that this is not a work of narrative or biography, but is inverted to begin with the subjects' deaths or, rather, their *political representations* of death. I begin in Part II by foregrounding death, the teleological 'end-point' of a life often submerged or hidden in/from the beginning of the text in conventional life-writing (biography and autobiography); and try to pay strict attention throughout, to the im-mediate or unmediated contexts in which Kanno Suga and Kaneko Fumiko spoke of their selves in relation to death and life, and to the audiences to whom they spoke. Further, since my object is not to determine in empiricist fashion 'the Truth' of the life-construct of any particular speaker, in Part III I compare and contrast what Suga and Fumiko said about their lives with what contemporaries – comrades, families, intimates – had to say about them.

What my remarks so far should suggest is that structuralist and post-structuralist theory has partly informed my approach, not only to representation and power, but also to life-writing. Regarding the latter, it has led me to doubt that Suga and Fumiko set out to construct themselves as the 'unique, self-creating I' of liberal–humanist autobiography.[3] As I have argued elsewhere, Suga or even the very egoistic Fumiko was very much the creature of her world; thus each had a collective mission while *simultaneously* being engaged in carving out for herself a Subject-position that created her in the role of the autonomous individual.[4]

My hypothesis and approach concerning self-presentation and empowerment, moreover, have hinged partly upon a critique, common enough these days, of the tendency in early 'second-wave' metropolitan feminism to represent female historical actors solely as victims. In our justifiable concern with women's oppression there was long a tendency to lose sight of women's agency: the ways in which women were/are or can be *both* objects of oppression and agentic individuals.[5] Perhaps this blindness to agency has been the case particularly with works of history about Japanese women. It seems that the 'Madame Butterfly' construct of Japanese femininity is long in the deconstructing, to wit: 'The "treacherous" *Japanese* subjects of your research were not just *anarchists*, but *female* ones?' [*sic*] Hence, this book is about the subjectivity claimed by two prewar Japanese women who might have achieved notoriety because of their treachery, but were none the less no less agentic than many other Japanese women and men who earlier this century resisted, in a multitude of ways, imperialism and/or the emperor-system.

Since Foucault's rethinking of power relations has been found useful by many a feminist,[6] I will henceforth continue with my reflections on power, agency and 'eulogies' to 'martyrs', ultimately with further reference to his observations about his 'in-famous men'. There is always a danger that martyrology might degenerate into martyrolatry. But this at least suggests not pity for a victim so much as esteem for a fighter. It might be natural to eulogize fighters such as Suga or Fumiko – lament the conditions of their passing due to power arbitrarily abused – but one needs, none the less, to be careful to recognize the part they played in bringing about their own 'destiny'. Martyrdom implies varying degrees of voluntary action on the part of the 'martyr'. While individuals might be put to a death they did not actively seek, if it was for persisting in a faith or political practice, then that in itself implies an element of choice or free will.[7] On the other hand, a concern with agency might lead one to represent Suga and Fumiko as having been more in control of their fates than their circumstances would suggest. Women have too often been represented as the passive victims of patriarchy, capitalism, society, men or, in Japan, the family- and emperor-systems, but one still needs to be wary of overreacting to this and making it appear as if they were/are not victims at all. Nor should one forget that some women were/are happy to help create and further systems based upon an oppression of women.

In works about revolutionaries, active opponents of the state often, upon 'defeat', suddenly become its passive and innocent victims – arrested unjustly, 'framed', and so on.[8] To remind oneself that the losers had been engaged in a fight, which perhaps continued even after their arrests, does not necessitate making a judgement about whether or not the combatants were equally matched and the fight fair or by the rules. Whether Fumiko was 'framed' or not, one must acknowledge the creative part *she* played in determining her own fate, both before being arrested and during the trial. By defiantly admitting or even inventing their guilt or by using the courtroom as a political forum, surely Suga and Fumiko were using what power they had at their disposal. Merely the telling or writing of their life-stories during their imprisonments must have been *meant* to empower them because they ascribed meaning to their own lives and deaths, and presented their versions of social reality, in an explicitly counter-hegemonic ideological fashion.

Concerning my readings of what they meant, moreover, by arguing that meaning is social or cultural, not locked up inside the heads of historical actors, June Philipp has rejected claims that ethnographic historians concerned with meaning are, in effect, reviving traditional positivist history.[9] Other scholars working in the area of the 'new history' in Japan Studies, like H. D. Harootunian, have also questioned the positivist assumption that human motivation or intention is knowable. He argues for a need to focus on discourse, thus seeking to avoid the problem of intentionality.[10] Likewise, the author of a work specifically on postmodernism, Hilary Lawson, speaks of a 'gradual abandonment' since Nietzsche of a focus in traditional philosophy on the unique 'experience, morality, choice and will', hence motives, of the individual (humanist) subject.[11] Indeed, a deconstructive project such as this, which is focused on discursive representations of the meaning of death and life, is premised upon a perceived need to circumvent the problem of 'getting into heads'. *As far as is possible*, I avoid ascribing conscious ('private') intention to the subjects, though even a project concerned with constructs, with effects rather

than motives, cannot entirely avoid the problem of intentionality –
that is, if 'any meaning is to some extent intentional', as Paul de
Man once observed. He went on to explain that this is not to say
that the subject necessarily controls altogether, its own discourse or
mode of meaning: the way in which 'I' mean may not be intentional
because I am forced to depend upon linguistic devices not made by
me.[12] Meaning is not simply a matter of individual psychology because
it is not only linguistically, but also socially produced and shared. If
one seeks to understand what Suga and Fumiko *meant* when speaking
to various audiences, one needs to try to put oneself both into their
'shoes' rather than their 'heads', and also listen with an ear attuned
to temporal and cultural differences.

The subjects' constructions of death and life were not produced in
an historical or social vacuum. Suga and Fumiko each participated
in an ongoing political discourse about death and life. The ways in
which they constructed (the social realities of) life and death must
therefore be viewed through a culture shared with others: 'Getting
inside actions . . . is a means of reconstructing the experience and
meanings expressed by people in the past who were conversing, in
public, amongst themselves.'[13] If, for Philipp, the meanings of actions
are not private, but public or social, interpreting them does not require
a foray into the realms of psychohistory or psychobiography. Nor
does it justify letting the texts speak for themselves and accepting surface meanings that appear to be self-evident – despite distances of time
and culture, and also a 'confusion of tongues'.[14] Historical actors
expected 'that their actions could be and would be read and understood', Philipp explains, warning that the 'process of expression,
expectation, communication, and understanding, was historically situated; it was situated in a particular context of shared or common
experience and familiar forms of discourse.' For historians to be
able 'to read past action', or try to grasp the sense they had in that
time and place, they must try to reconstruct its context.[15]

MORE DEFINITIONS: POWER, IDEOLOGY, POLITICAL CULTURE

The issue of eulogies to 'martyrs' demands a reconsideration of the
nature of power. Foucault, the historian for whom power is omni-
present, seems at first sight in 'The Life of Infamous Men' to concep-
tualize it as omnipotent. In this essay, state power, the sort of power
usually seen to be hovering threateningly above, first *appears* to be a
reified, personified sort of power because it looked down upon and

'lay in wait for' people; it was something 'which spied on them, which pursued them, which turned its attention' to them and, finally, 'marked them with a blow of its claws'.[16] This *seems* to have been a (state) power that could be 'collided with'; that was separate and apart. Thus far, the language Foucault uses (and I have also used) seems to suggest a binary opposition, whereby there are two poles; with no grey area, for one either has power or has not, one either *is* 'power' or is not.

However, Foucault proceeds in this essay to point out that one could see petitions to a king for a judgement on the actions of a third party as a sharing in so-called 'absolutist' power: 'Everyone could make use of the enormity of absolute power for themselves . . . and against others'; everyone had the potential to become 'a terrible and lawless monarch for another' by using petitions, the 'mechanisms of sovereignty'.[17] What he seeks to do here, as elsewhere, is undermine dichotomous conceptions of power. Here we see how an individual, who might appear to be powerless in the face of a source of obvious, apparently overwhelming power, can 'appropriate this power, at least for a moment, channel it, tap it and inflect it in the direction one wants . . . make use of it . . . "seduce" it'.[18] This is another way of saying *with Marx* that people are seldom, if ever, mere creatures who passively allow forces to act upon them. They too act, and continually participate in creating their own circumstances. People are *both* creatures and creators of their worlds.

It cannot be denied that Kanno Suga and Kaneko Fumiko were the 'victims' of power – its objects – but it must be allowed that they were also its subjects. However great the imbalance of power, we do not have to see them as either power*ful* or power*less*. While many authors recognize the defiant stand taken by both women, in my view they have not gone beyond surface appearances to consider the *many* ways in which Suga and Fumiko interacted with state power. Hane Mikiso suggests that there was a part of Fumiko that did not want to escape the net she was caught up in, but he does it in such a way as to imply a dismissal of her as psychologically unbalanced: 'Kaneko seems to have been driven by a *death wish*.' He says of both Suga and Fumiko that they 'courted death' – were 'driven to the edge in their *fanatical* determination to stand up to the authorities [my emphases]'.[19] Despite the fact that looking at power from another angle has the potential to be equally one-sided, we may be able to come closer to grasping some of the complexities of power relations by considering how to some extent these 'victims' chose and even directed their own destinies – or at least wanted to be *seen* as being in control of their own fates. I do not seek to prove that it was Suga and Fumiko who were power*ful*, that they really 'won' in the end, though this might have been what *they* were trying to prove.

These two women have often been treated almost as if they were drawn against their will into the final round of a fight, which of course they could not 'win'. This has been the case particularly with Fumiko. But they were engaged in this fight both before and after their respective arrests. When in prison, moreover, they said what police, prosecutors and judges believed *could* not be said about the 'living god-father of the nation', the emperor. As each of the trials progressed, the subjects' treacherous statements would have been enough to convince the authorities of the need to secure a conviction for the supreme 'thought crime' of a lack of reverence for the emperor and respect for his agents. Whatever the precise facts of these 'conspiracies', Suga and Fumiko had already made their political choices regarding radical ideas and alliances. These choices were, by definition, opposed to the emperor-system; and they were informed choices. In a political climate that was undeniably repressive, neither woman could have discounted the possibility that her political practice might in one way or another decide her 'destiny'. John Crump has pointed out that left-wing treatments of the 'iniquity' of the Meiji High Treason Incident have been somewhat naive: it is as if the capitalist state's monopoly of the means of violence to enforce 'law and order' (in the interests of 'all') could be expected to be 'fair'.[20] Fumiko, certainly, had no such expectation. Her nihilist subject-position or, for that matter, Suga's anarchist one, was in itself a declaration of war.

Also concerning 'power', I should note that whilst I might speak of their strategies of self-em*power*ment, of course neither Suga nor Fumiko used this or similar terminology. For them, *P*ower (or 'authority') was something separate and apart; something that they had no relation to, and wanted no share in.[21] They tended to conceive of power as state power; their perception was of a world divided into those with power and those without it, even if they themselves were actually engaged in a (power) struggle with it. They treated it as their own exclusive opposite. Thus, for Suga its future negation would be 'anarchism'; while for Fumiko (only initially during her imprisonment) 'nihilism' represented the negation, in her words, the 'annihilation' of power, humanity and Life.

If Suga's and Fumiko's perceptions of power were more dualistic than dialectical, this also raises the issue of their notion of 'ideology'. Amongst Marxist and other theorists there have long been critics of conspiracy theories of ideology as the exclusive possession of the ruling class and necessarily a deception or deliberate 'mask' for reality.[22] Suga and Fumiko, however, would have seen no reason to dispense with such theories. For them the production of an 'ideology' was the preserve of 'Power'. Therefore, while I myself might be inclined to speak of ideological production generally, on occasion referring to 'dominant' or 'hegemonic' as well as other ideologies, when discussing what Suga and Fumiko seemed to be intent on doing I prefer to put it in terms of their countering, contesting, or even *unmasking* 'ideological deceptions'.

A final point about power and ideology relates to the 'isms' (*shugi*) with which each woman set out, often quite intentionally, to fight or negate 'Power'. One needs to consider at some length what 'anarchism' meant to Suga and 'nihilism' to Fumiko. Rather than defining such terms in advance, I prefer to allow their meanings for the subjects to unfold throughout the text. That being said, however, the one thing that does demand some explanation is 'nihilism' which, in a Japanese context, has at least three common meanings: 1) a political doctrine associated with nineteenth-century Russian populist terrorism; 2) philosophical moral nihilism associated particularly with Nietzsche and others like Max Stirner; 3) negative dialectics in Mahayana Buddhism (for example, Zen). The second of these is the most pertinent to Fumiko's understanding of it, though I suspect that her nihilism was an amalgam of all three.

Attempting to define such 'isms' in advance with confident precision would not only imply the use of a yardstick made elsewhere, in Europe, for example; it would also suggest a static treatment of doctrines that the subjects continued to utilize and develop in a discourse about life, death and social realities. One certainly could not take even the ideas they adhered to when imprisoned to be finished, immobile products, for this would be to ignore the impact of their trials and incarcerations. According too much prominence to such 'recognizable' doctrines could also be taken to mean that only the *explicitly political* ideas of the subjects are pertinent. One needs to be wary of narrow definitions of politics, that, in line with public–private distinctions, would exclude from, say, a 'political' biography aspects of an individual's experience deemed unimportant because 'personal'. As my interest is in the subjects' *social* constructions of death and life, the focus here needs to be broad enough to encompass a *political* discourse that includes both mundane and ontological, even 'metaphysical' considerations.

Hence I look at the death- and life-constructs of Suga and Fumiko within the context of a 'political culture' that I define broadly, both in this sense and in the sense that this culture was internally differentiated and dynamic. It was not singular but subject to complex internal variation, contestation and change. Further, it was not 'purely' Japanese but subject to external influences. The approach to Meiji and Taishō 'political culture' which is taken here, therefore, firstly involves a recognition that that culture had diverse strands. Secondly, it represents a dialectical attempt to take a 'middle way' between two conceptual tendencies: one that too narrowly focuses on cultural difference (e.g., Japanese 'uniqueness'), and another that, in too totalizing (perhaps 'West'-centric) a style, opts for generalities or universality in human behaviour and organization.[23] I therefore look closely at the question of the subjects' Japanese cultural identity in Chapters 5 and 6, at the extent to which it had a bearing on their political commitments and strategies.

PATERNALISM AND PATRICIDE

Concerning the 'patriarchal fictions' referred to in the book's sub-title, I would first observe that in a political system founded on a complex metaphor of paternalism that extended all the way up to the monarch as another supreme 'god, the father', it is to be expected that some would come to entertain thoughts of the ultimate form of 'patricide'. Suga certainly did, while Fumiko at least lauded the idea in court. Paternalism was a pervasive metaphor for social relations of all descriptions from Tokugawa (1603–1867) through Meiji and Taishō and beyond. This brings to mind the bitter criticism of the Tokugawa socio-political system by Andō Shōeki, a samurai doctor and scholar. In the mid-eighteenth century Andō had argued that in an ideal state of nature:

> there is no distinction between between high and low . . . no exploitation of those below for luxury and greed. . . . Since there are no selfish teachings . . . there are no distinctions between the sages and the foolish. There are no samurai who criticize the misconduct of the common people and strike them on their heads. . . . Since there is no teaching about filial piety, no one flatters or hates his parents and no one commits parricide. Since there is no artificial teaching about benevolence, there are no fathers who drown themselves emotionally in the love of their children, nor parents who hate their children. . . . The world is a unity. There is no duality.[24]

Here Andō explicitly referred to the logical connection between the
ideology of 'benevolent' paternalism and parricide, while also dismissing the ways of the sages, buddhas and gods as mere 'ideology . . . an
excuse to rob the people'.[25] Paternalism was an intrinsic part of
late Tokugawa ideological orthodoxy, the core of which was neo-
Confucianism with its emphasis on fixed and eternal binary distinctions between heaven and earth, rulers and ruled, fathers and sons,
men and women. By the early 1900s, however, it took on an expanded
political meaning.

Even before the Meiji Imperial Restoration of 1868 there had begun
a gradual mythological construction of the emperor as 'divine father
of the nation'. In Meiji this came to obscure demands for unquestion-
ing political obedience and loyalty ('filial' piety) towards those who
ruled in his name beneath a 'veil' of quasi-religious mystification.[26]
Carol Gluck comments on this remaking of the emperor as follows:

> [T]he late 1880s and 1890s saw the emperor become the manifesta-
> tion of the elements associated with national progress as the Meiji
> elite defined it, and the symbol of national unity, not of a political
> and legal, but of a patriotic and civic kind. Then . . . [he] was
> also turned toward social ends. As the patriarch of a family-state
> he became the symbolic representation of harmony and as the
> descendant of the sun goddess, the deified evidence of the ancestral
> ethnicity of the Japanese.[27]

According to this grand patriarchal familial myth, the Japanese people
were all children of this 'living god' whose family claimed direct succession from a deity said to be the highest in the pantheon. Ironically,
this was the female sun god, Amaterasu Ō-mikami, offspring of the
('imperial' tribe's > clan's > family's) founding gods of Japan. The
people of Japan were therefore children who could expect to live in
a divinely bestowed condition of 'harmony' so long as they paid
heed to their 'benevolent' fathers, both supreme and lesser.

I shall leave it to Jon Halliday to explain further about this 'familial'
nation-narrative:

> Though the 'family-state' ideology incorporated earlier elements, it
> cannot be identified with the forms of repression practiced at the
> start of the Meiji period. Only in the late Meiji period did the
> system take on its full distinctive form. . . . The Confucian-type
> familistic ethic provided the real foundation for the society, and
> increasingly, from the late Meiji period on, Japanese ideologists
> spoke of the nation as an 'extended family'. The nation was not

like a family, it really *was* a family. This national family, supported from below by the socio-ethical patterns of individual households, was then 'sanctified from above by Shintō beliefs which imbued it with a quality of sacredness.' The 1889 Constitution contributed to this by declaring the Emperor 'sacred and inviolable.'[28]

Speaking of the Ministry of Education's final revision by 1910 of school textbooks, Halliday proceeds to discuss how these now incorporated the hegemonic family-state ideology in language simple enough even for elementary school children.

> These new 1910 texts demand filial piety and obedience, and seek to transfer familial loyalties upwards to the Emperor by identifying Emperor-loyalty with filial piety. The favourite expression in these texts is *chūkō no taigi* ('the great loyalty-filial principle') in which loyalty (*chū*) and filial piety (*kō*) are fused into a single concept. Emperor-loyalty is then fused with patriotism . . . into one expression: *chūkun aikoku* (roughly, 'patriotic Emperor-loyalty'). Finally, Shinto mythological tradition is mobilized to infuse Emperor-loyalty and patriotism with sacred absoluteness. Moreover, the 1910 texts present Shintō mythology as believable historical fact, thus further fusing history and myth – and, of course, by debasing 'fact', strengthening irrationality, mystification and repression.[29]

Such a mystification was well under way in Suga's time, but far more refined, socially diffused and therefore familiar to people throughout society by the 1920s. Fumiko would have had such an education. Partly due to this, no doubt, she opposed the emperor-system in a more systematic way than Suga, to the extent of responding directly to the above-mentioned State Shintō-derived 'irrationality'.

How, then, should we view the crime that Suga and Fumiko were accused of: conspiracy to commit 'regicide', 'deicide', or 'patricide'? When governmental and other ideologues create a deified father-figure for a 'harmonious' nation – and justify 'natural' social hierarchies and political repression in his name – one can be sure that some will come to note the contradiction, and see assassination as a logical counter-ideological step and symbolic necessity. Carol Gluck has remarked on increased social perceptions, by the 1920s and 1930s, of a glaring disparity between individuals' lived experience and emperor-system/State Shintō ideology.[30]

The light in which Suga and Fumiko each saw the emperor suggested a critique of his paternal aspect in the first instance (though a rather ambivalent one); and his godly one in the second. Suga confessed to an intention to blow up the head of state, who was not directly but symbolically responsible for repression; while Fumiko claimed she had participated in a plan to demystify (with bombs) the god-emperor, symbol of social inequalities. Their professed intentions to kill him could be viewed as more in line with patricide in the first case, deicide in the second. This has a certain logic for other reasons: for, even though Suga was a 'feminist', who might be expected to be automatically suspicious of patriarchs, she was mostly concerned about political repression in the name of a 'father' she partly *esteemed*. Fumiko's primary concern, on the other hand, was not only with a social but also racial/ethnic inequality that was partly derived from the notion of Japan as the 'land of the gods' (the imperial ancestors), and the Japanese race as the divine children of the gods. She had lived for several years in colonized Korea and had seen the brutal results of such a myth.

Referring to Suga, Irokawa Daikichi observes that this first treason incident revealed the fact that 'the emperor system was not a compassionate all-enveloping embrace but a tyranny that would stop at nothing to eliminate heresy'; it was 'a self-contradicting system that concealed within the shadows of its harmoniousness' a cold brutality.[31] Japan was/is usually styled as a uniquely consensual nation in which people knew their place in a social hierarchy guided by 'father-figures' of various descriptions, at various levels of society. Amongst them, there were some whose specific duty it was to mete out punishment to wayward children, bring them to submission and shame – and in many cases, then forgive them. Fumiko's case was just before the official policy of *tenkō* (encouraging political offenders to recant) was introduced in 1931, but already by 1928 evaluation of suspects' 'state of repentance' had become part of standard police evaluations.[32]

During their respective imprisonments, both Suga and Fumiko must have come into contact with any number of 'fatherly' officials, but each was favoured by the attentions of one in particular: Prosecutor Taketomi Wataru in Suga's case, and Preliminary Court Judge Tatematsu Kaisei in Fumiko's. Tatematsu was a very significant figure in the second treason case. Though only a judge in the Tokyo District Court, at the end of 1925 he was appointed to the Supreme Court pretrial because the defendants were more likely to co-operate with him. There might have been various reasons for their willingness to 'co-operate'. For example, after Fumiko's death the press got hold of a photograph taken by Tatematsu of the couple in an intimate pose *in the courtroom* – Fumiko sitting on Pak's lap, his left hand resting on her breast. When Tatematsu was accused by the press of having been too lenient toward the couple, it was said that he left them alone in the courtroom to indulge in their 'scandalous behaviour', allowed Fumiko ('conjugal'?) visits to Pak's cell, and so on. The accusations were partly true, probably because Tatematsu realized quite early that he would get no co-operation from them unless he humoured them. According to Pak Yeol, Tatematsu showed 'respect' for their political stand, yet there are signs that he played on their impulses to heroism in order to get them to incriminate themselves.[33] His presenting himself as a kindly father-figure concerned for the welfare of wayward children would not have been an unusual tactic at the time, especially given the state's efforts to foster the ideology of national familism in the interests of social harmony and political obedience. When dissidents were later encouraged to confess, recant and thereby be reintegrated into society as part of the official policy of ideological conversion (*tenkō*), a common ruse of interrogators was to harp on thought-crime offenders' lack of filial piety – to immediate and/or supposedly 'national' families.

Certainly by late Taishō, the paternalism metaphor was all-pervasive, but it was hardly 'unique' or unusual. Inga Clendinnen, writing about Spanish Franciscans and their Yucatan Indian 'wards', says that paternalism:

> is a comfortably capacious metaphor. We would be mistaken if we saw its content as solely or necessarily benevolent. There are fathers and fathers. Some loving fathers punish most tenaciously; the profound ambivalence of the consciously loving father towards his child-victim is only now beginning to be explored. In the very violence of the response of the Yucatan friars to that first discovery of the 'treachery' of their Indians we see something of the emotion-charged punitive rage of the betrayed parent.[34]

The Maya continued to engage in 'heathen' practices after baptism, and were therefore punished most severely by their stern but loving 'fathers'. 'Traitors' – amongst both the Maya in the sixteenth century and early twentieth-century Japanese rebels – suffered for acting upon a view of reality that did not accord with that of their 'protectors'. Diego de Landa, the inquisitor, and Prosecutor Taketomi or Judge Tatematsu, it seems, had much in common. Rhys Isaac also refers to a 'comprehensive metaphor of fatherhood' or *'patriarchalism'*: his Virginian variant extended from the slave-owner who was both father and judge up to the Father-Creator.[35] An interesting point of difference between Isaac's Father-Creator and the Japanese emperor, however, was that the emperor was not represented as 'alternately harsh and merciful', only the latter, though others more stern acted in his name.

Suga and Fumiko may have recognized from experience the 'punitive rage of the betrayed parent' when they encountered it in Japan's prisons and courts. Apart from their own biological fathers who, according to their own accounts, fitted the image of stern fatherhood rather well, they remarked on others whose true character did not at all reflect the requisite balance of sternness and benevolence. But Suga's and Fumiko's counter-ideological representations of 'fathers' aside, what we need to keep in mind is that while some 'paternal' figures may well have been consciously practising a deception, it is possible that others were not – entirely. There is good reason to suspect that Prosecutor Taketomi was, for he was said to have bragged later that he 'buttered Suga up', getting her to talk of personal matters so she would see him as sympathetic and therefore 'talk'.[36] (She had at first refused to speak to him at all, because he was an old 'enemy' of hers.) But one could hardly fail to see the *ambivalence* in the relationship between Fumiko and Judge Tatematsu. His treatment of her suggests that some 'fathers' firmly believed in their paternal role of 'moral guidance'. It was, after all, Judge Tatematsu who delivered to a comrade of Fumiko's her prison memoirs. It was he who had first asked her to write an account of her life explaining further how her treatment by family and society had led her to nihilism. What, indeed, would have remained of her today, if not for the 'profound ambivalence' of this punitive and loving father?

In sum, it seems to me that this aspect of the emperor-system, its *all-pervasive* paternalism or 'patriarchalism', has been overlooked in works of prewar Japanese history. While any number of works of women's or feminist history of late do, of course, note the strongly patriarchal aspects of Meiji and Taishō legal, institutional and familial history (both traditional and reinvented),[37] to my mind they do not engage adequately with paternalism. I can think of no work that attempts a thorough, sustained critique of the way in which paternalism was fostered anew in Meiji and came to permeate, not just labour–management relations, for example, but society as a whole. Perhaps we need to direct our attention more to those individuals who contested it, particularly those most likely to be patronized – and not only in the family but also in 'public' life, for example, the legal system. Suga and Fumiko themselves might not have *explicitly* opposed any 'fathers' other than their biological ones, but their critiques of the emperor-system and their justifiable suspicions concerning the father-figures with whom they came into contact when charged with treason, demand a closer look at the profoundly *paternalistic–patriarchal* aspects of the emperor-system.

ENDS AS BEGINNINGS

To begin with the critique of conventional life-writing implicit even in the structure of this book, I would first note that biographers and other commentators on the lives and ideas of Kanno Suga and Kaneko Fumiko seem to have spent too little time in self-reflexive historiographical reflection. They have not reflected upon issues like how their subjects' texts might have been affected or even *effected* by the conditions under which they were produced; and by the audiences for whom they were produced. A related problem is a tendency to engage in reconstructions of the subjects' life-stories in teleological fashion without reflecting upon how their ends (impending death) had already determined their 'beginnings'. Certainly in the case of Kaneko Fumiko, who both told and wrote her story under threat of execution by the state, the production of such a life-story must have been greatly influenced by the immediate context of the narration.

This brings to mind Herman Ooms' critique of teleology: 'The project of going back to a beginning is engaged in only because a pressing present has drawn singular attention to some item of the past,' he remarked.[38] Here he was making a general point about how the historical beginnings or *origins* of a phenomenon can be invented and mythologized.[39] However, we can also apply his remarks to an autobiographical project, the real beginning of which might not have been, for example, the mistreatment and oppression that Fumiko suffered as a child, but rather her struggle against state and society as an adult. The 'pressing present' of the autobiographer in this case is a need to explain an end, her death or 'destiny', so the focus switches to childhood oppression as the 'beginning' of something that is not as clearly stated in the life-story as it might be. Childhood experience, in short, takes on a meaning that is not situated so much in its own present or context, but rather in the subject's future: the writer's present. We can see how such a confusion of ends and beginnings might lead to one aspect of a subject's early life taking on an exaggerated importance in what is presented as a complete and balanced linear life-story centred on one meaning (an 'autobiography'), but is really more an unstated explanation of an end. The story presented is one where ends have determined beginnings, and death, life.

There are various lessons to be learned also from the constructions scholars have placed upon the lives, ideas and actions of Kanno Suga and Kaneko Fumiko. Regarding teleology, one cannot pretend that one does not know that both died in a final clash with state power, but one can try to prevent such knowledge from *determining*, or having too great an influence upon, how one sees their earlier lives. While it might seem natural to ask what *brought* Suga to an execution at the hands of the state, or Fumiko (apparently) to death by her own hand, one needs to be careful that the way in which the question is framed does not commit one to an assumption of continuous causative development toward a predetermined end. The point at issue here is the *scholar's* ascription of meaning to a life. For, particularly when a subject dies in extraordinary circumstances, the nature of her death often determines the ways in which her life-story is told. In cases where the death is highly unusual – self-inflicted, perhaps, or violent or heroic – the manner of death can loom large in biographers' ascriptions of meaning to the life.[40]

In the existing works on Fumiko in both Japanese and English, authors have apparently seen it as unproblematic to reconstruct her life almost entirely from her own account written in prison in the mid-1920s.[41] But wouldn't it be natural for someone in that situation to look back over her life from the vantage-point of a clash with power and focus on aspects of it that seemed most relevant to the social making of a traitor or 'nihilist'? Would we not expect such a person to prioritize certain things, however consciously, and impose certain silences on herself? Though in Suga's case it is possible to determine whether there was a contrast between her early and late life-narratives – whether she represented her life/Life differently after almost a decade of political struggle – this is not possible with Fumiko because of the limited nature of the extant sources. Particularly in her case it would make no sense to begin this study with her account of her life, when its *im-mediate context* was a trial for treason and the threat of execution.

In ascribing meaning to their lives when facing death, Suga and Fumiko were not unlike any person about to die who may ask, 'Has my life had some significance? Has it had some ethical meaning that I can assert as I die?'[42] But with these 'traitors' there must have been an additional reason for such a concern, whether entirely conscious or more subliminal: the need for a counter-knowledge about their ideas, actions and identity; one which would signify to the world the 'true' meaning of their lives and deaths. When facing likely execution, they must have also suspected something of the ways in which they would be seen in the future by those who believed them to have been 'justly' executed – perhaps even by those who represented them as having been 'martyred' by the state. As a nihilist-egoist, Fumiko, I might observe at this point, was suspicious of the notion of martyrdom.

Jean-Michel Raynaud questions the use of autobiographical works for 'factual' detail about a subject's life when he asks:

> What is hidden in transforming an object into a document, that is a new semiotic object, and then a document into facts, and then isolated facts into a continuous and coherent story? What happens when various objects left by a person during his/her life are taken as able to stand for the entire life? Is a life reducible to a meaning? Is a life a text? Is a life a story?[43]

One can hardly fail to think of Fumiko while reading this and might well ask in return: What happens when that person herself seems to want certain objects to stand for her life, seems to want to reduce her life to a certain meaning? Fumiko and also Suga certainly seem to have presented their stories as 'the struggle of a subject . . . against an anti-subject' in a manner pinpointed by Raynaud:

> A biography is always presented as the struggle of a subject, the main character, against an anti-subject, more difficult to define; for example, a rival, society, illness, and at least death. The subject wants to carry on an action which will give it [*sic*] a certain object of value, fame, success, and so on . . . actually, biography does not limit itself to the telling of a life. Biographies do not finish with the death of the hero. The last words at least always indicate the repercussions, the consequences of such a life, of which this actual biography is an illustration in itself. As if to a story telling the triumph of death over a [hu]man was added a story telling the triumph of an individual over death.[44]

Isn't this what Fumiko's memoirs represent: her triumph over death, and over other anti-subjects like power and society? Suga, moreover, had an explicit concern with revolutionary immortality, so almost all of the elements are there. Raynaud has neatly summed up what Suga seemed to be doing with the objects (particularly prison diary and poetry) she left to posterity. She could be seen to be struggling toward the end of her life with all of the anti-subjects listed – a rival (or rivals, and their constructions of her life and its meaning), society, illness (TB), and certainly impending death – and her actions did appear to be premised partly on concerns with her own value, fame

or success. In her last days she often seemed at pains to counter constructions of her actions as meaningless, or pictures of herself as not
only infamous but a 'failure', since nothing had come of her plans
to rise up in revolution. *Do* we, then, simply re-tell their stories of
life? Or should we rather *read* them in terms of their narrative-political
strategies?

Since the first part of this study is concerned with Suga's and
Fumiko's counter-constructions of death, it partly entails looking at
them as 'historians of their own ends'. If the state could determine
the moment and manner of death and then inflict it as well, would
either of these 'traitors' want to permit it to monopolize the meaning
of the death too? We do not need to portray them as consistently setting out quite deliberately to wrest the meaning of their deaths and
lives from their enemies. Nevertheless, they must have wanted a say
in something at once so personal and so public.

And what of their 'beginnings'? If Part III concentrates on their
counter-constructions of 'Life' itself, and thus largely entails looking
at Suga and Fumiko as 'historians of their *own* beginnings', it seems
to suggest that they were both radical solipsists: 'Life = *my* life'.
Yet one's own experience is usually the most convincing of evidence
for one's view of reality. Fumiko, both in court and in her prison
memoirs, used her life-story as evidence of widespread social inequities
in prewar Japan. And even when Suga was writing social criticism in
newspapers between 1902 and 1909, her own personal experience
(past and present) was probably never far from the surface. Looking
at Suga and Fumiko as historians of their own beginnings in narratives
about Life therefore involves using both autobiographical and other
sources.

The fact that in prison and earlier they used their experience of life
as evidence for the correctness of their political views suggests that the
subjects' personal histories were counter-ideological weapons in a fight
for self-legitimation and empowerment. This recalls Ooms' remarks on
how historians go about locating the beginnings of an historical phenomenon under scrutiny. They still have a ring of accuracy when
applied to Suga's and Fumiko's own historiographical endeavours.
Finding a beginning, he observes,

> entails more than bringing clarity to a diffuse past. There is no inno-
> cence about such an undertaking. The project of going back to a
> beginning is engaged in only because a pressing present has
> drawn singular attention to some item of the past. . . . Phenomena
> for which a beginning is projected increase in reality, and are not

simply spoken of more easily because of their clearer identity. They may acquire an identity because they have been assigned a beginning. They are thus spoken of differently. Authorized more fully, such phenomena have a thicker layer of legitimacy.

Thus it appears that beginnings are often not 'real' beginnings but real talk about beginnings. Such talk of beginnings often serves concrete interests and it is thus itself ideological.[45]

Here Ooms is referring to a rather different 'phenomenon', but these remarks are equally pertinent to Suga's or Fumiko's concern with her own beginnings. There was certainly a 'pressing present' – what Suga perceived to be the appalling condition of women in Meiji society, for example – that led Suga as early as 1902 to narrate particular episodes of 'her' past. And in the process did she herself not 'increase in reality', come to have a 'clearer identity' (as a social critic), and more 'legitimacy' in the eyes of her audience through revealing a past that justified her criticisms of the present? We can at least see how the phenomenon of women's subjugation might increase in reality for many through her stories about 'her' own personal trials. Whether or not the beginnings she spoke of were always 'real' – they were not necessarily so, for example, in her 'semi-autobiographical' works – her talk of them was certainly (counter-) ideological. From 1902 to 1911 she was engaged in a struggle against dominant ideology and power structures, part of which struggle was to invoke the miseries of 'her' past in opposition to the ideological deception of the existence of social harmony and benevolent paternalism.

In portraying life itself, Fumiko and Suga often used their lived experience as proof of their moral and/or political correctness – as a weapon in their respective struggles with power. Hence, the meaning that Suga and Fumiko generally ascribed to life *when in prison*, their metaphor for life, was 'struggle' – against both visible and not so visible opponents. This is what we might expect of someone in such a situation. But was it so for Suga in 1902 when she wrote her first journalistic articles and stories? Immediately before her final imprisonment in 1910 she certainly represented Life in such a way. These texts of Suga's do reveal that even then she was engaged in an all too violent 'clash with power'. But whether she saw it in that way as clearly in 1902 as she did in 1909 or 1911, is questionable: in 1902 she had no reason to define, or metonymically reduce, her life *entirely* to one meaning in such a way. This Fumiko did in her prison memoir, however, which is why it has much more to tell us about her political struggle in the mid-1920s, than about her so-called 'real' beginnings, her childhood.

When in prison each woman talked about her 'beginnings' in different ways. Fumiko narrated her story of the social origins or making of a nihilist, just as Suga described in her trial testimonies in 1910 her beginnings as a 'direct actionist' two years earlier. They invoked their experience of life's realities against the ideological 'unrealities' presented by a succession of advocates of dominant morality and paternalism. This was a battle of life-constructs or constructs of the world (intensifying over the period of a decade in the case of Suga) where two individuals were saying what amounted to: 'You represent this "reality" as universal, but it is not mine!'

The analysis in Part III does not seek to piece together a supposedly complete story of these women's lives but, because interpretation of their representations of life requires contextual understanding, one is likely to encounter some of the same difficulties as a biographer. When one turns to ask what was happening in the subject's life at the time of writing, it might be necessary to consider the above mentioned 'semi-autobiographical' works. In the existing biographies of Suga there is included as evidence information from so-called semi-autobiographical novelettes she wrote about heroines she did not name as herself.[46] For my purposes, however, it does not much matter whether 'Akiko' or 'Tsuyuko' *was* the historical Suga. If one sets out to interpret her *representations of life*, Suga-invented (perhaps Suga-like) heroines are just as useful.

There are many difficulties encountered when trying to 'read' the life-story of Kanno Suga that has been pieced together by a succession of biographers. If one adds to the problem of 'semi-autobiography' the fact that the parts of the story that Suga herself put together were narrated at different times between 1902 and 1911, one is confronted by other anomalies: it was not only the contexts in which she wrote that were different; she must also have had different concerns at different times. Then there is the matter of different audiences. One might also want to ask to what extent representations of her life by contemporaries have been explicitly brought to bear on the story, and how critically they have been treated. Arahata Kanson's representations of Suga's 'past' and character need to be treated with extreme caution,[47] yet in a work focused on the picture/s she painted of life, such contemporaneous constructions of her life can be utilized – not to add to the coherence or truth of Suga's own life-story, but rather as an hermeneutic aid in understanding the context of her representations of life.

STRUCTURE

I have divided the remainder of this work into two parts focused upon constructions of 'Death' and 'Life' – 'Engagements with death' and 'Life-narratives'. This is both for the reasons discussed above (in order to treat ends as ends and beginnings as beginnings), and also because such a division accords with the *apparent* tendency of Suga and Fumiko to construct themselves as victors over death, and yet victims of life. This was only apparent because both women indicated that there had come a point in their lives when they decided that they would take no more; life would no longer victimize them. Chapters 3 and 4 are thus devoted to the first step of an interpretation of the self-empowering meanings ascribed to death by Suga and Fumiko, while contextual discussion is largely carried out in the two subsequent chapters. I first set out what each said about death, attending to immediate questions of linguistic or cultural meaning, and also discuss the occasional action-statement of apparent symbolic significance. Here I also refer to pre-prison texts of Suga's, but as we would expect, she did not discuss death as much before her final imprisonment as she did in her last days. I have found certain broadly death-related political themes – immortality, self-sacrifice, revenge, ontological pessimism–optimism, and death-affirmation and romanticization – to be useful for structuring a discussion of Suga's treatment of death, and thus apply them also to the case of Fumiko. This will reveal both a number of similarities between the two, but also some important differences.

In Chapter 5 I focus on the more abstract themes in the subjects' constructions of death, for example, ontological pessimism–optimism and also 'immortality', interpreting them in the light of contextual 'discourse on death and beyond'. Here it will be seen, for example, how im-mortality, the negation of mortality, can be a means of self-empowerment, particularly in the case of an individual who is facing a death represented to be not of her own choosing. However she represents that ontological continuity, it can be a symbolic statement that death is not so powerful an 'enemy' after all: 'immortality', in short, can become a weapon in a fight over the *political*-ontological meaning of death and life. In this chapter I consider the religious and philosophical ideas that might have influenced Suga's and Fumiko's constructions of death. The chapter is introduced by a brief, critical consideration of thanatological works, particularly those related to death in Japan and that apparent cultural monolith usually referred to as 'the East'.

Chapter 6 represents the second part of my interpretation of the subjects' political representations of death against the background of their discursive-cultural contexts – in this case the 'action-contexts' of their statements on death. By this I mean the influences upon the more action-oriented elements of their constructs, those related to 'direct action', heroic death, self-sacrifice/assertion, a romanticization of political death, and so on. Here I discuss the less abstract ways in which, in ascribing meaning to death, Suga and Fumiko empowered themselves, or presented themselves as victors over death, destiny and, last but not least, their enemies. This chapter is largely a consideration of the subjects' political culture, and thus focuses on how they acted on the basis of shared understandings in their own time in Japan about political action, resistance and self-empowerment. This involves looking at contemporary, socially constructed patterns of political heroism and heroic death; and at how Suga and Fumiko appeared to model themselves on two common but different types of political heroes present both in Japan and elsewhere. Therefore, while in Chapters 5 and 6 I concentrate my attention upon the subjects' immediate political-cultural contexts in order to interpret their representations of death, I also discuss foreign influences upon Japanese ideas and action-models.

In Part III, Chapter 7, I divide Suga's adult political career into three distinct periods in which she produced texts for different audiences. Any method of dividing up Suga's career might be arbitrary, but the division in Chapter 7 has a certain logic because it mirrors *ostensibly* major changes in her political career. I emphasize, in other words, that such changes in her texts or in her constructions of life do not rule out continuities. Such an emphasis helps to undermine the teleological tendency whereby pictures of the early Suga can be overly influenced by what she ultimately became. Suga had been rejecting dominant discourse and knowledge/s about life for much longer than Fumiko, yet despite the availability of texts in which she did this (from as early as 1902), the picture of her that has been handed down to posterity has been unbalanced by notions of who she ultimately was in 1911. One starts, in other words, with a picture of what an anarcho-terrorist is, then looks back to see what sorts of linear stages would logically precede such an identity; and since one is looking for a preconceived rational progression, one finds one. What is therefore produced are a few ('reduced') snapshots taken at different times: one of a Christian moralist-women's emancipationist, another of a reformist socialist, and finally, the one of the anarcho-terrorist. But the trouble with snapshots is that they might fix one for all time in a certain costume that was not always worn at that time.

Chapter 8 focuses on Fumiko's constructions of life from the year before her imprisonment in 1923 to her death in 1926. There are a few brief pre-prison magazine articles of Fumiko's extant, and these will be discussed here. None the less, of Fumiko, we have only one *clearly focused* snapshot that froze her in one costume in one place. Fumiko left behind one complete, perfectly rounded-off life-story in her early testimonies and her memoirs, and much of her 'real life-construct' can be gleaned from this. Though it is not necessarily the case that the meaning that life held for Fumiko, or the meaning she pre*sent*ed, is more easily interpreted than Suga's, *pres*enting her texts is less complicated because they were mostly produced in one period and context.[48] Most were also produced, at least initially, for one audience: Judge Tatematsu. After a brief introduction to her immediate political culture, her life-construct will be discussed (like Suga's) in sections marked by headings indicating the different types of intended audiences.

Finally, to reiterate: in this book I consider the extent to which, and the *many* ways in which, Kanno Suga's and Kaneko Fumiko's representations of death–life were strategies of self-empowerment. This need not imply that they always fully consciously set out to avail themselves of power, but I still maintain that there was little ambiguity in Suga's and Fumiko's self-presentations as victors. Even when in prison they admitted to having *once* been the victims of life, it was as if they were determined to emphasize the contrast with their present *complete* selves. And when death was staring them in the face, it was depicted as controlled if not entirely 'vanquished', and held to be a beginning, not only an end. Death can come to symbolize both individual im-mortalization and a more social 'revitalization'.[49] If for both women, death was held to be life, if destruction was construction and ends, beginnings, this in itself indicates both the personal *and* *socio-political* nature of their engagements with death and narratives concerning life.

Part II
Engagements with death

3   Kanno Suga: 'The unswerving path'

> Knowing it to lead
> to a fathomless precipice, I
> hurry along –
> never once glancing back
> down the unswerving path.[1]

Suga reached such a precipice in her twenty-ninth year when at eight
o'clock one morning she was escorted to the gallows. At 8:28 on the
morning of 25 January 1911 she was pronounced dead. When she
made an entry in her prison diary the day before, she was unaware
that it would be her last, and on the day of her death she did not
know that her eleven comrades had preceded her to the scaffold.[2]
According to the Buddhist prison chaplain, her countenance did not
betray that this was a day out of the ordinary: she 'went to her
death as if happy, wearing a smile, and composed'.[3] Another witness
to her execution repeated her last words. An instant before the stran-
gulation commenced, she was said to have yelled: '*Ware shugi no tame
shisu, banzai!*' ('I die for the cause, banzai!')[4] One newspaper described
the hanging, and the amount of time it took Suga to die, in graphic
detail; while another inveighed against her 'vanity' in seeing herself
as 'a pioneer among Japanese women', against her 'godlessness' and
her self-indulgent habit of reading about Russian revolutionaries
who had died for their 'so-called principles'.[5] (She had said during
the trial that she admired Sofia Perovskaya, leader of the five Russian
populists executed in 1881 for assassinating Tsar Alexander II.)
   The surviving Meiji socialists were deeply shocked and grieved at
the outcome of the trial, and what was particularly saddening was

their knowledge of the innocence of most of the defendants.[6] But we need not dwell overlong on the attitudes of comrades toward Suga's death, except to note one point. When Arahata Kanson wrote later of his feelings at being confronted with Suga's brutalized body (after it had been collected from the prison), he also mentioned that Sakai Toshihiko had tried to drown in sake his grief at the loss of *so many* friends, and then took up a cane and went off smashing street lamps in the dead of night to let off steam.[7] When visiting Suga a few days before her execution, Sakai had let slip the telling remark, 'I thought Kōtoku and you would die for [us/the cause], but . . . '; he was then unable to go on, in anguish over the fact that so many (initially twenty-four) had been sentenced to death.[8] What he was expressing was a common expectation that some would choose or even consent to die for the cause. Hence, while her execution was clearly profoundly saddening, for some of her comrades, Suga's death came as no great surprise.

Suga was buried by friends in the cemetery of a Tokyo Buddhist temple, Shōshunji, next to her younger sister, Hide, who had died of tuberculosis four years earlier. In connection with arrangements she made before her execution for the continued care of her sister's grave and for the disposal of her own remains, Suga had made quite clear one aspect of the meaning she ascribed to death. Indeed, in order to make sense of some her remarks about death in her diary, one first needs to be aware of the fact that when talking of it she often spoke as a socialist materialist. In a letter written two days before her death she had asked Sakai and other friends to take some money to the temple to pay for the care of Hide's grave, because she had neglected this.[9] She was not so 'superstitious' as to believe that sutras could save souls, she said in her diary that same day, but she wanted to make sure that Hide's grave would be cared for.[10] We might simply note for the moment that her remarks seem to suggest an acceptance of the existence of a soul, her association of religious belief with superstition notwithstanding.

Despite Suga's ambivalence about both Buddhism and being buried herself at Shōshunji, her friends must have felt that she had really wanted to be buried with Hide.[11] They could not have known then of her last words on the subject in her diary. There she partly repeated what she had told them in person about wanting to be buried in the prison cemetery. The cemetery for executed criminals would be good enough, she wrote: it mattered little to her if her ashes were 'scattered to the wind or thrown into the river'. But since she knew that this would not be possible, perhaps because it would be thought unseemly or disrespectful to the dead, she had asked comrades to see to her burial in a way that would not be too troublesome for them.[12]

Before discussing further the contents of Suga's diary it should be emphasized that she expected that her comrades would be able to read it after her death. In a letter to Sakai Tameko and Sakai Toshihiko she had said of the diary: 'I'll record in it frankly, reminiscences, feelings, confessions, desires, whatever occurs to me. I guess you'll be able to read it sometime.'[13] In another letter to Yoshikawa Morikuni (also a socialist), she explained that she could not write much in letters because of censorship, so she was recording everything in her diary, which she hoped he would read later.[14] That comrades were prominent amongst her intended audience might have a bearing on the fact that in the diary she seemed to be at pains to present herself as a materialist who rejected religion entirely – to appear as if nothing but mundane matters connected with her coming death were of concern to her. Her diary entry of 23 January suggests that she was less concerned about her own burial than with what her younger brother might think if he returned after a long absence in America to find Hide's grave looking like the unmarked, unkempt graves of people with no surviving relatives. (Kanno Masao was by then the only other surviving member of the immediate family.) In the note she wrote to Sakai and other friends she had asked them to ensure that Hide had a new, clearly marked tablet, and requested that her brother erect a tombstone for Hide on his return. She said nothing about funeral or later memorial services for herself, nor about anything pertaining to her future spiritual well-being.

Suga intimated that earlier she had stopped visiting Hide's grave both because the rituals associated with such visits were 'mere superstition', and because the Shōshunji priests were disagreeable. In 1908, nearly three years before making these remarks in her diary, she had published an article which referred in passing to the rudeness of the 'arrogant and mercenary' head priest and his 'cold-hearted', equally greedy assistant.[15] (She volunteered the information here that Shōshunji was Shinshū, the True Pure Land sect of Buddhism, so this might have been the family religion.) Burying Hide at Shōshunji was something she clearly regretted later, for she said in that article that she would rather remove her sister's remains to a public cemetery than have to deal with its priests. Because she had no money to pay for their services or give them gifts, she was 'treated by them with contempt'. But despite the 'mercenary' attitude of the priests and their rudeness to her, Suga seemed at the time almost to forgive them their faults and 'hypocrisy', pointing out that it was unreasonable to expect them to be any different from anyone else just because they were 'religious men concerned with people's salvation'. After all, reciting sutras and tending people's graves was their livelihood.

Another point where Suga spoke as a materialist in her prison diary was in noting how absurd and inconsistent of herself it was still to place food that Hide had been fond of, or flowers and incense, before her portrait on the domestic altar. At death the body 'becomes smoke or disintegrates into the atoms from whence it came', she said, adding that she did not believe that the soul survived to appreciate such gifts. Yet she had still continued to do this through 'the force of habit of many years, only because it gave her a little consolation' or helped her to come to terms with her sister's death.[16] She also intimated that when she herself had breathed her last and her body had become a mere 'piece of flesh', she little cared what happened to it. She did put some thought into the sort of coffin she wanted (a Western, full-length one), and also considered what she should be wearing when dead, only in case imperial loyalists should decide to disinter and, presumably, desecrate her remains.[17]

In her last days Suga appeared to be concerned only with practical, worldly matters, which is to say that if she had any faith in another life to come, there is little sign of it. Yet in her diary she often suggested that to have revealed a concern with anything spiritual in connection with death would have been a sign of weakness. Her materialist position was closely bound up with her identity as an anarchist, and to relinquish that would have meant not only a loss of face, but also disempowerment. Whether in this or other connections, in her last writings, Suga must have imposed some silences upon herself, whether consciously or unconsciously – speaking to different audiences differently, depending upon whether they were lawyers, family or comrades.

Thinking of
my last day soon to come,
I ponder
my eternal life
and smile.[18]

Only a few days before dismissing notions of the soul's survival after death, Suga copied this tanka into her diary. The reference in the poem to an 'eternal life' is clearly at odds with the remarks cited above where she seemed at pains to present herself as a scientific materialist; there she explicitly discounted the possibility of an after-life. This poem leads one to wonder whether her consolation in 'living eternally' was of a spiritual nature. It is doubtful that in it she was merely referring, say, to revolutionary immortality, despite the fact that she assumed this would be accorded her and her comrades.

Suga recounted a conversation with the prison chaplain, Numanami Masanori, that was specifically about the subject of salvation and life after death:

> He spoke of how impressed he was that Mineo, one of my fellow defendants, had been blessed with a new faith in salvation since being sentenced to death, and doesn't show a trace of anxiety. Then he encouraged me to find solace in religion as well. I replied that I could hardly have more peace of mind than at present. (For a true anarchist [crossed out]), it's a bit of a joke that an anarchist who categorically denies all power should suddenly in the face of death cling to one such power, the Amida Buddha, claiming he has found peace of mind. Still, I think that what Numanami said was fair enough given his position as a religious man and chaplain. I, however, have my own sort of preparedness and solace.[19]

(The defendant Mineo Setsudō was a Rinzai Zen monk but, according to Numanami, when facing death he converted to Numanami's own Shinshū sect.[20]) What Suga was specifically rejecting was the possibility of salvation through faith in the benevolent intercession of Amida Buddha. She explained that her peace of mind, readiness for her execution, and consolation had nothing to do with religion.

> Sacrifice is a step that some must take. . . . It was only after many sacrifices were made following the coming of the Sage of Nazareth that Christianity became a universal religion. Bearing that in mind, (I feel that [crossed out]) the sacrifice of so many of us is not so significant after all.
>
> These feelings, which I spoke about in the courtroom at the end, are always with me. I am confident that our sacrifice now could never be futile; it cannot fail to have some meaning. Therefore, I firmly believe that right up to the very last instant on the gallows, I will embrace in death a precious feeling of self-respect and wonderful solace in being a sacrifice for the cause; [I firmly believe that] I will attain a peaceful death free of uneasiness or anguish.[21]

Her emphasis in the first paragraph on 'so many of us' is significant because she too bemoaned the fact that so *many* comrades had been sentenced to death. She was angry and guilt-stricken that so many had been implicated 'because of the actions of five or six' who, she said, had been intent on sacrificing themselves for the cause. That she would draw a parallel between Christian martyrdom and sacrificing one's life for one's beliefs is not surprising given Japan's own tradition of Christian martyrdom (mostly in early Tokugawa),[22] and also because many Meiji socialists had either once been or were still Christians. Suga herself was baptized in a Protestant church in Osaka in 1903, and remained a practising Christian for a few years.

Suga had already stated more than once that her solace was not religious but political, yet in her diary two days later she mentioned another visit from Chaplain Numanami when he remarked that it was clearly 'because of [her] faith or political ideals that [she] had found peace of mind'. Some might have regrets if they were not closely involved in the conspiracy, he continued, but her 'preparedness came of [her] commitment to it from the first until the last'. Suga wrote that she was gratified by his words, also because he did not try 'to press religious comfort' on her again.[23] Her statements indicated her dismissal of any sort of religious comfort, either Christian or Buddhist.

Beyond the 'eternal life' Suga spoke of in her poem, we have not uncovered any further indication of an inconsistency in her materialist position. Yet it was not only into the diary that she transcribed this particular poem, for she also included it in postcards to Imamura Rikisaburō and Ishikawa Sanshirō, on 13 and 14 January.[24] It could be significant that the two people to whom she sent the poem about eternal life were a defence lawyer, Imamura, and the *Christian* anarchist,[25] Ishikawa Sanshirō. In the letter to Imamura dated 13 January, Suga included two poems as expressions of her gratitude to him for delivering a message to Sakai Toshihiko. The one that followed 'my last day soon to come, I ponder my eternal life and smile' was:

> Amidst
> limitless time and
> space –
> what could tiny beings have
> to squabble about?[26]

Her use here of the same word '*kagirinaki*' ('eternal' or 'limitless') strengthens the possibility that she used it in the first poem in a metaphysical sense. The suggestion of the unimportance of the human world in the second does not suggest that in the first it was merely the thought of revolutionary immortality that made her smile while pondering her 'eternal life'. To Ishikawa on the fourteenth she wrote that she had generally been 'in surprisingly good health and spirits'; and it was in illustration of that fact that she included the poem about her 'eternal life'. What is thought-provoking about her sending the poems to these two individuals is the fact that while she went to great pains to explain in her diary – which she would leave to posterity (to her comrades and perhaps future socialists) – that her consolation was not spiritual but pragmatic, to a lawyer who was not a comrade and to a comrade who was a Christian, she offered no such explanation. This may have been unconscious, perhaps a mere coincidence, but it may have reflected inconsistencies in her thinking about religion because of the power of her upbringing or past.

Suga had been a Christian for some years, though she indicated that Christianity was ultimately displaced in her ideals and commitments by socialism. Well after she became a socialist late in 1904, however, she still observed Buddhist rituals. (Of course, she may have even while still a Christian). For example, she said in 1911 that she had continued to make offerings to Hide's portrait after 1907 out of habit and because it *consoled* her or lessened her grief at the loss of her sister; not merely, for example, because Hide would have expected it. It might simply have been her way of keeping her sister's memory alive, a ritual empty of religious significance for her. Yet Hide was not only buried in the graveyard of a Buddhist temple; on the forty-ninth day after her death, Suga had also observed the Buddhist ritual of offering up sutras for safe passage.[27] This was four years earlier but it was after Suga had become first a Christian and then a socialist. It was also despite the fact that Sakai had reported in a socialist newspaper at the time of Hide's death that her ceremony was 'without Buddhist or Shinto priests, without flowers or flags'; it was a good ceremony based upon 'only true human feelings'.[28]

Particularly in a culture often described as unusually eclectic and syncretistic in religious matters, it is difficult to know how much importance to ascribe to inconsistencies such as these between materialist beliefs and religious practice. Suga may not have seen such rituals as meaningful, but still we cannot ignore the possibility that she observed them for reasons that had more to do with spirituality than practicalities like keeping her sister's memory alive, or conforming to the expectations of Buddhist priests regarding safe passage ceremonies so that they would continue to care for Hide's grave.

On the other hand, we certainly cannot read too much into Suga's saying while in prison that she would 'pray' [*inoru*] for the long life or good health of friends; she did not say she would pray to God or to the Gods or Buddhas. To 'Takeo' (a niece of Kōtoku's) she wrote, 'From the bottom of my heart, I will pray for good health for all of you.' And she asked other comrades to pass on the message to former lover and estranged friend, Arahata, that she would 'be praying for his good health right up until the moment [she] mounted the scaffold'.[29] But, her Christian and Buddhist background notwithstanding, there was no suggestion at all in Suga's letters or diary that she would meet friends again in a 'great beyond' (whether 'heaven' or Pure Land). In fact, more than once she said that this would be a *final* or *'eternal'* parting. What also serves to confuse the issue of whether her representation of death was consistently materialist or contradicted by a belief in life after death is the fact that she also wrote: 'From beneath the earth at Zōshigaya [the prison graveyard], they are watching [me]'.[30] Was this merely a poetic reference to death's awaiting her?

Born in
a very small land,
I sacrifice
my small life for
a small hope.[31]

As we have seen, Suga insisted that she found solace in her last days in the belief that her devotion to the cause would be respected by future generations of revolutionaries. Sacrifice for the cause as 'consolation' in the face of execution was a recurring theme in her construction of death in her prison diary and poetry, but it is also apparent in her letters and testimonies, often in connection with her motives for revolutionary action:

> I heard from Kōtoku Denjirō ['Shūsui'] that Miyashita was a very resolute man, and I took it into my head that together with him I might be able to achieve an important task [*daiji*]. . . . Then we exchanged letters and discussed sacrificing ourselves for the cause. I think it was around that time [January, 1909] that I received a letter saying that Miyashita was researching the manufacture of bombs.[32]

While in this excerpt *'kenshinteki ni yarou'* is ambiguous in the sense that it could be rendered as 'devoting ourselves to' rather than 'sacrificing ourselves for' the cause, Suga was often more explicit in speaking of 'dying' (*shinu* or *taoreru*) or 'laying down her life' (*karada o sasageru*) for her ideals or the cause.[33] She also associated doing something 'important' (*daiji*) with death for the cause, which in turn suggests a view of heroism that involved achieving a 'great' death through an heroic act.

The lawyer-writer, Hiraide Shū, made clear in his ('fictional') stories based on the incident the fact that he had found Suga's romanticization of self-sacrifice hard to stomach. As Jay Rubin puts it, he thought her 'absurd, her talk of sacrifice ludicrous', and he also noted the irony that the government's overreaction to the incident had ensured that she and her accomplices would have their moment of glory.[34] He held Suga and the other plotters partly responsible for the fates of innocent defendants. Hiraide reported her ('Mano Suzuko's') last defiant statement in court, which she ended with a plea for the lives of her innocent comrades. Rubin observes that 'Suzuko's' insistence on their innocence is consistent with the real Suga's diary, doubtless because in that diary she said she had spoken of sacrifice on that day. What seems rather out of character for Suga, however, is 'Suzuko's' implied equation of failure with womanhood, even if most of the statement is consistent with her late writings.

> We've put you to a lot of trouble for quite some time now, but today at long last the affair has come to a close. I have nothing more to say. And I have nothing to repent. For me the only disappointing thing is that the [two characters censored, probably 'revolution'] we put so much effort into ended in complete [two characters censored, perhaps 'failure' or 'suppression']. It's because I'm a woman – and women lack spirit – this is my shame. Among our predecessors there were many who died courageously setting us an example of decisive action. I feel I have failed those predecessors. I will die with good grace because this is my destiny. Those who sacrifice themselves are always most honoured and esteemed by later generations. I too have become such a sacrifice, and will now die.
>
> I believe that a time will come someday when my aims will be vindicated, so I have no regrets. There is one favour I would ask of you. I am quite prepared. I was prepared from the beginning when we made these plans. I will not be at all discontented however severe my punishment. But there are many others apart from myself. These people had no connection with us at all.[35]

In one early cross-examination Suga had said something similar about only being disappointed that the plan had ended in failure. Asked by the judge whether she had understood the law against inflicting injury on the sovereign, she responded: 'I don't know anything about that. But it must be the heaviest penalty of execution. If we had achieved even part of our purpose I'd be determined to sacrifice myself, but the real pity of it is that we were caught because of silly [mistakes] and it has turned into this sort of case.'[36] Both in claiming a solace that came from her belief that she would be accorded the respect due a (willing) political martyr and in expressing regret only at the failure of her plans for revolution, this revolutionary proclaimed that she was not about to concede defeat.

In mid-May 1910 Suga wrote three letters to Kōtoku that reveal something of her tendency, even before her imprisonment, to romanticize self-sacrifice and heroic death. The last was sent just two days before she was due to begin serving a prison sentence of a few months for contravening the publication laws the year before. It was a week or so after her imprisonment that her co-conspirators were arrested, and the high treason case began. Suga ended the second letter to Kōtoku on 12 May as follows:

> I must resign myself to going [into prison]. There's no point in wasting my days of freedom hoping. . . . I ask affectionately that you please take care of yourself. If you keep in good health, I won't mind how many years I'm in prison. I won't even mind dying.[37]

Compared with her other two letters at that time, this was calm and quite reasoned; it was affectionate, and indicative at least of self-effacement, if not necessarily abnegation, with regards to Kōtoku. In this letter she was apologizing for a previous letter which was in her own words 'wild', 'hysterical' and 'morbid'. Yet on 16 May she again seemed rather 'morbid':

> When you hear of my current illness [a bad cold], you'll probably tell me I must postpone going into prison. But I will go resolutely. I'd rather sleep in prison than here. It'd be better to die in prison than linger on and die here. That would have some meaning. Then there would be some consolation in death.[38]

Suga's use of terms like 'consolation' (*isha*) or 'solace' (*ian*) here and where she spoke of her solace in being a sacrifice for the cause suggests that she may not have been as prepared to die as she insisted elsewhere. But perhaps the amount of consolation she needed depended upon *how* she was to die. She apparently believed that the best way to meet death would be while attempting some important task. When she spoke of lingering on and dying, it seemed that consolation was all the more necessary because this would be such an undramatic death to no purpose. She did not glorify death in general, only heroic death. Suga had actually said in an article four years earlier that what she most hated was the thought of dying of a lingering illness (like her sister, Hide): she would rather die in a bold, resolute (*omoikitta*) sort of way. Only a few weeks later, moreover, she wrote in a highly romantic fashion about her ideal lovers – the ideal lovers' ('double') suicide, she argued, would be one where a man and woman fought for a cause (*shugi*) and died for their ideals (*risō*) together.[39] By the time Suga wrote these letters to Kōtoku in May 1910, both she and he were suffering from serious consumptive conditions, and it was natural for her to wonder whether she would survive her prison term. Yet she implied that even dying of illness would be meaningful so long as it happened *in prison*.

In speaking during the trial of sacrifice for the cause as a means of making the movement survive and grow, Suga was both warning her opponents and scoring some points in this rather deadly game of power. Time and again she expressed her conviction that the police and courts might be able to kill off anarchism, but it would be born again through the sacrifice of the defendants: 'the tall tree falls only to put forth new shoots again', she wrote. This scarcely veiled threat was also evident in one of her tanka where she used the metaphor of regeneration or 'reincarnation' again:

> Do not search
> for a seed lost
> in a field –
> pray wait for a day in spring
> with an east wind blowing.[40]

Here she likened herself and her comrades to seeds putting forth life again after death. It was as if she were saying that in death there is life – ends contain within them beginnings. After referring to the tree, she went on to say that 'in these spring days in the world of thought' those like her 'who willingly took on the role of pioneers [had] no need to look back to past days of autumn and winter'; they must look ahead, 'forge ahead, looking toward the bright future anticipated'.

Implicit in Suga's use of these springtime-growth metaphors was a threat that the authorities had only appeared to win this round. She had also made it clear in her testimonies that her belief in the necessity of sacrifice so that anarchism might continue to live, or live again, was not only a post-facto consolation that helped her come to terms with her imprisonment and sentence. She insisted that, on the contrary, her vision of heroic sacrifice had been bound up with her initial decision to make an attempt on the emperor's life, hopefully as part of a 'revolution'. Early in the Pretrial Hearing she explained that when she had used the term 'uprising' to refer to their immediate aims, the prosecutor understood it inappropriately as 'meaningless violence'. Therefore she retracted the term and substituted 'revolution', which meant similar sorts of tactics as in the French revolution: 'carrying out assassinations, temporarily halting transportation facilities, also arson or setting fire to various buildings, in short, showing that the spoils could be taken back from the spoilers, even if just for a while.'[41] (The last few words suggest that she did not necessarily believe that this 'revolution' would be victorious.) What is clear is that she represented a belief in the necessity of self-sacrifice as *both her initial motive and ultimate consolation;* for it had initially contributed to her choice of death, or her readiness to die in a heroic act.[42]

Perusal of Suga's later trial testimonies also reveals frequent usage of the phrase, *'shugi no tame ni'* (for my/our/the ism or cause/beliefs/ideals), followed by at least five variations on 'to die'. The theme of either dedicating one's life to one's ideals or dying for them had also run throughout Suga's earlier journalistic works in a way that has a quite Christian ring to it, though Christianity was only one of several likely sources of inspiration for it. The following exchange between Suga and the prosecutor during one of her later interrogations suggests layers of cultural meaning that go far deeper than the surface description of their strategy for *anarchist* revolution. This is suggested partly by the prosecutor's use of the phrase *'kesshi no shi'* (the closest approximation of which is 'warriors determined to die').

Ques. 17: During November of that year [1908] did Kōtoku ever talk to you about forming fifty *kesshi no shi*, distributing bombs and other arms, gathering together the poor in Hibiya Park and attacking the wealthy, then taking advantage of all this to destroy government offices and march on Nijūbashi [the palace], invade the Imperial Palace, inflict injury on the Imperial Family – wanting to bring out a state of anarchy in just one day?
Ans: There was that sort of talk sometimes. But at that time we didn't consult about anything concrete . . .
Ques. 19: Didn't Kōtoku reveal his ideas about violent revolution to Sakamoto Seima and tell him to go about the area agitating and recruiting *kesshi no shi*?

Ans: Kōtoku often told Sakamoto to go around agitating and I think he directed him to recruit comrades, but I don't know whether he told him to recruit *kesshi no shi* for the revolution.[43]

(Sakamoto was one of the twelve first sentenced to death, then to life imprisonment.) In the phrase '*kesshi no shi*', it is clear from the context that '*shi*' meant samurai-style fighters. While '*kesshi*' is sometimes rendered as 'death-defying', one is not merely risking death, but rather embracing it, being *determined* to die.

The conceptualization of 'revolution' in this exchange was almost certainly influenced by patterns of samurai rebellion in Tokugawa and early Meiji. According to the now famous seventeenth-century samurai text, *Hagakure* (Hidden Among Leaves): 'Where there are two ways to choose, let your choice be that one that leads to death. . . . When your mind is set on death, your way through life will always be straight and simple'.[44] It seems that '*kesshi no shi*' was a catch-phrase at the time, though not necessarily amongst socialists. Unlike 'sacrificing oneself for the cause' or the masses, socialists may not have seen it as very modern. In the past it had often implied selflessness, however, which was a popular ideal also in Meiji Christianity, 'new' Buddhism and socialism, as well as in the developing hegemonic ideology centred on the imperial-centred State Shintō. Perhaps Kōtoku's apparent unwillingness to use '*kesshi no shi*' implied that he associated it with earlier imperial 'loyalists', and thus saw it as reactionary:

Ques: Was your purpose in sending Sakamoto on a propaganda tour to recruit *kesshi no shi*?
Ans: If there were earnest people about, I told him to find them.
Ques: Doesn't what you call earnest people amount to *kesshi no shi*?
Ans: That is what it amounts to.[45]

When asked again about discussions between himself and Suga about recruiting these 'samurai', Kōtoku responded that of course they 'may have talked sometimes about being ready to die and starting a revolution for the sake of the cause', but they did not consult about anything 'concrete'.[46] In sum, even if the defendants did see the phrase '*kesshi no shi*' as anachronistic, their alternative of 'direct actionist' seems little different in meaning from samurai heroism, since both involved similar tactics (assassination) and were closely tied to an elitist, altruistic form of self-sacrifice (for the people, nation, Cause or 'masses').

There are lots of people I'd love to scare out of their wits if I could return as a spook or ghost, starting with the supreme court judge/s. How delightful it would be to see them scream 'Aaiee!' petrified with terror. Ha![47]

Revenge was another quite traditional theme that appeared often in Suga's testimonies and late writings. It was intimately connected with her emphasis on a heroic, 'great' death, and with her positive view of self-sacrifice for her ideals. She could have been half-serious when she spoke here of coming back from the dead, at least in the sense that it reflected her frustrated desire to avenge herself on those responsible for the persecution of socialists. Before making these remarks in her diary about haunting judges and others, she mentioned that Prosecutor Taketomi had promised to visit her grave with flowers and incense if she was executed. When she told someone about this, her listener thought the prosecutor must have been 'superstitious', or afraid, presumably, that Suga might come back and haunt him, adding that it would be funny if when he did visit her grave she grabbed him dramatically by the sleeve.[48] It was in this context that Suga went on to laugh about the fun she might have as a 'spook'.

Furthermore, *if* the account by Hiraide (discussed above) of 'Suzuko's' last declaration at the trial in the Supreme Court can be taken to be an accurate representation of Suga's words, there too she may have been trying to menace court officials and police. 'Suzuko' concluded her final plea with these halting words: 'Innocent people may be killed just because we made these plans. If I should see such an unjust outcome, I . . . I . . . even when I die . . . I may die, but death will not be the end of me.'[49] Existing translations of this do not quite grasp the sense of her expression of being literally unable to die really or truly ('*shindemo . . . shinde shini-kiremasen*'),[50] which has a sense of dying yet not being extinguished or quelled by death, having to take regrets or anger beyond the grave, being unable to rest in peace. In Japanese folk belief an uneasy spirit, especially one who died harbouring a deep resentment or anger toward 'evildoers' (e.g., its murderers), will not let go of its attachment to the phenomenal world and will be imbued with a terrible, vengeful supernatural power.[51]

Suga's first statement to the Prosecution had been much more explicit about her desire for revenge. There she actually threatened to kill the same man who later promised to visit her grave. Voicing her readiness to talk to anyone but Taketomi, she explained that ever since he had prosecuted her in two earlier incidents, she had been determined to pay him back for his 'severity and heartlessness':

> While I was in prison then, I resolved not to rest until I killed [you] Prosecutor Taketomi, the enemy I'd grown to hate. And when we raised the revolutionary movement, I was determined that the first thing I'd do would be to hurl a bomb at your head. If I hurled a bomb at you, I imagine your life blood would gush with just about as much vigour as you had when delivering that [court-room] address, wouldn't it?
>
> In the months after my release from prison in September last year, 1909, my resolution to kill you did not waver. Also when I was told after my collapse in October when I was feverish and unconscious that I'd raved in my delirium about Prosecutor Take-tomi – that I bore that deep a grudge against someone – it was enough to make me laugh. Then someone, I don't remember who, said that Prosecutor Taketomi – was not that brutal person-ally, and my antipathy subsided a little. Also, because I had much to do for the cause and my own affairs to attend to, until today there has been no opportunity to kill you.[52]

Suga vowed that now she was in prison again she would kill him, if she could get 'a bomb or a blade'. She reminded him that others bore deep grudges against him too and had 'a debt to pay' him. He would be 'fortunate to die a natural death', she sneered, before reiterating that she would not tell him, her despised enemy, anything.

This did not mean that she would not talk about her role in the affair or of that of her co-conspirators. Subsequent statements were given to other prosecutors, and she answered questions put to her by judges during the pretrial hearing readily enough. Her final words to Prosecutor Taketomi in this first statement were:

> If I were involved in this affair, since the offence carries the death penalty, naturally I'd be very determined and therefore tell all and not keep anything back. It's only you I won't talk to![53]

In connection with this statement two points are of interest: firstly, there is the suggestion that the likelihood of the death penalty was all the more reason for Suga to be resolved and admit to her role in the conspiracy; secondly, there is the related point that she had every intention of admitting her guilt – to anyone but him. She seemed in part to be playing a power-game with Taketomi, 'getting back at him', perhaps trying to deprive him of some of his 'glory', though she also said that she did not trust him to record her words faithfully and not twist them. At least at this point, if not necessarily later, it seems that this was one 'fatherly' individual Suga was suspicious of.

Taketomi was not the only enemy Suga had had in her sights, for naturally she mentioned the emperor, and also Yamagata Aritomo. Yamagata, one of the Meiji oligarchs and a former prime minister, was implacably hostile to liberal democracy, not to mention socialism, and was largely responsible for the removal of the more liberal Prime Minister Saionji from office in July 1908. Saionji's replacement was one of Yamagata's coterie, General Katsura, who intensified police efforts against the spread of 'dangerous thought'.[54] Hence, in Suga's view Yamagata was largely responsible for the repression of socialists. She went on to say later that she would happily throw a bomb at Yamagata. He had long been their target and she 'hated him the most' because he was the 'most reactionary among the *genrō*' (elder statesmen); he had played the greatest part in preventing the attainment of democracy, and had 'persecuted' socialists incessantly. For him, she was only too willing to take on the role of parricide.

In relation to the emperor, however, Suga was not a very willing parricide, as intimated above. She did not have a personal grudge against him, because he was only a symbol of state power and, though he would have to die because of it, she felt this was regrettable. Her final words in this statement might sound out of character for an anarchist:

> Though I actually feel it is a pity to do away with the current sovereign in his capacity as an individual, as sovereign of a system that oppresses us he is the one who stands at its apex, and it is therefore unavoidable. It is necessary, that is, because he is the leader of the spoilers. The reason why I think it is a pity is that he merely leaves things up to his government officials, and cannot know anything firsthand about society. I think that if we were able now to speak with him a little in person about democracy, he might come to understand and put a stop to this persecution. But in the situation there is today there is no hope of our having an opportunity to speak to the sovereign. He is a noble and great person, so it is regrettable but truly unavoidable.[55]

The theme of the (fatherly) ruler kept in ignorance about social ills and evils by officials is familiar from Russian, Chinese and Japanese traditions, as is the wish that the ('benevolent' and 'innocent') lord or sovereign could be petitioned directly.[56] Here, Suga tended to take as given the paternalistic aspects of emperor-system ideology, even to the extent of according this 'father' final responsibility for such ills.

Suga emphasized during the trial that she had begun to entertain the idea of retributive assassination and insurrection seriously after being arrested in 1908. There is no doubt that she meant the authorities to understand that they had brought the incident upon themselves by oppressing people such as herself:

> When I was imprisoned in connection with the Red Flag Incident in June 1908, I witnessed the brutal behaviour of the police and became utterly indignant, realizing that in these conditions it was impossible to disseminate our ideas by peaceful means.[57]

The 'Red Flag Incident' will be discussed below, but it might be noted here that Suga said that it was not just police brutality that had outraged and radicalized her, but also the unjust treatment meted out to some socialists who had not really been involved in it.[58] In this way she impressed upon her interrogators the fact that it had been from mid-1908 that political tactics and revenge had come to be closely connected in her mind – the authorities had only themselves to blame for 'creating' her. Actually, she had used the *rhetoric* of violent struggle as early as 1906,[59] so there is reason to doubt that her vision of revolutionary tactics had actually changed all that much over the years. Clearly, however, in 1910 she had sound political reasons to stress that it was not until a desire for vengeance was added to her anger at social inequalities that she came to believe in the necessity of violent struggle. As she told it, by mid-1908 high on her 'hit-list' were particular prosecutors and politicians, police and judges because, like others in Japan long before her, she had wanted to wage a moral-political rectification campaign against the corrupt and evil – all those in power who were lacking in the justice, mercy and benevolence they preached.

All day long I've been feeling pessimistic. Senseless human existence! I've long breathed [life's] chilly air, but I can no longer endure it. Life! The agony of life. To what purpose do mortals continue on their journey of meaningless wretchedness?[60]

This is most of the letter to Kōtoku referred to above, that Suga described as 'wild and morbid' in her second letter to him in mid-May. And in this pre-prison text of Suga's we do find a suggestion of quite a negative, 'pessimistic'[61] attitude toward life. Was it a logical consequence of this that she affirmed death so resolutely later when in prison? It is not surprising that she would despair of life in January 1911 when under two 'sentences' of death.

We saw above how Suga was already very ill before the high treason case when she expressed this weariness of life. It might be tempting to conclude that it was her not having long to live anyway, that made her want to take hold of her own fate by dying for the cause, but she had fantasized about dying 'well' long before her final imprisonment. The fact that it was from as early as 1906 that she romanticized a revolutionary heroic death (the year before she contracted tuberculosis) does not suggest that her later readiness for a political death was only due to her, probably terminal, illness. Also, it was from the latter part of 1908 that she and her comrades had talked about laying down their lives for the cause. Thus, these early statements of Suga's determination to fight, perhaps even die for the cause were made at a time when death itself was not yet an enemy to be conquered.

By the time she wrote the letters to Kōtoku in May 1910, however, death was not Suga's only foe: now she had another enemy that was only too visible, the repressive state. Therefore her apparent ontological 'pessimism' in mid-May must have had some decidedly political causes. Indeed, if before her third and final imprisonment her construction of death was already markedly political, we can expect to find it more so during the treason incident. Then her affirmation of death and related negation of life were not at all abstract. She seemed in effect to be saying to her interrogators that she was not only determined to die – in a manner she had decided *herself* – but would welcome the release that death would bring, the escape from a world they had made insufferable. Fighting back in whatever form or forum was available to her, Suga in her prison diary stated in anger that a life without freedom was not worth having:

> Poor, pathetic judges! In order to retain your standing, *solely* to safeguard your own positions [knowing it to be unjust, knowing it to be outrageous – deleted], knowing [that inhuman decision – deleted] it to be unjust, knowing it to be outrageous, you must have been compelled to hand down that inhuman decision.
>
> Poor, pathetic judges! Slaves of the government! More than being angered by you, I pity you. Here I am constrained by this barred window, yet I spread my wings in the free world of thought; you appear to us to be shackled or restricted by no-one, yet in truth you are pitiable human beings – pitiable [brutes – deleted] human beings

who live your lives as humans but have no human worth. One may live a hundred years without freedom, in servitude, but what would such a life be worth? Poor, pathetic slaves! Poor pathetic judges![62]

One suspects a touch of sarcasm in the remark about the 'free world of thought' given official concerns at the time with controlling 'dangerous' thought, definitions of which were far broader than merely anti-imperial ideas. None the less, here her message to the judges is clear: she may have been facing death, but had lived her life 'freely'; she had been physically 'shackled' before and was so again, but continued to exercise her freedom to *think*. One often gets the impression that she was raging inside at her impotence, though wary of revealing it too clearly.

Suga had long been fond of suggesting that her ideals would determine her fate. Both before and after her final imprisonment she often presented herself as much more than a passive victim of destiny. In an article in 1909 she said in the context of police harassment and suppression of socialists that the situation was such that they were being *forced* to choose between giving up the struggle and pushing on toward revolution.[63] She followed this with: 'Thus, our precious government of Japan does us the favour of creating many conspirators [*muhonnin*, also meaning rebel or traitor].' This seems to indicate a choice imposed by an outside agent, but we could also take it to mean that the ideals she had herself chosen would not allow her to give up. Here she represented 'destiny' as something decided *both* by herself and others.

When in her diary she struck out at her foes with the observation that servile judges and the like, who were not permitted to think for themselves, were locked into a sort of living death, Suga was saying that she had at least been able to choose freely and live by her ideals. The life judges lived, on the other hand, was equivalent to slavery. Implicit in her remarks was an equation of rebellion with truly living, even when it led to death. Death through rebellion was associated with freedom, for it was the result of free thought. Given the situation she and her co-defendants were in, this association comes as no surprise. (Fumiko said much the same thing.) But Suga was still critical of comrades who turned their backs on the struggle. At one point in her diary she wrote in anger:

There are some who discard their ideals like worn-out sandals, afraid of government persecution, looking out for their own safety. Ah, the vicissitudes of fate! How faint-hearted is the human spirit! Let those who would quit, quit; let those who would die, die![64]

After contrasting those who quit the struggle with those who remained true to their ideals, she went on to make the remark about the tall tree (of anarchism) falling yet putting forth new shoots. She seemed to be suggesting that for those like her who had truly lived and were therefore about to die for the cause there would be a sort of life in death, while those who had opted for life, servitude or safety were as good as dead.

Suga's apparent negation of life before and during her imprisonment was expressed on the one hand by referring to human life as 'senseless' and to people's journey through life as 'meaningless'. On the other hand, life for political radicals like herself was held to be impossible. In a situation where the state seemed to be 'calling the shots', the only self-willed, agentic way left open to them seemed to be rebellion and death. Her view of rebellion implied death since she believed it to be symbolically necessary to kill the emperor. But if she sought death because she really believed that human life was senseless, meaningless or inherently bad, we might wonder about her apparent desire to sacrifice herself for an ideal future society.

Ultimately, then, she seemed to be at pains to present herself as *optimistic* about life; for freedom *would* come. More to the point, particularly during Suga's imprisonment her apparent 'ontological pessimism', and its corollary of an affirmation of death, were obviously means of showing her political resolve and her defiance. Hence she continued to 'spread her wings' despite the physical constraints of the courtroom and her prison cell, recasting the threat of death as a promise, thereby asserting to her judges and executioners (also to her comrades) that death was something she had chosen and would happily embrace. In short, the constructions she placed upon death were, in effect if not always by conscious design, weapons in an ongoing political struggle that partly hinged upon contesting meanings of death (and, by extension, life).

Watching
the evening skies
slowly
clouding over –
a raven, forlorn.[65]

This poem evokes a feeling that could only be described as 'black,' whether or not the raven (in Japan, a symbol of death) was an allegorical allusion to herself. Apart from the gloom or darkness implied by the words 'forlorn, raven, evening, clouding over', there is also the suggestion of a deeper blackness yet to come, both with the night and with the storm. The poem is in marked contrast, therefore, with many of Suga's pronouncements in her prison diary and letters that seem markedly, perhaps suspiciously, bright.

In this final section I therefore look at the darker side of the picture, at moments when Suga seemed to let down her guard. It is not so much Suga's positive pronouncements about death that concern me here as her 'contradictions', and the silences she might have imposed upon herself particularly when in prison. The problems involved in taking her remarks at this time at face-value – as statements of how she 'truly'/consistently saw death or life – are self-evident. But like her diary, even her earlier journalistic articles had probably largely been aimed at a political audience in whom she wanted to encourage resistance; also partly at 'persecutors' to whom she wanted to broadcast defiance. Toward prosecutors and judges later she clearly wanted to be a defiant and brave combatant, and thus was all too ready to implicate herself and her co-conspirators, though protective of those she knew to be innocent. And perhaps she was merely being solicitous toward her friends in personal letters, wanting to appear in good spirits in order to lessen their worry and grief. In her diary we might detect that same solicitude, coupled with a concern with how she would be seen after her death. When considering Suga's constructions of death when in prison, therefore, we also need to think about what she might have suppressed.

The issue is not Suga's frankness, however, for she was probably as candid as she could be under the circumstances. Not only in the letters to friends already mentioned but also in her diary she stated her desire to try to be honest with herself:

> This is to be a record written very frankly, without whitewashing myself, without pretence, without deceiving myself, from today when I received the death sentence until I mount the scaffold.[66]

Two days later she repeated that it would 'record the naked Kanno Sugako without any falsehood or affectation', and later again she wrote the following which reveals rather more than her desire to be completely frank about her feelings:

> 22 January. Fine weather. Last night I was in low spirits for the first time since entering prison. That tragedy of a final parting really strained my [sensitive – deleted] nerves. Although since 2 June

last year when the affair was detected, I have wanted to be quite in control of myself [my nerves – deleted], if I can be overwhelmed even for one night by such singularly indefinable emotions, I really am a worthless individual. I am a little disgusted with myself. If this sort of faint-heartedness [persists], what will become of me?

Still, this was probably a natural human response. That special human characteristic of Eastern heroes, not showing their joy or anger or revealing their true feelings, is impressive in one way, but it is also a definite deception, an affectation . . . [but] for ordinary people with their capacity for emotions without falsehood or pretence, there is no reason to exist in such an insensible way. I am a small person [i.e., not a 'great' one]; I'm an emotional, an extremely passionate person. I hate lies, detest affectation, hate anything unnatural. I cry; I laugh. I rejoice; I rage. It's fine with me if I reveal my lack of sophistication. It doesn't matter to me how others measure my worth. If I can end my life without deceiving myself, I'll be content.

But today I'm in very high spirits. My feelings of last night have been buried with the night, and I wonder why I felt like that.[67]

It is quite clear in this passage that she was trying to be brave and resolute; and that she wanted to be seen as being in control of herself. She later justified her outburst during the 'final parting' from her friends, Ōsugi Sakae, Hori–Ōsugi Yasuko and Sakai Toshihiko, explaining that, while she had 'plenty of resolution' any other time, seeing their faces had inexplicably brought on tears. To Sakai she wrote that she was very depressed after their visit for the first time since her imprisonment.[68] She did at times let down her guard with her comrades and partly admit to her periods of despair, but it was specifically in connection with an unwillingness to say goodbye to her friends.

It is not the case that Suga's diary consists only of political protestations about her long-held willingness to sacrifice herself for the cause and consequent preparedness for such a death. It often reads as though she jotted down spontaneously whatever she was feeling at that moment. At one point fond memories cause her to feel 'both happy and sad'; at another she wonders why she feels so restless, and worries about whether enough time remains for her to take care of the things that still need attending to.[69] At another time, warm and relaxed after her weekly bath, she feels the best thing would be to 'just melt away, drifting into an eternal sleep'.[70] Moreover, upon reading the 'exaggerated verdict' coerced out of the judges, she is deeply depressed and unable to lift her spirits to write anything.[71] When she opens her eyes every morning, she thinks, 'Oh, I'm still alive!', and it seems like a dream. And told a story of an unknown samurai reprieved on the way to his execution, she remarks cynically on how she 'admires the depth of experience' with which this chaplain 'preaches Buddhism . . . coming up with such timely stories'.[72]

Yet to get a clearer view of the shadowy areas of the picture Suga painted of her last days and the fate that now stared her in the face, we could turn again to her poems. These are the most revealing of her writings precisely because they suggest the contradictions that go hand in hand with human emotions and human projects. By focusing upon Suga's explicitly *political* representations of death – specifically her apparent determination to appear in control of the meaning and value of it – perhaps we automatically relegate to the unfocused margins of the picture the moments when her mask slipped to reveal someone not nearly so strong. These three tanka express emotions not at all in evidence in her statements to the Prosecution or to judges, and not so explicit in most of her diary: sorrow, fear and uncertainty.

> The wounded –
> kept up late in the night
> weeping,
> with the pain of
> wounds old and new.

> Frozen
> in my chill bed at night,
> how often
> I listen to the
> stealthy sounds of sabres.

> Brave, brave
> child of revolution; timid,
> timid child of tears –
> are they one and the same?
> I look at myself and wonder.[73]

If the nature of Kanno's intended audience (comrades) did lead her to impose certain silences on herself most of the time in her diary and last letters, to the extent that she did so consciously, it could have been partly out of a desire to spare her friends pain. She did seem to want to act in a manner befitting a willing revolutionary martyr, at least partly for their benefit. But we cannot lose sight of the context in which she was writing them, her cell, because what that suggests is that she was simply unwilling to reveal to her *immediate* audience, her enemies – possibly even to herself – what fear she did have of death, or how much she lacked confidence in her mission, or how sad she was to part from the world. Therefore, expressions of sadness, fear or uncertainty were rather submerged in her last texts. They, after all, were largely designed to show the world that still in her last moments she was resolute in her resistance to a state that would legally murder so many for the 'patricidal' fantasies of a few.

4 Kaneko Fumiko: 'The will to die'

One's limbs
may not be free
and yet –
if one has but the will to die,
death is freedom.[1]

On the morning of 31 July 1926 the news headlines in Tokyo read:

> From a hemp rope tied to iron bars, death by hanging in the bright
> morning sunshine. Kaneko Fumiko hanged herself in prison under
> the very noses of those checking on her every ten minutes or so!

Beside this account on page one of the *Asahi Shinbun*, more headlines
ran: 'Body taken secretly to prison cemetery during the night'. Below
there was more: '"It is not that we permitted her to commit suicide",
insists the head of the prison branch; the lawyer, Fuse Tatsuji, says
"Responsibility lies with the branch".'[2] This was the Tochigi women's
branch of Tokyo's Utsunomiya Prison where, in April, Fumiko had
begun serving her life sentence. (Pak Yeol had been sent to Chiba
Prison). Fuse, Defence Attorney for Fumiko and Pak Yeol, was
quoted as saying that because the defendants had each been refusing
to eat, he and their friends had wanted permission from the Assistant
Chief of Police to visit and try to reason with them. The police official
had also been concerned about the possibility of suicide, given that
they had been pardoned by the emperor – for if they killed themselves
no apology to 'His Benevolent, Gracious Majesty' would be enough to
atone for the insult – but he still refused their friends permission to

visit. The surveillance of each of them was 'perfect', he insisted; there had been 'no cause for concern'.[3]

Fumiko's death had actually occurred a week before it hit the news. The death certificate gave her time of death as 6.40 a.m. on 23 July 1926.[4] The cause of death was recorded as suicide by suffocation caused by severe throttling of the throat by a hemp rope. According to prison staff, Fumiko had not only been refusing to eat, but steadfastly refused to co-operate in doing the work assigned to women prisoners, weaving rope from hemp. But then she asked to be allowed to work and was given the hemp. She worked hard that day, and the next morning the guard on duty looked in on her at 6.30 to find her diligently twisting the rope; yet when she was checked some ten minutes later, she was found hanging limply from the same rope now attached to bars at the window. She was immediately taken down and given artificial respiration, but it was too late; the doctor who arrived within twenty minutes also could not revive her. An autopsy was performed by the prison doctor with a local doctor in attendance, and their report expressed amazement at the 'determined, carefully premeditated, and calm manner of suicide'.[5]

Prison authorities did their best to keep Fumiko's death a secret, informing only her mother by urgent telegram on the same day, asking her to come and collect the body. When she refused, they petitioned her again, but ultimately decided to bury Fumiko in the graveyard nearby used for criminals with no relatives. Because of the gravity of the matter of Fumiko's death, the head warden had warned staff who knew of the 'calamity' to keep it quiet. The reason he gave for the secrecy, both then and later when he was quoted in the newspaper, was the 'shock to society' and strife the news might stir up amongst anarchists and sympathizers. He, too, hinted at another reason when he told her mother, lawyer and friends that he had increased surveillance of Fumiko because he was worried she might try to commit suicide: he believed that if she did manage to kill herself, he might be dismissed or have to resign in apology.[6] One point that should be made about the possibility of foul play is that if Fumiko had been murdered – or forced, encouraged or 'allowed' to commit suicide – it would have been tantamount to a countermand of the emperor's 'divine command' that she live. Thus, even if she was particularly unpopular with prison officials and guards, they might have deemed it wise to let her be. Once again, the apology the head warden alluded to, therefore, would have been to the emperor, indirectly at least.

One person who certainly did beg forgiveness for Fumiko's death was her mother, Kaneko Kikuno, but it was for her daughter's ingratitude:

> I did not have any idea that Fumiko was in Tochigi Prison until I had in my hands the urgent telegram I received at four p.m. on the twenty-third, advising me to collect her body because she had died. I was so thankful that Fumiko was saved like that from the death penalty that I never dreamed she would commit suicide. . . . There is nothing I can say that would be enough to apologize to everyone for Fumiko's killing herself when they went to so much trouble to save her like that.[7]

In 'everyone' she probably included the judiciary and government (for arranging an imperial pardon), as well as the emperor himself. The fact that Kikuno did not know that Fumiko had been transferred is an indication of the degree to which Fumiko was distanced from her family. Her comrades knew, however. One anarchist friend of Fumiko's, Mochizuki Kei, had been allowed to visit her about ten days before she died, and many years later he said that the two had been permitted to sit in the garden unsupervised, There he did a sketch of her.[8] But she had not been in contact with either of her parents for years, so to the journalist Kikuno explained that she had assumed the prison would have Fumiko cremated and her ashes delivered to Pak's older brother for burial in Korea. She must have been told by prison authorities that Fumiko had been legally registered as Pak's wife not long before she died.[9]

Because of the secrecy surrounding Fumiko's death for at least a week, some of her intimates were initially suspicious of the story put out by the authorities. What Mochizuki said about his meeting with Fumiko ten days before her death might suggest this because he said she had not appeared to be in a suicidal frame of mind. There were 'traces of sadness' in her face, he recalled, but she seemed in reasonably 'good spirits, calm as always, not much changed at all'.[10] But comrades certainly thought it strange that her lawyer had not been informed, though Fuse would have been regarded with suspicion by the authorities. Advertisements for Fuse's legal help – for help, that is, from 'The Proletariat's Friend, Rebel in the World of Lawyers, Fuse Tatsuji' – ran in radical publications in the 1920s, including those put out briefly by Pak, Fumiko and their group, the Futeisha (Malcontents' Society).[11] And before long he himself was imprisoned.[12] If the authorities wanted to keep news of Fumiko's death out of the papers, Fuse would have been the last person for them to inform.

It was after Kikuno told Fuse that the story broke. Then, because of the secretiveness of prison officials, some of Fumiko's friends felt they would not be satisfied until they saw her with their own eyes, so on 30 July a party comprised of Fuse, Kikuno and friends set out for Tochigi Prison. The exhumation was at dawn the next day, but, deciding it was too late for a post-mortem examination, the group took her immediately to be cremated.[13]

There was no way anyone could have known for certain that Fumiko killed herself, even if it was clear that the cause of death was hanging. After all, as Elise Tipton has noted, out of about 6,000 people prosecuted between 1928 and 1943, 'some hundreds suffered from torture and some dozens died in police custody'.[14] This notwithstanding, some of Fumiko's friends and also others connected with the trial seemed ready to accept that she had taken her own life. Kurihara Kazuo, a Futeisha comrade who had been present at the exhumation, wrote only a few years after her death, 'We know only too well the fact that Fumiko hanged herself.'[15] There was good reason for this ready acceptance of Fumiko's death by her own hand, for comrades and even some prison and judicial officials had actually *expected* her to try to commit suicide after her death penalty was commuted to life imprisonment. The widow of Judge Tatematsu also said many years later that her husband 'had been very worried about Fumiko because he had a presentiment that she would die after being moved to Tochigi'.[16] Involved in her case since its beginning, Tatematsu had known Fumiko well.

As for her lawyer, twenty years later at a welcoming reception held on 17 December 1945 to celebrate Pak Yeol's release from prison, Fuse made a speech that was more about Fumiko's death than Pak's survival. In that speech he assumed she had taken her own life. Responding to requests from the audience of assembled Korean and Japanese comrades and sympathizers, he gave the 'true facts' about her death as follows:

> We are moved by compassion to ask 'Why did Fumiko die in prison?'. We cannot help but be moved by Fumiko's determination. . . . You [to Pak] fought to survive today, but pure-hearted and stubborn Fumiko could not see that far. She couldn't take such a far-sighted view. . . . I wonder what the significance of her life was – as a wife devoted to Pak Yeol, as a Korean national devoted to Korea – even while she was living it in a Japanese prison under a life sentence of penal servitude that plundered her of body and soul. The fact that she died dedicating her life to Pak Yeol and her

bones were buried in Korean earth, becoming Korean earth, reveals to us the determination with which Fumiko dedicated herself body and soul to Korea. I believe that her death in prison truly put into practice the pure self-sacrifice of women; in going to death Fumiko was magnificent. I feel she died well for us. I want you, Pak Yeol and the whole assembly of Korean comrades here, to pay homage to this model Japanese woman who put into practice a glorious love of her comrades that crossed the national boundaries between Japan and Korea. I want you to praise the determination that kept Fumiko from the joy of being with us on this platform at this reception in celebration of Pak Yeol's wonderful survival.[17]

(Hence the title of his biography of Pak: *Victor Over Destiny*.) This was Fuse's welcome for Pak, and elegy for Fumiko. In explaining the reasons for her death, he used the term '*junjō*' (pure-heartedness or self-sacrificing devotion) twice and '*sasageru*' (to dedicate or sacrifice one's life) four times. From his remarks both about her stubbornness and her feminine '*junjō*', it is clear that, for him, Fumikos' taking her own life was an example of typically feminine self-sacrifice for a husband or family. His reference to Fumiko as a 'Korean national' could only have meant that he believed she styled herself in that way, even if she had not legally become Korean through marriage. In colonized Korea, Koreans were deemed Japanese, albeit second-class citizens. Thus, the 'true facts' of her death that he shared with the assembly were mainly that she had given her life for her husband, comrades and Korea. A knowledge of Fumiko's presentation of herself as a nihilist or egoist renders Fuse's interpretation of the 'true facts' of her death rather dubious, as we will see, but, given his emphasis here on the 'truth', we might wonder if some present on that day were still suspicious of the circumstances of Fumiko's death. Yet apart from his choice of words which could be taken to imply suspicious circumstances – his repeated use of the verb '*gokushi shita*' (died in prison) rather than, say, '*jisatsu shita*' (committed suicide) or '*ishi shita*' (hanged herself) – there is no other suggestion in his speech or elsewhere in his biography of Pak that Fumiko did not take her own life. And in the liberal atmosphere after the war, Fuse would have had little reason to conceal any doubts he may have had.

More recent sources, both in English and Japanese, also take it for granted that Fumiko's death was from suicide, and this includes even anarchist publications by Kokushoku Sensensha.[18] But there is good reason both for the above-mentioned expectation of intimates that she would kill herself and for this general acceptance that she did.

Perhaps one can never know for certain what happened in her cell early that morning on 23 July 1926, but in her own declarations there were a number of implicit suggestions or explicit statements to the effect that this was what she had intended. It was not only that she challenged judges to sentence her to death; on the other hand, she also continued to affirm death. She insisted that her *will to die* stayed firm, both early in her term of imprisonment when she tended to negate Life itself or later when she affirmed it. Thus, her death by her *own* hand has been seen as a natural consequence of her ideas. Like Suga, Fumiko's insistence that she had chosen death and would embrace it readily was clearly a means by which she sought to mitigate the power of her accusers. Suga's 'ontological pessimism' was only apparent, however, while for Fumiko it was for a time a weapon in her armoury, albeit one she ultimately replaced by an affirmation of both life and death that for her was truly 'nihilistic'.

The moon
shines, it shines
and yet,
people still follow
an endless dark road.[19]

Whether Fumiko meant to depict life as an endless road of darkness and suffering or was more concerned with human ignorance, this poem well captures a negativism about humanity that she often expressed. It conjures up a picture of life as a path along which people blindly grope their way, though the path is illuminated by the moon and should be clear. Thus, it suggests classical Buddhist 'pessimism', since in Buddhism ignorance and suffering are intimately connected and the moon has often symbolized enlightenment. The theme of death as freedom and thus a release from life ('an endless dark road') recalls a similar emphasis by Suga.

When in prison both Suga and Fumiko represented (death through) rebellion as the true aim of life. Fumiko's equation of the 'will to die' with 'freedom' is clear in the poem heading this chapter, but her attitude becomes even clearer when one considers her words while ripping the *imperial* pardon to shreds in anger in April 1926. As if this action-statement, completed before Ichigaya Prison officials and chaplain could overcome their shock and stop her, was not itself enough to consummate her 'blasphemy', she was also reported to have said at that moment:

> You toy with people's lives, killing or allowing to live as it suits you. What is this *special pardon*? Am I to be disposed of according to your [plural] whims?[20]

She was probably not just directing her comments to the official handing over the pardon to her, but at the authorities generally, including the emperor. There is little doubt that both in word and deed she was often trying to make it clear to her adversaries that it was not they who were in control of her situation and destiny.

Yet there had been many occasions during the trials when Fumiko said she wanted to die or insisted that it was she who had chosen her own death. She repeatedly demanded that the authorities sentence Pak and herself to death. Two years before she tore up the 'benevolent' pardon from Japan's supreme paternal figure, she had said in court:

> If you want to prevent an incident materializing, now is the time. You'd better kill me. However many years you keep me in prison, if you let me out into society once more, without fail I'll show you I can start afresh. I'll show you I can annihilate myself, and save you the trouble. Come, come, send this body of mine anywhere you like – even to the scaffold, to Hachiōji Prison. Bodies only die once. Do as you please. If you do something like that with me, it will just be proof-positive for me that I've lived my life to the full. I'll be satisfied with that.[21]

Her final words show that for her the way in which one died was the measure of one's life. The 'incident' mentioned was an imperial assassination attempt. She had just explained that the imperial family was manipulated by those she most 'abhorred', the government and their agents who were 'the holders of real power'. None the less, she said that she and Pak had discussed throwing bombs at the imperial family because they were the most obvious symbols of social inequality, even if said to be representative of national 'harmony'.

Fumiko was able to declare that she had chosen death partly because, according to her own testimony in the Supreme Court in 1926, she had lied about the extent of her guilt. That is, she had long pretended that she and Pak together laid practical plans for an imperial assassination attempt. One part of the plans was arranging to send their Korean comrade, Kim Choon Han, to Shanghai to procure explosives. But Fumiko now admitted that she knew of this plan only when it had already fallen through, hastening to add that she had not objected when she did find out about it. She had claimed much earlier in the trials that she had offered to go herself to Shanghai because a Japanese woman would not be bothered by police. (Pak was both Korean and a known radical.[22]) Of course, this may not have been true either. Perhaps it was *partly* because of such inconsistencies in her testimonies that before the Supreme Court trial judges decided to subject her to a psychological examination to see if 'madness' might be grounds for sparing her from the gallows. While they might have expected a woman to be more than usually 'emotional', they probably could not comprehend her alternating fits of reticence and outbursts of passion and hostility – especially when it came to greater and lesser father-figures. It is difficult to know whether to describe their finding her 'sane' to be predictable or strange, given the all too obvious 'confusion of tongues' between her and her 'protectors'.

Fumiko's 'confession' in 1926 about her *lack* of guilt was as follows:

> Even supposing that Pak had discussed the matter of Kim Choon Han with me, it's open to question whether I actually would have opposed it. No, I probably would've had faith in him and let him get on with it. The result is certainly as I'd expect, and I guess it's now over. I would not have censured Pak then. *No, no* [in English], quite the contrary, I would've been very happy about it.[23]

This was part of a memo she drafted the night before she read it out in court. In it she suggested that by this time such an admission would make no difference, and it did not: her 'blasphemous' statements about the imperial family and her threats against them were enough to convict her of high treason.

The only explanation Fumiko gave for now denying knowledge of Pak's attempt to import bombs was that she 'could not bear deceiving herself'; it was not that she 'felt any duty or responsibility' to tell officials the truth. What she meant by deceiving *herself* is unclear, but perhaps she simply disliked the pretence and wanted to set the record straight. The statement she read aloud in court ended as follows:

> I know Pak, and I love him. Whatever his faults and weaknesses, I love him. Now I unconditionally approve of the mistakes Pak made that affected me as well. So, to Pak's friends I say: 'If this incident seems stupid to you, go ahead and laugh at us both. It's only our affair.' And to the officials I say: 'Please go right ahead and hurl us both under the guillotine. If I can die with Pak I'll be content.' And to Pak I say: 'Even if the sentence handed down by the officials should separate us, I'll never let you die alone.'[24]

Presumably, the 'mistakes' she mentioned were in connection with Pak's getting caught, while the reference to his friends might have meant those who had been arrested with them, but were then released. Perhaps Fumiko thought they were laughing at Pak and herself for implicating themselves and taking a futile, 'heroic' stand.

Apart from the questions it raises about the extent of Fumiko's guilt and about whether she was intent on sacrificing herself for Pak, this statement shows that her 'confession' was not a last-minute attempt to evade the death penalty. It suggests also that for a long time during the trials she not only refused to defend herself, but co-operated with the authorities in establishing her guilt. That she was guilty of anti-imperial treachery was clear from the start, but the extent to which she had played a part in the 'conspiracy' is not clear, even if one of the Futeisha members, Niiyama Hatsuyo, had testified that Fumiko once let it slip that Pak had received a letter from a member of the Korean independence terrorist group, the Ūiyōldan.[25] In her statement Fumiko emphasized that she still accepted the tactic of imperial assassination theoretically, but whether there had been any serious 'intent' on her part is impossible to know. Despite all her protestations that there had been, she may have deliberately lied about this too to force the hand of her enemies.

As intimated above in connection with Fuse's representation of Fumiko's motives for suicide, discussion of the constructions she placed upon death (and life) could not be conducted without reference to her 'nihilism'. The most important of her nihilistic influences was the egoist, Max Stirner, whom she often quoted, but she also mentioned in her memoirs an interest in Nietzsche.[26] Because her understanding of nihilism changed significantly during her prison term, I might proceed by contrasting a few of the early statements in which Fumiko negated life itself in pessimistic style, with some in the Supreme Court in 1926. In her second court testimony in 1924, in answer to Judge Tatematsu's question about how she came to embrace nihilism, she narrated her full life history. This was her conclusion to that narration:

> I don't bear a grudge against my father or mother, but it is true that much of my life was spent in extreme hardship. I was cursed by it everywhere I went, and this made me want to die as I do, annihilating everything, cursing nature, cursing society, cursing all that lives.[27]

In her next testimony she repeated that 'the total destruction of all life' was the goal of her nihilism, at another point 'the annihilation of the human race'.[28] It seems that here Fumiko used 'annihilating' literally: she was not expounding a radical solipsism whereby the ego and what it creates are the only knowable and existent things, and thus all would be annihilated with its destruction. While such an emphasis on annihilating humanity might not suggest it, she explained her ideas quite rationally, if not always coolly, in her Twelfth Interrogation Record and elsewhere. However, she did get carried away with the rhetoric of 'destruction' or 'negation' at times; and said as much herself later in 1926.

Fumiko's early declarations about the nature of her nihilism imply that for her it first meant a negation of Life. Thus, it is unclear whether she was then aware of Nietzsche's condemnation of 'nihilism' – of the 'life-denying, pessimistic and dualistic' systems of Christianity, idealism, and so on. He distinguished two types of nihilism: the 'passive', negative type prior to himself; and the 'awakened or active', positive type.[29] Perhaps we could term Fumiko's earlier nihilism, negative and her later nihilism, positive. To give a further indication of the former, we might turn to a letter she wrote to Judge Tatematsu in May 1925 which was largely inspired by a third nihilistic influence, a Russian novelist named Mikhail Artzibashev.[30] She quoted Artzibashev in this letter which she signed 'Kaneko Fumi' and dated simply the morning of the 21st (of May 1925).

After six in the morning. For something to do before breakfast, I opened up and looked through the collected works of a Russian writer which was sent in to me a few days ago. I was impressed by one paragraph I came across by chance, and I'll take this opportunity to preach to you: 'It's a joke to admonish a person who wants to live not to want to live. Likewise, it's a real joke to turn to a person content with life and tell him his life is very unhappy.'

So I say to you: 'It's a joke to admonish a person who doesn't want to live to want to live. It's a real joke to turn to a person not content with life and tell him his life is very happy.'

For me life has no value. Value comes through a person's having joy in life. Everything about humans is individual, but nothing is more coloured by individuality than the issue of life and death.

Here she stated that life had no value and she did not want to live, though we could hardly fail to note that this statement was *to a judge who was probably trying to tempt her to recant* so she could be 'absolved'. Equally noteworthy is her reference to the highly individual nature of life and death and her refusal to beg – presumably for her life:

For the person who says 'I want to live', even if it's as a beggar, clearly life itself is the highest value. But, for the person who wants to die rather than being a beggar, life in itself has little value.

For the person who wants to live to see 'life' as the object and drag the person who doesn't want to live [back] to 'life' is a joke, ridiculous, an unwanted favour. It reveals [that person's] own superficiality and blindness to reality.

A person can fully live only when the *process* [English word] of life itself is happy for him [*sic*], or when his life is given meaning by something.

Say there is one certain person . When [this person] wants to cast off a reality full of pain, or rather wants to go to the darkness with joy, who has the right to pull him [*sic*] back to endure that pain?

Finally, Artzibashev said: 'Only those who find joy in life should live; those who don't see anything in it must die.' Finally, I say: 'The person who wants to live – live! The person who wants to die – die! That's the reality of life.'

Judge, your half-measures bother me. I don't know why you understand me so little. You should consider well the words and feelings I've expressed here, then come and see me.

Give me back my letters soon, please – what [you've] 'prohibited'. May is almost over, you know. Come and see me soon.[31]

Fumiko's reference to the judge's 'half-measures' probably meant he was too 'soft', or that he was dilly-dallying.[32] Otherwise, it must have been Artzibashev's *Sanine* that she cited, because its hero did say at one point: 'He only ought to live who finds joy in living; but for him who suffers, death is best'.[33] This letter reveals the familiarity between Fumiko and Tatematsu, as well as the ambivalence of their relationship. It is also an indication of why he had thought Fumiko might die in prison.

At the end of 1925, in one of the many statements where she declared that she alone controlled her destiny, Fumiko retracted her earlier (negative nihilistic) call for the 'annihilation of all life'. She wrote out a long untitled statement for Supreme Court Judge Itakura in which she expounded her nihilist thinking yet again. In this statement Fumiko explained what she *now* meant by negating or affirming life, both life in general and her own life:

Formerly I said 'I negate life'. Speaking scientifically, that is so . . . [but] a negation of life does not originate in philosophy, for life alone is the origin of all things. . . . Yes. My negation of all life was completcly meaningless. Negation is not created from negation.

The stronger the affirmation, the stronger the negation created. That is, the stronger the affirmation of life, the stronger the creation of life-negation together with rebellion. Therefore I affirm life. I affirm it strongly. And since I affirm life, I resolutely rebel against all power that coerces life. . . . Thus you officials might ask, 'Then why did you pretend you were trying to destroy your own life?' I would answer: 'Living is not synonymous with merely having movement. It is moving in accordance with one's own will. . . . One could say that with deeds one begins to really live. Accordingly, when one moves by means of one's own will and this leads to the destruction of one's body, this is not a negation of life. It is an affirmation.'[34]

Her comments on 'life-affirmation' suggest an influence from Nietzsche and/or Stirner. At about the same time as making this statement, Fumiko declared that up until then she had 'overstated' what she had been saying about 'annihilating all things'. This was just 'bombast' because she really only intended to 'eliminate' those with power over her.[35] She had also got a bit carried away with 'cursing life', she said in the Supreme Court in February 1926, when really she ought to 'affirm life . . . affirm everything'; she 'could not accept the thinking that aimed at the annihilation of humanity'.[36] But, as Morinaga indicates, affirming Life still did not mean that she was telling the Supreme Court Judges that she wanted to live.

For the purposes of this preliminary discussion of Fumiko's use of 'nihilism' as a discursive weapon, the most important point in her later untitled statement is her assertion that an affirmation of Life is *creative*: it creates both one's own physical negation, and one's affirmation (will to rebel, perhaps 'will to power'). Self-creation and ego-assertion are central themes in Stirner, who also said 'the *own will* of Me is the State's destroyer'. Fumiko insisted that an assertion of will (through 'deeds') was positive, notwithstanding the negation-destruction of one's physical self. 'Life-affirmation' for her seemed to mean something like it did for Stirner: en*joy*ment of life meant using it up, 'consuming' it (or 'annihilating it'), while also consuming or 'dissolving' oneself.[37] In an earlier statement of Fumiko's, without the emphasis on life-affirmation but still rather similar, she had said that her (terrorist) 'plan' was both negative and positive: 'negatively, it is the denial of my individual life, while positively, its aim is the eventual collapse of all authority in this world'.[38] She had no qualms about applying the word *'tero'* (terrorism) to her aims, but hers was said to be a 'philosophical' rather than 'political' form of nihilism.[39]

An early testimony of Fumiko's, the twelfth, which she gave in May 1924, has been taken as representative of her thinking throughout her stay in prison.[40] It is most often cited in discussions of her ideas because in it she went into great detail about various aspects of her ideology. It contains an explanation of why she opposed the emperor and emperor-system. Yet the problem with taking this testimony as representative of Fumiko's nihilism, is that it is an early statement of her ideas which she continued to develop throughout her stay in prison. She was not nearly so pessimistic about life later, for example, which is to say that she was more careful to expound a death-affirmation that was not merely the logical consequence of a personal negativism about life.

Fumiko believed her ultimate 'affirmation of Life' was consistent with her nihilist-egoist philosophy. Even late in the trials she still said she wanted to die, though if she first took Stirner's assertion 'I do not love [the world], for I *annihilate* it as I annihilate myself' literally, now she was careful to differentiate between destroying all life, and destroying just those in power. This threat that she often hurled at the authorities while expounding her approach to death and life could hardly have been more explicit. She clearly meant that, one way or another, she too would be destroyed in or through acts of rebellion. Amongst her 'acts of will', moreover, were *symbolic* acts or 'deeds'. One has been mentioned – her ripping the imperial pardon to shreds. One wonders if Fumiko's audience, like Suga's before her, could have failed to see the contrast she was setting up between those who lived a *living death*, and those like herself whose death through a Life-affirmative, self-willed rebellion would be proof of the fullness and truth of a life.

My soul
will perish, and yet –
washing my hands
of the ugliness of the
human world is fine by me.[41]

We often find Fumiko indicating her disgust with the human world – in another poem, her 'blazing hatred for humankind'. In the above, however, we also find the hint of an ambiguity in her view of death and beyond. She did not, like Suga, set out to prove herself a scientific materialist and dismiss continuity after death, and one can see in Fumiko's writings signs of a spiritual consolation in the face of death that she apparently saw no reason to conceal (even if she meant to leave her memoirs and poetry to comrades). In this poem about the ugliness of humanity Fumiko first categorically states that her soul will perish, cease to exist or be destroyed (*waga tama horobi*), but then specifies that it is the world of *people* that is ugly, and therefore that it is this she will leave. At the very end of her autobiography she wrote:

> My existence will probably soon vanish from this world. But I believe that even though phenomena are extinguished as phenomena, they continue in a real eternal existence. Now, tranquil and composed I lay down the brush with which I wrote this memoir. Blessings on all those I love![42]

Whether she used 'blessings' (*shukufuku*) with a consciousness of its religious connotations or used it as a formality, out of habit rather than conviction, is not a question that can be resolved. Her use of 'blessings' is reminiscent of Suga's 'praying' for her friends' good health and long lives. Yet there is little doubt that she was expressing a belief in some sort of continuity after death when she referred to her 'real [non-physical] existence', which would be 'eternal'. It might seem as though Fumiko merely meant that matter is conserved even if not in the same form, but the way she expressed herself in this entire passage suggests otherwise. Firstly, she spoke of vanishing from 'this' world (*kono yo*), then said that like all phenomenal things she would be extinguished, but suggested that she would none the less continue in a non-phenomenal form ('*Shikashi, issai no genshō wa genshō toshite wa horoboshitemo . . .*'). If, however, she only meant that she would continue in some other phenomenal form, why would she have described this continuity as not only a 'real/true existence' (*jitsuzai*), but also one that is 'eternal' (*eien*)?

It would certainly be reading too much into Fumiko's words to ascribe to them a Judeo-Christian-like concept of the soul (a permanent continuity of individual personality) – even if she did once experience a dramatic though brief conversion to Christianity – but her suggestion that there is a reality which is eternal, which is not phenomenal or connected with this material world, has a decidedly spiritual ring to it. About her own 'soul', moreover, she also penned the following:

Deploring
the war of two minds
within –
of the spirit and the flesh.
That's me these days!

My spirit!
Here I am in prison,
driven
to hoping
it's immortal.[43]

There is no ambiguity in Fumiko's use of 'spirit', because she used '*tama*' (also the 'soul') in both cases. The two poems remind us of Suga's smiling when she pondered her 'eternal life', but Suga had flatly denied that her consolation in the face of death was religious. Fumiko made no such declarations, and when she hoped for 'immortality', she was speaking of the survival of her 'soul', not revolutionary immortality. Her hope for 'immortality' was like Suga's in one way – a consolation when death was approaching, and probably a way of strengthening resolution. And apart from the similar political function of their conceptions of 'immortality', the two also had in common a fantasy about vengeance from the grave which indicates a frustrated desire for this-worldly retribution.

Imagining me
a vengeful spirit
stripped of
the fetters of flesh,
paying evil in kind.[44]

Neither Suga nor Fumiko merely *imagined* vengeance from the grave: they expressed their fantasies in words, in texts that would certainly be read by some among the 'evildoers' they had in their sights. Was this a way of menacing their enemies by hinting that not even death would stop them? Fumiko often indicated that a desire for revenge had been one of her motives for deciding to carry out assassinations and rise up in rebellion. In her autobiography she gave two reasons for drawing back at the last moment when about to commit suicide in

Korea at the age of 12 or 13. She had lived there for six years with her paternal grandmother and aunt who were wealthy colonists.[45] Apart from the fact that she was suddenly struck by the tranquillity and beauty of nature, which she contrasted with the 'cruel, unfeeling' human world, the other reason she did not throw herself into the river was her desire for revenge:

> Thinking in this way, I'd already decided, 'I *won't* die. Yes, together with people made to suffer like me, I must avenge myself on those responsible for our suffering. That's right. I *won't* die! And I settled back onto the riverbank again, and threw away one by one the stones in my sleeves and fastened [in the slip tied] around my waist.
>
> That pitiable young girl decided to die, and almost did. How dreadful and unnatural to seek relief in death at an age when she should have been reaching up like a young blade of grass; how dreadful, and how sad to continue living with that one desire, revenge.
>
> I stepped up to the threshold of the realm of death, but suddenly turned back. Then, I returned to the home of my aunt, a hell in this world. Having returned, one gleam of hope shone within me, a gleam melancholy and dark. But then I had the strength to endure any amount of suffering.
>
> I was no longer a child – more like a little demon with a thorn lodged in her.[46]

Fumiko indicated that she still had that 'thorn lodged in her' many years later when penning the memoirs that were largely an indictment of her family.

On 15 July 1925 she wrote two poems that suggest her desire for a very personal sort of revenge, directed at the family in Korea who had tormented her. Both tanka have an 'I'll show them!' theme:

> Memories of
> being under Aunt's care
> in Korea –
> all of a sudden I
> yearn for fame.

> At times
> I wanted to be a woman of
> renown,
> just so I could say
> 'Look at me!'[47]

Fumiko could have meant either 'notoriety' or 'fame/renown'; either way there is no doubt that she wanted her aunt's family to know about her situation and be shamed. Assuming that this was because they 'had made her like that' is consistent with her accounts of mistreatment by her family, particularly in Korea, which she said had played a large part in leading her to rebel. At this time Fumiko was well on the way to 'notoriety' as the poems were written just two days before she was indicted for high treason.

One difference between Suga's stated desire for vengeance and Fumiko's is that while the former wanted to avenge herself on individual prosecutors, and politicians, the latter was more class-oriented: she may have mentioned her relatives in Korea in this connection, but it was not only her own suffering she wanted to avenge; her sights were set on the ruling class as a whole. (She said she once planned to throw a bomb into the midst of the Diet, for example.) Later in her memoirs, she explained that she had developed years before an empathy for others who were exploited and oppressed, including colonized Koreans. In short, while Suga said she wanted to avenge specific political evils like the suppression of socialists, Fumiko indicated that she sought revenge for social evils like discrimination based on wealth, nationality or birth. Fumiko had been an unregistered child, and as such had not officially existed so had not been readily accepted into schools.[48]

Yet, like Suga, whose desire for vengeance was directed at those responsible for the repression of comrades, Fumiko did write one poem that was explicitly about avenging the murders of political friends:

> Sadly
> I recall the vow
> I made
> to the spirits of departed friends.
> It's September 1st![49]

There is little doubt that Fumiko meant an oath of vengeance, for 1 September 1923 was the day of the Great Kanto Earthquake. She was obviously referring to a vow made (in prison) to murdered Korean or Japanese comrades, most probably some of the socialists killed by military or civilian police during the period of martial law after the earthquake.[50] The 'departed friends' might even have been the anarchist couple, Itō Noe and Ōsugi Sakae, the former a well-known anarcho-feminist publicist, the latter the leading anarchist theorist of the day. Fumiko wrote a poem on 16 September 1925 about reading Ōsugi's autobiography in prison, which was one of the few she dated: on that day two years before Ōsugi and Itō had been arrested by military police and later murdered. Thus, the poem written two weeks earlier on 'September 1st' about the 'departed friends' to be avenged could well have been about them. While in this poem Fumiko might have been bemoaning the fact that she had been unable to carry out her vow, her many references to vengeance in this life or the next must have been meant to demonstrate how much of a threat she was either to society in general or specifically to those in power.

In earnest
about hurling
dynamite,
over the floor
s/he threw cold tea.[51]

This poem suggests a romanticization of political heroism amongst Fumiko's peers. It conjures up a picture of a radical activist with romantic notions of performing a *great act* and, according to Japanese popular traditions of heroic action, probably dying in the act. Fumiko must have been talking of someone amongst her own set of friends. The vision of heroism that she and her nihilist comrades shared, however, differed from that of Meiji socialists somewhat because not so closely bound up with altruistic selflessness, idealism and grand causes. The differences, in fact, in Suga's and Fumiko's views of action, political heroes and causes are differences we would expect between a (collectivistic) anarchist and (egoistic) nihilist.

It should be acknowledged that Fumiko was capable of making a remark in her prison memoirs like 'Ah, how I want to . . . fight to the extent of sacrificing [*gisei*] my life for our pitiable class'.[52] But this notwithstanding, she was far from consistent in her acceptance of the ideal of self-sacrifice as part of her construction of heroic action and death; actually, she was often scathing about the notion of sacrifice for a grand cause. In one early testimony she explained why she had been attracted to Pak (more than a year before their arrests). It was because they shared the same ideas and approach to political action. She had seen him as the sort of person who would 'act on his ego, and stake his life for the Movement',[53] which was partly a reference to *jiga no shuchō* ('self-' or '*ego*-assertion'). What is significant is her emphasis on *self-sacrifice* for a 'class' or a 'movement' (the Korean Independence Movement), but for 'egoistic' motives. She might have mentioned class here, suggesting a socialist utopian vision of the future, but Fumiko also insisted that she did not have a 'far-distant, idealistic purpose': she did not believe in a future ideal society based on the 'well-being' of all people.[54] And someone who did not believe in utopianism would hardly see her own death as a noble contribution to such a cause. Fumiko may have dreamed of a heroic death, whether on the scaffold or if ever released into society again, but willing martyrdom for a cause did not seem to be a consistent part of that dream. The self-denial it implied was doubtless out of place in her construction of herself as a dangerous, amoral, egoistic nihilist. Stirner meant by ego-assertion the opposite of self-'denial' for any cause but one's *own*. Similarly, Fumiko said in an early court testimony that part of the reason for her earlier abandonment of socialism and then anarchism, was her disillusionment with romantic views of the masses.[55] Part of her scepticism about socialist (including anarchist) idealism was that she had come to see the farmers and workers as too passive – 'stupid' in their too-ready acceptance of their 'chains'. There is no sign here of an altruistic notion of sacrifice for the (noble) masses. This 'nihilist' was aware of the contradiction inherent in her wanting to sacrifice herself for a class or an ideal, even if sometimes she lost sight of it.

But did she want to sacrifice herself for Pak? One can see already the need to question the remarks by her lawyer about her sacrificing herself for Pak and for Korea. In January 1924 she had pointed out that she sympathized with the goal of independence for Korea, and was certainly not 'prejudiced' against Koreans; yet she did not have any particular 'esteem' for them either, and had not decided to co-operate politically and live with Pak out of mere sympathy.[56] She and he shared the same ideas, as well as a similar vision of a 'task' in life, a task that connected with concrete and immediate action. In the context of the nature of her 'task' Fumiko also said: 'I am not living for the sake of other people. Must I not earn my own true satisfaction and freedom? I must do this myself.' A little further on she wrote about herself and her nihilist friend, Niiyama Hatsuyo:

> Even though neither of us had ideals regarding society, we both thought about having something we could call our own true task. It wasn't that we felt it had to be fulfilled. We merely thought it would be enough if we could look upon it as our true task.[57]

Fumiko's comments about her task in life are quite 'egoistic': she emphasized living for the moment and for herself, rejecting ideals connected with society and finding her own task. She also stated that the task need not be fulfilled, suggesting that the action – Act-in-itself – was important.

Toward the end of her autobiography, Fumiko spoke of the sort of obstacles that would have prevented her from joining forces with Pak. Significantly, she said that if he had been active in the Korean Independence Movement, she would not have co-operated with him politically nor lived with him. Narrating the circumstances of her rather lame 'proposal' to Pak, Fumiko said she had first ascertained that he was not prejudiced against ordinary Japanese people, and then had continued:

> Well then, there's something else I want to ask you. Aren't you in the Korean People's Movement? I was in Korea a long time and feel as if I can understand somehow the feelings of people active in the Movement. But however you look at it, I'm not Korean and not oppressed by Japan in the same way as Koreans, so I don't feel I want to work together with someone active in the Independence Movement. Therefore, if you are an Independence Movement activist, I won't be able to join you though it's regrettable.[58]

Certainly by the time she was writings her memoirs, Fumiko did not envisage herself working toward the goal of Korean independence.

The remarks of her lawyer and the way she has been represented in historical sources notwithstanding, Fumiko did not represent her political stand as a sacrifice for Korea or for Pak. Quite unlike Suga, in her remarks about him and Korean liberation there is not even a hint that she saw herself (or wanted to be seen) as a martyr for the Korean or any other external cause. She probably wrote this account of the beginning of her life with Pak in the first part of her prison term, but if her attitude toward self-sacrifice underwent a change later, there is no sign of it. In fact, in the untitled statement written at the end of 1925, Fumiko expounded Stirner's ideas as follows:

> People cannot love others; it is their own selves they love. All people are egoists. But one's self is not fixed. The ego is flexible. Sometimes they extend [that love] to the nation or to humanity, and sometimes you see a conflict within the individual between the self and others, so social cohesion amongst people is sustained just by this elasticity of the ego. . . . So what is virtue? Virtue in human society is the situation of co-existence and co-prosperity. However, the inevitabil-

ity of the survival of the fittest violates this law of existence; it prevents it. So here I proclaim: 'Rise up and rebel! Rebel! Rebel against all power! It is participating in the checking of power that is virtue. That is, rebelling against the oppressors is a virtue for those oppressed, a virtue for all humanity.[59]

Stirner was implacably hostile to notions of selflessness and martyrdom, and derided conceptions of 'the Good Cause' (whether God's, humanity's, justice's, my people's, my fatherland's, etc.). He also wrote about one's task, but rejected the notion of a 'calling', implying a destiny controlled by something/one other than oneself; for him, it was not one's 'task' but one's Act. On 'love', he said, 'I love . . . everyone. But I love them with the consciousness of egoism; I love them because love makes me happy, I love . . . because it pleases me. I know no "commandment of love".'[60] Moreover, there is no suggestion of sacrifice on behalf of others in this statement of Fumiko's, but rather an equation of self-satisfaction, creation or assertion with rebellion. At most, one may be able to find in these comments a hint that Fumiko's 'egoistic' quest was at times in conflict with the demands of love.

In the declaration in the Supreme Court where she started by saying that she loved Pak and ended by stating once again her desire to die with him, Fumiko also said that this was despite his 'faults, weaknesses, and mistakes'. When she clarified her nihilism in the Supreme Court she first said, 'I don't know whether Pak negates life or not'; and then followed this with, 'but I must affirm life, affirm everything, so I cannot accept the thinking that aims at the annihilation of humanity'. Here she even distanced herself from Pak philosophically. Distancing herself from him in terms of their shared political commitment or the penalty they should receive for their 'treason' was obviously the last thing she wanted; being true to her own ideas was probably foremost in her mind, even if that meant criticizing his understanding of nihilist philosophy. Fumiko, in short, wanted to be as much or more a nihilist than Pak, which is why she made a point of relating how she had once told him that if he should ever be corrupted politically and collaborate with those in power, she would immediately renounce him.[61]

Yet in what was doubtless another symbolic action-statement, Fumiko and Pak registered their marriage in prison on 23 March 1926, two days before being sentenced to death. If not partly a political statement against the imperialist state that condemned her 'malcontent' Korean partner and herself – one more way of shouting her defiance – one wonders why Fumiko had appeared in the Supreme

Court on 26 February, the first day of the trial, in Korean dress. Setouchi Harumi simply states in her earlier full-length biography of Fumiko published in 1975 that Fumiko wore ceremonial Korean dress on this day, while in her biographical article published six years later in 1981 she refers to it as a bridal dress. The symbolism of the action would be even more interesting if the latter were both true and deliberate (that is, if Fumiko had specifically asked comrades to get her a wedding dress), but I suspect that neither was the case. Kim (a Korean and Pak's biographer) simply says that Pak wore ceremonial Korean dress and Fumiko white Korean clothing. Fumiko herself, moreover, wrote a poem (which is included below) where she said only that the dress was Korean and white.[62] In any event, such acts are, no doubt, partly why Fuse and others have described her death as a sacrifice for her husband and his country. But there is more than one way to read such actions. Perhaps she wanted mainly to show her disgust with the imperialistic Japanese state by rejecting Japanese nationality. It is difficult to imagine Fumiko affirming any nationality when she had already insisted that the struggle for Korean independence was not hers. Moreover, the fact that she and Pak were *legally* married immediately before being sentenced for high treason may have also been meant to underscore the obvious irony in the fact that the Japanese state had united them legally in life before uniting them 'legally' in death. Whatever Fumiko meant by such apparently symbolic acts, the picture of the 'noble, self-sacrificing wife' is more the all too obviously gendered, imaginative construct of others.

On various occasions Fumiko threatened that, whatever the court decided, she would die with Pak. (Clearly, she was afraid that only he would be executed because only he, really, was guilty of the charges.) In the Supreme Court she cried, 'I'll never let you die alone!'; and near the close of her memoir, she claimed that four years earlier she had vowed: 'I'll always be with you. When you're ill, I'll never let you suffer. If you die, let's die together.[63] We'll live together, and die together.' But dying *with* Pak is not synonymous with dying *for* him, and in any event this statement about an early desire to die with Pak was *written* when they were facing the death penalty. Clearly, Fumiko was a passionate woman (at least when in prison), and much has been made of these sorts of statements in works about her. But because this was written at a time when she was probably worried she would not be executed with Pak, it is not reliable evidence for an intention four or more years before to kill herself if he died. It is quite possible that there was a political death-pact between Fumiko and Pak, made either before or during their imprisonment; but even if there had not been, Fumiko's romanticization of death *with* Pak is reflected by her repeated challenges to judges to sentence them *both* to death, and by her insistence that, whatever happened, he would not die alone.

Even if we do assume, firstly, that Fumiko took her own life and, secondly, that she was carrying out her intention to die with Pak (thinking that he would die or kill himself in prison), we do not have to read her action as a sacrifice for him. It might not have been *for* anything or anyone, in fact, unless for herself. Her statement cited above about her own physical negation as derived from her resistance/affirmation of life does not suggest that selflessness was an essential part of the meaning she ascribed to her death. Perhaps she did choose death for the second time, as her biographer Setouchi says, in one final act of rebellion.[64] This would certainly be consistent with her nihilism: 'Am I to be disposed of according to your whims?' And if she did annihilate herself, she would have *wanted* it to be seen by friends and foes as an affirmation of life, an assertion of her *Self* and will. For Fumiko, taking her *own* life may well have been the ultimate symbolic action-statement, a symbol of her power.

Alone
feeling sorry for myself,
rubbing
the numbness in a
trifling pen-callous.[65]

Like Suga, Fumiko insisted that she did not like pretence; therefore, when facing death directly she wanted to set the record straight in her testimonies. Also, however, throughout her imprisonment she wrote poems for herself (some of which were published by her comrades while she was still alive) that, in very 'Zen' style, perhaps, expressed the emotions of the moment very frankly. As with Suga, when one looks at her poetry in particular, one gets glimpses of a different, possibly contradictory but certainly more complex picture than that derived from her testimonies and memoirs. The latter were more clearly statements of defiance to self-empowering ends because intended for an audience of judges. In her poems, on the other hand, she spoke of things on which she was otherwise silent. Firstly, in them she was capable of a cynical sort of humour that was often directed at herself or her situation, as both the poem above and the earlier one about revolutionary zeal indicate. There are signs in them of an amusement at the absurdities or bitter ironies of the world. But Fumiko's tanka express a broad range of emotions, including self-mockery, pessimism, grief and depression, anger and frustration, rebellion, love and hatred, and distraction *almost* to the point of 'madness'.

Amidst the varied and conflicting emotions expressed in Fumiko's poetry, however, fear is not as strongly in evidence as in some of Suga's poems. Possibly, this was the only emotion to which Fumiko would not admit – even to herself. One poem might be taken to suggest it:

> Tiny nameless weeds
> entwined about my fingers.
> Abruptly I
> pull them up, 'I want to live!'
> they cry faintly.[66]

The use of 'nameless weeds' is consistent with Fumiko's view of herself: for a long time she had had 'no name', was left untended and grew wild, at least in the sense that she had no-one to care for her. She wrote another poem about pulling out weeds in the prison garden, and there she strengthens the probability that the weeds were an allegory for herself: 'uprooted, trodden on, writhing in pain – their forms both hateful and pitiful.' On another occasion, she referred to herself as 'ugly' (though not physically) rather than 'hateful':

> Forlorn
> I gaze at my ugly heart,
> my body
> wrapped in a pure-white
> Korean dress.[67]

All this strengthens the likelihood that in the poem about pulling out weeds, it was the *will to live* in all living things – including herself – that she was expressing, however 'faintly', and not fear of death at all! (This, too, could be taken as an indication of her ultimate, positive-nihilist affirmation of life.) Similarly, she wrote more than one poem apparently mourning the number of people (comrades?) who had died in prison, though this also does not necessarily indicate a fear of sharing the same fate. One of those poems was:

> Is it the souls
> of those perished under
> the guillotine,
> that vermilion of
> the garden azaleas?[68]

She must have been saddened to think of others before her who had spent time in this garden and never regained their freedom.

Fumiko was willing to reveal her sadness and fits of depression in her tanka, and also her self-doubt or derision. In the poem in which she refers to her white dress, presumably a symbol of purity, she implies that her (red) heart is polluted. She uses word plays on the colours of red and white again in the one about 'red azaleas', and yet again refers to her picking such a flower in the flickering sunshine in the prison garden and seeing it turn into 'pure-white cremated bones'. While white generally represents purity in Japanese folk religion and red can symbolize pollution, in Buddhism red is the colour of desire that brings about retribution. (Thus, prisoners wore red uniforms.) But this final poem might have been written when Fumiko was in a less sombre mood, and probably needs no further comment beyond stating the obvious that at that moment she found it hard to treat something – or someone – seriously. If not herself, had she been sporting with someone else?

> I ask my heart
> if I am jesting or
> in earnest,
> and it doesn't answer –
> it just grins broadly.[69]

5   Commentary: discourse on death and beyond

Thus far in my interpretation of how Suga and Fumiko presented themselves in relation to death, I have commented only on some contextual issues. In order to make sense of the sense they made to those they were conversing with, however, an understanding of their respective discursive contexts is necessary. This first requires a consideration of the general 'discourse on death and beyond' in which they participated. In this chapter, therefore, my focus is on the more abstract discursive context: the religions, philosophies, ontologies that might have influenced Suga's and Fumiko's constructions of death. After some preliminary remarks on thanatology, particularly as it relates to Japan, Tenrikyō and Christianity will claim my attention. This will be followed by a discussion of Meiji and Taishō 'physics' and metaphysics, much of the latter part of which will concentrate on Fumiko's philosophical influences. Finally, five modes of symbolic 'immortality' said to be universal,[1] will be utilized as a framework for interpreting further the ways in which, when facing death, Suga and Fumiko each expressed a sense of continuity with life. This interpretation of the more abstract, 'grey' areas of the subjects' engagements with death will also hinge upon of the centrality of the issue of power. Even the literal sense of 'immortality' implies that one lives on, that mortality is negated: death, in short, has lost its 'sting'. And when the context of such a symbolization of immortality is a courtroom or cell where one is being threatened with death, it can also be seen to be empowering not just in relation to the 'last enemy' of death, but also other opponents.

We have already seen how the religious attitudes of both women would best be described as ambivalent. Yet their occasional suggestions of a 'life' after death represented a defensive–offensive mechanism with more subtlety than notions of heavenly, paradisial or nirvanic rewards. When they voiced a 'pessimism' about this world or life, it did not hinge on an 'other-worldly' longing for the next. If, at times, they denied the value of life, it was to demonstrate that they had come to terms with quitting it. We could not assume from this that either was an unusually 'pessimistic' person, but would expect to find that this apparently 'ontological' negativism had much to do with her immediate political context. Perhaps scholars today are less inclined to reduce the question of the apparent pessimism of individuals like Suga or Fumiko to individual psychology or 'Oriental' (Buddhist) metaphysical tendencies, however, since a post-Idealist, post-'Orientalist' approach to an individual's construction of death requires a recognition that it could not have had only metaphysical influences, nor been due to a static essentialist identity, whether cultural or psychological. What is more to the point is the manner in which these 'traitors' contributed to a discourse on the quality of life possible in their world – broadcasting their apparent 'ontological pessimism' *while in the custody of the state.*

There is too large a body of thanatological literature available in English for it to be treated in depth here. I might simply note, therefore, that much of it is informed by a binary logic of East/West difference and thus refers holistically to a denial of death widespread in that cultural monolith, *the* 'West'. Its being seen as a 'taboo' subject associated with fear, anxiety, pessimism, obsession and even obscenity[2] is commonly traced back to Judeo-Christian views of death as an 'evil' or to Pauline notions of it as an 'enemy'. But Philippe Ariès in *The Hour of Our Death* argues that death-denial has largely been a twentieth-century phenomenon in Europe and North America, a consequence, in fact, of death's gradual individualization.[3] In their psycho-biographical work, *Six Lives, Six Deaths: Portraits from Modern Japan*, Robert Lifton and co-authors note this thesis when positing an apparent increase in individualism and thus also death-denial in Japan in modern times, their assumption being that *the* Japanese did not hitherto suffer from this 'Western' death-denial.[4]

Early representations of the Orient as the 'other', as fundamentally different and inferior, doubtless played a large part in bringing about the assertions of Eastern *superiority* that one now encounters in some works on Eastern philosophy or thanatology. It has been common for Asianist scholars to counterpose a general Eastern monism to a general Western dualism; or contrast the approach to life and death in the West with an 'Eastern' view of an 'inclusive wholeness of reality' where life and death are not seen as mutually exclusive or in contradiction, and neither is denied.[5] The argument for Western dualism – said to involve an extreme dichotomy between life, which is good,

and death, which is not – suffers from the same indefensible general-
izations found in related arguments for Eastern monism. While the
hierarchy of value is reversed, these are characterized by the same
binary logic their authors are engaged in criticizing, for they represent
East and West as poles in exclusive opposition.[6] We find subtle assertions of this Eastern metaphysical or moral superiority in works that
seek in holistic fashion to define Japan's *'essential'* philosophical or
ontological assumptions, and approach to life and death. Internal divi-
sions of class, gender, generation, area and ethnicity are largely ignored
in such works. Hence, *the* Japanese are said to be inherently optimistic
and 'this-worldly'; their approach to death is largely group-oriented;
they lack any deep 'metaphysical *angst* about the meaning of life;
and tend not to deny death'.[7]

Comparatively speaking, Japanese religions may not have placed *so*
strong an emphasis on post-mortem judgement and punishment. (The
thematic content of medieval Nō plays at least suggests an attempt to
soften such an emphasis.) It is therefore possible that the fear of what
awaits one after death may have been less than in Islamic or Judeo-
Christian cultures. In popular streams of Japanese Buddhism like
the True Pure Land, even the evil ('being saved in one's sinfulness as
it is') have long been eligible for salvation.[8] From early medieval
times there were various forms of *rokudō bakku* popularized –
means by which one might easily escape from karmic retribution in
the six samsaric existences.[9] Now there was *less* reason to fear what
one might become after death: a hungry ghost, perhaps, or an otherwise vengeful or malevolent spirit.[10] Thus, the argument of Lifton
and co-authors for less death-denial in Japan makes some sense
when related to fewer reasons for fear specifically of post-mortem
experience. But this is surely only one reason amongst many for a
fear and denial of death.

In any case, pursuing an 'Orientalist' quest to situate Fumiko's or
Suga's representations of death and beyond only within an allegedly
pure Eastern or Western cultural tradition, would mean 'chasing
one's tail'. Particularly in the case of the very 'intertextual' Fumiko
it would be difficult to ascertain *which* religio-philosophical influences
to focus upon, because among the European philosophers who interested her were some whose thought systems were closely related to
Asian religio-philosophical doctrines. One could easily assume an influence from Buddhism when it had actually come from Nietzsche, or vice
versa. If, moreover, we wanted to argue that Suga and Fumiko were in
their 'Japaneseness' this-worldly and life-affirming, ultimately denying
neither life nor death because they adhered to traditional ontological

views, we would be forced to overlook the fact that the 'culture' in which each woman produced and was herself produced was as much political as religio-philosophical.

'RELIGIOUS' ENCOUNTERS

From 1903 in Osaka, Suga contributed articles to a Protestant magazine, *Kirisutokyō Sekai* (The World of Christianity), though simultaneously she also published in a Tenrikyō magazine, *Michi no Tomo* (Friend of the Way). By the time she was baptized a Protestant on 8 November 1903 she had also been active for six months in the Osaka section of the Nihon Kirishitan Fujin Kyōfūkai (Japanese Christian Society of Women for Moral Reform).[11] The society was strongly influenced by North American temperance unions.[12] Suga became a salaried official of the organization in December, and also became involved in Christian charitable works. Continuing to publish in the Tenrikyō journal until early 1905, she contributed more to it, however, than to *Kirisutokyō Sekai*. This was probably more related to publishing opportunities (since her literary patron then was the editor of *Michi no Tomo*) than to her religious identity or commitment. There were, in any case, no notable differences in the religious tone or content of her articles, whichever magazine she published in.

Tenrikyō was one of the first of the so-called 'new' Japanese religions which seem to have arisen in three main waves, roughly between 1800 and 1860, during the 1920s and also after the Second World War.[13] It was also one of the Meiji sects that ultimately had little choice but to take upon itself the not very meaningful appellation of 'Shintō'. Tenrikyō was recreated, in other words, much in the manner of State Shintō in that disparate elements in it that were traditional were lumped together under the umbrella category of 'sect Shintō', while elements that were new were simply redefined as 'traditional'. But, as to what Tenrikyō actually was, firstly, it was not unlike other 'new' religions in seeing nature as sacred. According to one author: 'To be harmoniously related to nature is one of the highest aims in Japanese religious life.'[14] Other than that the 'new religions' commonly had millenarian tendencies; they are often said to have been 'this-worldly' in the sense that they looked forward to a regeneration that would bring about a better life in this world rather than the next. Their this-worldliness is said to have been even stronger than in the traditional religions because now a material sort of paradise, not just spiritual salvation, was possible in this world.[15] This is a logical development both from earlier Buddhist millenarianism focused on the future Buddha, Miroku, who would 'renew' the world, and from the idea in some streams of Japanese Buddhism that enlightenment is possible in this life, though one could hardly ignore other non-Japanese influences upon either this nature-centred 'Romanticism' or modern millenarianism.

Concerning this-worldly 'paradises', Suga's later conception of a future socialist society had something in common with the belief in salvation in this world of the new Japanese religions:

> In the doctrine of Tenri-kyō a humanism centered on people and this world, and the equality of man and woman is clearly taught . . . a new quality absent in feudal religion, the insistent call for the material and spiritual relief of the masses, became Tenri-kyō's unique characteristic. At this time the hope of the masses was for world renewal such that by the virtue of the *kami*, the world would instantly change and an ideal world would materialize.[16]

Suga's progression from Christianity and Tenrikyō to socialism and anarchism was not particularly unusual, moreover, for the new Japanese religions might have preached salvation in this world but tended not to involve themselves with practical social reform. Tenrikyō's founder, Nakayama Miki (1798–1887), one of the female shamanistic leaders of the new religions, bitterly criticized the arbitrary rule of the government, yet her panacea for social ills was for people to 'take care of their hearts, reform themselves, and lead moral lives . . . [to] bring about an ideal world'.[17] If it seems that this approach would hold little attraction for Meiji socialists, I might note that one of the defendants in the Meiji Treason Case defended by Hiraide Shū was said by him to have confused Buddhist millenarianism with Utopian socialism: Takagi Kenmei spoke of 'a future heaven-on-earth of perfect equality', and recognized the existence of no authority but that of Amida Buddha.[18] Jay Rubin observes that it was this that made him a dangerous *anti-imperial* 'anarchist' in the eyes of his accusers! A similar logic was involved in the repression in Meiji and later of new religions (like Ōmotokyō) for worshipping their own principal god/s even as the true founders of Japan – in competition, that is, with the official emperor-system mythology that accorded such a feat to the emperor's own ancestral gods.

If adherents and accusers alike could confuse religious millenarianism with political radicalism, it was partly because both were part of the same broad reaction against 'modernization' after the Meiji

Restoration of 1868. There was 'a marked strand of millenarianism' in many new religions because they were, broadly speaking, attempts to make sense of and cope with a rapidly changing material and ideational environment.[19] In modern times within Japan and without, there have been many who, doubting the benefits of capitalization, advocated a return to 'Nature', implying at least a desire to return to simpler forms of social organization, if not a yearning for a past Golden Age.

In Suga's case, then, there were various aspects of Tenrikyō that might have attracted her by 1903 – its emphasis on sexual equality, its (female) founder's critique of modern society, its millenarian tendencies – even if her baptism in November suggests that her commitment to Christianity soon became greater. Yet a commitment to one does not necessarily rule out a continuing interest in the other. And if it seems strange that she could be so eclectic in her early connections with different religions, it might be emphasized that there is an internal consistency in the religions that, certainly by 1910–1911, constituted her background. All three – if we can assume that her family religion was True Pure Land Buddhist, and add it to Christianity and Tenrikyō – had monotheistic tendencies. Indeed, authors have often speculated about a possible Christian influence upon the other two. Since early medieval times, Pure Land Buddhism has been quite monotheistic in its focus upon a heaven-like Western Paradise and 'saviour'-figure of Amida Buddha.[20] On the other hand, Tenrikyō's saviour and principal *kami* was *Tenri-Ō-no-Mikoto* or *Tenri Daijin*.[21] This was an absolute, parental (apparently asexual) God in 'heaven', an 'omnipotent' creator of humankind who taught universal love to its children.[22]

In addition, both Suga and Fumiko had encounters with the religion that not so long before, in Tokugawa, had been known as the 'evil creed from South Barbary'. In Suga's case, however, it was somewhat more than a passing acquaintance. She was a practising Christian for at least a few years, and if there was one particular area in which the religion might have continued to have an influence on the way she represented death, it was her tendency to idealize self-sacrifice and martyrdom. She was not alone in this, however; one of those executed in 1911, Ōishi Seinosuke, had expressed the expectation years earlier that revolutionary leaders would have to shoulder 'the heavy cross of suffering'.[23] But there were various reasons for the wide popularity of Christianity among intellectuals after the Meiji Restoration. Some authors emphasize the attraction of certain individualistic ideals associated with it:

Christianity and Christian missionaries were the most important influences on the formation of the new, internalized ideal of individualism; it was the Christian doctrine of the uniqueness of the individual's inner life that indirectly inspired the development of a new ideal of private self-cultivation.[24]

While there had been a concern with 'private self-cultivation' in Confucianism, it had been more the individual's role and duties in society that had been emphasized. Now moral conscience was seen to be more a private concern. Christianity was also seen as the basis of Western civilization, a perception that owed much to the efforts of missionaries who taught that religion and science were natural allies in the West.[25] Thus, in early Meiji, amongst those in pursuit of *bunmei kaika* ('civilization and enlightenment') for their new nation of Japan, some had encouraged Christian conversions.

Christianity came to be associated with social equality and reform in the minds of its advocates and critics partly because of the doctrinal emphasis on spiritual equality, since all were 'equal before God'; and also because of Christian charitable works and campaigns against 'uncivilized' Eastern practices like concubinage. Once the ban on Catholicism was lifted in 1873 and all sects were free to proselytize, Christianity soon came to be both a 'challenge and model' for Buddhist sects. Among other reasons for the early Meiji social–political reaction against Buddhism ('political' because the supposedly indigenous 'Shintō' was intended to displace such 'foreign' religions), it had long been common for Japanese critics of Buddhism to inveigh against its priests' moral 'decadence' and lack of social conscience.[26] Pre-Meiji literature abounds with cynicism about the laxity of Buddhist priests who cared little for the traditional disciplines and other moral prohibitions. The famous Genroku satirist, Saikaku, narrated many tales like one about a man accused of theft *because* he was a 'man of religion'.[27]

By Suga's time, there was co-operation between socialists and Christians in various areas. A popular maxim of the day even expressed the idea that socialism was 'materialistic Christianity' and Christianity 'spiritualistic socialism'.[28] Suga first encountered socialists in April 1903 through the anti-prostitution cause, her interest in socialism deepened, and by 1906 she had come to see Christian welfare activities as mere palliatives: only socialism could 'eradicate the causes of social misery'.[29] By 1906 'spiritualistic socialism' was beginning to lose its appeal for her. The fact that many Christian organizations had supported Japan's involvement in the Russo-Japanese War must also have been cause for concern.

Yet it was not only Suga who had once found Christianity attractive: Fumiko wrote in her prison memoirs that she had experienced a dramatic 'conversion' to Christianity during a Salvation Army prayer meeting in Tokyo late in 1920.[30] She was at that time penniless and in despair, so had gone to ask a young friend, Saitō Otomatsu, in the Salvation Army for help.[31] This friend (referred to in Fumiko's memoirs as 'Itō') was called as a witness during her trial, and he corroborated this part of her account. He said that he had tried 'to give her proper guidance and get her to join the Faith', but after she tore up the Bible he had given her he decided his efforts at spiritual guidance had been to no avail. Fumiko also said that she soon came to be critical of what she saw as Christian hypocrisy: no earthly or material 'reward' had come to her through her hard work (domestic labour) for the Salvation Army, so she became disillusioned with Christian professions of love, even if she had never believed in 'miracles'. She came to wonder whether Christianity was not just a 'narcotic' with which 'foreign demons bewitched people's souls', for Christians 'manipulated people's good faith and affections'. When Fumiko spoke of the Christian denial of love, it was partly because her friend had rejected her sexually out of fear of losing his 'purity'. (According to Saitō, he did lose it with her, and had deeply repented this one moral lapse ever since.) Thus she became critical of Christians' denial of natural human instincts. The influence of Christianity upon her ideas was by her own account short-lived and not very profound.

Concerning the subjects' religious encounters, then, late in their lives neither Fumiko nor Suga mentioned heaven or hell, and they did not express a hope for a Christian sort of after-life nor any fear of divine judgement. Suga in her last days did not once mention having faith in any sort of benevolent God, Buddha or 'parent kami' despite her broadly monotheistic background. Moreover, both indicated that they had embraced Christianity for reasons that had little to do with religious (metaphysical) doctrine. For Suga, an interest in social reform was doubtless not the only reason she went so far as to be baptized a Christian; among other things Christian sexual morality might have had an appeal for her.[32] Fumiko – writing years after the event about her disillusionment with various doctrines – suggested that she had been enticed by a promise of earthly 'salvation'. Both might have misinterpreted Christian doctrine. Though it is not so clear in the case of Suga that an initial misunderstanding of Christian doctrine ultimately led to disillusionment, her observation in 1906 that

Christian activities would not lead to fundamental social change (after all) suggests it.

Much more could be said, particularly about Suga's relation to Christianity, but not in the context of her 'engagements with death'. Perhaps before turning to 'physics' (evolutionary and socialist materialism) in Meiji and Taishō and to the Western metaphysics that attracted Fumiko, I might reiterate that the distance between religion and social or even socialist movements was not so great as one might assume. Socialist materialism was then still in its infancy.

PHYSICS AND METAPHYSICS

Beyond referring broadly to anarchism, Suga did not speak of specific political-philosophical influences upon her thinking. When in prison, it was only in the context of action-models that she mentioned revolutionary inspiration. Earlier, moreover, her interests had been more literary than philosophical. Nevertheless, for almost a decade Suga was a journalist and activist, and at least on the margins of the progressive intelligentsia. Even if she had never read Herbert Spencer or Darwin, she must have known of them. The importance she accorded positivism in her construction of death and beyond was not created *ex nihilo*. Certainly by 1910–1911, scientific materialism was a central part of her identity as an anarchist.

Fumiko claimed nihilistic inspiration mainly from Stirner, Nietzsche and Mikhail Artzibashev, though without saying much about how they influenced her. She said she was also a little acquainted with the ideas of Hegel, Bergson and Spencer. Social Darwinism of the Spencerian type came to play an important role in her thinking, and among the Western thinkers she mentioned, only Spencer had emphasized the 'survival of the fittest' (*yūshō reppai* or *jakuniku kyō-shoku*, literally, 'the strong eat the weak'). Similarly, however, the eighteenth-century rebel scholar Andō Shōeki (whose works had been discovered by Fumiko's time) spoke of how it was only after the sages came on the scene and human 'invention' overran nature that humans degenerated to the level of birds and beasts and the great started to 'eat' the small.[33] Fumiko often used such terminology, which was not necessarily an indication of having read Spencer (or Shōeki) but rather a reflection of the degree to which such ideas were still in currency in late Taishō.

Spencer's thought had been popular in Japan in educated circles since the *keimō* ('enlightenment') movement of the 1870s. For a time

Tokyo Imperial University was known as the 'University of Evolution-ism' because of his influence; and its first professor of philosophy, Inoue Tetsujirō, went so far as to complain in 1880 that Spencer had become the 'god of the time'.[34] Spencer, Darwin and Henry Buckle were read by some Japanese intellectuals as part of a reaction against arguments for a necessary relation between science or 'civiliz-ation' and Christianity.[35] Together with Rousseau and Mill, Spencer had also been part of the 'ideological armoury' of critics of the govern-ment when in the 1870s popular rights advocates enlisted his theories of egalitarianism in their struggle for representative government.[36] But even government leaders made use of Spencer's ideas – his social Dar-winism came to form part of conceptual rationales for expansionism in the 1890s. While some applied only a Spencerian form of moderate social Darwinism to a theory of the evolutionary history of nation states, others, like Katō Hiroyuki (first president of Tokyo Imperial University,) began to use more 'violently competitive rhetoric'.[37] Thus, while Darwinism in Meiji was often linked with competition amongst individuals – the idea of fighting one's rivals to 'rise in the world' (*risshin shusse*) – by the last decade of the century and the Sino-Japanese War it was common for nationalists to phrase their arguments for Japanese expansion in terms of the 'survival of the fittest'.

Fumiko was among those who later took social Darwinism a step further, applying it to the individual's struggle for existence against the state. Gino Piovesana writes that in the twentieth century *shutaisei* (lit. 'subjectivity'; or selfhood/individuality) had often meant 'the affir-mation of the self against the political and social reality'.[38] Ironically, self-assertion or advancement had earlier been inseparably connected in the minds of many with *risshin* (advancement) for the nation-state or family, but this change was a natural reaction against a modern state which was, to use Earl Kinmonth's phraseology, 'founded on denial of [the supposedly Western creed of] individualism'.[39] Spencer himself, however, had allowed the state no legitimate power beyond protecting the rights of the individual against the collectivity and pro-tecting the people against outside foreign enemies; if it was permitted to interfere more in social organization, society would be distorted and regress.[40]

It is conceivable that the positivism expressed by Suga in her prison diary, about the soul's not surviving death, was influenced by Spencer.[41] It has been said of *Heimin Shinbun*, the socialist paper first produced during the Russo-Japanese War of 1904–1905, that its socialism was more social Darwinist than a 'materialist critique of history'.[42] Presumably, its contributors applied a social Darwinist rhetoric to the competitive struggle between nations or individuals rather than classes. Suga did read the paper at that time, but was probably more influenced later by the socialist materialism of intimates like Ōsugi Sakae and Kōtoku Shūsui. With Fumiko, on the other hand, we can see how theories that placed so much emphasis on competition and the struggle to survive may have deepened her negativism about human society and life. Certainly, the 'strong eat the weak' idea was accorded a central place in her depiction of life generally as a battle. Yet she did not share Spencer's faith in evolutionary human 'progress', and her remarks on life after death did not suggest a self-consciously positivistic approach. Spencer's influence does not seem to have had any bearing on her representations of death, unless in the indirect sense of contributing to the pessimistic aspects of her construction of life. But we can certainly see how his ideas became part of her 'ideological armoury' in her struggle against the emperor-system.

It has already been noted that neither Suga's nor Fumiko's representations of death suggested a Christian eschatological influence. Indeed, if Fumiko was significantly influenced by Nietzsche, Stirner and Artzibashev, and at least interested in Hegel and Bergson, this should come as no surprise. Bergson was one of the 'philosophers of life', like Nietzsche, another for whom the assertion of the will was central. For him, as for Stirner, free will meant a freedom for individuals to develop their creativity independent of moral constraints. Bergson's likely influence on Fumiko was more in the area of conceptions of action, however, and thus will be discussed in the next chapter. His views on death could not have influenced her, because he expressed them only in works written after Fumiko had died.[43] On the other hand, we cannot know whether Hegel's ideas on im/ mortality had any impact on her. Like him, she rejected the existence of a personal God and the notion of *personal* immortality (eternal continuity of personality), but so did Nietzsche, Stirner and Artzibashev. Beyond a vaguely similar emphasis on some sort of 'real' existence after death – since Hegel believed that the Spirit is reconciled with itself after death when the finite negates itself and passes over into the 'other', the infinite, to become real 'living Being'[44] – there is little indication that Fumiko's approach to death could have been influenced by Hegel.[45]

Fumiko's positive view of the ego and her view of the will as entirely free narrows the field of her significant European influences to the philosophers she said had most inspired her. The first to consider, then, is one of the famous European 'Buddhists', an appellation that seems out of place given Nietzsche's emphasis on the 'will to power'.[46] Before continuing I should first note the possibility that some Nietzschean themes could have found their way into Fumiko's ideas indirectly – through her reading of Artzibashev. But to turn to Nietzsche's impact in Japan, he was known there from about the turn of the century, and was popular with writers like Takayama 'Chogyū' for his works on aesthetics, his individualism (especially in connection with the *Übermensch*, 'superman' or 'overman') and his conception of the 'will to power'. Takayama's case provides some insights into the reasons for Nietzsche's popularity in Japan, because his transition from the 'way of abnegation and sacrifice' to the 'way of will and power' was in the forefront of a broader philosophical trend that increasingly emphasized *jiga* and *jiga shuchō* ('ego-assertion') over *muga* ('ego annihilation' or 'self-denial').[47] The way to happiness was to satisfy one's instinctual drives (also a Bergsonian theme), irrespective of conventional morality. Among Takayama's heroes were Gautama Buddha, Nichiren, Nietzsche and Napoleon. Kinmonth writes that he lauded the thirteenth-century founder of Nichiren Buddhism as a Japanese *Übermensch*.[48] Another devotee of Nietzsche, Abe Jirō, had worked for the *Asahi Shinbun* for a time, and it was he who in 1919 published a commentary on Nietzsche's *Thus Spake Zarathustra*.[49]

For Nietzsche, death was an integral part of life, not its opposite, and if life should be creative and joyful, the same must be said of death. One must be powerful at death in order to meet it as it should be met, and to withstand any manipulation of the fear of it. Nietzsche's view that we should have control over our own deaths was based on his belief that Christianity abused 'the weakness of the dying to commit conscience rape'; thus he argued for suicide in some cases, partly to prevent Christians from abusing the hour of death.[50] Suicide for him was not a negation of life, for a love of life would lead one to die at the right time: 'To die proudly when it is no longer possible to live proudly. Death of one's own free choice, death at the proper time, with a clear head and with joyfulness.' Earlier in his life, Nietzsche had seemed to see death as merely a liberation from suffering (like Schopenhauer), but later he glorified it in a way that rivalled earlier Romantics: 'All that became perfect, all that is ripe wants to die. . . . Death has been made into bitter medicine by narrow pharmacist minds [but] one should make a feast out of one's death'.[51]

Fumiko might have been influenced by Schopenhauer, firstly because like him she represented death as both a 'joy' *and a* '*deliverance*'. Her approach to continuity after death was also quite similar to Schopenhauer's, as are some of her remarks on egoism.[52] Fumiko did not share his negative view of egoism, but was similarly 'pessimistic' in her earlier view of the world and life. Moreover, like nihilism in Zen, where negation leads to an affirmation of the Buddha-nature in all things, Schopenhauer advocated overcoming the duality of life and death through a pattern of negation in order to reach a 'Great' affirmation (enlightenment). In effect, Fumiko, too, negated life, then negated that negation to arrive at an ultimate 'affirmation of life' ('true nihilism') that she equated with rebellion 'unto death'.[53]

There is much in Nietzsche's ideas that is suggestive of Fumiko – certainly the emphasis on affirming death (and suicide), meeting it with joy, and powerfully. The nature of his influence upon others of the earlier generation in Japan also suggests something further about her case. Many in late Meiji had cited Nietzsche as an inspiration for their youthful romanticization of 'anguish' or 'melancholy', and aestheticization of death or suicide. His early tendency to see life as 'suffering', and later glorification of death and suicide may have had something to do with this. There is a certain irony in the fact that these young 'anguished' Japanese were attracted to Nietzsche,[54] who had declared himself the enemy of the 'nihilism' (life-negation) or pessimism of Christians, Platonists, Idealists, Schopenhauer, and so on. He affirmed death, certainly, but he also affirmed life. Nancy Andrew gives an interesting account of Seitōsha (Bluestocking's) founder, Hiratsuka Raichō's youthful interest in Zen and Nietzsche (late in Meiji): she mentions how in 1907 Hiratsuka was typical of the 'philosophic youth' then because absorbed in 'ethics, God and the meaning of life', but her account of Hiratsuka's interest in Nietzsche more suggests a fascination with death.[55]

Another way in which Nietzsche had an impact on philosophical and political thinking in Japan is also related to pessimism, albeit indirectly. Kinmonth writes that Nietzsche had 'countered the idea that humanism was to lead to mass equality and prosperity' (Fumiko said the same thing about socialism, though this rejection of idealism about future progress was also a theme in Artzibashev's novel): humanism's real purpose was to produce an elite of 'model individuals' (*chōjin*/*Übermensch*) 'for whom the masses existed'.[56] Fumiko represented herself as having a special individual mission in life and at times expressed a disdain for the passive masses who did not assert their will. But though she said she was not so 'idealistic' as to believe in a future egalitarian society, she was none the less highly critical of social inequality and believed in the necessity of fighting against it. She might have seemed somewhat elitist at times, but in her memoirs she derided the notion of worldly success that earlier admirers of Nietzsche had found so appealing, and opposed authority or domination of any sort.[57] While the anarchist Ōsugi Sakae (who probably influenced Fumiko more directly) had been inspired by Nietzsche, he did not accept the idea of a superhero who would demand mass obedience; nor did he agree with intellectual leadership of the masses. What he found attractive in Nietzsche's thinking was the idea of an 'overman' who *over*came his own limitations through will power.[58]

Fumiko's will to die while rebelling against power was tantamount to the social Darwinist 'struggle for existence', but hers was a competitive struggle with forces that did more than threaten to deny her access to worldly success. She literally saw it as a struggle for existence in the sense that if she did not rebel, her selfhood would be crushed. Hers was a battle of wills, in fact a 'will to power', but not to the sort of power that the ruling class had over the common people (or an *Übermensch* might have). The power that Fumiko sought was the power of an individual over her own life, not the lives of others. This was also true of Ōsugi; and he did not accept either popular interpretations of Nietzsche or the extreme egoism of Stirner, for to do so would lead to a complete isolation of the individual from society.[59] The fact that Fumiko indicated that Stirner had had the most profound influence on her 'egoist' ideas was part and parcel of her declaration of her complete alienation from society – according to her own account, even before her imprisonment. Stirner's work, *The Ego and His Own*, it might be noted, had been translated into Japanese by the well-known nihilist, Tsuji Jun, and published earlier in Taishō.

Stirner (a probable influence upon Nietzsche) did not have much to say about death, but what little he did have to say cannot be overlooked. I have already remarked on his attitude toward enjoying one's life – using it up, consuming or 'annihilating' it – and on how Fumiko first seems to have taken this annihilation of Life literally. The naturalist writer Masamune Hakuchō, a Meiji pessimistic nihilist, also spoke of both the universe and the self being annihilated simultaneously at death, expressing a radical solipsism like Stirner's.[60] By the 'enjoyment' of life Stirner meant living for the moment, risking life or getting the most out of it without any thought for anyone or anything else: one's life was one's *own*. Enjoying life entailed triumphing over the 'longing for life' or 'hope of life' of the religious. Those who expend their lives trying to prolong life cannot enjoy it, he argued;

while those who still seek for life do not have it and can little enjoy it: 'Christianity does not permit thinking of death otherwise than with the purpose to take its sting from it and – live on and preserve oneself nicely.' Christians would put up with anything, he observed, just so long as they can 'haggle and smuggle' themselves into heaven; they must not kill themselves, but rather preserve themselves and work at the 'preparation of a future abode'. This conservatism or 'conquest of death' is what lies at the heart of the Christian: 'the last enemy that is abolished is death'.[61] Thus, Stirner cited St Paul as the prime example of a negation of both life and death's reality, and was scathing about the meaning Christians ascribed to 'self'-preservation. This involved distinguishing 'myself from myself (my immortal soul from my earthly existence etc.)'. It was not just the belief in immortality that he denounced, but the very idea that one part of us, the spirit, is in dualistic opposition to another part of us; we are divided into 'an essential and unessential self'.[62] Preserving oneself also meant that one could not take one's own life: Christians, he said, had power over their deaths by 'preserving' or limiting their lives, living in accordance with the limitations imposed by morality. For Stirner, the only life one has is this life now, so one would hardly deny it (even in Hegelian style) for the sake of the 'true life' of the spirit in the here and now or hereafter. Fumiko also wanted power over both her death and life like (Nietzsche or) Stirner, and she did not deny life in the sense criticized by him. Nor did she deny death's reality in Christian style, even if one of her poems (about the warring of spirit and flesh) did have a suggestion of a Platonic or Christian-like dualistic split between mind and body. Her sense of 'immortality' had no relation to notions of an immortal soul.

Stirner anticipated Nietzsche's critique of (dualistic) morality and 'pessimism', life-denial or negation. He had also derided humanism as a new Idealist morality, a 'sacred fixed idea' according to which '[hu]Man' had replaced Christ as the Subject, the 'I of the world's history'.[63] Therefore, while Fumiko's own attack on morality actually cited Stirner, her advocacy of amorality and her rejection of the idealism inherent in humanist or socialist views of progress could have been influenced by either or both Nietzsche and Stirner. Broadly speaking, her attitudes toward life and death closely resemble the ideas of modern 'amoralists' like them and Artzibashev. More than Stirner, Fumiko might well be called an existentialist, because she at least expressed a 'despair' of, or 'disgust' with, Being or existence, and explicitly rejected anarchist optimism about the future and idealism about humanity.[64] Confronting a power intent on beating her into submission, she tried to walk a tightrope between a self-empowerment that came close to the self-aggrandizement implied in the works of Stirner or Nietzsche and, ultimately, a more social form of 'self-creation' and assertion. Ultimately, she advocated a need for individuals to mitigate (if not altogether negate) power, and at least ameliorate the unequal, repressive condition of society. But concerning death and its beyond, it should be emphasized that of all the Western philosophers discussed, Stirner most explicitly dismissed the possibility of an after-'life'. In a rather Zen-like fashion, his concern was for the moment, the here and now.

Fumiko's insistence in her letter to Judge Tatematsu that she would go to death with joy suggested an influence from Nietzsche, and her 'affirmation of life', synonymous with ego/will-assertion, could have been derived from Nietzsche, Stirner, Artzibashev or even Zen. But the fact that she spoke of a joyful affirmation of life only in the context of 'Nature', as opposed to human society, narrows the field to Artzibashev. Like him, she distinguished between the 'natural' and human world, finding joy only in the former. Artzibashev was the only European writer actually quoted by Fumiko in connection with death (and *Sanine* was largely about death, suicide etc.). 'Sanine' had said that death is the best course for those who have no joy in life, and this was also Nietzsche's prescription for 'negative nihilists' or pessimists. In *Sanine* Nietzsche is referred to, albeit rather critically, and the novel also contains many themes present in Stirner's *The Ego and His Own*: 'egoism' versus moralism, altruism and self-sacrifice. It might be added that the anarchist, Itō Noe, had written admiringly in 1917 of Artzibashev's hero, 'Sanine', the egoist.[65]

Sanine is a superior type. Disdainful of the idealism with which acquaintances embrace their various causes, he is concerned only with living his life to the full, paying no heed to the moral concerns of others. He brings about one suicide; recommends it to a pessimistic friend who takes his advice; and when asked to say a few words over the grave of yet another who killed himself (a revolutionary idealist unable to decide which cause he should sacrifice himself for), Sanine pronounces him a fool.[66] Neither the suicides he had a part in causing, nor the loss to the world of one more fool, nor the pain of the woman he forced 'to bend to his will' cause Sanine any remorse: one is alone in life, responsible only to oneself, and morality is an illusion. Bored with the mediocrities in his village at the end of the story, he departs, once more denouncing the 'vileness' of humanity and the brutishness and slavishness of the masses.[67]

There are far too many parallels between Artzibashev's novel and Fumiko's ideas for us to dismiss them as accidental. The themes in *Sanine* that we also find in Fumiko's texts are:

1) a decidedly critical, cynical view of Christianity (one character in *Sanine* declares in Nietzschean style that Buddha, the gods of Greece and Christ are all *dead;* Christianity had proved itself as 'impotent' in the face of human bestiality as any other religion, and it was due to the 'law of evolution' that all had had their day);[68]

2) an insistence that one can choose to die of one's own free will, especially if one has no joy in life;[69]

3) an expectation that the only grief one will feel at the point of death is at the prospect of losing the senses with which one enjoys life (defined more in terms of Nature);[70]

4) a negative view of humanity, or at least 'unnatural' society contrasted with a joyful celebration of Nature, which is 'free': 'All is beautiful', enthuses one character, 'man alone is vile.');[71]

5) an emphasis on one's being educated through one's experience of life rather than from books (interestingly, characters in the novel make negative remarks about Nietzsche on more than one occasion in the context of learning from life, not books);[72]

6) a cynicism about sacrifice for 'lofty' ideals of any description (dying for others was a fool's death, according to Sanine);[73]

7) a ('nihilist' or Russian populist) conception of social change as necessarily involving bloodshed and a view of life as conflict, coupled with disbelief in a future 'golden age' where all will be free and equal (for we might even regress to barbarism);[74]

8) a disdain for the 'slave mentality' and brutishness of the masses who are content to do nothing about their servitude and thus deserve it.[75]

In general *Sanine* is characterized by the sort of nihilistic amoralism that seems to have attracted Fumiko to Stirner. Echoing Stirner on how humans suffer from the illusory morality they themselves create, Sanine observes that people 'create for themselves phantoms, shadows, illusions, and are the first to suffer by them'.[76] And finally, a further parallel connected with the novel's main theme of pessimism and optimism, life and death is that it is those who (unlike Fumiko) are idealistic about humanity, altruistic causes, the future and 'progress' who (like Fumiko) are represented as having no joy in life now; and it is they who die. In mid-1925 Fumiko clearly identified with their taking their own lives because of a lack of joy in life, though she did not share their idealistic dreams.

As to Suga's and Fumiko's approaches to metaphysics, then, firstly there is no evidence to support the possibility that it was a Christian–Platonic notion of a permanent continuity of personality after death that Suga once posited – when she referred in one prison poem to the confidence and consolation that her 'eternal life' afforded her. Fumiko's case is more complex in the sense that the foreign philosophers she expressed an interest in, were mostly noted for their proximity to Asian philosophies: Nietzsche, Bergson, Hegel, and even Stirner have all been claimed as 'honorary orientals'.[77] While sometimes it is not possible to pinpoint precisely which Western philosophers influenced which exact areas of Fumiko's thinking, they *all* posited: amorality; a fairly general emphasis on the assertion of the will or ego; an affirmation or even in some cases a glorification of death; and also an explicit rejection of Christian doctrine. As for im-mortality, Fumiko did not use Christian or Amidist terminology like 'heaven' or 'paradise' or 'salvation', but expressed herself in terms more reminiscent of Mahayana sects like Zen: 'all phenomena perish as phenomena', she wrote, yet continue in a 'true existence' (a vague sort of 'essence', perhaps). Given that in Zen doctrine there is no soul that survives death, Fumiko could have been expressing a Zen sort of phenomenalism, according to which there is no duality of life and death, true existence is nothingness.[78] On her return from Korea she spent some time with a maternal uncle who was a Rinzai Zen priest, though she said that he was not particularly religious.[79] Therefore, on the whole Fumiko's remarks (as well as her silences) suggest a vague, impersonal, symbolic 'immortality' that was more in keeping with Zen than Christianity or other forms of Buddhism, but perhaps owed little to any systematized religious doctrine.

IM-MORTALIZING MORTALITY

Fumiko's and Suga's rather vague and inconsistent remarks on post-mortem states might be taken to suggest a particular, though un-systematized view of continuity after death which Lifton, Katō and Reich claim has been dominant in Japan in this century: 'dying into the cosmos'.[80] They also note that this has been common in non-Western societies. It refers to the idea that individual souls stay for a while but gradually fade away or disappear from the living cosmos. The individual soul belongs to a group, usually the family, but as time passes and living memory fades the soul disappears, becoming an ancestor god. Though there is a continuity of personality after death, the individuality of the soul is not eternal. Lifton, Katō and Reich maintain that Japanese religions have generally subscribed a group-oriented 'immortality' which is connected with this world through the family, social group, or nation. This 'larger connectedness' with this world is said to have lessened anxiety about death in Japan. Treating the dead as still part of the world and daily life, in other words, is thought to be an important aspect of Japan's this-worldliness.[81] Hence, what they refer to as 'dying into the cosmos' hinges upon a few interrelated aspects of Japanese religion commonly held to be its defining characteristics: this-worldliness (or 'optimism'/ life-affirmation); a part of which is a group-orientation rather than individualism; which in turns means a comparative lack of death-denial. Therefore, in order for Suga or Fumiko to present a 'typically Japanese' approach to life and death it would have to be inclusive or unitary (affirming both in 'Eastern' style); and it would have to be group-oriented. Let us see how they measure up.

Firstly, it would seem that the meaning that 'immortality' held for Suga or Fumiko was not other-worldly. Suga's attitude toward her sister Hide's death was not very consistent with her positivistic rejections of an after-life, but still it might be said to reflect this 'this-worldly' tendency to maintain an interdependence between the living and dead. Each woman, moreover, fantasized about staying in the world to wreak vengeance upon her enemies. Their inconsistencies re 'life' after death might suggest a split between the rational-political and a persistence of the sort of religious belief discussed by Lifton, Katō and Reich. On the other hand, presenting themselves as potential *vengeful* spirits could have political uses. This unwillingness to leave the world behind after being executed by the state was a special, not uniquely Japanese, sort of 'this-worldliness'.

Thus far, the dominant Japanese attitude toward 'immortality' posited by Lifton, Katō and Reich does not seem to be a very useful heuristic device. It seems likely that Suga's or Fumiko's determined affirmation of death was more a reflection of her immediate political situation than of Japanese 'this-worldliness' or unitary visions of life and death. When in prison facing the death penalty it would have served little purpose for either to have denied the reality of death; to have done so would have implied a lack of readiness and resolution, and thus, a loss of power. As to group-centred versus individualist approaches to death, moreover, we would already expect Suga to opt more for the former and Fumiko more for the latter. This had much to do with the respective ideologies they embraced, a collectivistic form of anarchism and 'egoism' or nihilism, both of which were largely foreign in origin. Further, while for Lifton and co-authors, death in Japan is 'less an individual event than an occurrence within the group or community', they do concede that in Japan there is an (undefined) 'elite' whose 'highly individualized' approaches to death involve trying to 'take hold of death with their own hands to ensure the meaning and purpose of their life.' If the great mass of Japanese people is not elitist-individualistic but group-oriented, how then do we account for Suga's elitist-groupist tendencies?

One way out of this quandary might be to put some thought into whether *women* conform to such models of elite–mass difference. Further, we might remind ourselves that, while there may indeed be aspects of ostensibly 'Japanese' symbolizations of immortality that bring to mind Fumiko's or Suga's case, the five modes of immortality discussed by Lifton, Katō and Reich are by their own account universal. They are means by which people anywhere posit their own continuity, thereby rendering death as not so powerful a foe after all. And on the other hand, as the authors themselves point out, individuals' symbolizations of their 'immortality' may combine two or more of these five universal modes of symbolic immortality – 'biological-biosocial, theological, creative, natural, and experiential transcendence'. Indeed, amongst these, all but one, the 'theological' mode, seem applicable to Suga and/or Fumiko.

To turn more directly, then, to the sorts of frameworks in which Suga and Fumiko laid claim to 'im-mortality', one form of symbolic continuity that is suggestive of Suga is the third 'creative' mode – continuity through creative works or personal impact on others. This is a collectively oriented symbolization of immortality, where the group might be familial, social, national or even universal. The individual's creative legacy could be scientific, artistic, literary or political. Suga wanted to leave her prison diary to her comrades, and more generally, symbolized her own continuity in terms of the revolutionary legacy she was bequeathing to the cause. But Suga's construction of revolutionary immortality probably encompassed both the 'creative' and 'biological-biosocial' modes because it extended a 'familial' continuity to a political group. Lifton includes the biosocial mode under the biological category, since the social group can become a substitute for familial continuity.[82] Suga exhibited a much stronger sense of connectedness with humanity through her expanded (transnational) revolutionary group than Fumiko, which is partly why her symbolic continuity was more group-oriented than individualistic. She also had almost no immediate family left by the time of her death, which may have contributed to her reliance on an 'adopted' family. A possible indication of the pertinence of the 'biosocial' mode of immortality to Suga's case is the fact that she was scrupulous about willing her few possessions to particular friends in the socialist movement.[83] She may have hoped to gain a symbolic continuity through passing personal possessions on to comrades. Her use of the term 'memento' (*kinenhin*) to refer to the items suggests this. On the other hand, however, since very few socialists were wealthy, she may have simply wanted her property to be handed on to those who would have a use for it; and she did say this herself.

It is thought-provoking that Lifton mentions a common fear of ostracism in individuals whose symbolizations of immortality fit the biosocial mode.[84] The security of the group can be seen as so important that death might be considered preferable to ostracism. Suga had been ostracized by many socialists when she and Kōtoku became lovers. (This will be discussed in Part III.) We cannot know for certain whether Suga's commitment to sacrificing herself for the cause had something to do with a need to redeem herself, but there is no doubt that once executed she was seen by the movement to have atoned for her sins against 'socialist' morality.[85]

In Fumiko's case the biological mode is almost certainly not pertinent – she would not have wanted to 'live on' in a family she was alienated from. Nor did she voice a biosocial expectation of living on in the memories and traditions of future generations of revolutionaries. However, she did leave a 'creative' (political) legacy for comrades or society: her prison writings. Her autobiography she first dedicated to comrades who might find it 'useful' for pedagogic purposes, then to 'the parents of the world'. But she immediately added, 'No, I think I want all people to read it, not only parents, but also teachers, politicians and social theorists who want to reform society'.[86] Fumiko represented herself quite consistently as a determined egoist and anti-social nihilist, but her words here (and elsewhere) sometimes have a ring of altruism. Perhaps she sought a personal continuity through her creative works – which included some poetry published by comrades while she was still alive – but, unlike Suga, she did not use a strong identification with a group or society as armour against the threat of annihilation.

The modes of symbolic immortality that are clearer in Fumiko's representations of continuity are 'Nature' and 'experiential transcendence', which are closely related. 'Living on in Nature' refers to 'the perception that the natural environment around us – limitless in space and time – will remain, and that something of oneself remains a part of it'.[87] 'Living on in Nature' is said by Lifton to have been 'especially vivid in Japanese culture, steeped as it is in nature symbolism', a legacy in part of the animistic tendencies of indigenous folk religion. It now begins to sound as if Fumiko were the more 'Japanese', since she more than Suga claimed a special relation to Nature in connection with both life and death; but while nature symbolism might have been particularly vivid in Japan, this 'natural' mode of immortality has been universal, one European expression of it being nineteenth-century Romanticism.[88]

One can see how Fumiko's constructions of death and symbolic continuity would logically come to be bound up with her general tendency to glorify Nature. But her this-worldliness or 'connectedness' with this world was a little one-sided, for she had wiped her hands of the 'ugliness' of the world of *humans*; her positive view of 'nature' did not extend to human society. The only time Fumiko explicitly remarked upon an ongoing relation with the human world, was in the context of wanting to avenge herself upon it. She wrote of finding joy only in the natural (not human) world, and often spoke of herself and others as corrupted by contact with society. When narrating the story of her intention to commit suicide in Korea because of mistreatment by her paternal relatives, she said that she had decided not to throw herself in the river after all because the cry of a locust suddenly reminded her that she would have to part from the things in Nature she loved. Later in her memoirs she added that people's fear of death was based on a sadness at parting from earthly phenomena.

Fumiko's general idealization of nature is clear at various points in her memoirs, where by 'freedom' she implied two different but interrelated meanings: firstly, being able to live in a pristine state of nature; and secondly, a separation from human society. The immediate influences on Fumiko's negative view of urbanized society and positive view of Nature and innate, uncorrupted human nature may have been Artzibashev, anarcho-communism (Kropotkin) and Japanese agrarianism. In an anti-modernist style akin to that of twentieth-century anarchists or agrarianists, Fumiko spoke of how the villages in Japan had been plundered and impoverished by the cities.[89]

There was therefore a multi-faceted meaning inherent in Fumiko's claim that in Korea she had felt 'free' only when she was sent to the mountains alone to pick chestnuts:

Ah, nature! In nature there are no lies. Nature is open-hearted and free. It does not warp humanity as humans [themselves] do. Feeling this in my soul, I was inspired to say 'thank you' to the mountains.

Meanwhile, I had suddenly recollected the life I led at the time, and wanted to cry. Then I did cry and cry. But there has not been another day in my life that changed me to the extent of that day I spent in the mountains. That day was the day of my liberation.[90]

Perhaps her writing of nature as a 'purifying' agent could be seen to be very 'traditional', especially given the spiritual importance of mountains in Japanese folk religious traditions, but it was at least equally 'modern'. As a means of contrasting the beauty, kindness and purity of nature with the 'distorted' and cruel characteristics of society, she also described what she saw that day from her vantage-point in the mountains: Korean prisoners being dragged out into a Japanese military-police compound, stripped naked and whipped! Fumiko did not have had a 'larger sense of connectedness' with the urbanized, modern capitalist and imperialist world. Still, it could be argued that even in early medieval times in Japan, 'renouncing the world' really meant the human-social world.

Fumiko's hermit-like desire to renounce the 'world' brings us finally to the last mode, 'experiential transcendence', whereby one achieves a state where time, death or a 'sense of mortality' are negated through 'losing oneself'. Japanese culture has long stressed 'quiet' forms of this mode, Lifton, Katō and Reich observe, in spiritual and physical disciplines like Zen. Classical terms like '*mujō*', '*hakanai*' and '*aware*' have expressed a poignant pleasure in the fragile, ephemeral beauty of living things; and a feeling that humanity is part of an eternal, ever-changing cosmos. The metaphorical suggestion is that human life is also short; and aesthetic appreciation of it can increase in direct proportion to its brevity. This is indicated by the likening of young samurai dying bravely in battle to cherry blossoms, long cherished in Japan partly because of the brevity of their beauty and vitality.[91]

Here also I need not quarrel so much with constructs of 'Japaneseness', perhaps, since Fumiko clearly was one in a very long line of Japanese poets who found pleasure or solace in depicting human fate and the destiny of a cricket, flower or bird as little different. Amongst Fumiko's poems one can readily find expressions of this originally Buddhist concept of the ephemerality of all things in nature:

> Cricket!
> Stop lamenting in the corner
> for I too
> follow the same road
> as yourself.[92]

> Three to five
> wild garden roses in their
> second bloom –
> lingering, it strikes me
> that this is my fate too.[93]

We might recall that Suga also seemed to liken herself to 'a raven, forlorn', though the picture she painted then was not serene but a threatening, gloomy one of a raven about to be enveloped in a storm and darkness.[94] Yet for either woman, waxing philosophical about her fate or the brevity of human life (a universal habit, albeit with particular cultural expressions) was still a form of 'immortalization'. Compared to others it was a less defiant one, to be sure, but, undeniably, 'experiential transcendence' was one of many ways in which they armed themselves against death and, by extension, also against those who brandished it.

CONCLUSION

The difficulties involved in deciding whether Suga's or Fumiko's discourse on death and beyond was recognizably ('essentially') 'Japanese' suggests something about methodological approaches that give undue explanatory weight to cultural identity. Though it might be tempting to resort to stereotypical essentialist notions of inclusive/unitary attitudes toward life and death in the 'East', we could hardly conclude that either embraced death with an apparent readiness or serenity only because of a specific cultural identity or, indeed, special psychological make-up. Perhaps a denial of death was not a real option for them, because to refuse to accept it would imply fear. How they confronted death and represented themselves in relation to it had rather a lot to do with their immediate situations: with politics and power.

The various ways in which they went about claiming a symbolic continuity – an im-mortality – were clearly part of their refusal to accept that their destinies were in the hands of others. *If* in their cultural context this signified that two hitherto obscure women had joined the ranks of a social elite, moreover, surely it was largely because they had few other options when facing the threat of execution; they could either protest their innocence and beg their 'benevolent fathers' for mercy or 'take hold of death with their own hands to ensure the meaning and purpose of their life'.[95] One aspect of the latter was the symbolic continuity implied in leaving behind works, either to ensure a personal continuity after death, or merely in the hope that they could have the last word. In the final analysis it is ironic that Suga's and Fumiko's 'annihilations' would ultimately be negated through their being immortalized in history. Irony must indeed be the principal trope of history,[96] for, the expectations of their enemies notwithstanding, ultimately they were not silenced.

6 Commentary: martyrs, nihilists and other rebel heroes

INTRODUCTION

Reconstructing the respective contexts of the subjects' strategies for power in the area of their representations of death also demands consideration of the more explicitly political aspects of their culture. Within this political culture, they acted and interacted with others on the basis of a shared language about resistance and heroism, and also 'rebellion unto death'. Shared 'languages' notwithstanding, however, the political culture Suga or Fumiko was a part of was internally differentiated and dynamic. Twentieth-century Japanese radicals, too, were capable of 'picking and choosing' from existing models of rebellion and resistance – both indigenous and imported – accepting, appropriating, reworking and contesting them as they saw fit.

My focus in this chapter is on the more practical aspects of the subjects' political influences; on constructs of political action and political death. Taking account also of likely 'exotic' influences, I first consider how Kanno Suga and Kaneko Fumiko seem to have modelled themselves on two particular kinds of 'traditional' rebels, before proceeding with further discussion of the constructions Japanese heroes have placed upon 'dying well' (and the 'Great Death'), upon politically motivated vengeance and an aesthetics of death. Once again, a central problem addressed in this chapter is 'Japaneseness' – the degree to which cultural identity can explain the constructions Suga and/or Fumiko placed upon political action. If, in 'universalist' style, hitherto I seemed somewhat dismissive of its importance, *in this context* I will be treating the issue more seriously.

Nevertheless, both this and the last chapter seek to avoid defining Meiji and Taishō activists *only* by reference to either indigenous ideational or action models, or the European-derived 'isms' they embraced. To say, for example, that Suga and Fumiko were inspired by European and other radical theorists and activists is not to deny that their own indigenous culture, in all its internally differentiated forms, played a significant part in influencing their ideas and actions. No doubt their critiques of Japanese society and their ideas about political action were sometimes inspired and sometimes *reinforced* by foreign-inspired ideas current in their respective revolutionary groups. Political resistance and rebellion had, after all, been carried on quite effectively in Japan long before the advent of 'liberal democracy', 'socialism', 'anarchism' or 'nihilism'.[1]

Whether the subjects' constructions of political action and death were part of a discourse that was *more* indigenous or more alien is not really the issue, however. Those who embrace foreign doctrines may not recognize the degree to which their conceptions of rebellion are influenced by traditional patterns. The political effects of acknowledging traditional precedents may even be considered undesirable in a context where a modernizing state and emperor-system is bent on both furthering and reinventing 'tradition' for its own uses. Such difficulties, however, do not obviate the need to acknowledge that indigenous and other inspirations reinforced and acted upon each other, resulting in influences upon the subjects' thinking that may have been deeper than a mere borrowing of 'exotic' views would suggest.

The syndicalist slogan of 'direct action' may have been embraced by many Japanese radicals with a sense of recognition or familiarity;[2] just as some Japanese philosophers or activists took up European intuitionism and action-oriented ethics because they seemed 'Oriental'. The exaltation of decisive action in political circles from Bakumatsu (1853–1868) to the Taishō era and beyond, which was partly informed by Yōmeigaku (a heterodox, individualistic style of Tokugawa Confucianism), came to be augmented by recourse to the ideas of European philosophers like Henri Bergson and Georges Sorel.[3] Action was so central to Bergson's system that Bertrand Russell categorizes his as a 'practical philosophy', which is to say that in it action is regarded as the 'supreme good'.[4] Whether directly, or indirectly through theorists like Ōsugi Sakae, Fumiko may well have been inspired by Bergson in the area of action. He had posited an instinct to, or desire for, action without purpose or idealistic vision (a theme which modern Japanese admirers of Yōmeigaku also cite). Sorel, the author of *Reflections on Violence,* was influenced by Bergson, and therefore advocated a revolutionary labour movement without a definite goal. Thus, foreign influence may have been the more immediate inspiration in some areas, even accorded prominence by Fumiko and Suga themselves;

none the less, one still cannot overlook the likelihood that, in some respects, indigenous traditions paved the way for an acceptance of the 'new' model for political action.

The glorification in Meiji and Taishō radical circles of ostensibly Western ideals – for example, direct action and ego/self-assertion – had some indigenous roots. Yet it is not always possible to determine the degree to which those Japanese who embraced such 'Western' ideas did so with a conscious sense of familiarity. Philosophers like Nishida Kitarō, Nishitani Keiji and others, attracted to Western thinking partly because they found correspondences between it and Eastern philosophies, may have been exceptional. Matsumoto Sannosuke makes some pertinent remarks on cultural borrowing in an essay on Confucian foundations for ('Western') natural rights theory:

> When a nation which has already developed a highly sophisticated culture encounters and begins to absorb another from outside, the preexisting culture intervenes to provide a frame of reference. Foreign cultural components are selected and digested in terms of familiar concepts and vocabulary. This tendency is most pronounced when cultural learning is the result of independent choice, as in the case of Japan's encounter with the West. Japanese intellectuals of the Bakumatsu and early Meiji periods, seeking to adopt modern political ideas from the West, often understand these ideas in terms of Confucian concepts. They employ existing terminology as well, which they redefine appropriately.[5]

'Culture', of course, is rather more than 'ideas' and 'concepts', comprising a shared vocabulary and understanding, a shared recognition and ongoing contestation and reinvention of signs, symbols, rituals, codes of behaviour or action.[6] But what comes to mind in connection with Matsumoto's remarks is Inga Clendinnen's account of the indigenous 'concepts and vocabulary' that the Maya in Yucatan brought to bear on their interpretation of Catholicism.[7] Her account raises the problem of whether such an intervention of a preexisting culture is particularly the case with an 'independent', more or less voluntary acquisition of new beliefs. Fumiko's eclecticism was voluntary; but even if it had not been, her partly borrowed philosophical system would still not have been as 'new' as might be supposed from her remarks about Stirner, Nietzsche or Artzibashev.

Cultural borrowing or influence, moreover, is seldom unidirectional. Suga played a part in a discourse about rebellion that extended beyond the boundaries of Japan to at least North America. She was memorialized along with her eleven executed comrades by

Emma Goldman and other anarchists in the pages of *Freedom* and *Mother Earth*.[8] (North American anarchists had organized a campaign earlier in support of the defendants). Suga was therefore one of the group of Japanese revolutionaries who came to have a place in a transnational libertarian culture. And this was not the first time that Japanese socialists had come to the attention of like-minded people in other parts of the world. Katayama Sen's famous handshake with the Russian Social Democrat, Plekhanov, at the Amsterdam Congress of the Socialist International in 1904 during the Russo-Japanese War had been seen by many to be a powerful symbol of socialist solidarity and internationalism.[9]

In some respects Suga's and Fumiko's responses to their immediate political environments were remarkably similar to the responses of radical contemporaries in Japan and in other parts of the world. They did not live in an historical vacuum, and their environments were not so different from elsewhere in the world that discussion of their indigenous political heritage could lead one to conclude that Japanese radicals were politically aberrant. It is instructive to compare remarks by the Meiji anarchist, Arahata Kanson, about the political situation in Japan in the first decade of the century with an account of the state of affairs then in Russia by the Russian anarchist, Voline. Both intimated that a state that brutally suppressed almost any form of political opposition was bound to produce a violent reaction.[10]

Thus, we look next at different types of popular heroes in (and out of) Japan, two in particular, the 'noble' and 'nihilist', whose differences in style largely depend on the type of motivation for political action. At this point two cautions need to be raised, however: firstly, that I am speaking of a *model* along the general lines of which Suga or Fumiko seems to have constructed herself; and secondly, that I am referring to *socially produced motivation*, not individual psychology. Concerning the first point, the fact that each woman styled herself on a particular type of particular hero does not rule out the possibility of inconsistencies. Suga, the self-sacrificing fighter for a grand cause, was also capable of glorifying action almost as if it were an end in itself; and Fumiko, the amoral egoist, might have been more altruistic and 'noble' than she cared to admit. Concerning the issue of motivation, on the other hand, one thing that underscores the social nature of this apparently personal question of motivation for action is the above-mentioned fact that a broad emphasis on *muga* ('egolessness' or selflessness) in Tokugawa and early Meiji had given way to *jiga* and *jiga shuchō* (ego-assertion) in some circles by Taishō. While once even radical critics of hegemonic power and ideology mainly tended to construct themselves in the more familiar mode of self-denial, now 'egoism' could be openly advocated as part of political discourse. Selflessness was no less a part of the new emperor-centred hegemonic ideology, but now it had to contend with a more extreme expression of individualism that was buttressed rather than altogether created by new, foreign inspiration.

HEROISM, NOBLE AND 'NIHIRISUTO'

Fumiko and Suga both represented rebellion and revolution, respectively, as necessarily involving death; and Ivan Morris has argued that a real Japanese hero is one who dies in an act of valour. He, however, has attempted to explain *the* (singular) 'pattern of Japanese failed heroism' in Japanese history by reference to noble heroes who 'fought bravely for a doomed cause'. Morris' remarks seem accurate enough in the case of Suga – who remained committed to an act of heroism for the cause – more accurate than in the case of Kōtoku, whom he mentions.[11] Yet Fumiko, a popular hero today in Japan at least on the Left and amongst feminists, denied that she had a 'cause' outside herself. 'Failure', therefore, could only be pertinent if she had not been true to herself. In general, the 'act in itself' that was important to Fumiko (resistance, or the heroic 'deed') meant the rebellious 'assertion' of her ego, self-creation and control of her own destiny. We may well ask whether the actions of popular Japanese heroes always had to be centred on a worldly cause. In cases where they did seem important, we might still want to ask whether having a cause has necessarily had much to do with their popularity. Morris' emphasis on pragmatism or practical failure leads him to ignore the possibility that some of his *failed* heroes might be admired simply because they *acted*; or because they turned a worldly failure into a 'spiritual' sort of success. He himself describes 'failed', tragic heroes as admirable because of the 'courage of their sincerity in carrying out brave but hopeless *resistance*' (my emphasis).

In the context of the influence upon Restoration imperial 'loyalists' of an action-orientation in samurai ethical codes ('Bushidō/Budō/ Shidō'), Yōmeigaku neo-Confucianism, and Nativism (Kokugaku), Thomas Huber notes of the 'romantic' faction among his 'men of high purpose' (*shishi*):

Their aim was not in the external world of concrete results, but lay rather in the realm of emotional gratification that lay within themselves (but also in such observers, present or vicarious, as there might happen to be). For them, such gratification was derived from moral conduct, that is from exceptional and charismatic acts of loyalty. . . . Such acts were to be carried out with maximum public visibility, in the name of loyalty to the emperor, that is, devotion to the communal good.[12]

There is a tension here between the emphasis on internal gratification (even an aim that was a 'profoundly satisfying' sort of 'spiritual fulfil-ment' through action), on the one hand, and the references to *moral* conduct, loyalty and even 'devotion to the communal good' on the other. We cannot know which really was central to individual Restora-tion 'loyalists' [*sic*] – the cause or the act itself – though Huber suggests the latter when he observes that 'direct political results, if any, had nothing to do with it' because what was deemed important was how individuals conducted themselves. Terms like 'moral conduct' do not necessarily fit the bill, therefore, as simply taking 'action', whether seen to be moral, immoral or amoral, may have been more important in some cases.

Not surprisingly, the existence of this style of more egoistic than 'groupist' hero has only been hinted at in English works on Japanese history or culture. However, another commentator on Japanese hero-ism (unto death), Ian Buruma, actually calls this type of 'rebel' hero a 'nihilist' in a sense that is vaguely related to Fumiko's construction. Buruma's main example of the 'nihilist' hero is from a postwar film genre about *yakuza,* yet there is much in his description of this popular hero that is suggestive of the appropriation by *yakuza* today of (real or imagined) samurai–Zen–Yōmeigaku traditions. *'Nihirisuto'* are admired in contemporary popular culture, he claims, because they are 'cynics' stripped of the 'codes and rituals' that usually keep them 'in check', smashing their way through the 'tight web of Japanese society'.[13] In a sense derived from Zen they are 'ego-less', victors over the mind/rationality and emotions (thus violent and 'anarchic'), or in common parlance, 'super-individualists' in a society with little time for individualism. Setting aside Buruma's rather reductionist assumptions about this monolithic society of conformists (for it seems that in Japan the price for being an individual is death!), we should note that this nihilist type of hero is not a recent phenomenon in Japanese history. Buruma further defines his popular nihilist as one who seeks 'enlightenment through the Way of the Sword', one who is, moreover, violent, anti-social and bad.[14] There is an obvious contradiction in his suggestion that this 'ego-lessness' applies to 'super-individualists', but what he is suggesting is in fact a popular representation of a hero who in 'Zen'-style is ego-less because *amoral*.

Buruma's comments about the 'nihilist' hero bring to mind a somewhat submerged point made by Albert Craig about amorality:

> In the basic Tokugawa ethic, loyalty was not justified primarily in . . . Confucian terms. Rather, it was based on the duty of a samurai to fulfil his obligations (*hōon*), a duty that was to be performed selflessly (*muga ni*). Thus, the same idea of loyalty, that on a scholarly level was sanctioned by the moral Confucian universe, was justified on a deeper level by a Buddhist concept of the annihilation of the self and the release from a universe or morality and immorality. In an everyday secular setting the annihilation of the self became the denial of the self.[15]

We might first note his acknowledgement of the way in which Buddhist 'ego-annihilation' came to be interpreted secularly in more Confucian terms as 'selflessness'. But the crux of the matter is that self-annihilation is said to be equivalent to a 'release from morality and immorality'. Broadly speaking, this is in keeping with both the Buddhist doctrine of amoralism whereby worldly morality is irrelevant and also modern European nihilism where social morality is rejected because oppressive to the individual.[16]

There is much in Buruma's portrait of the Japanese 'nihilist' hero that is similar to descriptions of European nihilists.[17] This comes as no surprise, since the important sources of European nihilistic intellectual inspiration – Stirner, Nietzsche, Turgenev, Dostoevski – were popular in Japan. But together with Buddhist amoralism, there were in Japan other traditional sources for a 'nihilistic' form of heroism focused on the purity of the Act itself. However reworked it was over time, the dialectical approach in Mahāyāna Buddhism to action as one with realization or liberation (the 'oneness of means and end') was almost certainly one of them. It is often said that in Zen liberation comes through practice, not conceptualization. Thus, for many in medieval Japan, practice came to be the measure of the life of both monk and samurai. According to Dōgen, the thirteenth-century founder of Japanese Sōtō Zen:

> In the Buddha Dharma, practice and realization are identical. Because one's present practice is practice in realization, one's initial negotiation of the Way in itself is the whole of original realization. Thus, even while one is directed to practice, [one] is told not to anticipate realization apart from practice, because practice points

directly to original realization. As it is already realization in practice, realization is endless: as it is practice in realization, practice
is beginningless.[18]

As Abe Masao adds, 'practice ("becoming pure") and realization
("being pure") are inseparable and dynamically one'. He emphasizes
that the duality of 'potentiality and actuality' is overcome by Dōgen's
'oneness of practice and enlightenment', as is the 'duality of means and
end'.[19] What this implies is an emphasis on the purity (hence in
popular parlance, also the 'sincerity') of the action, whether we
happen to be speaking of Zen meditation or secular, even political
action. Regarding amorality, furthermore, if one sees things in terms
of this 'oneness of means and end', a 'Zen hero' does not have to
be, or be seen as, noble or evil in accordance with worldly morality,
motivation or goals. So, to return to the contemporary *yakuza* films
Buruma discusses, what this can also imply is a pseudo-spiritual justi-
fication for a genre that is extremely violent: for shedding the blood of
others is not immoral, but 'amoral'. Since purity comes to be associated with violent (but 'sincere') action, moreover, the act seems to
symbolize a purification (not 'pollution') through bloodshed, as
Buruma indicates.

If one applies the notion of amorality and this monistic approach to
means and ends to samurai patterns of heroism, which were undeniably influenced by Zen, it raises questions about the centrality of
goals, causes and outwardly directed loyalties – all of which are
usually said to have been central to the [*sic*] samurai code of ethics,
honour and action.[20] If historians of Japan had not been so inclined
to treat Confucianism and neo-Confucianism as the sum total of
samurai and 'Tokugawa Ideology',[21] respectively, a more complex
and convincing picture of samurai codes, 'Bushidō-s', might have
emerged. Ivan Morris himself implies the one-sidedness of this
Confucian-centred/Japan-as-'groupist' thesis (though soon loses sight
of it) when he says of his noble, failed heroes that when facing
defeat they would typically take their own lives – in order to 'avoid
the indignity of capture', preserve their honour, and demonstrate
their sincerity.[22] (Cutting oneself open, of course, was supposed to
demonstrate the purity of the 'heart'.) What is suggested is a rather
individualistic approach to self-completion, self-assertion and even
self-empowerment that is not necessarily *so* intimately bound up
with mindless obedience/'loyalty' to authority or group expectations,
morality or causes as often argued. Morris even notes on occasion
that his historical heroes did not bother to plan their actions or

rebellion at all carefully, citing Mishima Yukio (a Yōmeigaku fan) who once said, 'It is the journey not the arrival that matters.'[23]

Therefore, while such historical heroes as are described by Morris faced and perhaps even 'chose' death, they need not be seen as 'tragic failures'. Connected with this Zen-derived equation of action with realization, whereby ultimate practical goals are deemed either irrelevant or secondary, we should recall that Fumiko mentioned a 'task in life' that did not have to be 'fulfilled'.

Fumiko's ego-assertion or fulfilment was the apparent opposite of the doctrinal Buddhist 'ego-annihilation. But while it might have been largely inspired by the 'egoistic nihilism' of Max Stirner and an individualistic form of social Darwinism, her act of seeking within herself for liberation was not entirely 'foreign'. It is noteworthy that ten or so years earlier, Itō Noe had criticized her second husband, Tsuji Jun's personal solution approach to politics;[24] this was a 'nihilistic' approach that was ostensibly modern, yet Tsuji himself identified the inspiration for his self-liberation as Stirner's 'sutra of the ego'! (*Jiga no Kyō* was the title he gave his translation of *The Ego and His Own*.) A highly individualistic, personal liberation approach to philosophy or politics in early twentieth-century Japan was certainly influenced by foreign ideas and behavioural models, but it raises once more the possibility of indigenous religio-philosophical inspiration.[25] The two broad approaches to enlightenment or salvation in Japanese religion had long been *jiriki* (the self-empowered approach of Zen etc.) and *tariki* (the reliance on another's power as in Pure Land schools). It is not difficult to see where the samurai emphasis on self-reliance and self-assertion in part originated.

Thomas Huber hints at a deification of practice/action when he observes that for some *shishi* – literally men of *will*, not necessarily 'purpose'! – 'romantic courage' was more important than 'political pragmatism'. This tradition would partly explain why later left-wing radicals would respect reactionary heroes like Saigō Takamori. E. H. Norman once noted that though many (ex-samurai) government leaders fell victim to violent attacks or assassination, the Meiji government did not really try to suppress groups of patriotic terrorists because such 'sincerely motivated' tactics were not so alien to Japanese samurai tradition.[26] 'Sincerity' was/is a quality admired in revolutionary heroes, whether or not the admirers agree with their convictions, tactics or goals. Irokawa Daikichi notes the degree to which people's rights advocates in the 1880s respected Kumoi Tatsuo, executed in 1870 for having led discontented samurai in a plot to re-establish the shogunate. His pro-democracy admirers saw Kumoi as an example of 'resolute revolutionary resistance'.[27]

Whatever the precise reasons for the popularity in certain circles in Japan today of revolutionary heroes like Suga and Fumiko, it is clear that the one styled herself more along the lines of a 'noble', self-sacrificing, idealistic and altruistic hero (for whom the collective group, revolutionary movement, the 'people' and even humanity were important); while the other represented herself as an amoral 'nihilist' or egoist for whom a highly individualistic form of action/resistance was more important than worldly goals or success. In Fumiko's terms ends were the same as means. While we should remind ourselves at this point that her philosophy of political action probably owed much to European philosophies, none the less, the action-oriented vocabulary of Fumiko (or Suga) may well have been partly derived from Japanese philosophies and models of heroic action.

Suga's idealization of self-sacrifice for a principle, her revolutionary movement and the people seems more in keeping with Morris' 'noble' hero. This, too, suggests indigenous influences, though once again we cannot ignore the importance of foreign models. She herself emphasized that she had taken Sofia Perovskaya as a model for action, and Russian populists had exhibited the same sort of altruism as Meiji socialists who wanted to reform society *for* the 'ordinary' people. (John Crump refers to this as typical Confucian-style elitism: the masses could not be expected to do anything for themselves.[28]) As early as the 1880s there had been a spate of Russian nihilist novels published in Japan; also works specifically about the lives and fates of Russian terrorists. The assassination of Tsar Alexander II in 1881 by Perovskaya and others of the People's Will had sparked a wave of interest in Russian populism: there were thirty-one works about nihilists published in Japan in 1881, and thirty-four in 1882.[29] Still in Suga's time, moreover, works at least partly about Russian populism were being produced (for example, Kemuriyama Sentarō's *Kinsei Museifushugi* or *Modern Anarchism*, published in 1902). In the years that followed, Japanese radicals continued to look to Russia for inspiration, particularly in the area of tactics, no doubt increasingly so as repression intensified. Another reason for the increased interest in the doings of Russian revolutionaries in the middle of the first decade of the century, however, was the 1905 Russian Revolution. Crump discusses how, paradoxically, now there was again in Japan a spate of articles on the nineteenth-century Russian populists. In articles on Vera Zasulich, Perovskaya and others, *socialists* were urged to go 'to the people'.[30] Given the regicidal example set by

Perovskaya and others, it is not difficult to see why five years later Miyashita Daikichi, one of the small group of anarchists who, with Suga, was involved in plans to assassinate the Meiji emperor, said under interrogation that he had believed it to be impossible to realize socialism while a superstitious reverence for the imperial family permeated society: 'I made up my mind to first make a bomb and then throw it at the emperor,' he said. 'I had to show that the emperor too was a human being whom blood could flow from just like the rest of us.'[31]

Contemporaneous gender constructions were probably among the factors that led Suga to accord self-sacrifice such value. According to Confucianism, women were expected to devote themselves entirely to their families, submitting first to the authority of fathers, then husbands, and finally eldest sons. This hardly changed once Japan entered the 'modern' era, except that from about mid-Meiji a renewed state and social androcentrism led to the dissemination to all classes of once-samurai patriarchal codes and forms (in some areas an imposition of them through law). Again the official attitude toward the social role of all women was a narrowly 'private'/familial one, now expressed by the slogan, *'ryōsai kenbo'* ('good wife, wise mother'). The virtuous woman was still to be all that negative definitions of femininity in Buddhism, Confucianism, Bushidō and so on had implied: in short, a non-person, since such constructions of feminine subjectivity had been centred upon an effacement of the self.

Yet in Meiji the field to which women could devote their *non*-selves was widened. No longer was it a case of a woman's having no 'lord' but her husband to deny herself for; now she could serve husband (and still *his* sons), father, and other paternal figures of authority right up to the father of the nation. The service now expected of her was to a whole range of masculine figures all rolled up into one grand patriarchal, national Cause. She was, moreover, officially discouraged in a variety of legal and other ways from playing any more 'public' a part in building a modern nation, unless of course it was in the direct service of nationalism and the emperor-system. Whilst political activity by women was outlawed in 1887 under the Peace Preservation Ordinance, the state from late Meiji defined the 'political' narrowly to mean anything leftist or otherwise 'unfeminine' – in fact, women in a variety of acceptable political (e.g., nationalist) organizations were encouraged to keep up the good work.[32] If the 'family state', in which the highest loyalty was due to the paternal figure of the emperor, appeared flexible in its definition of the public sphere, it was because in reality the only permissible 'public' role for

woman now hinged upon an extension into public life of her private/
familial duty involving selfless, nurturing service.

Suga was hostile toward the notion of 'good wife, wise mother', and
once explicitly rejected the sexual double standard it implied, but even
late in her life she did not seem particularly critical of the demand
for self-denial it rested upon. In this she was quite unlike Fumiko
who, certainly in this respect, was a much more thorough critic of the
familist emperor-system ideology as it pertained generally to model,
patriotic citizens; but Suga was not unlike some of the female Russian
revolutionaries she so admired. In their search for a moral purpose to
replace the earlier emphasis on devotion to the family, some seem to
have redirected their self-sacrifice to a social and political level.[33]

It is possible that in 1909 Suga had had a desire to sacrifice herself
for Kōtoku. The circumstances of her publishing under her own name
in 1909 (his) anarchist magazine *Jiyū Shisō* (*Free Thought*) will be discussed in Part III, but there is little doubt that in this case she had
placed a higher premium on Kōtoku's health, freedom and value to
the movement. Both were quite ill with consumption, yet it seems
that *he* would not have survived a prison term. However, it is likely
that *later* she saw her sacrifice (for the cause) as a political one
rather than a merely personal one for her common-law husband.
During the trial, at least, she represented her own (activist) and
Kōtoku's (proselytist) contributions to the anarchist movement as different but equal, for he was 'a man of letters more suited to publicizing
socialism than to carrying out radical measures.'[34]

Selflessness was an ideal long in vogue in Japan, but in and after
Meiji it took on different 'colours'. Earlier, martyrdom for a cause
both revolutionary and nationalistic had been a common theme
amongst people's rights advocates as well as still earlier *shishi*, as the
following ballad suggests:

> For our more than forty million countrymen,
> we're not afraid of wearing convict red,
> Promote the national interest and the people's welfare,
> Foster the people's strength!
> And if we can't,
> Dynamite, Boom![35]

This interest in dynamite was probably partly inspired by the example
of the Russian populists, but it was not such a great jump from sacrificing one's life for the sake of the people ('*banmin no tame*') in late
Tokugawa, to dedicating it for the sake of the nation ('*kuni no
tame*') in and after Meiji. The latter was a phrase constantly used in

Meiji nationalistic discourse.[36] And from there it was no great leap to dying for the sake of a principle or the cause (*'shugi no tame'*), a constant in revolutionary discourse in Suga's time.

The subject of political heroes' being galvanized from apparent motives of selfless 'nobility' brings to mind the case of Kawakami Hajime, a prewar Marxist, who had first come to Christianity and socialism in late Meiji, at about the same time as Suga. He was attracted to the Christian teaching of 'absolute unselfishness', and created his own personal synthesis of Confucian selflessness, Buddhist egolessness, Christian unselfishness, Pure Land Buddhist 'selfless love' and, finally, also Marxist 'sacrifice' for the masses.[37] Later in the 1920s, Kawakami was criticized by young Communist Party members for not being enough of a materialist and for emphasizing sacrifice too much. (These communists had probably internalized the individualist anarchist and nihilistic emphasis on *jiga*, the ego, more than they might have cared to admit.) It is significant that Kawakami, one of the older generation of radicals by the 1920s, would have laid so much emphasis on selflessness – and been criticized for it by younger comrades. Clearly, by the 1920s the tensions between noble selflessness (*muga*) and a nihilistic assertion of the ego (*jiga shuchō*) had taken a clearer form within radical circles. Suga and Fumiko were very much the products of their respective political environments, since by Fumiko's time social critics were probably more able to see clearly the uses to which self-abnegation could be put in the service of emperor, nation, economic productivity (for the nation), the family (as microcosm of the state), and so on.

Akiyama Kiyoshi, a well-known anarchist theorist, has distinguished 'mere terrorism' from nihilism in Japan on the basis of living for the sake of others ('renouncing the ego') versus recognizing and acting upon the subjectivity of the ego. The former, he argues, is mere sentimentality and a philosophy of death, while the latter is a true philosophy of life: ego-preservation, in short, not ego-annihilation.[38] One can hardly fail to see the correlation between these remarks and Fumiko's ultimate affirmation of both death and life, and her representation of death (through egoistic resistance) *as* life. It was noted above that the egoism that had gained popularity by Fumiko's time was of a specific type, for individuality had come to be seen as necessarily a struggle for existence against the state.[39] This transition had nevertheless accompanied a shift from the revolutionary elitism of Meiji socialism, the self-sacrifice of leaders for the impotent masses, to the Taishō anarchist attitudes of those like Ōsugi Sakae who had faith in the latter's potential for self-liberation and were suspicious of intellectual or other elite leaderships. This trend was, in turn, challenged in radical sections of the socialist movement by authoritarian socialists, including communists, in the mid-1920s. But we should recall that Fumiko did not share Ōsugi's idealization of the masses. No doubt this was one more way in which she not only identified herself with nihilism, but also distanced herself from anarchism. Neither her nihilism, however, nor Suga's selfless 'nobility' had derived only from foreign sources; the two differed greatly in their constructions of heroic political action, but such differences had long been part and parcel of resistance, Japanese-style.

A GREAT DEATH

In *Six Lives, Six Deaths* Katō argues that the way one approaches 'dying well' has in Japan been 'defined by one's membership in a particular group'.[40] The statement seems somewhat tautological, but what is useful for my purposes is his discussion of premodern Japan's 'most important special group with its own rules for dying': the Tokugawa samurai class. The tactics (assassination) both women advocated had much in common with samurai vendettas – but there is yet another way in which they might have been modelling themselves on samurai-style 'rules for dying', which is again related to a Zen or Buddhist concept, the 'Great Death'.

In speaking of ritual suicide as social control in Tokugawa, Katō notes that samurai not only had to be 'prepared for death' in order to be able to take responsibility for their own 'offences to the community' or clan, or the offences of others in the clan for whom they were responsible; they had to be *determined* to die putting to rights the wrongs committed by outsiders. Perhaps no other historical drama has so captured the popular imagination in Japan as *Chūshingura*, one rendition of tales of the 'forty-seven rōnin' who had in 1703 avenged their lord before following him in death (*junshi*). This and other cases of ritual suicide apparently inspired by loyalty to superiors – for example, that of General Nogi for the Meiji emperor in 1912 – came to be constructed as 'models for patriotic behaviour' in prewar and wartime Japan.[41] But also among the various reasons for voluntary suicide in premodern times was registering a protest against an unjust decision or treatment by superiors.[42] This was clearly influenced by the Confucian view of the right to rebel if rulers did not fulfil *Ōdō*, the 'Great Way of Governance', through their 'heavenly mandate'.[43] Needless to say, however, it was a conveniently inwardly directed form of rebellion.

Katō's emphasis on conforming to group expectations of how one should die is part of the thesis that death in Japan has long been more often a group-oriented than individual event. While Lifton, Katō and Reich imply that samurai traditions were more likely to be individualistic in various ways, they fail to emphasize traditions in Japan that were strongly so: 'self-empowered' or self-determined paths to enlightenment in schools of Buddhism like Zen, for example; or the strong emphasis amongst samurai on personal honour, integrity, self-assertion and -completion. Nor do they note the tendency amongst peasant rebels or other commoners to appropriate such 'samurai' individualistic traits, casting themselves in the role of noble warrior heroes and claiming virtues that were supposed to be the monopoly of the ruling class. Samurai were not, of course, the only popular heroes in Tokugawa Japan or later. To give but one example, the seventeenth-century peasant leader and political martyr (*gimin*), Sakura Sōgō, became a hero of kabuki plays in the nineteenth century. Both in Tokugawa and in Meiji, peasant rebels often acted in a fashion that samurai or former samurai clearly thought was their preserve. One farmer in the Chichibu uprising of 1884, for example, selected a posthumous Buddhist name to write on his headband before going into battle (against state and even emperor), and set off 'with no intention of returning alive'.[44]

Janet Walker expresses one aspect of traditional individualism in Japan well when she observes that,

> Zen, by stressing the individual's personal experiencing of the truth, contributed to Japanese culture a concept of the individual as a free being somehow outside of or transcending the social hierarchy. This paradoxical idea that the individual was socially unfree though experientially free continued to affect Japanese culture even after Westernization began in the late nineteenth century.[45]

This 'experiential freedom', however, was not merely a concept, but rather an incentive to action. On occasion, even samurai resisted the social–ideological pressures to be loyal, obedient and conformist. People's behaviour anywhere and at any time must surely conform in many respects to larger cultural or small group expectations, yet in other ways might be quite individual. Thus, 'dying well' in accordance with group expectations is in one sense particularly relevant to the case of Suga, for whom her revolutionary culture was very important. Not only Suga, but also Sakai Toshihiko and (like her) another defendant in the Meiji High Treason Case, Ōishi Seinosuke, all expressed the conviction that some would have to die for the cause. In fact, it was years before the treason incident that Ōishi Seinosuke expressed the view that it was up to revolutionary leaders to sacrifice themselves:

> Of course, not all people would sacrifice themselves. But at least the leaders of the revolutionary movement will not be able to arrive at the heaven of the joyful new society without entering through the narrow gate which Christ talked about and accepting the heavy cross of suffering.[46]

There are various strands here that are pertinent to Suga's construction of death: revolutionary elitism; the common ideal of self-sacrifice for the cause, and the Christian influence upon that; and also the notion of a good (revolutionary) death.

Suga might have exhibited an acceptance of group rules for dying, but in her diary she also gave the impression that she resented feeling constrained to act in ways deemed fitting for a revolutionary. On one occasion she dismissed 'that special characteristic of Eastern heroes', which was to suppress their 'joy or anger' and not reveal their 'true feelings'. She went on to say that she did not care how others might measure her worth, suggesting that she did not care to conform to others' expectations of her. In facing death, she was group-oriented, certainly, but not entirely so, just as Fumiko did not completely fit the egoistic role she cast herself in. Fumiko's construction of dying well tended to be more individualistic, though she suggested at one point that her group of comrades ('Pak's friends') thought Pak and herself 'stupid' – presumably for taking the unnecessary stand they did by refusing to deny their guilt, thus playing into the hands of the authorities.[47] Her implication was that their nihilist friends thought they were being unnecessarily 'self-sacrificing'. The nihilists in Pak's and Fumiko's group seemed cynical about any hint of idealism or altruism. Possibly, with Fumiko's immediate group it was not so much a case of having rules for dying as a code of *egoistic* self-preservation that may or may not have involved dying.

One would expect a glorification of heroic death mainly by an elite class of charismatic warriors to continue to have a broad popular appeal in modern times, but samurai tradition was also part of both Suga's and Fumiko's family heritage. Fumiko, however, was utterly scornful of her father's pride in his family's pedigree and name.[48] Her generation, of course, was farther removed from the days when samurai ruled than Suga's. Suga and her comrades clearly did take samurai as models for their rebellion. During the trial there were frequent references to the fact that Kōtoku and others had thought that

Kumamoto in Kyushu would be a good place to recruit such determined fighters. It had been a centre for samurai rebels opposed to the new Meiji regime. John Crump also remarks on how the *shishi* were 'the ideal types on whom the Meiji socialists sought to model themselves' (which partly explains their tendency to elitism).[49]

The samurai emphasis on 'dying well' had been influenced by the Zen idea of *daishi* or *taishi ichiban* (the 'Great Death'; death of the ego or delusion in Buddhism),[50] which when secularized came to be interpreted as literally a great physical death. One model for samurai was the medieval Zen monk whose 'equipoise' in meeting death voluntarily was illustrated in a vast number of stories about the 'Great Death'.[51] Since fighting, warring and death were then the business of the samurai, it is not difficult to see how this concept would also come to have a somewhat different meaning in secular parlance. LaFleur gives some indication of how the term 'Great Death' has been used in Japan, in both a doctrinal and popularized sense, in this description of its influence upon 'ways of the warrior':

> The calm of the Zen monk's mode of life as well as the equipoise with which great Buddhists . . . met the end of their own lives had an obvious attraction for the warrior. . . . However, even if the 'Great Death' of the Buddhist monk served the samurai as the effective model for his own death in battle, it was the death of the samurai rather than that of the monk that appealed to the popular imagination. It was not the death of an aged monk voluntarily and calmly moving into death . . . but, rather, it was the swift death of a brave and young warrior in battle, an index to his bravery and loyalty to his lord, which became the primary model of a great death during the feudal period in Japanese history. In this context the aesthetics of dying had new importance.[52]

A reference to the romanticization of the deaths of *kamikaze* pilots during the Second World War is perhaps enough to illustrate the persistence of this sort of model, though the continued use of violence by radicals as 'a means of government suasion' through the Meiji era and beyond is also pertinent.[53] E. H. Norman noted the fact that Meiji inherited from the Tokugawa era, when there was no other means of 'concerted political action' available to samurai, 'the weapons of the vendetta and assassination'.[54]

The above description of the 'calm and equipoise' in the face of death of monks and samurai makes more sense of the remark about 'Eastern heroes' that Suga made when admonishing herself to be calm, resolute and in control of her feelings in the face of execution.

When she then insisted that she would 'cry, laugh, rejoice and rage', however, she was not suggesting that she had not herself taken hold of death voluntarily. When Katō distinguished between elite and mass views of death in modern Japan,[55] paradoxically, he observed of the former that 'in a way similar to the samurai elite, the self-control they show toward their individualized deaths depends on a sense of resignation'. This, however, is not the more group-oriented resignation leading to passivity, which is *said* to have characterized the common people.

One often encounters an emphasis on the importance in Japan of the Buddhistic conception of *akirame*, a 'resignation' to one's destiny. Partly for this reason, Tokugawa peasants are often characterized as having been passively resigned to their lot.[56] But *akirame* has long had two sides to it: there can be a 'resigned acquiescence in resistance'.[57] The 'apparent abandonment' beneath an 'exaltation of activity' or resistance referred to by Spae is not unrelated to Katō's point about resignation making 'self-control' possible (the ability to take hold of one's destiny), but the latter's assumption that this has only been true of conventional social elites in Japan is questionable. I implied earlier that the cases of Suga and Fumiko suggest something about the difficulties inherent in defining what constitutes a member of an 'elite': unlike the six subjects studied by Lifton, Katō and Reich, both were women, neither were from fortunate backgrounds, they had both had little formal education, and were not even leaders in their political movements. Yet still their constructions of political action 'unto death' fit Katō's description of elite, individualistic self-control. Perhaps this is partly because the political authorities helped to create them in the role of antagonists, and thus equals (as they had peasant *gimin* earlier).

VENGEFUL SPIRITS

Assassination for motives of political revenge has almost certainly been common in all parts of the world. Yet Matsuda Michio once suggested that revenge-motivated anarchist terrorism was a distinctive feature of Russia and Japan.[58] Some, like Alexander Berkman in the United States and August Vaillant in France, made attempts in the 1890s on the lives of individuals or groups they held responsible either for particular acts of repression or social iniquities more generally.[59] Perhaps, therefore, Matsuda was thinking specifically of acts of vengeance in response to the legal or extra-legal murders of revolutionaries. The prime example of the latter is that of Ōsugi Sakae and Itō

Noe, murdered by military police after the 1923 earthquake. There were a number of incidents of revenge-motivated anarchist terrorism in Japan in the mid-1920s. Furuta Daijirō of the Girochinsha or Guillotine Group of Osaka was ultimately hanged together with another member, Nakahama Tetsu; they had intended to exact vengeance for the deaths of comrades by assassinating the crown prince (and had gone to Korea to try to buy bombs with that aim in mind).[60] There was another incident involving a Girochinsha member, Tanaka Kōgō, who was unsuccessful in his attempt to kill the nephew of Captain Amakasu Masahiko of the military police unit responsible for the murders of Itō and Ōsugi. Wada Kyūtarō and Muraki Genjirō, on the other hand, both of whom had been union activists in Ōsugi's circle, tried to kill General Fukuda Miyatarō, who had been the commander of martial law after the earthquake.[61]

In Japan's own history of assassination for motives of revenge – from samurai in premodern times, through anti-foreign zealots in late Tokugawa and critics of Meiji government policies, to left- and right-wing radicals in the twentieth century – the rectification of evil was a common theme. In accounts of village movements for people's rights in the 1870s and 1880s (as in accounts of peasant protest earlier), the idea of a need to purify, rectify or avenge 'evil' is often in evidence: the capital was the site of 'the wicked and evil'; and 'evil rulers' were to get the 'heavenly punishment' they deserved.[62] Traditional influences may not have been necessary for a desire for revenge to become part of Suga's or Fumiko's representation of political action, however. Both accused society or the authorities of inflicting various sorts of torments upon them and their comrades or friends. Nevertheless, we cannot deny the extent to which heroic vendettas have been romanticized in Japan. One need hardly mention how common the theme of revenge had been in popular culture, in kabuki, bunraku, and so on. Moreover, *goryō* (restless, malevolent or vengeful spirits) have long been part of the Japanese pantheon.[63] Such restless spirits are unable to let go of their attachment to life, sometimes because of their thirst for vengeance. In ages past *goryō* were enshrined and worshipped, partly in order to appease the desire for vengeance that came from their untimely, often unjust deaths.[64]

When in prison, Fumiko did not only imagine herself as 'a vengeful spirit . . . paying evil in kind'; she also used the simile of a 'demon' when describing her earlier desire for revenge. In Korea she had been like a 'little demon with a thorn lodged in [her]': something had been nagging at her, needing to be attended to in order to ease her pain.[65] On more than one occasion she expressed a desire to avenge social inequities and evils. Apart from the imperial family (who symbolized inequality and were a screen for the real wielders of power), she did not target particular individuals as Suga said she had. Rather, Fumiko claimed she had once planned to throw a bomb into the midst of the 'riff-raff' or 'rabble' (*uzōmuzō*) in the Imperial Diet.[66]

A desire for revenge amongst those who have suffered political repression is probably rather common anywhere. None the less, one can see how such a desire might be strengthened by indigenous traditions of romanticized vengeance. Thus, whether or not revenge had been part of their original political motivation, once in prison Fumiko and Suga certainly did imagine themselves as avenging spirits. Perhaps, since neither had been able to exact their vengeance in this life, they both fantasized about being *goryō* in the next. What they each seemed to be saying to some unspecified audience was that if their opponents thought they had won this round, they might yet have a surprise in store.

ROMANTICIZING DEATH

The subjects both romanticized heroic political deaths in various ways. I have referred already to Suga's early romanticization of revolutionary 'double suicide'. Closely connected with this, moreover, is an 'aestheticization' of death evident in LaFleur's description of the young warrior's death. This, he adds, came to be equated in feudal times with the cherry blossom, a symbol of impermanence or the brevity of beauty: aesthetics, in other words, attenuates any violence that might be connected with death. Since in Japanese religious culture death and blood have represented pollution this also indicates a tendency to see such a beautification as equivalent to purification. (Buruma also implied something similar about the film genre he discusses.)

Lifton, Katō and Reich note that Japan is often described as a 'death-haunted' culture, meaning that in Japan it has been common to romanticize death and violence.[67] This is by no means peculiar to the Japanese (the tendency of European Romantics to romanticize death was remarked on earlier, and there are other obvious parallels in US, European, Australian or other popular culture/s today concerning a romanticization of violence). But an association of death with beauty is writ large among the imagery associated with Japan: charismatic samurai cutting down all in their path; their vendettas and their ritual suicides; and also the erotic suicides of star-crossed lovers. Films about the martial arts also often feature a romanticization (partly a Zen-derived mystification) of violence. Earlier discussion of the 'experiential transcendence' mode of symbolic immortality also indicated that there has long been a broad tendency in Japan to look for beauty in death or attempt to see it in aesthetic terms. We need not, however, find in the latter an 'obsession' with death-as-'spectre', but rather a natural human tendency to want to come to terms with death and accept its inevitability.

Like countless others facing death within Japan and without, in modern times and earlier, both Suga and Fumiko looked for and found beauty or 'joy' in death – at least that is the impression they seemed to want to create. Suga had a romantic view of her heroic sacrifice for the cause, while Fumiko reverted to classical expressions of the ephemeral beauty of all things in nature. Both probably romanticized going to death together with their lovers, influenced no doubt by the popular tradition – in the performing arts and in reality – of double 'suicide'. The above-mentioned Nietzschean 'Bluestocking', Hiratsuka Raichō, was in 1907 drawn to a novelist, apparently largely because of his talk of death and beauty, and there was a public scandal after they attempted double suicide.[68] Dying together, presumably, was meant to be the supreme act of rebellious love, as Suga once suggested. Yet while Suga in 1911 might have been about to die together with Kōtoku physically, in her last few days she was clearly grieving over her recent estrangement from him:

> We go
> to our graves
> you and I,
> our hearts estranged
> like the seas east and west.[69]

Also in the poem already cited about her being 'kept up late in the night weeping with the pain of wounds, old and new', it is possible that she was referring to his recent reconciliation with his wife. Suga often referred to Kōtoku in her diary, and may have had some consolation in the fact that, while they would not now be living out together what little remained of their lives, they would be going to death together. An indication of the many-layered nature of inspiration for such a romanticization of ('revolutionary') double suicide, moreover, is that Suga had earlier visualized this in quite 'samurai' terms, similar to a samurai's committing *seppuku* or ritual suicide after a desperate battle. She had even counterposed revolutionary *shinjū* to the traditional 'weak' form of lovers' suicide where couples typically just gave in to social pressure: killing themselves, presumably, because social morality would not permit them to be together (a popular theme in the theatre).[70] Fumiko, too, often stated her intention to die with Pak. A general romanticization of 'rebellion unto death' – with their partners – was part and parcel of the representations of heroic political action and death of both women.

CONCLUSION

Lifton, Katō and Reich acknowledge that death symbolism can be 'a source of vitality and continuity': possibilities for 'revitalization' can be found amidst destruction.[71] They also comment on the use of death symbolism both by adherents of hegemonic emperor-system ideology (the case of General Nogi, for example) and by its opponents (revolutionary martyrs as inspirational models). Suga's threat that anarchism or a future ideal society would be born from deaths like hers, or from the destructive–reconstructive task to which she and her comrades had been committed, is an example of such a revitalization, as is Fumiko's emphasis on the need to check authority and domination through the individual's self-assertion, rebellion and death. In their 'engagements with death', victims became victors, and death also became life; not only in terms of how they symbolized their own personal continuity despite the 'annihilation' of death, but also because death came to represent social reconstruction. Ultimately, in both cases an affirmation of death meant also an affirmation of life.

Suga and Fumiko were 'haunted' by death only in the sense that they tended to romanticize it, like revolutionary 'martyrs' or rebel heroes anywhere. We do not need to 'get inside their heads' to suspect that this romanticization of heroic death must have played a part in their choice of tactics or political associations, as well as in their actions while in custody. Their representations of a political death drew upon both foreign and indigenous sources of inspiration which formed part of a broad discourse in Meiji and Taishō about radical political action. Themes such as self-sacrifice, revenge, the importance of acting, taking hold of one's own destiny, the aesthetics of death and 'dying well' were not specific to Japan, but all had a special place in indigenous traditions. In Fumiko's case there are also signs of an 'ego-fulfilment' that had something in common with both a classical Buddhist vision of seeking inside oneself for liberation and a modern conception of egoism. Many indigenous traditions were doubtless reworked through appropriations of foreign ideas or action-models perceived as similar: conceptions of Nature, amoralism, an idealization of selflessness, an exaltation of action, and also self-empowered approaches to 'salvation' or liberation.

In sum, neither grand theories about 'Oriental pessimism' and Eastern 'unitary visions of life and death', nor holistic notions about *the* group-orientation or *the* pattern of heroism of the Japanese are of much use in interpreting the complex, many-layered meanings ascribed to death by individuals like Suga and Fumiko. Nor, to my mind, would a psycho-biographical approach be if it meant *reducing* such meanings (or motivations) to 'youthful identity crises', 'death-wishes' or 'survivor guilt'.[72] What needs constantly to be borne in mind when reading their writings on death is the fact that such texts were mostly *produced in prison under threat of death*. Evidently, the approaches to death of different individuals are determined as much by their immediate circumstances as by the religio-philosophical and political cultures of which they are a part. There is no doubt that the subjects' testimonies and actions in prison were often meant to wrest from society and the state the significance of their own deaths – and lives. And it is to the latter that I turn next to see how each constructed herself as a victim of society, yet in so doing, seemed to be trying to empower herself. It is clear that the theme of victimization was used as a weapon by both Suga and Fumiko against androcentric nation-narratives that to live in Meiji or Taishō Japan was to live amidst a 'familial harmony' that came of benevolent (imperial and other) paternalistic rule. Herman Ooms has observed that this was a deception that had its roots in Tokugawa; and if ideology then was 'a continuation of warfare with other means',[73] a war of ideas was just what Suga and Fumiko were engaged in when they put forward what they saw to be the realities of Life.

Part III
Life-narratives

7 Kanno Suga (1902–1911)

TEXTS AND CONTEXTS

Biographical descriptions of Kanno Suga's childhood have drawn upon the 'semi-autobiographical' novelette of 1902, 'Omokage' ('Memories'), the heroine of which was named Akiko. There are a few parallels between information contained in it and a very brief account Suga gave of her background during the trial, but there is no doubt that her youth is more a matter for speculation than has often been admitted.[1] Because it is often difficult to ascertain whether details about her youth and early career have been derived *only* from her 'semi-autobiographical' writings, here secondary sources will be treated with caution in attempts to piece together contextual information about her background. The strength of autobiographical traditions in Japanese literature partly explains this assumption that Suga's stories about Akiko or Tsuyuko were actually about herself. But even if we could justify on these grounds treating such works as factual, problems like the extent of political or dramatic licence would still remain. There is also the issue of to what degree her hindsight moulded her retelling of events that had occurred years before. These are problems inherent even in autobiography where authors explicitly proclaim the truth of their 'own' life-stories. Yet in a project where one's concern is rather with how the subject *represented* the reality of life – whether her 'own' lived reality, or that of fictional characters like Akiko and Tsuyuko – such issues are not so problematic. When one's object is not the reconstruction of a life, but rather an interpretation of narratives about life, a consideration of political purpose is not only an intrinsic part of the interpretation, but also helps to bring into sharper relief the contexts in which the subject wrote.

Before turning my attention to texts written by Suga between 1902 and 1905, I should first to make some observations about the discursive context and literary style of her works. Doing so should also explain why scholars have been happy to assume that heroines named Akiko or Tsuyuko were the historical Kanno Suga. Suga's narrative style was influenced by two distinct but related streams in Japanese literature, one of which was the modern *shi-shōsetsu* or confessional 'I-novel' about to emerge as a recognized genre. A strongly introspective tendency had partly been inspired by the enthusiasm for individualism amongst Meiji intellectuals; also by the strong tendency in Japanese naturalism toward confessional self-exposure (equated with rebelling against society).[2] Donald Keene says of the Japanese 'I-novel' that it is 'a story so closely based on personal experiences as to be a kind of dramatized diary'.[3] Yet Keene's emphasis on the preservation of true experience seems a little too positivist when contrasted with Noriko Mizuta Lippit's emphasis on irony and self-dramatization in I-novels. She also notes that Japanese literary critics have consistently identified these confessional novels with the actual lives of the authors. This, no doubt, has contributed to historians' readiness to treat Suga's 'fiction' as fact.

The other stream in Japanese literature that influenced Suga's style was 'female-school literature', which formed the basis of modern autobiographical writing in Japan, and had its beginnings about 1,000 years ago.[4] Lippit and Kyoko Iriye Selden note that women then developed the poetic diary in which they recorded 'their private thoughts, feelings, and observations of the people around them'. This sort of 'private, autobiographical writing' was one important influence upon the development of Japanese fiction. They add, however, that in modern times the existence of a distinct, recognized school of women's literature became restrictive because female writers have been *expected* to confine their writing to private autobiographical works about their personal feelings, relationships and commitments. The greater proportion of Suga's early works do fit this description. Even some later articles that one would expect to be 'impersonal', from their explicitly political titles and subject-matter, are in fact descriptive narratives of particular incidents in the heroine's life and how she personally responded to them. Yet Suga, no doubt, would have agreed that 'the personal *is* political', much like the proletarian literary movement writer, Sata Ineko, who later 'strove to combine a [political] vision of her society with the exploration of the emotional needs of the individual'.[5]

Almost all of the texts Suga wrote during her early career as a journalist were published under her pen-names: 'Sugako', or 'Yūzuki-joshi' later shortened to 'Yūzuki-jo', 'Yūzuki', 'Yū' or 'Tsuki'. 'Sugako' she wrote in Chinese characters with a sense of congratulation or celebration, which perhaps referred to her debut in journalism. Itoya Toshio notes that five years later in 1907, Suga was one of only two women working as journalists in Tokyo. Yūzuki-joshi' might be best rendered as 'Madam Hazy Moon' ('*joshi*' does not signify marital status), the character for '*yū*' having a sense of the supernatural or, since here it was used in a pen-name, mystery or secrecy. Suga seldom signed her surname to her works, and at times unrecognizable pseudonyms must have been meant to obscure her identity further. Her writings were, on occasion, implacably hostile toward fathers, stepmothers or mothers-in-law. Given that some of her works were at least partly inspired by her personal experience, sometimes she would have wanted to avoid public recognition of her authorship. Yet Suga wanted her readers to know that she was a woman – perhaps to indicate privileged knowledge about the topic she most often wrote about in one way or another, women, or simply because she was proud of her unusual achievement. If she had not wanted her audience to know that she was female, she would not have signed herself in ways that were gender-specific. 'Yūzuki-jo' was her most common signature at this time.

1902–1905

Addressing intemperate gentlemen and chaste ladies

Suga's writing career began in mid-1902, the year in which she turned 21. By the time she became a journalist, she had left and divorced her husband, Komiya Fukutarō. She had been married in September 1899 and left the Komiya (merchant) family in January 1902.[6] At the request of her invalid father, Kanno Yoshihige, she left Tokyo to return to their home region of Kansai with him and her younger sister, Hide. Suga said under interrogation in 1910 that she had married into a merchant family, but 'loved reading and disliked business', so two and a half years later she left her marriage on the 'pretext' of nursing her father.[7]

The family managed to survive somehow for half a year with Suga working to support them. In the meantime she had come to know her brother's patron, an influential playwright, and asked him to help her become a novelist. Udagawa Bunkai must have been surprised at her petition: firstly, she was a woman, and, in addition, she had had only an elementary school education, and no relevant work experience. It is possible that Suga had worked as a nurse, a hair-dresser, and done some factory work,[8] though the source of this information about her former occupations might have been her 'semi-autobiographical' stories. Udagawa, in any case, overlooked her lack of formal education, and she embarked on her literary training in the usual fashion, as an apprentice. With his recommendation she was able to start writing for a small, relatively conservative newspaper, *Ōsaka Chōhō* (*Osaka Morning Report*), at the beginning of July. In this paper she published novelettes as well as social commentary.

Before turning my attention directly to 'Omokage', a story ostensibly narrated to the writer, Sugako, by Akiko, I should first note that Suga wrote that the heroine had been born into a wealthy family, the eldest daughter of a mining entrepreneur whose business later failed.[9] This story has therefore been treated as autobiographical because when Suga was interrogated in 1910, she said that her family had been very wealthy until she was 10 years old, but then the mine operated by her father failed and the family became destitute. Arahata Kanson said much the same thing about her childhood.[10]

In 'Omokage' Akiko's mother was said to be delighted with her new daughter, but, because the little girl was thought very plain, the mother was taunted by her female in-laws. The mother must have done something terrible in a past life to invite the karmic retribution of an 'ugly' daughter. She consoled herself by vowing to raise her daughter to be a well-educated, refined young lady. But her work was cut out for her, as the little girl soon proved to be a 'tomboyish' child who resisted her mother's attempts to 'pretty her up' with 'feminine clothes and sweet hairstyles'. The mature Akiko was critical of the fact that people had often said she was a 'cute' child only because of her splendid outfits. Society, she complained, judged girls only by their 'external appearance'. Akiko observed that though little girls then were brought up to be feminine and sweet, there had not been much chance of her becoming a conventional young lady: 'like father, like child', she had been 'eccentric' from an early age. Here the author seemed to be lauding a father for unconventional traits, yet she would soon change her tune.

The heroine's narration of the story of her childhood largely dwells on her early years as the pampered child of a rich family with a number of servants. Much to the chagrin of the young Akiko, she was seldom allowed out of the nursemaid's sight, all the more so after nearly being drowned in the river nearby while playing with the local boys. Still, much of 'Omokage' is about the general contentment of a small child loved and spoiled by her mother. Why then, we wonder, is the heroine introduced by the writer as a young woman whose life had been wretched, for family and society had caused her 'nothing but pain and misery'?[11] Clearly, Akiko's troubles must have begun when her father's mining business failed and the family sank into poverty. Suga continued this 'riches to rags' story by explaining that there were times when there was no food, and they huddled together for warmth on cold nights. Yet the father was 'stubborn and inflexible': he had 'sworn not to give up mining as long as he lived'.[12] To make matters worse, the mother had been seriously ill even before the business failed.[13] (Suga said during that same testimony in 1910 that she had lost her mother, Nobu, when she was 11, a year or so after her father's business went into decline.)

'Omokage' reveals that Suga in 1902 already had a critical view of her world and a quite developed 'feminist' consciousness. Her remarks on attire and physical beauty as the most important criteria for judgement of a girl's merit have a decidedly modern ring to them, as do her complaints about Akiko's being forced into what we would now refer to as a stereotyped sex-role. 'Gender-bias' was clearly an important concern of hers at this time, and there are early hints of what certainly amounted in her later works to a thorough critique of a 'patriarchal' familial system. Here we see women and children suffering because of the pride and selfishness of a father, whose decisions brook no argument. We see the young wife suffering the effects of the patrilocal aspect of a partriarchal system, tormented by the women on the paternal side of the family. The ways in which the family and social system made women suffer was a theme that Suga would often return to in other works, ostensibly only literary or personal, where she again took the opportunity to proselytize.

In Suga's professional life at this time she was involved with a rather different sort of father-figure, Udagawa Bunkai, her literary patron. She was hospitalized for a week in early November 1902 with dysentery and, in a serialized non-fictional article explicitly about herself, 'Isshūkan' ('One Week') published shortly after, she referred to an unnamed 'master' or 'teacher' who could only have been Udagawa. This was a man who visited her ('Sugako') in hospital, arranged nursing for her, looked after her father and sister in her absence, and, finally, also gave her advice about how to improve her writing skills.[14] It was with his encouragement she first read the Bible while in hospital. It is clear that Udagawa was kind to her, for the emotions Suga expressed in 'Isshūkan' range from esteem and gratitude to real affection for this mentor.

A lack of evidence notwithstanding, it has generally been assumed that Suga became the lover or 'mistress' of her married, disfigured and much older patron.[15] Some authors, moreover, take as given Arahata Kanson's story that she did so because of the professional and economic assistance he could offer her.[16] As Sievers notes, this jilted lover of Suga's has been the source of historical 'knowledge' of her promiscuity and lack of literary talent, but I would also attribute to him her reputation for being mercenary and manipulative. Suga, according to him, 'sold' herself to Udagawa in return for professional and economic assistance.[17] Depicting her life in Osaka as 'dissolute', he said she had had to rely on her teacher's help and 'pay for it with her chastity'; and then after becoming a journalist she 'fell into despair', sinking 'deeper and deeper into a life of debauchery', drifting from one love affair to another.[18] His tale of Suga's 'debauched' life in Osaka ended on the note that she soon developed an 'abhorrence for herself and drew closer to Christianity'. But if Suga had been exploited sexually by Udagawa, in turn using her sexuality to gain material benefits, her writings about her patron in 1902 (or later) contain no hint of it. Even if we would not expect them to, need she have been quite so expansive in her praise of him? Would she have written about him at all, especially in such a glowing way if, as Arahata indicated, her colleagues suspected her to be his 'mistress'? Arahata's account is of interest largely because of what his attitudes reveal about conventional sexual double standards then – even amongst socialists later since his memoirs were written decades after these events.

What is even more interesting is that Arahata's account raises the possibility that Suga inadvertently helped to construct an historical view of herself as immoral, by confessing certain things to her readers or by not choosing confidants very carefully. It is possible that his account of her relationship with Udagawa was derived from Suga herself, either directly or indirectly. Arahata said that in 1908 a journalist who had known her five years before in Osaka told him about her 'past'.[19] However, he also said that 'on the whole' he had heard about her 'debauched' background *after their own separation*, so we cannot know how much of the information offered by this unnamed journalist was gossip, and how much (if anything) came from Suga herself. Had this anonymous journalist impressed upon Arahata in 1908 how fortunate he was to be out of the clutches of this woman who was so well-versed in 'seduction'?[20] The tone of Arahata's account of Suga's history is rather reminiscent of the tales of the sexual adventures of the famous 'evil' women of Meiji scandal-sheet literature.[21] It also sounds much like a Buddhist sermon on women as temptresses, 'daughters of evil' who lure men away from the paths of purity, ensnaring them in the polluted world of desire and delusion.[22] As Suga's own writings in 1902 only indicate that she then felt a respectful affection for her 'teacher', therefore, it would be ironic if, by confiding *later* doubts about the relationship to a friend, she herself contributed to the historical view of their 'mercenary' relationship. Even if she had been his lover, her early writings contradict such a view of her motives. Assuming for the moment that she had been, if she did become critical of her own motives, it must have been after some profound changes in her thinking and situation had occurred. It is possible that the Suga of later years was too hard on the Suga of 1902. 'Autobiographers' are not necessarily the kindest judges of their own character or motives, especially when it means applying new moral-political attitudes to previous actions or episodes in their lives.

Whatever the exact nature of Suga's relationship with her patron, it lasted till well after May 1903 when she joined the Christian-influenced Ōsaka Moral Reform Society; and well after she was baptized that November in Ōsaka's Tenmabashi. She said in 1910 that she had studied with her teacher for about two years (thus until about mid-1904); and a story she wrote in December 1904 and January 1905 referred to visiting 'my teacher, Master Udagawa' due to 'an urgent need to consult with him'. They were probably not estranged until after early 1905. Shimizu suggests that their estrangement was because of Suga's new political commitments. Udagawa, however, was reported by *Heimin Shinbun* late in 1904 to be sympathetic to socialism.[23] If she did become critical of herself because sexually involved with Udagawa, it may have been more because of her new connections with Christian groups. Sievers notes that one of the Society's activities was an anti-concubinage campaign to defeat parliamentary candidates who had concubines, and also argues that Suga's connection with the Society was consistent with their goals – the personal and economic independence of women – and that her experience as a 'mistress' was not unlike that of leaders of the Society.[24] Therefore, *if* we can assume that Arahata's story had some basis in fact, we can see how Suga might have developed a moral distaste for the life she was leading, if only because she was a married man's 'concubine', not necessarily because of her 'mercenary motives' or 'promiscuity'.

Even if Udagawa had not been her lover, however, she was still dependent upon his influence at this time, and it is noteworthy that it was only later that she expressed frustrations with a lack of professional autonomy. It seems that personal-economic autonomy for women was not as high on her early list of priorities as we might assume from a familiarity with her later works. Her construction in 1902–1905 of the realities under which women lived and worked was far from a systematic critique of patriarchy. Arahata might have been correct about unhappiness in her personal life helping her to gravitate toward Christianity. The only clear indication in her early written works of the reasons for her attraction to Christianity and the Moral Reform Society, however, was that she shared with them a commitment to charitable works, and social reform, 'temperance'-style.

One social 'vice' that both Suga and the Society were deeply committed to fighting was legalized prostitution, and she shared with these genteel women a tendency 'to castigate the "fallen woman"'.[25] The tone of Suga's articles on 'prostitutes' in 1903 was of moral outrage. The event that outraged her was an officially sponsored exposition to promote industry held in Tennōji, Osaka, where the entertainment included dancing and singing by geisha.[26] In Suga's view and that of many of her contemporaries, being a geisha was tantamount to being a prostitute. She denounced this entertainment by 'prostitutes' as a 'defilement of the dignity of the exposition'; it 'dishonoured the nation before the eyes of foreign visitors', so she called on the ladies and gentlemen of Osaka to co-operate in banishing the 'prostitutes' from the exposition.[27] Both in her tendency to berate 'fallen women' and in her concern with how Japan might appear to foreign visitors, Suga's views resembled both the Reform Society and earlier Meirokusha. From the 1870s when some of these early liberals championed the rights of legal wives while blaming Japan's parlous moral state on concubines and prostitutes, monogamous marriage had been deemed one of the hallmarks of Western-style 'civilization and enlightenment'.[28]

Suga depicted public dancing by geisha as an affront to respectable women, and argued that geisha entertainment lowered the tone of the exposition. Furthermore, she suggested rather cynically that for Christians to participate in such an exposition lowered the tone of Christianity. This was not the place for missionaries to attract serious-minded converts, only people who would treat it as the day's entertainment.[29] In her early works, there is more than a hint of moral judgement and elitism: implicitly in the tone she adopted about certain lower classes of people; explicitly in the concerns that seemed closest to her heart, like preventing impure women from flaunting their shame in public.[30] But this notwithstanding, Suga saw this campaign as part of the broader fight against prostitution, which recalls Sievers's remarks about the attitudes of the ladies of the Reform Society toward the 'traffic in women':

> Then, as now, any discussion of the 'traffic in women' led inevitably to much wider criticism of the place of women in the society as a whole. What began as an apparent critique of Japanese society, voiced by women whose Christian morality was offended, easily became a feminist argument about the exercise of male privilege and the repression of women in the society.[31]

In Suga's case, however, this sort of progression was not so fast nor so complete a change as Sievers' words might suggest. In many cases, no doubt, the Christian moralist and women's emancipationist continued to coexist in the one person. It was not until the first half of 1906 that Suga started to call for thoroughgoing social change. None the less, when we compare the Suga of 1903 with the Suga of 1906, there are some significant differences. Earlier she was not at all consistent in countering idealized constructions of society, or woman.

Prostitution was an issue that many social reformers were concerned about at that time. At a lecture meeting that Suga attended in April 1903, one speaker, Shimada Saburō, delivered an address on the need to close the 'red light' district in Osaka. Suga wrote that she spoke with Shimada after the meeting and at his suggestion attended a socialist meeting the following evening where the Christian socialist, Kinoshita Naoe, raised (at Suga's request) the issue of the official use of geisha entertainment at the exposition. Overjoyed that she had two such 'influential allies' in Shimada and Kinoshita, Suga 'listened attentively' to the rest of the latter's lecture on socialism.[32] This was Suga's first contact with socialists, and there was an impressive line-up of speakers that evening, among them Kōtoku Shūsui. But from her reports of the meeting in the newspaper, it was clearly the Christian socialist, Kinoshita, who most inspired her. Suga developed an awareness of socialism from this meeting; nevertheless, she still had deeper interests and commitments in other areas at least until the latter part of 1904. In May 1903, just over a month after the meeting, she formally joined the Moral Reform Society, and later became one of its full-time workers.

Calling on pacifist patriots!

Suga continued to write and publish throughout 1903 despite the fact that her former newspaper had ceased publication in April, but now she was an occasional contributor to the two religious magazines: *Michi no Tomo* (Tenrikyō) and *Kirisutokyō Sekai* (Protestant). Since Udagawa was the editor of the former, once again it was through his influence that she could contribute to it, which might have led to feelings of frustration at still being dependent upon his assistance. Whatever the precise reasons for her attraction to the Reform Society and Christianity, it is likely that her search for new inspiration and commitments was connected with her own personal situation – whether because of shame at her own 'moral laxity', or more because of frustration over her inability to be independent, even in a occupation that (for women) was well paid. Alone, she might have been better able to survive, but she was still supporting her father and sister. Her salary as a journalist while at *Ōsaka Chōhō* was higher than wages for the more usual occupations for women, but women's wages then were only about a third of men's.[33]

Between the end of 1903 and the first half of 1905 some of Suga's writings were about war. The Russo-Japanese War did not formally begin until early in 1904, but from about 1901 the two countries had been in contention over their respective spheres of influence in Manchuria and Korea. War was officially declared by Japan on 10 February 1904, lasting until the Portsmouth Treaty was signed on 5 September 1905. Four days after Suga published a seemingly pacifist short story entitled 'Zekkō' ('Severed Relations') in October 1903, two of the most prominent socialists in Tokyo, Kōtoku Shūsui and Sakai Toshihiko, resigned from the newspaper they worked for over its change to a pro-war stance.[34] When Kōtoku and Sakai began in November to publish a daily anti-war paper, *Heimin Shinbun* (*Commoners' News*), Suga became one of its readers. As a member of the Reform Society, she probably already saw herself as a pacifist.

Most writers have set out to trace the origins of Suga's political career, and have thus looked (teleologically) for her most explicitly 'political' writings – those that would present a neat picture of how she logically developed into an anarchist. Suga the anarcho-terrorist of 1908–1911 has overshadowed Suga the moral reformer, Christian 'pacifist' *and nationalist* of 1902 to about 1905. Commentators on Suga's political career therefore treat 'Zekkō' as the most significant of her works in 1903–1904.[35] Kondō Tomie claims that the socialist meeting in April 1903 had so deep an influence on Suga that her subsequent writing exhibited a new authority and confidence.[36] But, if an inspiration from socialism had been the cause of this, we would expect to see some sign of it in her works in this period, even if the two magazines she was writing in were religious ones.

Socialism was not the only new influence upon Suga, nor yet the deepest. Thus, the style of her writings on the war is of either a Christian or humanist (rather ambivalent) 'pacifist': there is no sign of socialist arguments against imperialistic, capitalistic warmongers, or for proletarian internationalism. If she was familiar with socialist writings on the war through the *Heimin Shinbun,* it is difficult to see any distinct influence from it.[37] One would have to look very hard for any mention, much less discussion, of socialism in these articles of Suga's. They oppose the war (rather inconsistently) on *moral* grounds, expressing support for 'our boys over there' and sympathy for their families, sometimes with a patriotic tone about somehow restoring peace in the Orient by 'doing one's bit' to raise money *for* the war. Suga was not entirely enthusiastic about what she termed the 'splendid' labours of the Women's Patriotic Association (Aikoku Fujinkai), however, for she did say that it was complacent to think that one was doing enough to support the war effort just because one had joined such an organization. Women could work for the war by nursing, tightening their belts etc., so that Japan would no longer have to endure insults from the likes of Russia.[38] In this respect she was little different from Yosano Akiko who in September 1904 published her in/famous ('anti-imperial') poem begging her little brother not to die in the war. As much as Yosano hated war she apparently believed that everyone in Japan had to work toward a quick *Japanese victory and* peace.[39] Similarly, there is little doubt about Suga's nationalism in 'The War and Women', published six months after 'Severed Relations'. She did, however, use the necessity of self-sacrifice for the nation in time of war as an argument against men's keeping concubines or visiting (still 'shameful') prostitutes.[40] The money men spent in such pursuits could have been put toward the war effort. Even if she was using the issue of the war as a forum for bringing women's issues to the fore, this was far from a systematic critique of imperialism or patriarchy; and her patriotic tone cannot be explained away by reference to editorial self-censorship (because of the threat of a post-publication ban on the magazines). It was not until April 1904 that the most radical opponents of the war, the Heiminsha, had their paper banned. The tone of the *Heimin Shinbun* was cautious, certainly, but hardly nationalistic.

The title, 'Severed Relations', refers to an argument between two teenage girls about the likely war with Russia. One, the daughter of a pastor, musters various arguments against war, the most significant being that there can be no 'righteous' cause for it; for war implies a descent from civilized to 'barbaric' behaviour.[41] At the end of the story, the younger sister of one of the Sino-Japanese War heroes, flounces off in disgust, announcing that she will have no more to do with the Christian pacifist: a 'cowardly, disloyal' traitor with no under-standing of the Japanese spirit because of her foreign religion[42]. A 'true' Japanese could not stand by while Japan was 'shamed' or under threat. In this story, a connection between pacifism and Christianity is asserted by the Christian, though she admits that not all Christians are pacifists.

If Suga had been writing this after the war, she would have had more time to become critical of the weakness of Japanese Christians' commitment to pacifism. Kōtoku, for example, wrote of the Japanese socialists' eventual disillusionment with Christianity in a letter (in English) dated 18 December 1906:

> The Japanese diplomatists . . . suddenly began to put on the mask of western civilization, and eagerly welcome and protect [Christian-ity], and use it as a means of introducing Japan to European and American powers as a civilized Christendom. On the other hand, Christian priests, taking advantage of the weakness of the govern-ment, got a great monetary aid from the State, and under its protec-tion they are propagating in full vigor the Gospel of Patriotism. Thus Japanese Christianity, which was before the war the religion of [the] poor, [has] literally now changed within only two years to a great bourgeois religion and a machine of the State and militarism![43]

Many Japanese Christians supported the war in return for a new respectability that replaced the grudging recognition on the part of the Meiji oligarchs of a now inevitable Christian presence in Japan; which largely explains why the early Christianity–socialism symbiosis did not last beyond the war.

To readers with compassion

To round off this section on Suga's early texts, I shall turn to two pieces which are connected by allusions in each to rape. One is another serialized 'semi-autobiographical' novelette by Suga (this time, 'Yūzuki') that has commonly been treated as factual. 'Tsuyuko' (November 1905–March 1906) is about a marriage arranged for Tsuyuko by her father. The other, earlier text of July 1902, 'Kinenbi' ('Days of Remembrance'), is a short article in two parts about two days that this particular woman 'journalist' named Ōitako would never forget. The story in the second is presented as the journalist's own, but the name she appended to her article was not known to *Ōsaka Chōhō* readers, and not used again.

'Tsuyuko' has other points of interest: the symbol of evil and the cause of familial unhappiness, for example, is the (former geisha) step-mother. Suga's hostility toward 'geisha-prostitutes' was probably not only moral prejudice. She said in 1910 that when her mother died she was brought up by a stepmother (mentioned also by Arahata), and then her life was 'very unhappy'. The stepmother left the family, apparently, when the father had a stroke in 1901.[44] Like 'Omokage', the story that Suga called 'Tsuyuko' after its heroine coincides roughly with the rather scant record of her own life. Details about family mem-bers in the story fit her own family; and the main theme of the novel, an unsatisfactory marriage to a merchant in the Kanto area, parallels her experience. The name she gave this merchant, 'Miyamoto', was also similar to 'Komiya', the real name of her former husband. Yet the same problem as with 'Omokage' remains: that one can only guess at whether it was a faithful rendering of her own story. Thus, it is sufficient for my purposes to treat it as the story of a Meiji woman. Whether any part of her audience was meant to recognize Kanno Suga (or more accurately, 'Yūzuki') in Tsuyuko is not really the point. What is rather more pertinent is that Suga's representations of the trials life held for women, who were allowed no freedom to shape their own lives, were beginning to be tinged with impatience.

In 'Tsuyuko' the heroine's stepmother was described by Yūzuki as a woman with a 'disreputable' past who would 'sprawl unbecomingly in front of the brazier as if she had taken root, barking orders to bring or remove tea cups and blowing tobacco from a long, slender pipe into smoke rings'.[45] Her harsh disposition made the lives of Tsuyuko and her younger brother and sister a misery. When early in the story the heroine returns from Tokyo where she has been training as a nurse, she immediately knows something is wrong because her stepmother welcomes her effusively.[46] Tsuyuko is soon told by her father that arrangements have been made for her to marry a wealthy merchant. She then meets Kōichi and finds that he is a pampered adopted heir of doting parents, a cold, ignorant, dull-witted and uncommonly ugly man. She is expected to marry him for his money. Yet, despite her feelings of abhorrence for the marriage and disgust at her parents' avarice, she is 'bound by the chains of filial piety' and must 'sacrifice' herself for the good of her family. Furthermore, much like in 'Omok-age', Tsuyuko's father is described as a man who ought to be ashamed of his career of 'dabbling in speculation on the stock-market' when he 'cannot even feed his children'.[47] Once married, Tsuyuko finds other reasons to be unhappy with her arranged, loveless marriage: the mother-in-law disapproves of this 'vulgar ex-nurse' from a 'beggarly' family.[48] Again we see the theme of the bride not being welcomed into the family but harangued and mistreated by the mother-in-law. And there is another villain in the novel, a clerk. One day while the frail Tsuyuko is recovering from an illness, apparently the clerk sexually assaults her. She is found lying on the floor insensible, reviving with a gasp at the 'horrifying recollection' that the face of the clerk brings her.

Suga's references to a rape in this story are veiled, but at a time when the victims of sexual assault were even more likely than today to be held responsible by society, she was courageous to raise the subject at all. Three years before she wrote 'Tsuyuko' she had also alluded to rape in 'Days of Remembrance'.[49] It seems that she was prepared to take the risk of being judged unchaste by her readers – or by her journalistic colleagues who would know who the author, 'Ōitako' was. In implying that she had herself been the victim of rape, Suga revealed how important she believed it was to bring this aspect of the brutal treatment of women to the attention of the public. It also recalls the emerging literary tendency to equate a confessional style with social rebellion. For there is little doubt that merely in writing sympathetically of a *victim's* suffering, Suga was being much more radically 'political' than her words alone might suggest to today's reader. These two texts foreshadowed a more explicit concern later with women as the victims of both patriarchal double standards and sexual violence.

In 'Days of Remembrance' Suga had begun by speaking of two days of the year that always brought the writer painful memories: on both these dates, she was once 'struck down by the god of death' who 'snatched away', not her life but her 'respectability and virtue'. Though Suga did not use explicit terms like 'rape' here either, the signature that she attached to this article, literally 'girl-child of Ōita', also lends credence to the view that these two days were the anniversaries of occasions on which she herself was raped.[50] For an explanation of the significance of Ōita one needs to recall that Suga said under interrogation in 1910 that her father had been a miner. At one time the family had lived in Ōita Prefecture in Kyushu as Yoshihige once operated a mine there.[51] Arahata also wrote that Suga confided in him that her stepmother had been responsible for an incident that caused her unforgettable 'anguish'. The stepmother, he said, had ordered a miner to rape her in a 'sinister scheme'.[52] Suga's biographers (source unclear) have added to Arahata's account of the rape that the stepmother's intention was to alienate father from daughter, so the stepmother twisted the facts to make it seem as if the young victim of the assault had been the guilty party.[53] Hence, Suga might have had very good reason for her hostile representations of stepmothers, and also fathers, since hers had apparently believed her guilty. We cannot know the precise details, but Arahata's remarks together with her references to rape in these articles make it seem likely that Suga had been raped, and not just once.

To the remark about this 'sinister scheme', Arahata added that Suga had 'also confessed that despair over this aspect of her past had been the foundation of her rather dissolute life in later years'. The suggestion is that in 1903 she had seen herself as already impure and therefore it did not much matter if she led an unchaste life. There are hints of such an attitude in 'Days of Remembrance' where 'Ōitako' wrote that the 'god of death' had robbed her (permanently?) of her 'respectability and virtue'. Arahata, supposedly repeating what she had said, appeared to use the rape as an excuse for her later moral 'transgressions', which is to say that he felt that he was being sympathetic.

While again it can only be a matter for speculation about historiographical ironies, one wonders if, in both confiding in Arahata about rape and also writing about it, Suga contributed to the historical picture of herself as promiscuous and immoral. She did seem to have a habit of confiding in people – readers, intimates, even prosecutors – despite the fact that certain confidences could be misinterpreted or deflected away from the purposes she intended. In admitting she had been raped, Suga was probably intent on illustrating how women were brutalized by the social system; it is doubtful that she was merely looking for sympathy, because it was far from certain she would get it. She might not have been very consistent in 1902–1903 about how that system was founded upon a double sexual standard, but by 1906 this had changed.

Turning finally to Suga's increasing interest in socialism toward the end of the period, it should first be noted that it seems to have derived largely from the sympathy of some male socialists for women's problems. The issues that she felt most strongly about in these early years were clearly the patriarchal family system, prostitution and rape. According to Arahata, Suga had been deeply impressed with Sakai Toshihiko when he published an interview with a rape victim. Rape, he had said, was 'like being bitten by a mad dog', a misfortune for which the victim could hardly be blamed. It was for this reason, Arahata said, that Suga visited Sakai at the Heiminsha offices the year after.[54] She sought Sakai Toshihiko out in July 1904 while in Tokyo for a national Reform Society conference. Suga's meeting with Sakai was a significant one because he not only played an important part in drawing her nearer to socialism, but remained one of her close friends until the end of her life. In 1911 she wrote in her prison diary of his sincere sympathy for women.[55] After their first meeting, in *Heimin Shinbun* Sakai wrote that a 'welcome guest' had called in, a Miss Kanno Sugako who was a journalist in Osaka and a 'socialistic' (*shakaishugiteki*) thinker. Perhaps what he meant was that she was a socialist sympathizer. (She did say herself in her testimonies later that she started 'studying' socialism around that time.) He also commented that 'those in the women's community who are acquainted with our position [on women] are delighted'.[56] Apparently Suga was, because on her return to Osaka she helped organize a fund-raising campaign for the Heiminsha, and a *Heimin Shinbun* study group.[57] Suga, it seems, was now no longer merely 'socialistic', but an active socialist. And it was only a matter of time and opportunity before this change would be more clearly reflected in her writings.

Until May 1905, Suga continued to publish in *Kirisutokyō Sekai*; in *Michi no Tomo* only until February 1905. But it was in Wakayama in the first half of 1906 that she gained more freedom to flex her muscles – both because she was now working for a socialist paper, and because for a time she had editorial control of it. Suga started writing for *Murō Shinpō* (Murō News) at the end of 1905, contributing articles from Kyoto. It was not until she started writing for *Murō Shinpō* that she began to paint a picture of life in Meiji Japan that was less a reflection of dominant ideology and morality. This plus the fact that she now had a different audience combined to turn her then-current Life-construct into something more likely to bring ideological opponents to the fore.

1906–1908

One of Suga's earliest articles for *Murō Shinpō* contained the following:

> Our ideal is socialism, which aims at the equality of all classes. But just as a great building cannot be destroyed in a moment, the existing hierarchical class system, which has been consolidated over many years, cannot be overthrown in a day and a night. . . . So we [women] must first of all achieve the fundamental principle of 'self-awareness', and develop our potential, uplift our character, and then gradually work toward the realization of our ideal.[58]

This does not necessarily mean, however, that socialism immediately came to define her writings, nor that all of her texts were consistently socialist. The standard view of Suga then is that she was a reformist socialist. Accepting this view, however, might lead one to speak as if this necessarily displaced Suga the Christian; or to overlook early radical populist (or *shishi*) influences upon her so-called 'reformism'. Even at this time she was capable of speaking as if she accepted radical revolutionist, violent tactics, though whether she subscribed to a revolutionary vision of a socialist society is open to question.

To 'good husbands and wise fathers'

While in Kyoto in 1905, Suga had not been writing for any paper. In September she found some work teaching Japanese, apparently with the recommendation of both the Protestant pastor of the church she attended in Kyoto and Hayashi Utako of the Reform Society. But the following month she received a letter from Sakai Toshihiko asking if she was free to fill in for Mōri Saian, the editor of *Murō Shinpō*.[59] Mōri was being prosecuted for two counts of 'insulting' government officials in the pages of the paper, and wanted someone to edit it during his trial and likely imprisonment.[60] Suga could not see her way clear to leave Kyoto for Wakayama at once, perhaps because she had just committed herself to a new position, so Sakai sent Arahata Kanson to help out for the time being. Mōri interviewed Suga while on one of his trips to Osaka during the court case, and exacted a promise from her that she would contribute to the paper from Kyoto before taking up the post of acting editor.[61] Ultimately, Mōri was fined and sentenced to imprisonment for forty-five days. He was due to enter prison on 13 March 1906, so Suga arrived in Wakayama on 4 February to take up the editorship in his absence. Thus it was in the coastal town of Tanabe that Suga met Arahata and the two of them developed a close friendship. According to one source, this was because they had 'travelled a common road from Christianity to socialism'.[62] This, however, implies that they had already renounced Christianity, which cannot be said of Suga.

Suga's father had died in Kyoto on 3 June 1905.[63] She was then left alone with her sister, Hide, because her younger brother had gone to study in the United States. One might expect the death of her father to make Suga look a more kindly upon fathers in her writings, but in fact she became more severe on paternal authority. The first part of 'Tsuyuko' was published five months after Yoshihige's death. One event in her life in 1905 must have contributed to her obvious disdain for social constructions of fathers *alone* as moral role models. (Women, after all, had to be educated to become 'good wives and wise mothers'.)[64] Before his death, Yoshihige had called to his bedside a young man who turned out to be his eldest son by a woman other than his legal wife.[65] This was the first his two daughters knew of the existence of their half-brother and his mother. Suga wrote a short non-fictional essay entitled 'Yonin no Hahaue' a year later, in which one of her ('Yūzuki's') 'four mothers' was described as follows: 'The mother who gave birth to my elder brother and to whom I am bound by duty lives in Kyoto. She is a rare gentle person by today's standards.'[66] This was the 'mother' toward whom she felt 'filial'. Suga's 'biological' mother had died long before, and the other two were described as her 'compassionate' mother and her 'spiritual' mother. As Itoya argues, the stepmother was not amongst these 'mothers' she respected and felt a deep affection for.[67] Suga did not say much that was revealing about her 'filial' mother – 'who had been brought up as a young lady, and was thus innocent of the ways of the world' – though she did paint a sympathetic picture of her. A criticism of fathers in general was implicit in this essay that glorified only 'mothers', but one could also see the piece as partly a personal criticism of her own father. Her implication was that someone had taken advantage of the gentleness and innocence of this woman when she was younger.

In this article Suga also described her 'spiritual mother'. This was Hayashi Utako, the Christian leader of the Osaka Moral Reform Society and founder of the Hakuaisha. Sievers describes the Hakuaisha as 'a charitable institution functioning as an orphanage, nursery, day school, and shelter for mothers and children'.[68] For Suga, Hayashi was 'a woman of rare strength who was perhaps a little too austere for some'; she was a woman to whom she had been 'bound by God', and her 'clear thinking, burning religious faith and eloquence dispelled [Suga's] ennui with one sweep' each time they met.[69] This was the figure to whom Suga now looked for advice and encouragement, with whom she sometimes even argued. She was the only person with whom Suga could give free reign to the 'rational side' of her character. Hayashi had clearly replaced Udagawa as a mentor: she was, Suga said, 'almost like a loved and respected teacher'.

It is not difficult to see a Christian influence in Suga's writings for *Murō Shinpō*. There are often references to 'God' in her articles in 1906, when she thanks God, or even notes in the context of discussing the sort of ('bold' or resolute) political death she wants that He has not set her time yet; 'faith', moreover, is explicitly used in the religious sense.[70] In one article, however, she dismissed the Christian prohibition on suicide while expressing her desire for a spouse who would be so passionate in his love for her that he would be happy to die for the socialist cause together with her.[71] It might be making too much of this 'revolutionary'-samurai romanticism to suggest that it reflected an informed commitment to socialism, but Suga's writings in *Murō Shinpō* reflected changes in her ideas and rhetorical style which at the time would have sufficed to identify her as a socialist. In this early period when she was apparently still a Christian and still involved in the Reform Society, yet was moving closer to socialism, there is no sign in her works of a thorough knowledge of socialist theory, nor any doctrinal consistency. Nevertheless, it was clearly an important period in her professional and political growth. Her close friendship with Arahata may have had some impact on her political thinking, but now she was also able to work free of editorial control and actually expected to write in a socialist vein.

In order to comprehend how she now presented life and society to her new audience, one needs to look firstly at how the content and tone of her writings changed. To begin with, there was a marked difference between her earlier support of charitable works amongst the poor and also orphaned children, and her comment in April 1906 that people should not 'just cry at the sad plight of orphans' but rather 'curse the society which plants the seeds of their misery'.[72] She made this remark in an article about a charity concert for such children that she attended with her sister. Suga had been associated for some time with Hayashi's orphanage and shelter, and one of the Hakuaisha's greatest problems was coping with widespread tuberculosis. It is significant that her comments on the misery of orphans were made at a time when her own sister's consumptive condition was deteriorating. No doubt this contributed to the impatience with which she called on people to 'wake up to the fact that only socialism would eradicate the causes of misery in society'.[73] She never had the financial means to provide adequate medical care for her sister, and Hide's condition often came up in the course of her writings at this time.[74]

Another area in which Suga's constructions of life underwent radical changes is sexual politics. In 1903 she had sat in moral judgement of 'prostitutes' or 'fallen' women, but now she was more 'outraged' by a government that condoned a trade in daughters of the poor; appalled also by the many men who viewed women as mere playthings to be bought and sold.[75] Was there not a contradiction between the nation's claim to be civilized and its condonation of such tyranny? This, she felt, was an affront to *all* women.[76] Not surprisingly, now there was suddenly a liberal use of the editor's-censor's brush, both for this article and for a few lines on the same topic a few days earlier. (The system of censorship at this time was post-publication, so this would have been self-censorship by the editor to avoid publication prohibitions and fines.[77] Mōri had not yet gone to prison at this point.)

In the middle of April, Suga published another article, 'Hiji Deppō' ('Rebuff'), that highlights the degree to which her feminist critique of conventional morality had become more thorough. This time, once again, the issue was women's chastity, though now she denounced the habit men had of hypocritically harping on the subject. There should be some 'evidence of the speaker's competence to speak to such a subject before we agree to listen', insisted Suga; and she expressed the 'utmost cynicism and unbridled hatred for dissolute men who had not earned the right to talk about chastity and exhort women to be 'good wives and wise mothers'.[78] In 'Rebuff' Suga recommended that men look to their own chastity and try to become 'wise fathers and good husbands'. In Suga's representation of the ideal Meiji woman, chastity and purity was still the ideal, though she was now arguing pointedly that it should not be so only for women.

'Rise up, women!'

Once again in 'Rebuff', Suga told her readers that only socialism could provide a fundamental solution to the problem of hypocritical attitudes toward female sexuality, though she did not specify how. Here, at least, she seemed to expect changes in attitudes to follow automatically the abolition of capitalism. So according to Suga, a 'socialist solution' would address 'the root of the problem', but in the interim women still had to take up the struggle themselves 'not only against husbands but against the entire self-serving world of men'.[79] Drawing a parallel between women's struggle against a world that served only men's interests and the class struggle of workers against capitalists, she called on women to fight for, even shed blood for, their freedom.

Apart from a treatment of conventional gender constructions that was now decidedly oppositional, there is already a hint here that men could not be relied upon to champion the cause of women. Suga was rather inconsistent on the question of reform or revolution – unclear on what form the struggle for socialism would take. She did not speak explicitly about 'revolution', but she implied its necessity with her reference to the necessity of bloodshed in either struggle, just as she often suggested it by speaking even in this early period of socialists' giving up their lives for the cause.[80] (Increasingly, of course, radical publications at this time were catching the attention of censors and being banned, and this was particularly the case if they contained the word 'revolution'.) It is possible that these were just dramatic turns of phrase, but the person speaking about shedding blood had seen herself as a pacifist only a short time before; and sacrificing oneself for the cause does not suggest working for piecemeal reforms. All in all, these were strong words for a woman who, no more than a few years before, had bemoaned the lack of virtue in certain types of women and, only a few months earlier, had been re-elected as an officer of an organization dedicated to pacifism, limited social reform and philanthropic works. But Suga's 'revolutionary' language notwithstanding, concrete matters connected with socialist revolution or the nature of a socialist society did not claim her attention.

Mōri Saian, the regular editor of *Murō Shinpō*, was released from jail at the end of April, and three weeks later Suga resigned from the paper and returned to Kyoto. Arahata was already back in Tokyo, having left partly because his writings were too radical for many of the locals in Wakayama. Suga wrote on 12 April about how he could serve the cause of socialism better back in Tokyo.[81] Hence, her readiness to leave the paper might have been partly because she, too, found her audience too conservative, but on the other hand she had not been getting on well with Mōri. On his return her editor had expressed concern about the tone of her writing and censured her for being 'too extreme', but Suga then carried on her arguments with Mōri and male readers in the pages of the paper. She actually told readers of this reprimand, revealing to them the pressure she was under to moderate her views.[82] He began to append cautionary editorial notes to the readers about her articles or to print rebuttals of them. In one strongly worded refutation (of the article on double suicide) that was highly critical of her 'morbid ideas', Mōri lamented in patronizing fashion that this could come from a Christian socialist.[83] But, other than the paternalistic way in which he treated her, it is possible that there was another reason for the tensions between the two: Arahata claimed that Mōri had proposed marriage to Suga on one of their first meetings, but she was indignant to discover later that he already had a wife confined to a sickbed.[84]

In general, in the pages of *Murō Shinpō* Suga expressed her anger and frustration with a society in which women were at best patronized or ignored, at worst treated as merchandise subject to care or abuse in accordance with its value. During her time at Wakayama, her criticisms of men became what we might even describe as 'savage', and the 'extreme' views she expressed were probably born partly of frustration with the sluggishness of change. Many in the decades after the Meiji Restoration chafed at the 'two steps forward, one step back' fashion in which 'progress' was affecting women. To give just a few examples of this uneven progress: when women had gained the right to file for divorce with the Civil Code of 1898, men were accorded legal headship of the family unit; though female children had gained the legal right to primary education, it was not until 1913 that women could enter national universities; and, while men of means gained the right to vote and participate in politics, all women were barred from such unseemly public activities. Article 5 of the Police Security Regulations of 1890 had not only prohibited women from organizing or joining political groups and attending political meetings; Diet members had even gone so far as to try to exclude women from the gallery from which the 'public' were permitted to observe Diet proceedings.[85]

Suga now pulled no punches in how she represented life for Meiji women. On 6 May 1906, after Mōri's return, she declared in 'A Perspective on Men':

> There are no animals in the world as conceited as men. When they are paid even casual compliments by women, they immediately jump to conclusions and betray themselves with loathsome smirks. Men really are the personification of conceit. The more conceited [they] are, moreover, the more they tend to prefer faint-hearted people. In times of emergency, they clearly have more affection for women with no self-respect who first burst into tears, wailing 'Whatever shall we do?' at their wits' end, than for wives who give good counsel. . . . Many men dislike women with their own opinions. They prefer women who listen to what they have to say admiringly, even if they are utterly indifferent. Men who are very conceited treat women as playthings. . . . They hide behind their masks, looking grave, putting on airs and affecting dignity; and the more they talk self-importantly, feign cleverness, and take themselves too seriously, the more women are able to see through their downright stupidity.[86]

Her comment that men disliked women with strong opinions recalls her remark earlier that it was only with Hayashi Utako that she could express the rational side of her character freely. The article continued in this vein, concluding that women had long been deluded into thinking of men as strong and naturally superior when generally it was women who were bold and who took the initiative.

Given the obvious tensions between Suga and her editor, it is possible that much of this was directed at him. A few days later Mōri printed a rebuttal of this article written by a reader, and Suga in turn defended herself against this and Mōri's criticism of her 'extremism'. In this defence she complained that both the reader and her editor were only prepared to consider men's views on women, not women's on men.[87] It is probable that Suga's writings at this time were largely aimed at men she knew personally. One is able to detect more than a hint of her speaking from personal experience when in disgust she mounted an all-out attack on men's 'conceit'; on men who could not tolerate women with independent views; on 'debauched' men who employed sexual double standards by insisting that women be chaste, while they themselves could go to prostitutes and also keep 'mistresses'.

When Suga had spoken of 'the entire self-serving world of men' earlier in 'Rebuff' (15 April), it was clear she was representing sexual exploitation as part of the conditions under which all women lived. What appeared to be foremost in her mind were issues like prostitution and concubinage. These were institutions that far too many women suffered under, not only the prostitutes or concubines themselves, but also wives whose value depended largely upon whether 'they' could produce male heirs. The pitiable situation of wives had received ample attention since earlier in Meiji even from male liberals, and Suga herself had once joined in the fight to win good gentlewomen the protection, respect and affection they deserved. But now, only a few years later, she was expressing her concern also for the other victims of this 'world of men': the women she had once sat in judgement upon, some of whom might not have been so unlike herself, that is, *if* she too had been the lover of a married man. Whether or not Udagawa was amongst her men in 'masks' (he had, after all, actually worn a theatrical mask to hide his disfigurement), her remarks have a ring of personal affront as well as general outrage about sexual double standards and exploitation. It is highly unlikely that all of the objects of her 'utmost cynicism and unbridled hatred' were men she did not personally know.

Whatever the extent to which 'personal' problems with Mōri had contributed to her desire to leave Wakayama, it is clear that by the time Suga left she felt that women had to 'struggle for their freedom and equality with men' on their own behalf. Even socialist men were not necessarily allies in the fight for women's emancipation. It is also clear that she was beginning to see a commitment to socialism as 'a heavy cross to bear' – which is to say that it required dedication in the present and perhaps also the ultimate sacrifice in the future. She was beginning to see and represent life for such as her as synonymous with rebellion; and this was already romantically connected in her mind with death for a cause.

Rise up, people of will!

When she returned to Kyoto at the end of May 1906 Suga worked for a time doing office work at a university while still contributing occasional articles to *Murō Shinpō*.[88] In July Arahata visited her from Tokyo. Suga said in one of her court testimonies that their common-law marriage began in Kyoto at this time. On 12 October she moved with Hide to Tokyo, the opportunity to do so having presented itself when she was offered a position as a reporter for the social pages of a new Tokyo newspaper, the *Mainichi Denpō (Daily Telegraph)*. This was not a socialist paper, so perhaps what helped her to obtain the position was a short article she had written in September, which was published in one of the largest daily newspapers.[89] This dwelt on the memories that a present from her mother evoked of the days when her mother, father and older brother were all still alive (her older brother had died when she was fifteen). The possibility of her sister's death might have been weighing on her mind at that time. Hide's illness would have added to her desire to find employment before leaving for Tokyo, since Arahata the wandering proselytizer was unlikely to be able to contribute much. Suga sent word at the end of that year to her Wakayama readers and friends – also to some foes perhaps – that she and another former *Murō Shinpō* reporter were beginning a new life together in the new year.[90]

The beginning of 1907 was eventful for her in other respects. In January two socialist newspapers began publication: *Heimin Shinbun,* which was now revived as a daily, and the first paper produced by socialist women, *Sekai Fujin (Women of the World)*. Then in early February, a labour dispute escalated into an insurrection at the Ashio copper mine not far from Tokyo. Ashio was in the news at the time not just because of miners' struggles, but also because of an environmental struggle of much longer duration. The mine was responsible for pollution of the Watarase River which even by the 1890s was a problem of immense proportions. The government continued to refuse to close the mine and, instead, in 1902 came up with a plan (an unsuccessful one) to flood one area to contain the problem, limiting the poisoning of peasants' fields. Some villages were destroyed in the process in July 1907, Yanaka being the most famous.[91] Such

disputes led some to believe that the age of 'direct action' was dawn-
ing in Japan, this being particularly topical at that time because on
5 February 1907 Kōtoku Shūsui had published his well-known essay
on the subject, 'The Change in My Thought'.[92] Here in anarchist
style Kōtoku dismissed suffrage and parliamentary (indirect, 'political') strategies in favour of direct economic strategies like the general
strike. In so doing, he added the final touch to a developing split in the
new Japan Socialist Party, formed in February 1906, between 'politicians' (social democrats) and direct actionists. The Japan Socialist
Party was not given the opportunity of a final sectarian breach, however, for one year after its foundation, it was outlawed.

Because one would expect Suga to have been more interested in
socialist women's activities, it is worth pausing briefly over *Sekai
Fujin* and its organizer, Kageyama (Fukuda) Hideko, veteran of the
Popular Rights Movement of the 1880s. Hideko had close connections
with the Heiminsha, but she and others clearly felt the need for an
independent socialist forum for women.[93] *Women of the World* lived
up to its name: it established contact with emancipationists and suffra-
gettes around the world and reported on their activities; and through
doing so, brought the point home to Japanese women that they not
only lacked the vote, but could legally do little to bring about suffrage
and other reforms. While social democrats like her argued that women
must fight to repeal Article 5 (that prohibited women from any involvement in politics), later that year in *Sekai Fujin* Kōtoku invoked
Emma Goldman as authority for his view that socialist women
should not campaign to repeal Article 5. Parliamentary action and
the vote would not bring women freedom, he argued.[94] A final point
that should be made about *Sekai Fujin,* moreover, is that the group
gave only qualified support to the Moral Reform Society. Though
they supported the Society's struggle against concubinage and prostitution, they believed that rather too many of these 'upper-class', 'genteel' ladies were involved in the reactionary, State-sponsored Women's
Patriotic Association; too few of them, moreover, showed any concern
about women's lack of political rights.[95] Suga may not have been
directly involved with *Sekai Fujin*, but we will see shortly how the
group might have influenced her attitude toward the Reform Society.

Suga did not have the time to involve herself in any of this flurry of
socialist activity early in 1907, but she was not busy writing. She
apparently produced three short articles in the first week of January,
two more during the month, and only two in February. Arahata
returned from Ashio in the second week of February to find that
Hide's condition was deteriorating rapidly. Unable to scrape together

the money to hospitalize her, Suga and Arahata stood by helplessly until she died on 22 February 1907, three days before she would have turned 20.[96] There is little doubt that Suga was grief-stricken and embittered over her sister's death, but she may also have suffered from guilt. She had never been able to provide good medical care for Hide; her income could never have been more than what was needed merely to survive. She wrote one short piece in July about a dream in which Hide appeared to her, and stared hard at her until her eyes watered and a few tears fell. The suggestion is that Hide's spirit was uneasy, and reproachful.[97] Furthermore, in addition to Suga's likely feelings of frustration and guilt, she herself was ill. She, too, had contracted tuberculosis, so her prostration at the end of February must have been both emotional and physical. Early in May she went to a convalescent home where she spent two months. Perhaps her employers at *Mainichi Denpō* not only gave her leave from her job but also paid her expenses.

When writing for this newspaper or others she now contributed to occasionally, Suga most often signed herself 'Sugako', or even 'Kanno Sugako'. Presumably, she now wanted her audience to know her identity. One of the short pieces she wrote for *Mainichi Denpō* before Hide's death, 'Joshū to Jokō' ('Female Prisoners and Female Factory Workers'), was about a visit to both Hachiōji Prison and a silk or cotton thread factory.[98] As the title suggests, Suga was making the point that there was not much difference between the two, which was a reference to the appalling, prison-like conditions of many textile factories.[99] She also noted that both prisoners and textile workers were so because of a mere accident of birth: poverty. Both she represented as innocent victims of capitalism. The article was class-conscious to some extent, because there is in it a hint of a socialist critique of the function of both capitalist exploitation and penal systems. Suga also remarked on how daughters of the rich, with the opportunity to go to school without any cares, should be confronted with these pitiful children in the factories. Suga did not need to name the 'ideal society' against which she measured the reality she saw: the article was clearly written by a socialist.

Another article she published at the very beginning of January 1907 was called 'Risō no Fujin' ('The Ideal Woman'). Once again, this was largely about women as decorative objects, but also about the need for reforms in styles of dress.[100] She connected this with the issue of women as the 'playthings' and 'slaves' of men, and also urged women to resist 'shallow vanity' and the 'devils' who tempted the 'high and low, rich and poor' with finery and ornamentation. Interestingly, she also advocated that women throw away their restrictive *obi* (sashes); dispense with the uselessly long sleeves on *kimono*; and cease doing up their hair in traditional *Shimada* or *Marumage* styles that were artificially 'stiffened unhygienically with oil' and could not be managed alone (unlike Western styles). In advocating doing away with traditional means of distinguishing single from married women through coiffure and styles of kimono-sleeve, she was also implying that advertising one's marital status should be dispensed with too. Finally, she urged her female comrades to be brave and set an example for others. Her 'ideal woman' now was one who adopted new, simple styles of dress that would not restrict her movement. Even if she did not go so far as to advocate heavy boots and short hair,[101] one wonders if she knew of the strict codes for plain, *practical* dress of Russian populist women.

In July 1907 Suga was still attending Reform Society gatherings, though only in the capacity of reporter. She covered one conference where the issue of legal prostitution was discussed, and a pro-'monogamy' (anti-concubinage) petition to the government planned.[102] Though unsigned, there is no doubt that one report entitled 'Madam Yajima and Yanaka Village' was written by Suga. Her interest in the struggle against the destruction of Yanaka village might have come partly from Arahata who wrote a book on it in August 1907, although, as Hane notes, socialists like Fukuda Hideko had also been active in support of the anti-pollution fight and the campaign to save Yanaka.[103] In another piece, Suga reported on the women's condemnation of government officials for their lack of concern about prostitution, which was indicative of politicians' 'general contempt for women', and described the delegates to the conference as 'peerless warriors, full of religious faith and spiritual vigour'.[104] She might have still respected the moral commitment of women like Yajima Kajiko, the founder and national president, and Hayashi Utako, to whom she was personally indebted, but there is no evidence of her having further contact in Tokyo with Christian organizations. On the other hand, her expression of admiration for the spiritual faith of Reform Society women may have been an oblique way of saying that she herself no longer had that sort of faith.

Suga's underlying tone, particularly in the article about Yajima Kajiko, is of distance from the more conventional women of the Reform Society. There is a hint even of condescension in the way she expresses her admiration for them. She is there only in the capacity of observer, and, when she does once use a personal pronoun to state her own feelings, it is to say in a detached sort of way, 'On behalf of society and women's groups we are delighted with the fact that out of love the Kyōfūkai never ceases to be active, always focusing its attention on [bread and butter] issues of life.' But what is more to the point is that she admitted at least somewhat unfeelingly, that for her the high point of the conference was when the president, Yajima, raised as a postscript an issue that had nothing to do with the women's issues that interested the Society: the campaign to save Yanaka village. Given the above-mentioned *Sekai Fujin* criticisms of the apolitical stance of the Society, Suga's statement that this message of support and condolence from the Society was 'the thing really worth hearing during the conference' sounds like a political criticism – which might explain why the article was unsigned.

In the second half of 1907 Suga became much more a part of the socialist community in Tokyo, often attending Heiminsha meetings. This was when she became intimate with socialist women like Sakai Tameko and Hori Yasuko. Being more a part of the socialist community, moreover, accounts for her increased interest in prisons. In November she published an article about a trip to Sugamo Prison with Hori to welcome the latter's husband, Ōsugi Sakae, on his release. Suga described Ōsugi as a young anarchist imprisoned for five months for publishing translations of Kropotkin, and referred to Yasuko as a friend who was like a sister to her.[105] This article is mainly a description of the night that Suga, Yasuko and a young male socialist named Sakamoto spent at an inn in front of the prison while waiting for Ōsugi to be released early the next morning. Sakamoto got carried away with enthusiasm at one point after having observed that their imprisoned comrade, Ishikawa Sanshirō, might be nearby: 'Hooray for Ishikawa!' he yelled; 'Hooray for the Japan Socialist Party!'[106]

In general, the article was more about the horrors of the inn – bedbugs, noisy students, and drunken male neighbours – than about explicitly political issues. Once again, however, there is a hint of a socialist critique of prisons: Suga's 'heart was so full at wondering whether [her] nearly two thousand brothers inside the bars in this solemn prison . . . were keeping up their spirits by cursing the cruel society and having hopeless dreams, that [she] forgot her joy at being able to welcome a friend in a few hours.' She could not have been referring only to socialists, since there were nowhere near so many of them in prison. It is clear that what she was saying was that capitalism had made the inmates into criminals. There is no explicit condemnation in the article of the suppression of socialists, but it is interesting that she represented a prison guard as sympathetic to Ōsugi. He was at first 'arrogant' but his voice through the gate became 'very kind' at the mention of Ōsugi's name. It is almost as if the guard knew him to be especially innocent. Finally, while Suga was not in a position to offer a description of conditions in that prison, there is little doubt that this account of a filthy, frightening inn, which was the den of criminals and other undesirables, was allegorical, however inconsistent this was with her picture of a prison full of the innocent victims of capitalism.[107] Suga explicitly introduced the inn as a metaphor for the prison nearby when she noted that they found the room in the inn 'horrid' because it had 'a nasty association in their minds with the prison'.

Suga's editors tolerated her references to socialism, perhaps so long as her writing was not too polemical or radical. She was not as prolific after her sister's death as she had been in her brief period at the *Murō Shinpō*, and her writing overall was not much more radical politically. Given the fact that she was now close to some in the radical faction, it might seem strange that her writing did not reflect this more, though it is likely that this non-socialist newspaper was happier to have her reporting on women's colleges, covering the activities of the Moral Reform Society, or penning elegies for her lost sister than writing about imprisoned anarchists.

Suga did not actually declare herself an anarchist until after the Red Flag Incident of June 1908 when she was first imprisoned, but she was often in contact with members of the 'direct action' group during the year before. She was personally close to the Sakai family, and while Toshihiko (a 'hardline Marxist') was not part of the anarchist faction, he was none the less a good friend of its leader, Kōtoku. Other members of the anarchist group who were her intimates were Arahata, Ōsugi Sakae, Hori Yasuko, and perhaps also Ishikawa Sanshirō. Her surviving correspondence with him from early 1909 suggests that they were friends. Even in 1907 her sympathies were probably more with the radicals than the reformists – if earlier indications of a penchant for dramatic 'revolutionary' rhetoric are anything to go by – though later she indicated that she had been vacillating at this time. But then the Red Flag Incident occurred. This was during the last weeks of the relatively liberal Saionji government (January 1906–July 1908), which had ignored the formation of the Japan Socialist Party in 1906. Such 'tolerance', however, could not be expected from the new prime minister, Katsura Tarō, protégé of the authoritarian Yamagata Aritomo. It was during Katsura's second cabinet (July 1908–August 1911) that socialists were sentenced in connection with both the Red Flag and High Treason Incidents.

On 22 June 1908 Arahata, Ōsugi and others had been arrested after a meeting for marching down the street waving red banners reading 'anarchism', 'anarcho-communism' and 'revolution', singing revolutionary songs and yelling 'ana-ana-anarchy'. When police tried to stop them, an hour-long brawl ensued. The anarchists won the brawl, it appears, but were still all arrested, together with Sakai Toshihiko and Yamakawa Hitoshi who had only tried to stop the fight.[108] Concerned about their friends, Suga and Kamikawa Matsuko had followed them to the police station where they were also detained. Altogether there were then four women arrested, and by all accounts they and their ten male comrades were treated brutally during their imprisonment.[109] Sievers cites a newspaper that reported on the women's mistreatment in prison and their desire for revenge. The prisoners were held for about two months awaiting the trial, and then Suga and Matsuko were acquitted while the others received fines, and prison terms ranging from one to two and a half years.

This, then, was the turning point in her political career that Suga referred to during the treason trial. Her experience of the Incident and prison, she said, had made her realize that disseminating socialist ideas 'through peaceful means' had become 'utterly impossible'; thus she resolved to 'work hard to bring about rebellion or revolution, carry out assassinations and so on to rouse the souls of the people'.[110] She made similar references in her prison diary to the influence that this incident had had on her. In addition, after she was released from prison in August 1908, she was dismissed from the newspaper. With her health worse after two months in jail, she was therefore left with no means of supporting herself until she found a job as a housekeeper and cook in an inn. She often visited comrades in prison, including Arahata, though they had probably been separated since early in 1908. All in all, it is easy to see why the autumn of 1908 has been represented as the 'official' beginning of her radical period.[111] This incident was not such a radical break with her past as Suga indicated, however; for her the leap to anarchism was not such a big one. It was not just a matter of a pacifist, reformist socialist suddenly changing in June 1908 because, as her own words as early as May 1906 show, she had long had radical inclinations or assumptions about political tactics. Perhaps the change is best expressed as a move from a 'distant' view of socialism and romanticization of revolutionism to a commitment to immediate revolutionary practice.

Suga's writings back in 1906 had been more *radical* than earlier because by then she was painting quite a different portrait of the 'real-life' experience of Meiji women. I would not go so far as to say that this portrait was defined even by reformist socialism, however, for one cannot easily recognize as socialist many of the articles she wrote in Wakayama. This was probably due more to a lack of knowledge or confidence than to editorial self-censorship, whether by Mōri or Suga herself. Though there were some changes in her writing when she got to Tokyo, it was never so polemical in style as to give us a clear indication of what socialism or anarchism really meant to her. Like many action-oriented people in Japan and elsewhere, Suga was never a theorist. What is quite clear about this period, however, is that her presentations of life gradually took on a much more consistent counter-ideological tint than in the earlier period. Now she was not only presenting a very different picture of the reality that women faced, but was also exhibiting at times a consciousness of class.

1909–1911

For almost a year from the autumn of 1908 Suga did not publish anything. She may have been working too hard at her new domestic job, because by February 1909 she was so ill that she had to go away for a few weeks to rest and recuperate.[112] It was just before this, in January, that she had met the anarchist Buddhist monk, Uchiyama Gudō, who visited her at the boarding house where she worked and informed her that he had a hidden cache of explosives. It seems she was already known to be sympathetic to the idea of 'direct action'. Early in February, she was also present at a meeting at the Heiminsha with Miyashita Daikichi, who claimed he had succeeded in manufacturing bombs.[113] Later she recalled how after she met Miyashita she exchanged letters with him discussing sacrificing themselves for the cause. Kōtoku was interested in the idea of a rebellion only in 1909. The two were living together as a couple from June, some time after Suga had moved into the Heiminsha quarters to help out with political work. (Thus Kōtoku and his wife Chiyoko were now separated.)

In an atmosphere of intensifying repression when many of her comrades were in prison, it is not surprising that Suga did not publish much between the beginning of 1909 and May 1910, when she entered prison for the last time. This was partly because socialist papers did not last long before being prosecuted and fined, or banned. *Sekai Fujin*, for example, was banned several times during its two years of existence between 1907 and 1909.[114] Because in this period Suga published only a few articles in the short-lived *Jiyū Shisō* (*Free Thought*) of mid-1909, one is forced to look elsewhere – to personal correspondence, for example – for indications of how she represented life just

before her final imprisonment. The texts that will be used here therefore vary. They include written texts of different types for different
audiences (articles, poems, editorials, personal letters, and her prison
diary), and also oral testimonies.

These two years were Suga's most radical period. It was a time when
she embraced 'direct action' or, rather, 'propaganda by deed'. After
all, propaganda by word had become well-nigh impossible. This was
also a time when those who were her enemies began really to pose a
more direct threat to her existence. For now she was denouncing
such things as arbitrary abuses of power by the police and judicial
authorities in a way that revealed her desire to lash back. While
Suga's earlier texts suggest that she had often been engaged in a
struggle with figures of authority, in 1909 she seemed to present herself
as already on the road to a final clash with power. There was not, perhaps, so much of a contrast as we would expect in the ways in which
she represented life directly before and after her final imprisonment.
She herself implied that the more serious charge of high treason
served mainly to strengthen her resolve.

Dear free thinkers

We saw in Part II that when *Jiyū Shisō* was published in May and June
1909, Suga's name appeared as editor.[115] She was probably trying to
shield Kōtoku, as he (too) had tuberculosis. By that time, fines for
infringements of the censorship laws were heavy. Offenders were
imprisoned if the fines remained unpaid by a set date. It was Suga,
therefore, who was arrested on 15 July 1909 and who spent one and
a half months in prison awaiting the trial. Both she and Kōtoku
were ultimately fined, his penalty being lighter than the 400 yen or
100 days hard labour that she received. Both appealed the judgement,
but the appeal was dismissed the following April. After the journal was
banned in June, by which time many comrades were already in prison,
it was must have been clear to Suga and Kōtoku that socialists could
no longer disseminate their ideas legally.

Suga wrote two articles in mid-1909 in the second and final issue
of *Jiyū Shisō*, in which some of the reasons for the frustrations of
socialists were graphically portrayed. She was courageous and also
rather reckless to write them and, inevitably, the backlash was swift.
The first was an account of the Red Flag Incident twelve months
before. The article dwelt largely on the socialists' arrival at the
prison, their defiance despite rough treatment by police and warders,

and Suga's first impressions of prison conditions.[116] She first painted a bright picture of the camaraderie of the socialists who all went together to prison in two horse-drawn police carts, singing revolutionary songs and yelling 'Anarchist Party [*sic*] forever!' (Elsewhere parties were usually rejected by anarchists because 'political'.). But then the picture darkened as Suga noted their indignation at having their 'freedom shackled' when they had 'committed no crime'; and admitted that the group's optimism did not last long once the male comrades were handcuffed together in pairs and the women dragged away 'like baggage' and shoved into individual cells. These were pitch-dark and so narrow that they 'scraped their noses' if they tried to move around. Suga soon heard the 'clanking of a sword at someone's side' drawing nearer, and thankfully breathed a sigh of relief when the door was unlocked. 'You're not getting out. Here's your food', someone muttered while shoving a filthy box with a revolting mess of *miso* and poor quality rice toward her. Evidently, she and the other women had forgotten the warnings of their more experienced comrades before they were separated: amidst the chorus of farewells someone had yelled, 'However awful the food, you must eat it or you'll lose your strength!' Tapping on their adjoining walls and conferring on the subject of the 'feast' until they were roared at to 'shut up', the women were all of one mind: they could not summon up the courage to touch the stuff.[117] Doubtless, Suga was making a point about why it was that socialists returned from even short spells in prison in poor health.

At the beginning of this article, Suga promised to continue her account of the Red Flag Incident in the next issue where she would discuss the 'tragic scene at the Kanda Police Station lock-up, the wretched night at the Metropolitan Police Headquarters, and also the day at the Prosecutor's Office that [she] would never forget'.[118] (It was at this office that she first encountered Taketomi.) But she was not allowed the opportunity to keep her promise to reveal all. She never did describe in print the 'tragic scene' at the lock-up: the terrible beating that police gave Arahata and Ōsugi, who were stripped of their clothes, dragged along the corridors by their feet, kicked and stamped on.[119]

The other article that Suga published in *Jiyū Shisō* in which she expressed her political frustration was an editorial. Here she gave her readers graphic details about why the journal had to be limited to four pages; why, in fact, it was difficult for them to produce anything. The problem was police harassment of a kind that Suga said would have been 'hilarious' if it were not so 'regrettable' and trying. If any in her audience were under the illusion that Japan's modernization had brought political freedom, her portrait of the rewards of being a known social critic would have revealed it to be a fiction. This was her description of the *very* close watch that police kept on the offices of the Heiminsha:

> We were afraid we would be banned immediately, but we published the first issue anyway . . . secret publications appear in rapid succession, and it is clear that government officials are really in a panic. All of our comrades are being shadowed. . . . If it continues in this way, I believe we will arrive at our destiny – having to choose between the alternatives of starving to death or advancing to [the point of] an explosion. Thus, our refined Japanese government actually does us the favour of creating many conspirators/ rebels.
>
>   . . . recently there have been four plain-clothes men, eight eyes intently keeping vigil in shifts night and day, watching this office. There are two men at the front door and two at the back.
>
>   There is a certain residence nearby that has no connection with this Society and its comings and goings. Many days ago, the hedge there was torn up; they [the police] set up a tent with a ready-made red and white curtain for an entrance, and brought their cane chairs and camp stools almost as if they were having a garden party. I was struck dumb with amazement at these vigilant police sitting there dutifully taking notes.
>
>   They made this house of a midwife named Matsuda . . . their troop headquarters, and what is more, they now rush around . . . enthusiastically swarming like ants from the red and white curtain to directly in front [of our offices], letting nothing pass them by. It is both hilarious and regrettable, but at least they are giving the mistress [Matsuda] some publicity.[120]

It was fortunate that Suga could maintain a sense of humour in such circumstances. She did a good job of painting an absurd 'Keystone cops' sort of picture of the unwarranted attentions paid to socialists by the police. There is little doubt that her audience was meant to question the intelligence of both those in charge of the national 'good' and those they charged with domestic security. Furthermore, in her remarks about destiny and rebels/conspirators, she seemed to be warning the government that it might come to regret pushing them too hard, while also making a bid for public understanding in the event something 'explosive' happened.

Using such rhetoric was probably unwise, when police were on the look-out for violent conspirators already. Uchiyama Gudō had been arrested in May after his cache of explosives was discovered.[121] His connection with Kōtoku and Suga was known to the police and they, suspecting some sort of extremist plot, had stepped up their surveillance of the Heiminsha offices. As Notehelfer observes, one of the reasons for this was that there was a rumour abroad that Kōtoku was considering anti-imperial violence; but this he disdainfully denied in an interview published in the *Asahi Shinbun* on 7 June, asking how anyone could be so stupid as to even think about perpetrating such an act.[122] None the less, now Suga and Kōtoku could not go anywhere without their escorts.

This period between June and November was an eventful one. Perhaps by November, Kōtoku, who had withdrawn from the 'conspiracy', was already starting to regret separating from his wife, whom he had not seen as a fitting wife for a revolutionary. With Suga, he had thought he could live a life of 'perfect happiness' because she was 'direct', did not resort to 'flattery', and not only shared his ideals but 'worked zealously' for the cause.[123] Kōtoku seems to have respected Suga politically, but there are indications that his view of their relationship was a little one-sided: she was the sort of woman who could better support him in his remaining political career.[124] He did hope to be able to bring some peace into her life, however, because she 'had been raised in adversity from childhood and had spent all her life fighting', and he wanted to 'let her live out her remaining life in peace'.[125] Kōtoku also implied in 1910 that it was because of his concern for Suga's health that he had started to become ambivalent about the assassination plans. He had hoped that they would both be able to retire to the country, where he would continue writing and publishing.

Kōtoku had good reason for his concern over Suga's general state of health, for, by early October 1909, it had deteriorated to the extent that she collapsed in the street. Ironically, the man who had carried her home unconscious on his back was the policeman who had been tailing her – to and from the public baths! She was hospitalized for a month after this, her condition diagnosed as nervous exhaustion.[126] Her illness may have been aggravated by emotional stress due to a number of factors: her being arrested and held in custody for six weeks after which she was fined the enormous sum of 400 yen; the certainty that she would soon face another term of imprisonment if she could not raise the money; and also the fact that she and Kōtoku were being hounded by police. Her involvement in discussions of assassination attempts and her impatience to do something decisive probably also added to her tension, but a further factor that might have contributed to the strain she was under was the 'love scandal' over a supposed love triangle involving herself, Kōtoku and Arahata.

The relationship between Suga and Kōtoku was not received well even by comrades in the socialist community, largely because of an obvious misconception that she was still Arahata's common-law wife. Arahata did nothing to dispel this mistaken notion but, on the contrary, took the news of their intimacy in the spirit of a 'deserted husband', even going so far as to write to Kōtoku the following year threatening to kill him. Arahata admitted in his autobiography much later that there was already a 'fissure' in his relationship with Suga early in 1908, but he claimed that this had merely been a 'temporary' separation. According to Suga's account, it had not. The section in his memoirs on the 'love scandal' is entitled 'Jealousy, Envy, Anguish', which suggests something about his role in the scandal.[127] Probably, Arahata's state of mind at the time was closely connected with the fact that at the time he was in prison because he recalled in his memoirs being baited by prison warders about 'his mother' and her new boyfriend. Suga was five or six years older than him.

There may have been economic reasons for the separation too. Arahata's later remarks about Suga's character are interesting because of a connection with the issue of money, because he claimed that she entered into all of her relationships with men for economic or mercenary motives. Shimizu Unosuke observes that even when Arahata was in salaried employment at the Heiminsha, he was earning less than Suga, and his income lasted only from January to mid-April. She was apparently earning 25 yen a month and he 15 yen.[128] If Suga had hoped to have an easier life with him in Tokyo, this certainly did not eventuate. Also, she later wrote in her prison diary that their relationship was unsatisfactory for her because they had been more like elder sister and younger brother than husband and wife.[129] A testimony of June 1910 (extract below) shows that she saw him as a 'younger brother' partly because he was like another dependant.

The socialist concern with Suga's and Kōtoku's sexual 'immorality' was part of a broader public and governmental reaction to social 'decadence' and sexual 'depravity'.[130] The popular press contributed to the 'love scandal', making much out of this 'free love' incident. In one passage in *Jiyū Shisō*, Kōtoku bemoaned the lack even of sexual freedom in Meiji Japan: 'We have no freedom of speech, no freedom of religion, and still we do not have freedom in love', he said.[131] In general, even Meiji socialists were slow to recognize the challenge 'free love' posed to conventional Confucian–Western sexual morality and the 'samuraized' family.[132] Samurai familial practice had in many ways spread to the lower classes in Meiji, and even been enshrined in law – for example, primogeniture and male legal headship of the family – but, before Meiji, 'monogamy' had been held to be a virtue only for women. Socialists failed to recognize the highly political nature of 'free love', apparently, even after *Jiyū Shisō* was banned specifically for publishing an article advocating the destruction of the family or family system.[133] Nor did they question the conventional view of women as commodities: Kōtoku was shunned by other socialists, not so much because he had deserted his own wife, but rather because he had 'stabbed an imprisoned comrade in the back' by stealing *his* woman. Ōsugi apparently exclaimed that Suga had 'abandoned a foot soldier in favor of an officer', while Kōtoku 'stole the woman of a comrade in prison'.[134] And, of course, in the minds of socialist moralists then, in this so-called 'triangle', Arahata's claim to Suga was more important than Chiyoko's on Kōtoku.

Thus, there is good reason to suppose that Suga felt a need to vindicate herself in the eyes of the socialist community after she and Kōtoku had been shunned. Some tanka she wrote and included in the first issue of *Jiyū Shisō* under the general title of '*Chiisaki Kyogi*' ('White Lie/s') actually refer to this ostracism. Two of these five poems are particularly revealing, but I will also include the last:

> Since the day when suddenly
> I felt ashamed at how practised
> I'd become at white lies,
> I've been cast out by society.
>
> . . . .
>
> Silent people
> again today,
> cultivating
> their one fearsome power.
>
> . . . .
>
> Even on the day of
> the drum signal for the attack,
> I'll smile and think of the bliss
> of dying in your arms.[135]

We should first note that Suga signed herself 'Ryūko' (lit., 'dragon' + feminine suffix), which might have been a cynical reference to her being painted as a temptress. It has been said that Suga's stepmother hated Suga because she was born in the year of the dragon, which meant that she was evil and cunning.[136] Perhaps she was drawing a parallel between being seen as unchaste now and being blamed for being raped when a girl. Both the signature and the poems themselves are open to interpretation, but my reading of the first tanka is that the 'white lie' was Suga's pretence that she was still Arahata's common-law wife after the Red Flag Incident, in order to get into prison to visit him and other comrades.[137] She mentioned this in one testimony later. It was because of this pretence that she then suffered ostracism for deserting a 'husband' in prison. Furthermore, concerning the last two poems, though she might have to contend with the 'fearsome power' of people's silence for the moment, what seems to buoy her spirits up is the certainty that the day of 'reckoning' will come when she can die for the cause – with Kōtoku presumably – and prove that it is they who are the true revolutionaries. Suga seemed to be protesting her innocence, while also portraying herself as a genuine revolutionary misunderstood by her peers. Finally, here too there is a hint of some cataclysmic, heroic act yet to come, which will show her true worth.

Two points should be emphasized about this 'free love scandal'. The first is that it is possible that this was not the first time that Suga had faced the moral condemnation of colleagues, that is, if Arahata's story about her 'promiscuous' past when at *Ōsaka Chōhō* had any basis in fact. The second point to be made about the muddied reputations of Suga and Kōtoku is that this might have influenced her apparent 'pessimism' just before her final imprisonment when she painted life as a 'journey of meaningless wretchedness'. After all, in the wake of socialist censure for depravity had come suspicions of treachery against comrades and the cause. This was because by March 1910, Kōtoku and Suga had retired to a health resort in Yugawara on the Izu peninsula, which led to a belief in the socialist community that he had defected. There was some cause for his comrades to think this: a friend of Kōtoku's had arranged financial support for him to move to the country and pursue scholarly work; and this same friend had approached a high-ranking police official to stop the harassment of Kōtoku if he promised to retire from political activity. Even after their arrests, Suga was intent on refuting this charge of defection. In one court interrogation (included below), she denied more than once that by then Kōtoku had then 'abandoned the cause' or 'given up anarchism'.

Kōtoku implied in a letter to Arahata in May 1910 that Suga had added to his problems at Yugawara because her state of mind was unstable: he said that she had often had attacks of 'extreme hysteria' from the time she was released from prison six months earlier. After her collapse he had 'had doubts about her sanity', and still now she suffered 'a severe nervous debility'.[138] His description may have been somewhat exaggerated, however, because it is known that at that time they argued over the issue of political retirement. (Perhaps he saw her defence of her *political* position to be merely 'emotional'). She, however, seemed to feel that his attitude toward the assassination plans was too passive, and she was probably not very happy to be sitting around doing nothing in a health resort not knowing what her fellow conspirators were doing. During the Pretrial Hearing, Kōtoku said she had agreed at first to retire to the country, but while they were there she hated being inactive.[139] On 18 April Suga wrote to Furukawa Rikisaku indicating that she had not abandoned the plan for rebellion, and also saying that she had decided not to bother continuing with the appeals against the fines and would take the hundred days of hard labour.[140] Kōtoku was still trying to borrow the money to pay her fines at this point. On 1 May she left Yugawara for Tokyo, and less than three weeks later, on 18 May, she was accompanied to the prison gates by some comrades.

It has been argued that when Suga left Kōtoku in Yugawara, both knew that the relationship was over. This may have been true of Kōtoku, who later wrote to his wife apologizing and hinting at a reconciliation, but it was not true of Suga, as her letters to him in May illustrate. Prison officials were said to have baited her by showing her the letter from Kōtoku to his wife. Suga apparently felt betrayed and shortly after her imprisonment, she sent a letter to him in prison terminating their relationship.[141]

To friends and foes

Suga was not expending any effort at all on proselytizing just before her final imprisonment in 1910; she no longer had the opportunity to do so. The only writing she was doing, apparently, was in letters to friends, and these I look at first before turning to her pretrial testimonies. The latter, being texts to her 'foes', naturally show how she remained defiant, but one might question whether they reveal the heightened use of her lived reality as an ideological weapon that one would expect. In the third part of this section, I include once more a brief consideration of her last letters and prison diary, and it should be recalled that the latter was largely written for her comrades. In such texts one would not expect her to be trying to *convince* anyone of the dreadful iniquities of the social-legal system – for this would have been preaching to the converted – though she does bemoan them. But by this time, of course, her indignation at the persecution of innocent comrades was greater than earlier because of the severity of the sentences (for treason) imposed upon so many.

I

Suga's personal letters written in May 1910 are the only texts one can consult to see how she represented life just before her final imprisonment. They reveal that her statements later in prison or court about the quality of life, about what it meant to her to live and die well, were not solely knee-jerk reactions to a *final* confrontation with power. Suga's constructions of life and death did not change greatly after this imprisonment because her clash with power had been going on for some time, all the while intensifying. There are rather a lot of signs, in fact, that she had expected such a confrontation with her 'destiny'. Her letters to Kōtoku in May therefore show that grand questions of the meaning of mortality and immortality, direct meetings with power, and a quest for political self-empowerment in a situation where there were definite limits to possible action were already issues for her even before her third imprisonment. But these letters have a very personal dimension too, reminding us of various things: her love for Kōtoku and depression over a coming separation; her failing health; and also the horror of dying a lingering death that she had first mentioned years before.

These letters Suga wrote Kōtoku not only express the fact that at that point in time she was intent on dying meaningfully; they also show that she was wavering between worrying about going to prison and being resolved that it was the best course. The tone of each of the following three letters written over a period of six days is quite different. The first seems to have been written in despair, the second in a spirit of calm resignation, and the third with a feeling of determination. Far from constituting evidence of her general 'mental instability' by that time, they show her to be a human being reacting naturally to an extraordinarily difficult and painful situation:

> I just spent two or three hours sewing with my chest hurting feeling poorly perhaps because of the weather. All day I've been feeling pessimistic. Senseless human existence! I've long breathed [life's] chilly air, and I can [no longer] endure it. Life! The agony of life. To what purpose do mortals continue on their journey of meaningless wretchedness?

> 11 May, Evening. [Signed] Yū.

[The following was scribbled on the outside of the envelope.] 12th, a.m. Yesterday and today a letter had not come from you – are you unwell?

[To] My Beloved Sui-sama [Shūsui],
I sent that wild letter, then went to the bath-house, but am very unwell. And of course, even though I had written in such a manner, it was because I was impatiently waiting for a letter. Meanwhile your letter came, [leaving me] prostrated with tears, with inexpressible feelings of mortification and pain. Now I am feeling much better. When I looked at your graceful, dear handwriting, the things that were vexing me till now suddenly vanished like smoke. Your sending me such a kind letter makes it difficult to reply because I've caused you such pain. I'd resolved to enter prison without saying anything, but having seen your letter I feel I must write in humble apology. What manner of childish, foolish person am I? Please forgive me. I was thinking only of you and became hysterical like that, and I've also been unwell since I saw you. Thus I became a bit morbid out of love and loneliness. From now on I'll keep in good humour and write a letter every day during these [remaining] five days. I must resign myself to going [into prison]. There is no point in wasting my days of freedom hoping. . . . I ask affectionately that you please take care of yourself. If you keep in good health, I won't mind how many years I'm in prison. I won't even mind dying. This makes it my third letter today.

12 May. [Signed] 'Yū'

[In a postscript she noted that she also had a cold, and told Kōtoku to look out for some medicine she was sending him].

16th May, 2 p.m. Last night I had a terrible fever. I have no idea what my temperature was. I tossed about suffering. Today too, when I doze off I become soaked in perspiration. For the first time I took up my chopsticks for a meal. Naturally, it didn't taste any good. Tomorrow I intend to take it easy and go by rickshaw to see [Dr] Kitsuda. I didn't go out at all today. I wonder if it's because of the recent strain that my cold has worsened so much. But as you say, all is fate. When you hear of my current illness, you'll probably tell me I must postpone going into prison. But I will go resolutely. I'd rather sleep in prison than here. It'd be better to die in prison than linger on and die here. That would have some meaning. Then there would be some consolation in death. I'm tired so I'll write later.

5 p.m. Yoshikawa came and chatted for about two hours. There's some significant news too.[142]

Yoshikawa Morikuni was a socialist, but not one of the conspirators. It is not clear what the 'significant news' mentioned in the last letter was. Also, I have excluded what follows 'hoping' in the second letter because Suga did not say anything further about what she was 'hoping' for. There is a definite suggestion in the second letter, where she said that she would not mind how long she was in prison so long as Kōtoku kept in good health, that she viewed her sacrifice for him as worthwhile because she had spared him from prison.

At face value, these letters appear to reflect a confused state of mind. As to their contexts, however, the first was apparently written while Suga was depressed over both her illness and the fact that she had not heard from Kōtoku since coming to Tokyo. When she received a letter from him just after sending it, she clearly felt guilty about the tone of her first letter and sat down to write a calm and apologetic response. The tone of the first letter was not only one of despair but probably also accusation. Certainly, she was accusing him for not writing, but there might have been another accusation implied in her sending him such a depressing letter only a week before her imprisonment. He felt guilty enough about the fact that it was Suga rather than he who was going to prison.[143] In a letter to his family dated 27 September 1909, Kōtoku expressed his certainty that she would die in prison, and though he was 'at a loss to know what to do, he had to do something'. Raising the money for her fine was 'entirely [his] responsibility'. He was more explicit about the 'cruel sacrifice' he had allowed Suga to make in his letter to Arahata of 20 May. Hence, it is unlikely that Suga's letter of 11 May would have assuaged Kōtoku's guilt – quite the contrary – which is probably why she immediately wrote in apology on receiving a 'kind' letter from him. But, if there was only an implicit accusation in her first letter, where she told him of her despair just days before going to prison in connection with a publication not her 'responsibility', her tone of accusation was more explicit five days later.

Suga's letter of 16 May could be read as a show of bravado. Perhaps when she insisted that she would rather die in prison, she was trying to alleviate Kōtoku's frustration over not being able to raise the money for her fines. Was she simply saying that he should not worry because she herself did not care one way or another? Perhaps – and perhaps not. Her protesting her willingness to go to jail, and render her death 'meaningful' by dying in prison, would have been small consolation for a man accused of 'selling out'. Kōtoku, at this time, might have been going through a crisis of confidence, in despair partly because of the political persecution and resultant poverty, and partly because he seemed to believe himself to be ineffectual and lacking in determination.[144]

If Suga seemed inconsistent at this time, it was doubtless because she was wavering between despair and a desperate need to act. She must have often despaired at her physical condition, at the many problems in her personal–political life, and perhaps at life itself which (certainly on 11 May 1910) seemed to have no meaningful purpose. Furthermore, she could not work politically without being thrown into prison. At this point she gave the impression that if she could not do something purposeful before her death, she would ensure that the manner of her death (in prison) would render her life meaningful. When she wrote these letters, Suga had not ruled out the possibility of rebellion, because she hoped to be out of prison in 100 days if her health did not fail her. Unbeknownst to Kōtoku, the night before she was due to enter prison, she had met with her three co-conspirators, Miyashita Daikichi, Furukawa Rikisaku and Niimura Tadao, to make final plans for an imperial assassination attempt. Their meeting was on 17 May, the day after her third letter to Kōtoku. Here they drew straws to see who would throw the first bomb and Suga won.[145] By 16 May, then, she was no longer in despair but again 'resolute' that she *would* survive her term to follow in the footsteps of the Russian regicide, Sofia Perovskaya.

Yet even in the letter Suga had written to one of the conspirators, Furukawa Rikisaku, a month earlier, she had expressed her determination to go ahead with their plans. She ended that letter as follows:

I look at the newspapers and my blood boils. Rebellion! Revolution! My own lack of strength is so vexing I can't endure it. I'm constantly thinking of ways of shoring up my bodily strength a little, waiting for their guard [the state's] to slip a little, and then ending by carrying out an action that has meaning and is coloured with a little 'dedication'.

I'll probably return to Tokyo at the end of the month. The details I'll leave till we meet.

18th April,   [Signed] Tsuki.[146]

There is not much doubt that she was telling her co-conspirator that in her mind revolution was still 'on the agenda'. The only other thing of interest in the letter was her explanation that Kōtoku would remain in Yugawara until his refutation of Christianity was completed, which indicated that he had not withdrawn from the struggle.

Since socialists could no longer organize nor publish and even had difficulty surviving economically because of fines and the lack of employment opportunities, it is reasonable to assume that among Suga's motives for deciding on a violent course of action were frustration, desperation, a desire to prove herself, and also a determination to exact revenge on their persecutors. Many socialists then believed that violence begets violence, as noted earlier. Arahata might have condemned Suga for her 'putchism' much later but in 1907 he had justified retaliatory revolutionary violence.[147] Nor did Kōtoku ever completely condemn terrorism, even if he opposed it on theoretical grounds. During the trial he referred to it as 'more or less legitimate self-defence' on the part of 'hot-blooded youths [who] . . . lacked any other means of resistance'.[148] He also observed that Suga's view of 'revolution' was based on the Russian experience (Russian populist terrorism).[149]

II

When for the third time in as many years Suga entered prison on 18 May 1910, she did not have any idea that she was already under suspicion for involvement in an anti-imperial plot, and that her three co-conspirators would be arrested a week later. While she suspected that she would not leave prison alive, she could not have foreseen that within a year she would go to the gallows. The trial records reveal that when first charged with plotting to assassinate the emperor she was unco-operative, though this was due to the fact that her old 'enemy', Taketomi Wataru, was the assigned prosecutor. In the very first sentence of her first statement to the prosecution she flatly denied that she, Miyashita Daikichi and others had been 'conspiring to commit regicide by means of a bomb', though later she was happy to admit to it.

Suga's relationship with this 'paternal' figure, who apparently became more 'benevolent' in direct response to her refusal to talk to *him*, is of particular interest because she did end up trusting him with personal details about her life. She was aware that such knowledge might be used against her, but she had long treated her lived experience as evidence of the moral–political rectitude of her beliefs and actions. Yet unlike Fumiko, Suga did not explicitly use her life-story as a weapon against power *formally* during her trial – at least, not so far as one can see from the pretrial records. She only seems to have done this off the record when she swapped 'wretched' life-stories with Taketomi.[150] After a career of confronting audiences with her account of life's realities through the telling of chapters of her own life-story (or of women like herself), Suga did not now take the opportunity to proselytize in such a way during the pretrial hearing. She did not, like Fumiko, treat her enemies to a step-by-step, detailed account of the social construction of a rebel. She made statements or answered formal questions about her life in a very matter-of-fact manner without going into much detail. All she said about her family background was as follows:

> [From Declaration to Prosecution of 3 June 1910]
> My parents were quite wealthy in the beginning but when I was ten years old Father's mining business failed suddenly causing us to have great difficulty surviving. Then when I was eleven we lost Mother and I was raised by a stepmother, and had a very unhappy life. When I married into a merchant family at seventeen I was predisposed to enjoy reading and dislike business, so because Father had a stroke when I was twenty-one I left my marital home on the pretext of nursing him. After that I worked as a journalist and writer.
> My schooling was restricted to elementary school; otherwise I am entirely self-educated.[151]

Yet it was in this same statement that she spoke *at length* about being inspired by Sofia Perovskaya; avowed her readiness to die for the cause; described how she had first become a socialist; and also gave her reasons for joining the radical anarchist faction.

Prosecutors and judges were very interested in Suga's 'personal' [*sic*] connections with comrades, particularly the anarcho-communist 'ringleader', Kōtoku. But she said little about her personal life unless pressed to explain further. In that same statement to the prosecution on 3 June she said:

I had formerly been a comrade and acquaintance of Kōtoku Denjirō and had respect and affection for him as our mentor [*senpai*], but from before the Red Flag Incident of the year before last, my previous husband Arahata Kanson and I had separated by mutual agreement. Kōtoku and I were in love from that time. Therefore, from March last year I lived and worked with Kōtoku. We lived as husband and wife from June last year.[152]

In her first court interrogation the judge still asked for clarification of her marital status:

[From Preliminary Court Interrogation Record of 3 June 1910]
Q13: Are you anyone's wife at present?
Ans: I am Kōtoku Denjirō [Shūsui]'s wife.
Q14: Since when have you been in this relationship with Kōtoku?
Ans: Since June last year.
Q15: How did it come about?
Ans: Kōtoku was producing the magazine, *Jiyū Shisō*, from the Heiminsha and I helped out, putting it out under my name. My relationship with Kōtoku came about because of that.
Q16: Didn't you become involved because you were of like mind or agreed on political doctrine [*shugi*]?
Ans: I respected and had affection for Kōtoku as a mentor.
Q17: But weren't you the wife of Arahata Katsuzō [Kanson] at that time?
Ans: No, I was not. I had formerly had a relationship with him, but before I, Arahata and others were imprisoned in the Red Flag Incident in 1908, I had separated from him by mutual agreement and we were living apart. But because Arahata was stripped naked, kicked and violently beaten by policemen when detained by Kanda police in the Red Flag Incident, we were all moved to tears with pity. I really felt for him and consoled him, and on the basis of that the police declared that I was his wife. I was acquitted but Arahata was found guilty and, naturally, so I could easily take parcels into prison while he was in Chiba Gaol I kept up the pretence of being his wife. Thus, before my relationship with Kōtoku, I had already broken up with Arahata.[153]

It is highly unlikely that the judge did not know of the love scandal earlier and was simply trying to establish who Suga's husband was. What is more likely is that he wanted to know if Arahata was still part of their extremist circle after the separation from Suga. However, she was clearly on the defensive for another reason – the love scandal –

and thus did not take the opportunity to defend free love. She seemed to be more intent on defending her own moral character or chastity by denying that she had been sexually involved with two men at the same time. One wonders why a simple 'So?' did not suffice in answer to question 17, though one would need to exercise caution in assuming that she understood by 'free love' the same thing as anarchists else-where (Emma Goldman, for example). In Japan, then, even some of the anarchists of the day understood 'free love' to mean merely the freedom to choose one's *marital* partner.[154]

The possibility that on such issues judge and defendant were talking at cross-purposes is clearer in a later interrogation when the same Judge (Harada Kō) asked for more detail about Arahata. What he probably wanted to know was whether their separation had been over personal or political differences.

> [From Preliminary Court Interrogation Record of 5 June 1910]
> Q8: When did your relationship with Arahata begin?
> Ans: When the person in charge of the *Murō Shinpō* in Kishū [Wakayama] was arrested about four years ago on a charge of using abusive language about Governor Kiyosumi, I went to the paper as editor. I came to know Arahata at that time because he was helping out. When I had just returned to Kyoto during that same year a letter came from Arahata who had returned to Tokyo; and when he came to visit me in Kyoto we became involved.
> Q9: When was it that you definitely broke up with Arahata?
> Ans: The Red Flag Incident occurred in June 1908; it was a little before that.
> Q10: What was the main reason for your breaking up with Arahata?
> Ans: Because Arahata is four or five years younger than me, I dealt with everything in our life [together] as the big sister. Also, as a writer he might have managed, but as a socialist he couldn't get work, so it might have been all right to look after him as my younger brother, but as a husband he was not suitable. In addition, even on Arahata's side, because he was predisposed to treat me as an elder sister he was in awe of, we did not ultimately hit it off as husband and wife.[155]

What she inadvertently told the judge was that her differences with Arahata had only been personal, not political, that he was an anarchist too. It was fortunate for Arahata that he was one of those in jail for much of the period of the conspiracy and not in any danger of being implicated. Consequently, the judge now turned his attention to Kōtoku and the Heiminsha again: the authorities were not going to let him slip through their fingers. They could not have been very impressed by the (lesser?) role the guilty defendants accorded him. One of the lawyer Hiraide Shū's pseudo-fictional stories, 'Keikaku' ('The Plot'), depicts this view of Kōtoku when the heroine decides that even if the hero has a last-minute desire to rejoin them, she must save him so that he can continue with his revolutionary 'scholarship'.[156]

It is obvious that the authorities did use knowledge of Suga's personal life against her in some ways: for example, when they tried to alienate her from Kōtoku by harping on his reconciliation with his former wife. The judges were probably disappointed that it made little difference to the degree to which Suga would implicate him in the plot. The following makes their ploy rather transparent:

[From the Sixth Preliminary Court Interrogation of 13 June 1910]
Q10: Was Kōtoku the first in our nation to advocate anarcho-communism?
Ans: Yes . . .
Q11: Then you and the other defendants who participated in this plan all advocated anarcho-communism with Kōtoku's encouragement?
Ans: That's right.
. . .
Q14: When was it that Kōtoku vacillated about putting the whole of this plan into practice?
Ans: It was from about January this year.
Q15: Didn't you all agree that you wanted Kōtoku to survive you?
Ans: According to the plan, if Kōtoku survived when we died he would communicate the news to comrades overseas for us. If Kōtoku died with us, we wouldn't be able to send the news overseas, and this would not be at all beneficial to the natural development of anarcho-communism in Japan . . .
Q19: Wasn't it the case that Kōtoku believed that avoiding putting it into practice himself and keeping himself alive would be beneficial for the development of anarchism?
Ans: I don't know Kōtoku's intentions but that is what I thought. I said this to Kōtoku at Yugawara. And the others felt the same way.
Q20: Isn't it the case that by now Kōtoku has abandoned anarchism?
Ans: He has not abandoned it.
Q21: Didn't Kōtoku tell you that he was divorcing you and asking

his former wife, Chiyo, to come back?
Ans: I did not hear anything like that.
Q22: But doesn't Chiyo still now have a relationship with Kōtoku, living by means of his support?
Ans: Apparently she has been receiving 12 yen for her monthly living expenses from Kōtoku.[157]

The judge must have been rather deflated at her knowing about the money Kōtoku was sending to Chiyoko – if his intention was to undermine Suga's confidence in Kōtoku to the extent of getting her to implicate him further, he would have been disappointed. Even when she obviously felt betrayed by him, she did not change her story about his innocence. In the thirteenth pretrial court interrogation of 17 October she said no more than that he had *once* got carried away with the idea of assassinating the emperor and so on, but from January 1910 his 'revolutionary fervour cooled' and his attitude toward putting the plan into action was too 'vague' for the plotters to include him in further plans.[158]

It is clear that in Suga's testimonies she was saying no more than was necessary. She was not taking the opportunity to proselytize at length on any topic. Perhaps she did not see any point in expending energy on preaching to those unlikely to be converted. The only way she used her experience of life as a weapon against the socio-political system was when she pointed out in rather Mencian fashion that the state itself was responsible for the conspiracy because of its lack of tolerance for democracy and its unduly repressive actions. One does not find in Suga's trial testimonies a systematic counter-ideological use of her lived reality, though this is not to say that she did not continue to defy power in other ways.

III

Even some of her comrades might not have always been the best of friends to Suga, but at the very end of her life she was not embittered about humanity. Quite the contrary. She was not like the often misanthropic Fumiko. In Suga's diary she included reminiscences of happy times with family and friends;[159] and also wrote about the ideal society that would inevitably come. In her last written texts she was quite positive about humanity and life, if not about contemporary society.

Over her own regicidal–*'patricidal'* part in the affair, Suga expressed both guilt and pride. In a letter to Kōtoku's niece she expressed both 'resignation' and 'satisfaction' with her sentence. She sympathized with the family over Kōtoku's fate, but did not take responsibility for his coming death: rather, she flatly stated that it was both his and her 'destiny'.[160] In another letter to Yoshikawa Morikuni three days later she spoke of how happy and relieved she was that half the defendants had been granted a reprieve. She expressed the conviction that they must have been those she 'knew to be innocent', to which she added, 'Hearing this, half the burden on my shoulders was lifted.'[161] This would-be terrorist made no apology for herself in 1910–1911; she did not repent of anything but the fact that her actions had enabled the state to frame innocent bystanders.

Nor was she only looking for sympathy when she spoke of the misery of her past informally to Taketomi. In a manner not unlike Fumiko's she might have been saying, 'Look at what *you* have made me!' Yet she was not just representing herself as a social victim. In that same diary entry about speaking to Taketomi of the 'circumstances of her wretched past', she said that this was 'such that it had only been through [her] unwillingness to accept defeat that [she] had had the good fortune not to become a prostitute or girl spinner'.[162] What she seemed to be emphasizing was that it was through her determination that she had been able to transcend her powerless origins, and become the 'enemy' who now faced the judges. When talking to enemies in prison or court, this 'traitor' did not want to be an object of pity.

CONCLUSION

Throughout her career of almost a decade of political action, Suga engaged in dialogues with 'Power' in which she left little doubt that her view of reality was different from that of the mainstream. In presenting the harsh realities of life she had had little trouble seeing through the 'veils' that obscured the faces of *most* of her paternalistic opponents. When she first refused to talk about her past to Prosecutor Taketomi she was afraid that he would 'distort everything and use it against [her]' – nevertheless, to him she then narrated her whole life-story.[163] She added that 'only those able to bleed and cry, who care about social problems', could be compassionate about her story; she believed that his 'eyes' had told her that he was not just 'pandering to [her] ego', trying to get her to talk. Now he did not seem 'sinister' after all. It was clear to her from his stories about his own 'deprived' background that he was able to empathize with her story. Clearly, she had softened toward this man she had at first threatened to kill. Here we see the humanistic, perhaps even the still-Christian side of Suga. Her swapping tales about her life with him at this point was consistent with her use of her life experience as *evidence* of the correctness of her ideas and actions; but it also could have been related to an inability to think anyone (except, perhaps, Yamagata Aritomo) entirely evil.

In such a hostile situation she might have been unusually vulnerable to paternalistic figures. However, even much earlier when she told her 'story', Suga seems to have assumed a degree of understanding that was not always forthcoming. Betrayal of women by men is a theme that runs throughout Suga's constructions of life whether in her early writings or her prison texts, even if she did mention exceptions like Sakai Toshihiko. First there was her father: if he did not fail *her*, there is still the father in 'Omokage' who betrayed both dead mother and family by bringing his evil and cruel geisha mistress into the house improperly soon after the mother's death; and the father in 'Tsuyuko' who 'sold' her. Then, if we can take Arahata at his word, there was Mōri's offer of 'marriage' to Suga, and Arahata's own role in the 'love incident'. Finally, there was Kōtoku's attempt while in prison at a reconciliation with his wife.

It was probably as early as 1902 that Suga decided that she would no longer be a passive victim. Even her account of the destruction of Ōitako's purity by two men must have been a calculated attempt to change the ways in which she and other women were treated. Later she depicted more of life's bitter realities both when she wrote of 'conceit', hypocrisy and a view of women as commodities in a 'world of men', and when she described prison conditions or treated her readers to an account of her life at the Heiminsha headquarters with Kōtoku and their avid audience: both the police across the road having their 'garden-party', and 'socialist' moral critics.

When Suga ascribed meaning to life, through her telling of chapters of her own story, or that of a Suga look-alike, she often represented life as a fight against social iniquities and, increasingly, state power. Power was mainly personified in the figures of various types of patriarchs – men who brutalized, exploited, or ultimately betrayed women, and also the government, police, prosecutors, and judges who both patronized and persecuted their 'children' in the name of the emperor. Suga was a social being, and she was not alone in painting a picture of life in late Meiji as an *escalating* fight against power. Her early works, however, do not suggest that she then saw a struggle against power as life's *defining* characteristic. If her metaphor for life was 'struggle', it was particularly so from mid-1908, though there hints of such a representation from 1906.

The picture of Kanno Suga in 1910–1911 became the one most committed to historical memory, and this has tended to cloud other, earlier pictures. This has obvious implications for the biographer: for in some ways, Suga the moral reformer was still present in Suga the free lover, just as Suga the 'direct actionist' (or, rather, socialist *shishi*) can be detected in the earlier impatient reformist; Suga the Christian, moreover, might still have had some influence upon the traitor who was unable in the end to hate those who posed a mortal threat to her. Clearly, working from preconceptions about a lineal ideational progression (from moral reformer to women's emancipationist to reformist feminist-socialist to revolutionary anarchist) makes it difficult to come to terms with the complex, many-centred Kanno Suga at any given point in time. However long one gazes at the snapshot of Suga as she was last known, one will never 'know' the Suga of 1906, of 1902 or, most of all, of her earlier years. Yet what can be known is that however many adult Sugas there were, there was one who consistently countered what she saw to be ideological representations of life, and was not prepared to resign herself either to them or to a personal destiny determined by others.

8　Kaneko Fumiko (1922–1926)

TEXTS AND CONTEXTS

Accounts of Kaneko Fumiko's life have been based almost entirely on her memoirs; authors have seldom utilized other prison documents such as her testimonies extensively or to good effect, more rarely still put to use those of people called as witnesses during the trial. This notwithstanding, neither the nature of her immediate audience nor the extraordinary context of her writing has prevented scholars from taking her story of life at face value.[1] They have not asked what she meant by answering Judge Tatematsu's question about how she came to nihilism with a detailed life-story – and then, at his suggestion, following up with an even more detailed written version.

In order to make sense of Fumiko's construction of life when in prison, one must reflect on what she was *doing* when she told her life story or in other ways knowingly presented a view of reality that did not accord with that of her political opponents. One thing she was doing was saying to figures of authority, and not just judges and prosecutors: 'It was you who made me like this!' She illustrated her point about how oppressively unequal a society Taishō Japan was by using her own lived experience as evidence; it was one of the few weapons against state and society available to her after her arrest on 3 September 1923. Thus, one cannot forget that the ways in which Fumiko ascribed meaning to her own life and to life itself were inseparable from the immediate context in which she interpreted them. Impending death in a sense determined her ascription of meaning to her life, and this, moreover, was a death that would be inflicted by the state. So there are various reasons for the need not to treat Fumiko's life-construct as 'the Truth' in empiricist style, but to accept it merely as her (1923–1926) truth. Emphasizing that reality is partial is not to say that her discursive representations were entirely individual, however, that she did not perceive reality in a similar way to others because of shared experience (class, gender, ethnicity) or current situation.

An epistemological concern with the ever-changing, dialectical interplay between an individual's context and texts, situation and actions should lead one to ask questions about whether Fumiko would have acted in exactly the same way before and after being arrested (or sentenced). Would she have told her story in the same way if her final clash with society and state power had not come about? Almost certainly, she would not. Yet to say that the story she told must have been selective – 'partial' in both senses of the word – is not to say that she was consciously practising a deception. In the mid-1920s she probably believed that someone both with her experience of life and an ability to see through ideological deceptions would finally see state and society through the eyes of a 'nihilist'.

The irony about the life-story that Fumiko presented (in a prison cell or courtroom drama), moreover, is that biographers intent on demonstrating even its plausibility need not rely only on her account. Compared to Suga's case where only a few intimates participated in a public construction of her life and its meaning, with Fumiko many witnesses called to testify at the pretrial in the District Court supplied information about her background.[2] That Judge Tatematsu was so much more interested in Fumiko's personal background (her pitiable story) than officials in the former case is itself an indication of the further development of an emperor-system based upon the hegemonic 'family-state' ideology of harmony, benevolence and paternalism. And one rare, positive result of this 'familial' affection on the part of Tatematsu is that the researcher interested in Fumiko's personal–political career has access not only to the testimonies of other Futeisha members or defendants, but also to witness interrogation records from her acquaintances, former employers and family members. So it might first be noted that the testimonies by members of her family (particularly her mother and maternal grandmother) generally verified the 'facts' of the story that Fumiko told about her childhood and upbringing.[3]

In this chapter where I first discuss the life-story Fumiko narrated in her memoir and early testimonies, the witness interrogation records are also utilized. This is not to verify the 'truth' of her life-story, but rather to help interpret it or to provide supplementary contextual information about the episodes in her life she discussed. More importantly, at times this brings into sharper relief the degree to which her presentation of her story and representation of life were oppositional constructs: representations of social reality that differed, for example, from her father's. One would not expect Fumiko and her father to tell the same story; indeed, for her he symbolized the common authoritarian, hypocritical, paternalistic ideas that she set out to counter. In that connection I should also emphasize that the witness and other interrogation records reveal quite a lot about the patriarchal rituals that were going on in court – the judge's 'fatherly' performance of benevolence, for example, in looking for details in Fumiko's past that, ostensibly at least, were to be used in her defence.[4] (As for Fumiko herself, however, while she was clearly using her life-story as a defence in the sense that she insisted that she was partly the product of family and society, she also demanded that the judge find her guilty.) Some of those rituals in court and interrogation rooms, moreover, will be looked at again in the closing section of the chapter where I consider further what Fumiko's, Pak's and other Futeisha testimonies reveal about the trial itself and the question of her 'treasonous' (and, by extension, her 'treacherous') intent. Finally, use of these testimonies can also help one avoid repeating the *pseudonyms* Fumiko used for family and acquaintances in her original manuscript.

We already know that Fumiko from 1923, much like Suga late in her life, came to present herself as having been a continual struggle against power. This is not surprising, since she was now in the midst of what was likely to be her final clash with it. Her adult worldview, which she summed up with the word 'nihilism', Fumiko presented as the sum of her life experience; and on more than one occasion she explicitly insisted, in the fashion of Artzibashev, that her way of seeing the world and human existence had not come from books but from life itself. More than once she emphasized that amongst the things that had made her what she was first and foremost her family situation. She was scathing about her parents in her second court interrogation where she ended with a denouncement of social demands for filial piety. How could she be filial, indeed, to people from whom she had never received parental love, who had never been real parents to her? It was in her penultimate remark on that day (17 January 1924) that she insisted that she did not bear a 'grudge' against her parents for all the pain and hardship they had caused her, but because of that long period of hardship she had come to 'curse nature, society and all that lives, [and] want to die, annihilating everything'.[5] Part II revealed one Fumiko, the 'amoralist' critic of conventional morality, but when looking at the way in which she sometimes sat in judgement of her parents' moral laxity, we find that she was not entirely consistent in this.

Before turning to the 'family portrait' painted by Fumiko and comparing and contrasting it with others, however, we need to pause over the few brief pre-prison texts that remain to us, and consider what they suggest about how she presented life in 1922–1923 (before her imprisonment) to an audience presumed to be actual or potential social 'malcontents': Korean or Japanese radicals, whether independence activists, anarchists, syndicalists, nihilists or communists. By the time Fumiko started to publish the occasional article in the spring of 1922, she had already been in Tokyo for two years, so we also need to consider how this busy metropolis would have looked in the early 1920s to a struggling, self-supporting student who, according to her own account later, had been developing into a bit of a rebel for quite some time. If so, we would expect her soon to come into contact with the socialist community and that she did, apparently, almost as soon as she arrived.

1922–1923

The Meiji High Treason Incident had brought left-wing activity virtually to a standstill but, as Suga had forecast, in a few years Japanese socialism did 'bloom' again after its *fuyu no jidai* (winter period). In the atmosphere of shock at the sentences, some anarchists and state socialists ceased political activity altogether while others went into quasi-retirement. The anarchist magazine *Kindai Shisō* (*Modern Thought*), for example, was published in the guise of a purely literary journal by Ōsugi Sakae and Arahata Kanson from 1912.[6] Their radicalism was concealed within articles ostensibly only about aesthetics, philosophy and literary theory.[7] During the First World War, however, there was a spontaneous resurgence of organized labour, and within the more liberal environment after 1911 when Saionji Kinmochi again became prime minister, even anarcho-syndicalist unions began organizing. In 1917 anarchists formed an industrial union of printing and metal workers, the Shin'yūkai (Faithful Friends' Society), which was followed two years later by another anarchist printing union, the Seishinkai (True Progress Association).[8] Groups of like-minded comrades also formed study groups like the Hokufūkai (North Wind Society).

The general trend by 1919 toward radicalism both within and without the labour movement was accompanied by the creation of several anarchistic papers and organizations. Around this time anarchist activities included the publication of *Rōdō Undō* (*Labour Movement*) by Ōsugi, Kondō Kenji, Wada Kyūtarō and others; and also the establishment of the Tōkyō Rōdō Undō Dōmeikai (Tokyo Labour Movement League). Anarchists participated in a broad united front of socialists, the Nihon Shakaishugi Dōmei (Japan Socialist League), while some like Iwasa Sakutarō and Furuta Daijirō later formed their own organizations like the Kosakuninsha (Tenant Farmers' League).[9] The intense interest on the Left in the various streams of anarchism was also reflected in non-anarchist journals and papers. Students of Tokyo Imperial University had established the Shinjinkai (New People's Society) in 1919, and before long the Society's magazine contained articles on the thought of Kropotkin, Sorel and Stirner.[10] Before long anarchist women, too, were organizing, for example in the Sekirankai (Red Wave Society) of the early 1920s. Anarchism was virtually the only prominent radical doctrine until 1922 when the Japan Communist Party was formed. This, therefore, was the same year that the government reacted to the 'twin evils' of anarchism and communism by introducing the Law to Control Radical Social Movements. This bill was ultimately replaced by the more stringent Peace Preservation Law of 1925, after which repression of the Left again became severe.

To social misfits and malcontents

By the time Fumiko wrote the few short articles I will consider here, she apparently already saw herself as a nihilist.[11] In *Kokutō* (*Black Wave*) of August 1922 there are two articles by her; and she is referred to elsewhere in this and later publications as 'Pak Fumiko', a name she obviously used then and later to make a political statement.[12] This was a magazine put out by mainly Korean comrades who were a mixed group of socialists led by Pak Yeol. Fumiko explained in one of her interrogations that the Kokutōkai, established in the autumn of 1921, soon split into an anarchist and a communist faction named the Kokuyūkai (Black Friends Society) and the Hokuseikai (North Star Society), respectively. This paralleled the inevitable rivalry between libertarian and state socialists (both social democratic and Marxist–Leninist) that intensified with the formation of the Japan Communist Party in 1922.

Thus, the time at which Fumiko said she had become committed to anarcho-nihilism was a period of intense rivalry between anarchists and Marxists: the '*ana-boru*' (anarchist–bolshevik) split. Excited by the Russian Revolution and convinced that Marxism–Leninism represented the 'science of successful revolution', some Japanese anarchists and syndicalists converted to communism prior to the establishment of the Party; others moved camp after communists began to make some headway in the labour movement. Yet Ōsugi well expressed the scepticism amongst anarchists about communist motives for participation in any 'united front': their desire merely to exploit it and seize leadership.[13] Hence, many retained their suspicion of 'authoritarian' socialism and centralism and their commitment to libertarian ideals and modes of organization. Printing workers were not only in the forefront of some of the earliest anarchist labour struggles, but were also among the most enduring of Japan's militant prewar unionists.[14] It was as a member of the Seishinkai that Ōsugi spoke when on 15 October 1920 he reported on the outcome of a printers' strike. No doubt he had been one of the organizers, or he would not have felt a need to apologize to the rank and file for their defeat.[15] From 1920 or so, the Seishinkai and Shin'yūkai were increasingly influenced by Ōsugi, who became one of the most vocal opponents of the combined social-democratic and communist push to rid the social-democratic labour federation (Sōdōmei) of anarchist influence.[16] Thomas Stanley cites Ōsugi's insistence that workers' organizations be based on 'the principles of autonomy, self-government, and an absolute right to join or withdraw from an association at any time'. The right of the rank-and-file to make their own decisions regarding whether, when, and how to act in labour struggles was sacred to anarchists and syndicalists. Ultimately, however, state socialism won the battle in Sōdōmei. By early in 1923, anarchist influence in Sōdōmei was effectively neutralized; and thereafter libertarian unionists remained in their own associations, organizing independently. Some anarchists continued for a few years to participate in other areas together with state socialists – in the proletarian arts movement, for example, at least until communists engineered their expulsion.[17]

By May 1922 Fumiko and Pak had begun living and working politically together. Niiyama Hatsuyo testified that she visited Fumiko at home on 15 May 1922 but found that she had moved out. Soon a letter came from Fumiko asking her to visit her in Shibuya in Tokyo where Fumiko was living with Pak; they were organizing a nihilist-anarchist group and producing a magazine.[18] According to Fumiko later, the object of the group had been to promote fraternity between like-minded Koreans and Japanese and propagate radical thinking.[19]

What we find written by Fumiko in the first paper, *Kokutō*, are a couple of short works of interest, one of which is a quite cynical piece on Korean 'assimilation'.[20] Fumiko insisted on various occasions that she had never wanted to work merely for the goal of Korean independence, and the fact that she was involved with a group of anarchists and nihilists in 1922–1923 does suggest this. Articles in *Kokutō* do not necessarily reflect it, though Fumiko later explained in a testimony that the magazines they produced then had been deliberately 'moderate'. In this particular article in *Kokutō* Fumiko related how one 'illustrious promoter' of the assimilation of Koreans had argued in humanistic fashion that Koreans and Japanese shared the same ancestors, and the two races should therefore be on good terms. She pointed out that in elementary school everyone had learned that humanity had descended from apes; and then went on (a trifle irrationally) to ask Japanese assimilationists, who argued that both races shared the same historical ancestors, if they would be prepared to be clasped in an embrace by an ape and danced with, or if they would be happy to sit down at the same table and eat with apes. Then she insisted scornfully that those who were so 'showy' in 'parading their love of humanity' needed first to transform Japanese colonists in Korea into humans before Koreans there could assimilate with them. Japanese creditors, for example, who pretended to be the 'bosom buddies' of Koreans, were not above literally torturing Korean debtors to retrieve money lent at interest rates ten times higher than usual. Fumiko concluded her article by explicitly commenting on the ideological deception of Japanese 'humanistic' paternalism with regards Koreans, by recommending that if nothing could be done to give Koreans some humans to assimilate with, this 'gilded signboard' (saying 'assimilation', presumably) with its thin veneer of gold, already peeling, might as well be pulled down.

After Korea was annexed in 1910 and Japanese colonists had migrated there in increasing numbers, the colonial government did indeed attempt to 'assimilate' the two cultures: colonists turned most of the indigenous population into a huge lower caste, and later tried to suppress the Korean language and destroy Korean ethnic identity.[21] According to Lee and de Vos, by 1940 Japanese colonists numbered 700,000 or 3 per cent of Korea's population. The low social status of Koreans is illustrated by the figures they give for the number of ordinary labourers among Koreans in employment: 95 per cent of men and 99 per cent of women. The migration of Japanese people to Korea was paralleled by another of Koreans to Japan, and despite the fact that Koreans became an oppressed minority there, as many as 400,000 migrated in the decade following the First World War.[22] There were thousands of Korean students in Tokyo and, like Korean workers, they were natural candidates for radical organizations.[23]

Fumiko's second article in *Kokutō* was on nutrition, which might seem to be a rather unlikely subject.[24] Essentially, however, she was attacking bourgeois philanthropists for poking about where they were not wanted: in the diet of the masses! (Not literally perhaps, because she was sceptical about whether this nutritionist, Dr Saeki, had 'ever so much as peeped at the kitchens of the fourth estate'.) The bourgeoisie had a tiresome tendency to interfere, firstly because they needed something to do to stave off ennui; only secondly because they were concerned that the working classes did not get enough nourishment. Pity they couldn't be more quiet about their good works, thought Fumiko. She was every bit as scornful here as in her other piece about assimilation. Proudly admitting that in their circle they were lucky to get three simple meals a day, she added that they did not get invited to banquets at mansions where they could stuff themselves like these people who harped on 'nutrition'. 'We proletarians don't want to be saved by the lily-white hands of the upper class,' she insisted in anarchist style, 'We will continue to demand freedom and equality for ourselves. With our own hands we will do our damndest to liberate ourselves.'

It was in November 1922, a month or two after the anarchist Kokuyūkai had been formed, that Fumiko, Pak and friends put out the first issue of a magazine entitled *Futoi Senjin* (*Cheeky Koreans* in Chinese characters, but also written in kana as '*Futei* [rebel, lawless or malcontent] *Senjin*'). Either way, it was meant to be a parody of Japanese attitudes toward Korean 'trouble-makers'. Fumiko explained in a testimony that they had decided to use the more innocuous characters for 'futoi' (meaning audacious, bold, or cheeky, etc.) when they imagined how the officials in charge of censorship would probably react to the title by exclaiming, 'Futoi yatsura da!' ('Cheeky scoundrels!'). They had wanted the magazine to appear 'innocuous' and intended its contents to be 'harmless' because it was intended as a 'front' to mask their underground ('direct action') activities.[25] She remarked that the public still did not like the title and would not buy the magazine, so because of their need for funds in order to buy bombs they changed the title again to the even more moderate *Genshakai* (*Today's Society*) after the second issue. (The last issue was the fourth, published in June 1923.) They also needed to attract advertisers because advertisements in the magazine were likely to be their real source of funds.[26] While it is possible that actual advertisements in the paper, for example, for the Mitsukoshi department store, were due to (anarchist 'plunder': *ryaku*) extortion on their part,[27] they appear to have wanted to attract advertisers by legitimate means rather than with threats of reprisals if they refused.

It was the Futeisha they secretly established to carry out 'direct action'; and this Fumiko later defined as rebelling against all power or 'making trouble for you officials'.[28] There is some doubt about precisely when the Futeisha was established, since a couple of the defendants gave the date as the middle of 1922 while Fumiko said its *formal* establishment had been in mid-April 1923. Fumiko and Pak had specifically decided to propagate more 'moderate' anarchist thought in *Futei Senjin*, because the Futeisha were part of the 'above-ground' anarchist Kokuyūkai. Tactically, there were differences, but ideological lines were not always clearly drawn between the two overlapping groups. Well-known anarchists like Ōsugi Sakae lectured at Kokuyūkai meetings, and thus it was probably partly because the Futeisha were all assumed to be 'anarchists' that they came increasingly under surveillance by the police. (Fumiko often seemed irritated by the judge's ignorance about nihilism, and the differences between that and anarchism.) But, of course, Pak and his radical *Korean* associates had long been watched by the police, whether or not they were anarchists. The first sign that police were closing in was at the end of August 1923 when officers visited and questioned Niiyama Hatsuyo, who first implicated Pak in some sort of anti-imperial plot. The reason for their visit was a rumour circulating in the socialist movement that Pak had sent a comrade named Harazawa Takenosuke to Korea to procure bombs. Fumiko, also, soon admitted to various attempts to get bombs.[29] Harazawa had been a friend of Fumiko's since 1921, it seems, because one of the witnesses called to give testimony said that Harazawa, then in the Gyōminkai (a proto-communist party), had recommended her for a job in his restaurant.[30]

The title these 'cheeky/lawless/malcontent' Koreans chose for their magazine seems ill-advised, though it is only with hindsight that one can see that doing so placed them in danger from sources other than police. No-one could have foreseen the massacre of Koreans and Chinese by police and civilian mobs after the Great Kanto Earthquake of 1 September 1923. By the night after the earthquake which devastated the Kanto area, many unfounded rumours had spread, partly due to the efforts of ultra-rightists.[31] There were tales of Koreans setting fires, poisoning wells, rioting, killing Japanese men and raping Japanese women. They were said to have bombed department stores which had burned down in the aftermath of the earthquake, and it was even claimed that an invasion was being planned from the mainland. Paranoia was rife. On 2 September, the 'respectable' Tokyo

Mainichi Shinbun actually added its voice to the rumours, blaring out headlines that the government had *ordered* the killing of Koreans. Yet the smaller print which quoted government sources read: 'Koreans and socialists [are] planning a rebellion and treacherous plot. We urge the citizens to co-operate with the military and police to guard against Koreans.'[32] Then the government declared martial law and sent 70,000 soldiers into the city to control the expected riots. What followed was a bloodbath. Soldiers, police, vigilante groups and mobs of hysterical civilians butchered anyone 'different', and the number of Korean dead has been estimated as over 6000 in the Kanto area alone.[33] There were also a few hundred Chinese victims. Doubtless the Futeisha were arrested so quickly because already under police surveillance, and they were fortunate to survive both the hysteria on the streets and their protective custody.

An examination of *Futei/Futoi Senjin* gives some idea of how Fumiko represented life in the year before her arrest; it also gives an indication of whether it was the content of the magazine that had made police more interested in the Futeisha. The group had intended it to appear 'harmless' probably because they knew that any Korean group would be watched by the authorities. Hence, in the first issue Pak scoffed at the misconception in Japan that 'malcontent Koreans' were people who conspired to commit assassinations and wreak destruction.[34] But it is certain that the fine distinctions either he or Fumiko made between radical (nihilist) thinking and 'moderation' would have been lost on the authorities. Certainly, in the third issue (March 1923) there was quite a bit censored, presumably self-censorship before publication, and much of it had been written by 'Kaneko Fumi' – two entire articles, one two pages long. The long article was entitled 'To You Koreans in Japan'; and one still can read enough of the other to see that it was commemorating the March 1919 anti-Japanese riots in Korea, the 'March First Movement'.[35] It was entitled 'Anniversary of the Korean [blank, blank]' (probably 'revolution' since blanks were used for this elsewhere) and the second para started with something about 'March 1919'. One can decipher a few words like 'Manchurian troops', 'clamour', 'armed might', 'resistance', 'bravery', and finally that 'over seventy detainees were released'. It was also dated 2 March 1923. Fumiko's texts would not have seemed so 'harmless' to the authorities.

Otherwise, there were some editorial-like pieces entitled 'Yabureta Shōji kara'. It is unclear what 'From the Torn Sliding Door' signified, unless simply the shabby lodgings in which Fumiko and Pak lived.[36] These were generally written by Fumiko. In the second issue in late

December she noted that Pak had returned from a trip to Korea unwell, which meant that she was late getting the manuscript to the printers. She wished comrades well for the New Year, expressed her desire that they all work hard for the movement in 1923, and reminded them that it was open-house at their place on Sundays. In the second of these 'editorials', she reported on less happy circumstances, however, explaining the reasons for their not being able to publish the magazine between March and June 1923. Not long before May Day, Pak and a few other Korean comrades had been released from prison in very bad condition: one had nearly lost his sight in one eye, another was limping badly, one had terrible bruises all over his back, and Pak had been coughing up blood and was disoriented. They had been arrested in the first place for engaging in what they saw to be 'direct action' – beating up a Korean 'fake communist' collaborator – and had also tried to retaliate when police began to 'terrorize' them. Later Fumiko herself was arrested at the May Day demonstration and spent a night in jail wrapped in a blanket with a few comrades and many more fleas.

Fumiko wrote two other pieces, one each in the December and June issues, expressing her opposition to Japanese imperialism and prejudice against Koreans. Unfortunately, parts of both are illegible, but the one in the June issue is a conversation between 'S' and 'F' (Fumiko, no doubt) where 'S' expresses the opinion that, unlike Japanese people, Koreans have bad habits such as not being frugal. For example, they waste their money on food [*sic*].[37] 'F' responds that *if* so, it would not be unreasonable because the best way to keep one's money to oneself is to keep it in the stomach. From here the conversation jumps to conscripting Koreans into the Japanese army, presumably topical because some politicians had argued for it. 'S' asserts that this would damage Japanese culture, the suggestion being that Koreans are inherently inferior. 'F' retorts in disgust that compared to the other speaker even Japanese politicians are wonderful (*erai*), apparently because they at least do not see Koreans as so culturally polluting (of Japan's unique cultural purity) that they cannot be conscripted.

In the December issue of *Futei Senjin* Fumiko had written one more longish piece entitled 'So-called "Malcontent Koreans"?' in which she defined what the term meant to her.[38] Its common usage in newspapers and magazines notwithstanding, its true meaning was rebelling against Japanese imperialism. After pointing out the hypocrisy of people who would regard Koreans as brave and noble if they fought with Japanese imperialists against a common enemy like China or Russia or Western

Europe – even if it meant killing innocent civilians including the aged, and women and children – she concluded with the remark that 'revenge' was the only way for the subjugated. So long as Korea's situation remained what it was, there would always be people (like themselves) who would fight back: Japanese imperialism would always give rise to 'rebel Koreans'. If this is an example of Fumiko's 'moderation', it is not difficult to see why the police would have been watching the Futeisha. Apart from the dozen or so 'malcontents' in this group who were all too vocal in their ingratitude for Japan's paternal protection, there was also at least one Japanese national who spoke out as an eye-witness to Japan's 'benevolent' colonial administration of Korea.

1923–1926

For judges and other 'parents'

The Preface and Postscript to Fumiko's memoirs appear to have been produced between 25 March 1926, the day she was sentenced to death, and 23 July 1926, the day of her death. In the Preface she made a remark about wanting to ask Tatematsu to give the manuscript back to her; it was no further use to him, she explained, now that the trial was over. Thus, her memoirs must have been written between the beginning of 1924 and mid-1925 because Tatematsu used them in the pretrial. Fumiko's preface opened with a reference to the horrors that followed the earthquake.[39] Then she mentioned the rumours and violence that preceded their arrests, and followed with an account of her first meeting with Judge Tatematsu. Explaining about how he had started to question her about her background, and how he had asked her to write something more about it, she ended with the above-mentioned dedication to comrades, parents, teachers and politicians.

She did not actually give her date of birth, probably for good reason, for she was not sure of when it had been. We can be reasonably certain, however, that 25 January was not only the day on which Suga died in 1911, but also the day on which Fumiko had been born, in 1903. The fact that she was born 'illegitimate' has led to confusion about when she was born, so much so that one can find in the sources any year between 1902 and 1907 given as her year of birth.[40] Her birth was not officially recorded until she was eight years old, and the record then falsified: she was entered into the Register of Families as the legitimate child of her maternal grandparents, born on 25 January 1902. But the most reliable information about her date of birth came from her parents. In 1925 on different occasions they agreed, though they had been separated for about fifteen years, that she had been born in a year of the rabbit and was thus 21.[41] Her father added that her date of birth was therefore 25 January 1903; and 1903 was in fact a rabbit-year. The most common date given in the sources is probably the one that Fumiko herself gave (January 1904). Yet, apart from the fact that all this confusion underscores her early lack of registration, what is most noteworthy about it is that during her interrogations she was fond of taking the opportunity to sneer at officialdom about the inaccuracy and thus meaninglessness of their records.

I

> At six I learned
> prematurely
> the sadness of life.[42]

Social discrimination was one of the main themes in Fumiko's story of her life. Concerning the first part of her life, discussed under the title of 'Father', she indicated that it was due largely to Saeki Fumikazu's selfishness and snobbishness in refusing to marry her mother that she came to be treated as a 'non-person'. (By the time she was writing her memoirs she and her father were completely estranged.) It was still common then for women not to be registered as legal wives until they had produced a male heir, and if the marital union was never made legal, children would usually be registered under the mother's name as illegitimate. But Fumiko was not so critical of the fact that her parents had not been married; it was more that her father's pride had caused her to suffer discrimination as a *musekisha* (unregistered person).

As for her mother, it should first be noted that her real name was Kikuno. Fumiko used pseudonyms for family and others discussed in her original manuscript.[43] Officially, her name had been recorded as 'Kie', but she explained in court that she had always been known as 'Kikuno'. Thus, Fumiko was born the eldest child of Kaneko Kikuno and Saeki Fumikazu.[44] Her parents had met in Kikuno's village, Suwa, in the Enzan area of Yamanashi Prefecture.[45] To Kikuno, the illiterate daughter of a peasant family, this eldest son of a military officer from a samurai family in Hiroshima must indeed have seemed like 'a young lord'. The couple eloped and settled in Yokohama where Fumiko was born two years later. Kikuno testified in 1925 that by the time their relationship had become the subject of local gossip, she was also afraid that she had conceived a child. Saeki saw it differently, testifying that he could not bring himself to register Kikuno as his legal wife because their common-law marriage had been founded on the 'cold-blooded lie' that she was pregnant.[46]

In Fumiko's eyes it was her father's selfishness and pride that prevented him from marrying Kikuno for the sake of his children, and to this picture of his character she added other qualities like brutality and debauchery. Like Suga, Fumiko painted this unflattering picture of her father fully aware of the importance in conventional morality and family-state ideology of filial piety, particularly toward the legal head of the family. Her irreverence extended from denouncing her father as 'bestial' in her memoirs to elsewhere dismissing the supreme father-figure of the nation, the emperor, as a mere '[mental] patient'. It was common knowledge that the Taishō emperor suffered from mental illness, so referring to him as the '*byōnin*' (invalid, a sick or feeble person) was probably a snide reference to this.[47]

Fumiko was happy to paint Fumikazu as a proud and affectionate father at first, though she claimed he caused dissension in the family when he brought a young woman into the house. It was from this time that her father began physically to abuse her mother (and, when Fumiko tried to help her, herself).[48] She also remembered being taken to see him at a place she later realized must have been a brothel, implying that Fumikazu had also been responsible for the family's poverty. He gambled, and was too proud to work in most occupations. Kikuno actually testified to her opposition to the presence in the house of this young woman, and also spoke of how he used to waste his money gambling in the red light district.[49] Later again, there was another addition to the family when Kikuno's younger sister, Takano, came to the city for medical treatment.[50] Fumiko wrote that Takano's presence created tension in the house once more – and Kikuno, her mother, Sehi, and Saeki all backed up Fumiko's story that the two had soon become lovers. But needless to say, their assessments of this polygamy differed. For Sehi, Saeki Fumikazu was a 'scoundrel' who had 'abducted' both her daughters; he, on the other hand, believed he had been justified in being sexually intimate with Takano because he and his wife had not been getting along for some time. For Fumiko, the reality of the situation was that he was a spoiled, selfish lecher.[51] Grandmother Sehi once came to Yokohama to try to take Takano home to Suwa to be married respectably (rather than being a 'concubine'), but she was described by Fumiko as 'an ignorant woman from a farm in the country', and no match for Fumikazu, a 'cunning city person'. One of Fumikazu's arguments at the time was that Takano was too frail to be a farmer's wife, so he would arrange a marriage for her in the city. He testified in 1925 that he actually had tried to do this.[52]

In some senses, the adult Fumiko and her mother looked back over their lives and painted a very similar picture of their experiences. Certainly, for both, Saeki Fumikazu had been the main villain in the piece. Hauled before a judge of whom she must have been in awe, Kikuno seldom contradicted her daughter's story, even when it reflected badly on herself. But this is not to say that she was ready to defend Fumiko if she felt she had done something 'wrong'; the fact that in some respects the two agreed on certain events in their lives does not mean that they always interpreted their shared past or the society they lived in similarly. For example, Kikuno told the judge that when she believed that Fumiko had been killed in the earthquake she thought it for the best because, while she loved her daughter, 'her ideas had become quite twisted'.[53] Still, each told the same story about one occasion when Kikuno was badly beaten by Fumikazu for 'embarrassing' him in front of his friends by asking for money for food while he was gambling.[54] There were only minor differences in the two accounts, and it is likely that Fumiko was merely repeating what she heard from her mother later about this instance of domestic violence or other episodes in her life. The two were separated about two years after this incident, and Fumiko saw little of her mother after that.

Fumiko also wrote a poem in which she refers to Fumikazu's fierce temper:

> Sad legacy
> to me from Father:
> my quick-spoken, quick-tempered nature.[55]

No doubt it was also a cynical reference to the one and only 'inheritance' she – who was never legally recognized and even 'disinherited' as an adult – received from her father. Saeki was asked by the judge if he had threatened to disinherit his daughter for destroying the name of the family by living with a 'base Korean'; and he replied that it was true.[56] This was intimately connected with what Fumiko deemed to be his exaggerated notions of his family's social superiority. He had in his possession the family genealogy which traced his family back over a millenium to Fujiwara Fusasaki – the Fujiwara having been court nobles and, in late Heian, imperial regents – was thus regarded by him as a sacred treasure. Perhaps this was an added reason for Fumiko's scorn for the imperial family, even explicitly the (supposedly unbroken) imperial descent from the gods. It was Fumikazu's habit every morning to line the family up and insist on their making a deep obeisance to this Saeki genealogy. Especially later, when Fumiko was 16 and briefly reunited with her father again, she said he would try to impress upon her how fortunate she was to be descended from such an illustrious family. But she had never been fortunate enough to be officially registered as such, Fumiko said it was painful for her to be forced to venerate her *father's* ancestors. This practice also seemed to her to reflect aspects of his character for which she clearly had the deepest contempt: his pride, pretentiousness, snobbery and vanity.[57] In the early 1970s Fumiko's biographer, Setouchi Harumi, was shown this genealogy by the wife of Takatoshi, Fumiko's younger brother (Kikuno's son). Though Fumikazu had eventually registered Takano as his wife and Takatoshi as his son (in 1916 or 1917), still the genealogy ended with Fumikazu. Fumiko wrote in her memoirs that she heard from her aunt, Takano, much later that he had never wanted to register Kikuno, which suggested to Fumiko that the 'daughter of a peasant' was not good enough for a Saeki. And even if Fumikazu did legally marry her younger sister, the fact that neither Takano nor his son appeared in the genealogy bears this out.[58]

Fumikazu and Kikuno had lived together for more than eight years by the time he left (probably in 1909), surreptitiously, according to both Fumiko and Kikuno. Kikuno testified that he had told her he was going to visit the police chief in Shizuoka in the hope of obtaining a position as a policeman. She also said she went about looking for him until she discovered where he and Takano were hiding.[59] But it was before this time that Fumiko had begun to feel the effects of being unregistered. Of that time, she wrote:

> I wanted to go to school with my two friends, but I could not. I wanted to be able to read books and write characters, but Father and Mother did not teach me even one letter! Father did not care, and Mother was illiterate.[60]

But her father came home one day with the news that he had found a school for her. It was a sorry sort of school in one room of a house in a slum area, but Fumiko was ecstatic to be allowed to attend. Her joy was short-lived, however, because even the customary small gift for the teacher (in lieu of payment) was beyond the family's means, so she soon stopped attending. According to Fumiko's account, both her unregistered status and their poverty continued to interfere with her schooling. Kikuno had kept silent, it seems, about not being Fumikazu's registered wife, but once her child began to pester her about going to school, she wanted to register her as a Kaneko. Fumikazu would not allow it, however, and berated Kikuno: 'You fool! Report her as illegitimate? As illegitimate she'd never be able to hold up her head in life!'[61]

The next instalment of the life that Fumiko presented was entitled 'Mother'. When Fumikazu disappeared not long after the birth of their second child, Takatoshi, Kikuno was apparently forced to feed herself and the children by pawning what little personal property they had. Fumiko wrote that from her father there was no word (for several weeks), much less financial assistance. Fumikazu admitted in 1925 that he had sent the family no money while he was away, but protested that he had not 'abandoned' them and gone into hiding. His story was a little different from that told by Fumiko and Kikuno. He had not sent them money, he said, because three weeks later when he returned with Takano, Kikuno was already living with another man. He and Takano therefore returned to Hamamatsu in Shizuoka after a few days.[62] Kikuno had in fact allowed a man to move in with them to help out financially, but it seems that Fumiko took an instant dislike to him and he returned the sentiment, finding ever more inventive ways of dealing with this 'cheeky' child. The judge asked Kikuno whether the man Fumiko named 'Nakamura' had once gagged and bound Fumiko and left her dangling from a tree at a river's edge after she had gone out, and Kikuno's response was revealing: 'Since it was after I'd left, I don't know, but there was a river beside the house we lived in then . . .'[63]

Fumiko recalled overhearing not long after that her father had sent for the infant, Takatoshi. Her sadness at losing her brother abated a little, however, when she found that she would be going to school again. Because of Kikuno's persistence a school principal in the area had finally agreed to let her attend. This was a *real* school, unlike the previous one her father had sent her to: the 'school for social outcastes'.[64] But here she was struck by the contrast between her circumstances and that of the other students, many of whom had servants. Even after they moved house again and Kikuno had to fight to get her into another school with many more poor children, moreover, her 'outcaste' status trailed her. Again she remembered being either ignored or treated cruelly by the staff, recounting how once she was accused by the headmaster of stealing her monthly tuition fees out of the envelope she had handed to the teacher. Kikuno, however, blamed the theft on Nakamura both according to Fumiko and her own testimony.[65]

In this section Fumiko continued her narrative about the suffering her father had caused her, and also remarked on her mother's failings. Kikuno was a very 'dependent' sort of woman who could not survive without someone to rely on.[66] She 'just could not exist without a man'. (By this point in her narrative, she and her mother had left Nakamura.) The child Fumiko came to the conclusion, apparently, that men were trouble. The two barely managed to eke out an existence while Kikuno was working at a silk mill; but this 'solitary but intimate' lifestyle was soon ruined for Fumiko by another man named Kobayashi.[67] Though Kikuno was sure that they would be a lot more comfortable with Kobayashi supporting them, Fumiko had argued that he looked like a loafer. She also intimated that time had proved her right. Kikuno was asked during her interrogation whether she had cohabited with Nakamura and then Kobayashi after Saeki left her. She responded that she had, explaining that she had needed help to support her daughter. But both men turned out to be 'idle and useless', she added.[68]

Fumiko was not nearly as hard on her mother as she was on her father. Kikuno she portrayed as merely weak, selfish, and morally lax. The judge was interested in a story she told about how one night Kikuno was 'romping about unashamedly on the futon' with Kobayashi and sent her small daughter out into the 'scary', pitch-dark night on an errand to get rid of her; and Kikuno did not deny that this sort of thing happened. None the less, Fumiko was more inclined to try to balance the negative picture she presented of her mother, even if there was one crime for which she had clearly never forgiven her. The destitute family had already pawned almost all their 'commodities', when one day Kikuno took her daughter to an agent who dealt in geisha and prostitutes.[69] According to Fumiko, Kikuno *claimed* that she was hoping that through a career as a geisha, her child would have a chance to 'better herself'. It was only when she discovered that Fumiko would be sent to a place named Mishima (above the Izu Peninsula) that Kikuno backed out of the deal, lamenting that it was too far away. In narrating this story about almost being sold as a 'prostitute', Fumiko's moral (-political) indignation seemed to be connected with being treated as a 'commodity' to be sold into a 'slave trade'. She suggested that that the price offered Kikuno had simply not been high enough. But perhaps Kikuno did not like the idea of Mishima for another reason. Mishima is an *onsen* (hot springs resort) and, as Liza Dalby observes:

> The women of such resorts generally go by the name onsen geisha, a term with a derogatory ring and with overtones of sex for hire as well as low standards of artistic skill. . . . these geisha suffer a tarnished image in the popular imagination. . . . Onsen geisha is usually taken as a euphemism for prostitute.[70]

If Kikuno hoped that her daughter would become a geisha, she might not have seen Mishima as the sort of place for her to 'better herself'. Her expectation that Fumiko would be sent to a closer place suggests Tokyo, and geisha in Kyoto or Tokyo had the best reputations for refinement and artistry. She admitted that she had once tried to sell her daughter as a geisha, though she did not explain why she subsequently changed her mind.[71]

To avoid their creditors Kikuno, Kobayashi and Fumiko made their escape late one night. They found temporary lodgings on the outskirts of Yokohama in a cheap boarding house.[72] Fumiko's clearest memory of this period was of hunger and searching for food amongst garbage in the street, yet, to her impatience, Kikuno only bemoaned the 'predicament' (a pregnancy) that made it impossible for her to leave Kobayashi. Fumiko said she only realized much later that her mother had been pregnant then because she had asked Fumiko's playmates if they knew the whereabouts of a *Hōzuki* shrub (Winter Cherry, botanical name *Physalis Alkekengi*). Kikuno then took a piece of root home with her concealed in her sleeve, because it was believed to be an abortifacient. This suggestion of an attempted abortion was evidently part Fumiko's critique of her mother's selfishness in always putting her own needs before her children's. In her eyes Kikuno was ultimately guilty of abandoning all three of her children. After a short stay in Kobayashi's home village deep in the mountains of Northern Yamanashi Prefecture, Kikuno returned home to her family in Suwa with Fumiko, leaving the newborn baby named Haruko behind with its father. Most of Kobayashi's family had been happy about the birth of his first child, so it was decided that Kikuno and Fumiko could go so long as the baby remained in the village.[73] But Fumiko remembered being worried that something might happen to her baby sister, having implied that the possibility of infanticide had been raised.[74] She did not go so far as to represent her mother as completely heartless, however, noting that she was sobbing and reluctant to leave Haruko without feeding her one more time. But she wrote that she would never forget the wailing of her 'abandoned' little sister; and neither Fumiko nor Kikuno (as she said in court) ever heard whether the baby had survived.[75]

The didactic intent of Fumiko's memoirs is very clear in connection with her emphasis on the primitive *natural* existence in Kobayashi's mountain hamlet. Like Kropotkin, she basically extolled the virtues of mutual aid, advocated that farmers should be able to wear their *own* silk, and opposed the capitalist money economy. She waxed lyrical about the village's primitive barter economy.[76] The harsh but allegedly wholesome mountain existence was even a good influence on Kobayashi who, to Fumiko's amazement, *worked*, making charcoal to sell or barter. She also noted that the diet there was humble but healthy (better, she said, than prison food!). In general Fumiko idealized this healthy, natural existence, yet it was in connection with school that she raised one negative point about the village. Because her mother had not had enough charcoal to exchange for the customary present of sake for the teacher, Fumiko did not get her school certificate. Here even school certificates (and a prize for scholastic achievement in Fumiko's case) were 'bought', she seemed to be saying, perhaps suggesting that corruption could still exist even without money.[77]

The next event in this supposed child's-eye view of life – that is, the adult Fumiko's less than reverent account of parental character and authority – was about Kikuno's 'desertion' of her firstborn daughter. When they arrived in Suwa, Kikuno was sent by her family to a silk mill where she had worked as a girl.[78] One night Fumiko learned to her dismay that a marriage had been arranged for her mother. Kikuno would first go alone to join the household and return for Fumiko later, *if* it proved acceptable to her new husband. At this point Fumiko launched into a bitter attack on the parents of the world. She wrote that she felt like screaming a 'curse' at them because they loved and then discarded their children at their convenience.[79] Fumiko sometimes addressed her reader/s directly in a self-conscious way. Here she apologized to the reader for her excess of emotion, but insisted that her words well expressed the despair she felt at that time. She was not prepared to forgive this desertion, whatever extenuating circumstances there might have been. One of Kikuno's interrogations, however, suggests something about the pressures that she must have been under. She had caused her parents to 'lose face', she said, and indicated that it was due to family pressure then that she first went to work in a silk mill (where her health soon deteriorated) and then married again. When the judge asked her to comment on how 'Fumiko said that her mother only cared about herself and thus married into other families any number of times', she replied: 'I wasn't concerned about myself at all. It was unthinkable that I could stay at home, defy my parents and brother, and not marry.'[80] We would not expect them to interpret the episode in the same way, perhaps, but Fumiko was not always so unsympathetic toward her mother.

Fumiko resumed her studies once again in Suwa, and despite the usual discrimination, recalled that school was her 'only joy' because it filled the void left by her mother's departure. Although Kikuno did come to collect her not long after, the child did not like her mother's new husband, so soon demanded to return to Suwa. However, Kikuno told the judge that Fumiko was treated as a 'nuisance' by her new husband so she sent her home.[81] It was almost winter that same year, 1912, when her paternal grandmother, Saeki-Iwashita Mutsu, came to visit. Fumiko was surprised to learn that she was to be taken to Korea to be raised by her father's childless sister and her husband, and even become their legal heir. Mutsu had joined her daughter, Kameko, when she married Iwashita, a government official who had secured a position in Korea supervising the laying of railway tracks (probably the Seoul–Pusan line). It must have been at the end of 1912 that Fumiko was taken there because she was entered into the Kaneko Register on 14 October 1912.[82] Any reservations she had first had about the plan were swept away by the beautiful clothes Mutsu had brought for her, by the prospect of being loved and *wanted*, and by the promise of having a good education. The one hitch in the plan – her lack of legal status – was removed when her maternal grandparents agreed to register her as their own youngest daughter. Fumiko explained that it was because her paternal grandmother insisted that a family with the social standing of the Iwashitas could not adopt an unregistered *or* illegitimate child that it was decided to register her first as the legitimate child of her maternal grandparents. Fumiko's mother and father both said in their testimonies that the family in Korea had wanted Fumiko as their child, and this concern with her prior registration *as legitimate* suggests that the family in Korea did intend initially to adopt her as their legal heir. According to Fumiko's account, however, what she became there was the maid.

The section of Fumiko's memoirs where she wrote about Korea is a long and detailed condemnation of her paternal relatives, which reflects the fact that she wanted to impress upon her reader/s how important an influence this period of over six years in colonized Korea had been on her political development. A central theme in this part of her life-story was how the wealthy and powerful cruelly mistreated perceived 'inferiors'. The character sketch she gave of her colonist family – largely through casting in a lurid light the way they had brutalized both her and Koreans – was clearly meant to leave her audience in no doubt about the fact that despite all the ideological rhetoric in the papers, Japanese actions in Korea did not reflect much 'brotherly' love. Her portrait of life in Korea was the other side of the coin of her depiction of life in Taishō Japan: for while this country was on the receiving end of imperialist paternalism, it was no more harmonious a 'family' than Japan.

Fumiko began her account of what life was like for her in Korea by noting that once at the Iwashita home there was no sign of the books, fine clothes and toys that had been promised her. However, her uncertainty about her position in the household was removed not long after she arrived. One day a lady visited, exclaiming when she saw Fumiko, 'My, what a sweet child!' But this was met by a cold look from the grandmother, Mutsu, accompanied by the words:

> Oh, she's just the child of a slight acquaintance. She hasn't learned any manners and knows nothing but coarse language because she's the child of a terrible pauper. It's all a real embarrassment to us, but we felt so sorry for her, you know, that we just had to take her in.[83]

Then Mutsu had whispered menacingly to Fumiko that she had better not tell anyone who she really was because officially she and her paternal relatives were now 'strangers'. If the truth became known that the Register entry on her birth was a lie, both the child and her maternal family would end up 'having to wear red kimono' (go to prison)! It was only many years later when she looked back over her life in Korea that Fumiko thought she understood the reasons for her subsequent demotion to family 'maid'. Her aunt and grandmother seemed to believe her unsuited to the position of family heir because she had been permanently 'distorted' by being raised in adversity. She lacked the refinement required of a daughter of the Iwashita family, and in that role would surely disgrace the family name. They had an elevated social position to maintain. Fumiko said her uncle had taken up farming between Seoul and Pusan. His land included fields tenanted by Koreans and he earned income also through usury: high-interest loans to Koreans. (In one article in 1922, she had also decried the exploitation of Koreans by Japanese usurers.) The area they lived in was divided into social and administrative communities of Japanese and Koreans. In the ruling clique were landed gentry, usurers,

Japanese government officials, military police officers, the school-teacher etc.[84]

Fumiko's narrative about her life in Korea was one long indictment of the cruelty, pride, selfishness, vanity, snobbery, hypocrisy and meanness of her grandmother and aunt. She mentioned her uncle only in passing after describing him early in the piece as 'a gentle man of few words' who, presumably, neither contributed to nor could prevent the Iwashita house from becoming a 'hell' for Fumiko. Specifically, it

> scolded and tormented me, robbed me of every bit of freedom and independence, whittled away my good points from the edges, stunted my growth, and left me twisted, distorted and warped.[85]

Fumiko did not mince words about the Iwashita house, at least in her memoirs. When questioned about Fumiko's life in Korea, both her mother and father replied that they knew nothing about it. (Fumiko wrote that she told them very little.) Kikuno remarked that her character had changed for the worse by her return, but that she learned nothing from her daughter about what had happened to her in Korea. When Fumikazu was asked whether Fumiko had been mis-treated in Korea, he observed that his mother was an 'unusually severe person'. Fumiko might have been 'disciplined harshly' by her, he added, recalling that he had felt after her return that it would have been better for her sake not to have been sent there. He must have played some part in the 'adoption', since the family in Korea would have had no other way of knowing of Fumiko's existence and location.[86]

Mutsu and Kameko were said to have 'tormented' Fumiko by con-stantly harping on two aspects of her background – poverty and her lack of registration – drumming it into her that if not for the kindness of her paternal relatives, she would still be a 'non-person'.

> I cannot know how much my self-confidence was wounded by that term which was always used: unregistered person. I can't forget it . . .
>
> But was being an unregistered person *my* crime? I did not under-stand that I was unregistered. That was something only my father and mother understood, and should have taken responsibility for. Yet schools closed their gates to *me*. Strangers despised me. Even my blood-grandmother held me in contempt and menaced me because of it.

I knew nothing. All I knew was that I'd been born and was alive. Yes, I knew for sure I was alive. However much my grandmother said I hadn't even been born, I *had* been born and I *was* alive.[87]

Two aspects of Fumiko's attitude toward having been unregistered are quite clear. Firstly, she was bitter over being blamed and punished for something not her responsibility. Secondly, her painful memories of having been an unregistered child were largely due to her being treated as if she did not *exist* (she had had no official existence, so had not been 'born'). There is no doubt about this because in one interrogation she also said that the law 'denies real, natural existence', and was therefore a lie.[88] Hence she was excluded from games at school, for example, because not a 'real' student. We can see how being treated as a *nonentity* might have appeared to the mature Fumiko, a determined egoist, to be the ultimate social crime against an individual.

Fumiko was apparently allowed little freedom from the time she arrived in Korea. Playing with local children was denied her since they were 'vulgar paupers', but games at school were also out of the question because considered too hard on her clothes. She said she was once very embarrassed when she was forced to admit that she was not allowed to work on the school vegetable plot because her grandmother considered it too rough on her clothes. The teacher rounded on her with the sarcastic remark that everyone could indeed see how splendidly she was dressed: 'just like a little princess'.[89] Here Fumiko launched a savage attack on parents who refused to let their children play freely just to save themselves work and keep up appearances. If they were worried about their children's getting dirty, it would be better to dress them in old clothes rather than 'robbing them of their freedom and individuality'. If children developed their individual talents *naturally*, society would be the better for it. This was another point at which Fumiko counterposed 'nature' to human society, something she emphasized also in connection with her intention to kill herself when she was no more than 12. But having decided that avenging herself on humanity was a more fitting goal, Fumiko returned home, she said, and from that day developed a 'fierce thirst for knowledge' – which was not easy to quench in a household where all but school textbooks were denied her. It is clear that for Fumiko knowledge was a means to power, yet nothing came of Mutsu's original promise to send her to high school, let alone a ladies' college in Tokyo.

A point Fumiko emphasized was that Koreans were amongst the few people there who showed her any kindness. One Korean discussed was 'Kō', the Iwashitas' manservant. 'Kō' she described as an honest and hard worker, who was very poor because underpaid and terribly exploited by the Iwashitas; while also having to suffer various cruel indignities at their hands.[90] In the context of the formation of her antipathy toward those with wealth and power, she mentioned in a later section how she came to empathize with 'Kō' and others who like herself were 'oppressed, tormented and exploited'.

The underlying theme throughout Fumiko's account of her experience in the Iwashita household was that it was this period in her life that had done the most to leave her 'stunted and warped'. Here she had been denied affection, brutalized, deprived of her freedom, and robbed of the opportunity to develop her natural potential.[91] She related how she was even forced to become dishonest in order to avoid punishment for imaginary crimes. Fumiko was afraid that her account of her life in Korea might seem exaggerated and unconvincing. She imagined that readers might think that Mutsu could not have been that bad, that she was lying because her character was 'warped'. She was not lying, she insisted, though she was indeed 'warped' – and she wanted her readers to understand how she got that way.

Fortunately, early in 1919 when Fumiko had just turned 16, her relatives decided that they should send her home because she had finished her education and would soon be expected to marry. This she interpreted to mean that they did not want to arrange a marriage for her themselves because of the expense. Arriving in Yamanashi soon after, Fumiko was relieved when, without exception, the family welcomed her. Kikuno was married again, but returned for a visit when she was told of Fumiko's arrival. At this point in her story Fumiko was relatively sympathetic about her mother's situation, recognizing that Kikuno's family allowed her little control over her own life. She explained that it was not Kikuno's fault that her many marriages did not work out, that she could not find a good man for a husband. What else could a woman with a 'past' expect? That day Kikuno greeted and fussed over her daughter happily until suddenly she noticed the condition of her hands: the signs of frostbite and hard work. But Fumiko made a point of writing here that she had been evasive about how badly she had been treated in Korea, for she did not like speaking ill of people. Here and elsewhere she seemed concerned that her motives for writing her autobiography might be misread: it was no mere vengeful diatribe against family and society, but rather a consistent and reasoned social critique.

Fumiko acknowledged that she had been gratified by her mother's resentment about the Iwashita's broken promises and concern for her, but said she had quickly tired of Kikuno's incessant complaints about her current marriage. She soon began to take every opportunity to escape to the nearby Zen temple of one of her maternal uncles, Motoei; and in this peaceful environment she began to feel restored. Then one day the main villain of this part of her memoirs, her father again, came to visit. She recalled thinking his demonstrations of affection for her absurd, and being 'contemptuous' of him because he believed he still had some paternal authority over her. When he and Motoei retired to talk privately about a matter concerning her, she had felt rather anxious. Fumikazu gave her no explanation but that night she agreed to his request that she go to live with him, Takano and Takatoshi in Hamamatsu. He wanted to make amends for the past, he insisted; and she was impatient to leave the village.

Fumiko soon discovered another attempt to 'sell' her like a mere 'object', she wrote, this time by her father. He had promised her in marriage to her uncle, Motoei.[92] When Fumikazu was questioned in court in 1925 about this engagement, he did not deny his part in arranging it. According to Fumiko's memoirs and second court testimony, everyone but Motoei and Fumikazu opposed the idea.[93] Marriages between close relatives were still common in prewar villages, often between first cousins or uncles and nieces. In Ella Lury Wiswell's and Robert Smith's study of Suye village in the 1930s, however, villagers were sometimes disapproving of this, voicing the opinion that cousin marriages either failed or led to miscarriages or abnormal children.[94]

Fumiko's whole account of the plans to marry her to her uncle suggests a moral opposition to it tantamount to revulsion. She was disgusted because to add to the 'profanity' of trying to wed uncle and niece, it was clear to her that her father's motives were mercenary. Fumiko gave the same account of her father's motives – the wealth of the temple – as her grandmother. Sehi testified that she had opposed the plan. Fumikazu justified his actions to the judge by insisting that there had been no alternative to the plan because Fumiko and Motoei had already been lovers. His account differed from Fumiko's and Sehi's in various respects. According to Fumiko, it was Fumikaza who had initiated the discussion about marrying her to Motoei, and not a case of his having asked for her hand (Motoei himself was not called as a witness because he had already died of illness by then).[95] Motoei was no better than her father, according to Fumiko, for his motives were bestial; and the 'dirty beast' was actually a priest! She knew that he was on the look-out for a pure young virgin to 'wed'; he had told her as much himself. (Presumably, this was to be a common-law marriage since Motoei was a Zen priest.) But while she was fond of Motoei, her father's claim that she was in love with him was a ridiculous attempt to twist the truth in order to justify his own greed.

One interesting thing about Fumiko's construction of life in both her memoirs and testimonies is that, while one might not go so far as to describe her as a feminist, much of what she had to say revealed a decidedly critical view of discrimination against women and gendered expectations of them. This was in a range of areas including education, sexuality, arranged marriage, and women's general lack of independence. One reason she gave for the increasing tension between herself and her father at this time was that her hopes of getting a *real* education were disappointed. The only school acceptable to her father was a girls' school where she was to learn needlework in preparation for her marriage. Even in more formal women's colleges then, sewing and other domestic 'sciences' made up the largest part of the curriculum. So Fumiko said she hated this school and neglected her 'studies'.

Though Fumiko recalled having an ally in Takano and also being fond of her brother, it appears that life in Hamamatsu became more and more frustrating for her. This, for example, was when she had to put up with the daily worship of the Saeki genealogy. When she stopped attending the 'stupid' needlework school, Fumikazu was furious and they fought, so she was sent back to Suwa again.[96] There she hit upon a plan to gain entrance to a prefectural high school where tuition was free, and become a teacher. Motoei, she wrote, had agreed to be her guarantor, so she threw herself into studying for the entrance exams, only to have him refuse to sign her application forms. Her uncle then went to ask Sehi to take Fumiko back to Hamamatsu, and it was clear to the latter that she was in some sort of trouble. There her father flew into a rage, beating and kicking her savagely, calling her a 'whore', at which point she realized that her romance with a young student in the village, 'Segawa' (real name unknown), had been discovered.

According to Fumiko, it was because Motoei assumed that she was no longer a virgin that he now retracted his promise to marry her, though the fact that she was legally registered as his younger sister might have had something to do with it. At this point in her story, Fumiko again inveighed against the hypocrisy of both her father and uncle for damning her as a 'whore' when she had not done a fraction of what they were guilty of. One had wanted her as a 'plaything', while the other had seen her as a 'tool' to be used for mercenary ends. In her second trial testimony, too, she mentioned that her father had seen her as mere 'property' and tried to sell her, even demanding 'payment' from Motoei for taking her virginity.[97] (It was not actually made clear in Fumiko's memoirs or testimonies that Motoei had not, but the general sense of her accounts seems to be that he had wanted her while she was still a virgin.)

This section of Fumiko's memoirs about her uncle and her sweetheart also followed an account of a sexual assault by an unknown man. (She said she had thought at first that he was a relative.) She was not explicit about what happened, writing only that she shook off this 'devil' and escaped 'in a daze like a wounded beast'.[98] She admitted to her readers that she had never confided in anyone about this, but could now because she would probably not live much longer and there was no longer any reason to hide it. It was, moreover, important to her that she record everything that had 'had a great influence on her life, ideas and character'. Perhaps in writing about this (attempted?) rape she was revealing one more way in which she had been 'distorted'. Like Suga, Fumiko left the reader to read between the lines and appeared to be concerned that she, the victim, might be held responsible. She seemed to be trying to avoid censure by her reader/s by stressing that she had at first mistaken the identity of the man, that she was unwell at the time, and that she was still then innocent of the ways of the world.

Relations between Fumiko and her father were impossible, she said, after she upset his plans to marry her to Motoei. From that time they were like 'enemies'. He would not permit her to study to become a teacher, but was overjoyed when his son passed the entrance exams for the prefectural middle-high school. Fumiko described her brother as neither very good at his school-work nor particularly ambitious. None the less, his father insisted that the (now legal) *son* of a Saeki had to do law at Tokyo Imperial University and thus attain a government post, perhaps even become prime minister. There is an undercurrent in her account that suggests that she resented Takatoshi's being pushed toward a future he was not suited for and did not want, while she was more intelligent yet not permitted to attend even high school.[99] It was over her younger brother, apparently, that Fumiko and her father had the row that led to her departure for Tokyo, because she had been openly scornful about his meanness in buying a cheap school-bag for Takatoshi and pretending it had been expensive. While beating her, Saeki not only railed at her for being 'unfilial', a 'trouble-maker' and, more importantly, a 'bad influence' on her brother; like his mother in Korea, he was about to evict her from his house too.

Up to this point Fumiko's autobiography largely denounced familial and social abuse. Her severest criticisms were most often of men, and of the paternal side of the family which, of course, included her grandmother and aunt. (Her maternal uncle, Motoei, she was rather ambivalent about, despite the above description of him.) Now she turned her attention to her days in Tokyo as a self-supporting student, and thus to more of those who abused their positions of power to exploit 'toilers' like herself or treat her like a mere 'plaything'. Here in the metropolis Fumiko saw how the strong really did eat the weak; how she had to fight to survive. She had set off for Tokyo in the spring of 1920 at the age of 17 excited and full of hope. Now she could finally reclaim her own life. Tokyo was sure to be a 'paradise on earth', for here she would find what she had long dreamt of: independence.[100] She said her bitter past now became an inspiration to her, because her contempt for her family's ideas and lifestyle was what had led her to strike out on her own in search of something better.

Then, however, Fumiko arrived on the doorstep of the man she only called 'great-uncle' in her memoirs, Kaneko-Kubota Kametarō. She wrote that her father had not cared about how she would fare in Tokyo and gave her nothing, and also said that her great-uncle had had no warning of her arrival. Kubota, however, testified that Saeki had written to him asking him to look after her.[101] It is clear that Kametarō took the task seriously because he also lectured Fumiko about giving up the idea of an education. He said in his testimony that he had pressured her to do something more suitable for a girl and more profitable: it would be better if she learned to use one of the sewing machines in his house, so she could then marry a respectable merchant. She, however, had other ideas. She had a little trouble convincing a man named Furihata (called 'Shirahata' by Fumiko) to take on a newspaper-girl: she was, after all, more like a boy than a girl; being 'tomboyish' meant that she would be able to work hard and not get up to any 'mischief' with the men. Furihata remarked on her masculine character, gait, speech and general behaviour, recalling during his testimony that she used to loll about in the company of the boys, reading nonchalantly.[102] She moved into the newsagency, and asked for an advance on her wages so she could enrol at two private schools to study mathematics and English. Her first object was to sit the exam for a teacher's licence, but she was also interested in becoming a doctor of medicine. There were few girls at these schools, especially in mathematics classes, and this suited her well. At girls' schools, she complained, academic standards were low and one was liable to be caught up in 'annoying competition' regarding what one wore.[103]

After attending one school in the morning and the other in the afternoon, Fumiko apparently worked from four until twelve at night, selling papers. She did not have any time to study, and it was tiring and tedious work, as she indicated also in two of her poems:

> Once I even
> sold the evening news,
> propped up
> against Sanmai Bridge
> in Uenoyama.
>
> Dozing,
> dozing, yet still ringing
> my bell;
> how wretched I was
> five years ago.[104]

Nor did she earn much. She came to see that her employers exploited their workers (and she was expected to help out with housework and childcare too). But what seems to have convinced her that she should leave was that this household was just as bad as her own family. What she meant by this was that, like her father, this man was not content with one woman. Furihata admitted that he was still supporting his former wife and children, that his current wife had once been his 'concubine', and that she was causing trouble over his current mistress.[105] What Fumiko seemed to find particularly immoral about Furihata was that she and the other workers were being mercilessly exploited to support his decadent style of life.

Yet the newsagency job had held one attraction for Fumiko: the vibrant street culture on the bridge from which she sold newspapers. Soapbox orators came once a week. Firstly, there was the Salvation Army singing and beating their tambourines; then an opposition group, the 'Buddhist Salvation Army', preaching and singing; and finally also some socialists with posters and pamphlets.[106] Fumiko explicitly said in one of her testimonies that it was the Salvation Army that most attracted her at first.[107] Still, it was from that time that she also began to mix a little with socialists. Her employer testified that she must have been influenced by socialism then because she became friendly with a man who published and sold books about it. This same man had once worked at the newsagency but was dismissed because of his socialist activities.[108]

When Fumiko decided to leave the newsagency, she had nowhere to go and no money. In fact Furihata claimed that she owed him quite a sum. In desperation she had already appealed to a socialist friend to help her repay her debt, but he refused so she went to seek out friends in the Salvation Army, and her short-lived spiritual 'conversion' followed, as did her brief romance with Saitō Otomatsu ('Itō'). Meanwhile, she had assumed that Furihata had simply written off her 'debt', and it was not until some time later that she discovered that he had visited her great-uncle's house and Kubota had felt duty-bound to pay the money. Furihata explained to the judge that he had only employed her because her great-uncle was her guarantor. He also said that she had 'wilfully' left when he threatened to tell her uncle about her socialist connections.[109] (Even if true, Furihata was obviously at pains to distance himself from socialism before the judge.)

With Saitō's help Fumiko became a street-stall vendor and found a room. Selling packets of soap-powder did not earn her enough for food and board, much less school expenses, so she stopped attending maths classes and pawned some school-books. Then in the autumn of 1920 with the help of Salvation Army Corps Leader, 'Akihara', a woman whose real name was Motoki, she found a job as a live-in maid with a family (probably Christian) that had a sugar shop. The work was very hard, and she could neither attend school nor find time to study. Moreover, there were domestic tensions (immorality) in that house too, so before long she wrote to a school-friend named Hori ('Kawada' in her memoirs) of her depressing circumstances, and was gratified when she visited and pointed out that her socialist brother (Hori Kiyotoshi) was opening a printing shop: there Fumiko might be able both to work and continue with her studies. By this time Fumiko also wanted to separate herself from the Christian company she had been keeping, she said, but felt ungrateful to Saitō and Motoki. This was before Saitō decided that she was a threat to his 'purity'.[110] For Fumiko, Christianity was a deception, even if people like Saitō and Motoki really believed in it; for her, however, it was still a lie. The discussion at this point of her disillusionment with Christianity was the first part of a continuing theme in the latter part of her memoirs, for first it was Christianity that promised all and delivered little and then 'socialism'. One has to keep in mind that what Fumiko was doing when writing her memoirs was explaining how the world had produced a nihilist like her. By 1922 she had come to believe that nihilism was the ultimate political doctrine because it was so much more the negation of state and society than even socialism (including anarchism).

When Fumiko finally left the sugar merchants' household, she felt 'liberated'. It was the hardest work she had experienced so far. Yet when she opened her pay packet on the way to Hori's house, she was appalled to find that these 'selfish, arrogant and unreasonable' people who lived in luxury had paid her a pittance. Here she returned to the theme of the meanness of the rich. She explained that the grandfather kept a concubine, gambled and indulged himself with entertainment by geisha; his wife took more than two hours to dress up in her finery; and the whole family slept in, having talked far into the night stuffing themselves with delicacies prepared by the maids, who were seldom allowed to sleep for more than five hours. In the somewhat defensive testimony of the young master of the shop about his father's 'indulgences', which coincided with Fumiko's story, he even admitted that she had been underpaid by his mother.[111]

Fumiko remarked once in court that after this experience she 'free-loaded off a few activists', the Horis first presumably, though she said in one interrogation that she worked there doing typesetting.[112] She did not go into any detail in her memoirs about this brief period of staying with socialists from January 1921, but after her experience at the sugar shop she must have looked forward to congenial company. This she suggested in her third interrogation, where she pointed out that then she had wanted to put socialist theory into practice, but it was not possible with people like Hori Kiyotoshi and Kutsumi Fusako (referred to as 'Kunō'), who were socialists in name only. Fumiko went into detail in one interrogation about the hypocrisy of Hori the socialist printer who had a (country geisha) common-law wife and illegitimate child, but kept it secret so as not to harm his career. She also spoke more than once of Kutsumi, a well-known socialist then who, according to Fumiko, neglected her own children in order to fly about seeking publicity and glory, and was also selfish and materialistic.[113] Fumiko, the 'amoralist egoist', had a strict sense of moral behaviour for socialists, especially when it concerned children.[114]

Once she returned to her great-uncle's not long after, Fumiko promised to help out with the housework so she could resume her studies. She did not have enough money to buy books, but at least a socialist friend helped her political education along by supplying her with pamphlets and union bulletins, through which she was 'gradually able to grasp the thinking and spirit of socialism'. This friend she called 'Ōno' was an anarchist and/or syndicalist printer, a member of the Shin'yūkai. This is an example of Fumiko's often vague use of the term 'socialist' to refer to anyone on the Left. The picture is obscured even more when at various points later in her memoirs she spoke of rejecting 'socialism'. Here the style of her critique was plainly anarchistic, so she may have been criticizing only state, not libertarian, socialism. In any event, she said that at that time 'socialism' had 'suddenly ignited the fire of sympathy and rebellion that until that point had only been smouldering in my heart'. Even more now she empathized with those in circumstances like her own, people who were exploited by the wealthy and powerful. But she suggested that even after this 'ignition' her spirt of rebellion was vague: she was as yet 'powerless', lacking in direction, just a 'discontented, disaffected child full to the brim with rebellion'. Still, she had felt even then that she had to do *something*. There is little doubt that what she was saying here was that her time as a victim of society had then been nearing an end.

In explaining when in prison how socialism had first affected her in the early 1920s, Fumiko noted that it had merely 'verified' her life-experience and pre-existing spirit of rebellion. Having been poor all her life meant that she had always been 'pushed around, tormented, oppressed, exploited and controlled' by people with money: in short, 'plundered of [her] freedom'. No wonder she had developed a 'deep antipathy for people with this sort of power', as well as 'a heartfelt sympathy for others in similar circumstances'.[115] She therefore related how she had been drawn to radical Koreans, including one she met at the English school in 1921. This man she called 'Sir' (perhaps Sir Dong Sung who was later in the Futeisha) was 'taciturn and gloomy', always silently reading socialist magazines. By mid-1921 Fumiko had met another Korean radical through 'Segawa', her lover from Suwa. The latter had paid her a surprise visit just before she went to Hamamatsu again for the summer holidays (at her father's request). But again she and her father often quarrelled so she went next to visit the family in Suwa. Kikuno was again divorced and at the silk mill, so the family's expectation was that once Fumiko became a teacher she would look after her mother. She wrote in disgust that she had had no intention of being a dutiful daughter: she had not been wearing herself out working and studying so hard just to take responsibility for a mother who had 'deserted her to pursue her own security in life'.[116] So once back in Tokyo, she met 'Segawa' again, as well as two Koreans who lived in the same lodgings as him. One of them particularly interested her because 'Segawa' had said he was a socialist.

After Fumiko became disillusioned with 'Segawa' because to him she was just a 'toy' to be discarded when no longer amusing,[117] she again met this Korean socialist ('Hyun'), and the two discovered they had socialist friends in common. Fumiko said that because he was the only son of a wealthy family, thus a 'petty-bourgeois intellectual', he was not really accepted in the 'serious' or 'earnest' sections of the socialist movement. This suggests the anarchist sections of the movement: Ōsugi was well known for his theoretical attacks on 'petty-bourgeois intellectual' leadership of the labour movement.[118] After this meeting Fumiko and 'Hyun' became sexually involved, but before long she felt that he too was just using her as a plaything, so once again she was disappointed in socialists.[119] She emphasized two themes in this final part of her autobiography: her disillusionment with men (not always socialists) who merely used her, and, more generally, with socialists who did not put their politics into practice in their personal lives. While the former was certainly a political critique of men who treated women as mere sex-objects, it was also part of a prologue to her finally finding a man, Pak, who would treat her seriously. This paralleled her narrative strategy of describing the process of political negation – Christianity, socialism, anarchism – that led her to nihilism.

To add to her depression over 'Hyun', by this time the situation in her great-uncle's house had become increasingly difficult. Her great-uncle testified that at first she was a serious student, but then 'bobbed her hair, even though she was a girl', suggesting that she became wild, a '*moga*' (modern girl). When he scolded her she 'talked back, going on about things she did not understand'. The judge asked whether that meant she was infatuated with socialism, and he replied vaguely that he did not know anything about socialism and had thought she wanted to join 'Tenrikyō or something'. Presumably, he meant that she was influenced by some new 'radical' sort of thinking (it is possible that he was confusing Tenrikyō with Christianity). When then asked why Fumiko left his house, he answered that he 'hated Tenrikyō and socialism'; having a member of his household influenced by these would be bad for business. It seems there was not much basis for communication between Fumiko and her great-uncle.[120]

According to Fumiko, she had left of her own accord, and then found work as a live-in waitress at a small restaurant in Hibiya. The proprietor, Iwasaki, explained to Tatematsu later that Fumiko had been recommended by a socialist then in the Gyominkai. In the latter part of 1921, she therefore continued with her schooling by night while working during the day at this 'socialist stew' (*oden*) restaurant. The food must have been cheap because Iwasaki told the judge that he subscribed to the 'humanistic' principle that a society based on the idea that 'those who don't work shouldn't eat' needed to be reformed.[121] Fumiko might have been thinking of his words when she wrote this tanka:

> You don't work, you don't eat;
> You do work, your burden gets heavier.
> That's
> today's world.[122]

By this time Fumiko was nearing the dramatic finale (and real 'origin') of her narrative: her embracement of nihilism. According to Niiyama Hatsuyo, it was at night school that she first met Fumiko early in 1922.[123] This section of Fumiko's memoirs was entitled 'To a Task! To My Own Task!', and thus it was here that she introduced those who helped her to find and take up this work of her *own*: Niiyama and Pak Yeol. It was in this section that she introduced the mature Fumiko, the nihilist who was the sum total of all the experiences, inspirations and disillusionments that she had so far described. The final section of her memoirs is where she portrays herself as having left behind her: family; working for others and being exploited; 'socialism'; formal education and dreams of worldly success; and the last vestiges of an adherence to conventional morality.

Fumiko was not explicit about it in her memoirs, but in this last section where she had arrived at the end-point of her development into a nihilist, the life-construct she *apparently only now* presented was the world according to a fully fledged 'nihilist'. When she spoke now of how her attitudes toward education had undergone a significant change by 1922, for example, what she felt she was presenting was a nihilist critique of formal education and worldly success. The most important thing in her life had long been education. Now, however, she saw no point in trying to excel in the rigidly stratified society of the day: it was only people with wealth, privilege and opportunity who became more wealthy and powerful[124]. To Fumiko (and Niiyama, apparently) the very concept of worldly success was meaningless, but there was still something she could do, some 'task' in life that was more important than 'greatness' in the eyes of others. As for her criticism of socialism and revolutionary leaders, Niiyama, it seems, had also despised the people in such movements and been sceptical about revolutionary idealism. Fumiko wrote that like Niiyama she, too, doubted that one could really change society in such a way that would lead to the well-being of every single person. Still, through *acting* ('on one's ego') one could be fulfilled and free, which was not the same as working toward a distant utopian ideal. Overall, one can see that what mostly constituted her 'nihilism' was a negative critique of society, state socialism and existing revolutions to the last influenced by anarchism (of all types);[125] a positive view of violent tactics and individualistic rebellion inspired largely by nihilism-populism (also individualistic anarchism); and a dismissal of revolutionary utopias derived from egoistic nihilism (probably Stirner and Nietzsche).

Fumiko was, according to her own account, already a nihilist by the time she met Pak Yeol in February 1922. Now she had finally found a kindred spirit. She had wanted to meet him from the time a Korean communist friend showed her a short poem of Pak's that was so 'powerful' she was 'enraptured' by it. Hence, she begged the friend she called 'Chung' to introduce her. Fumiko did not include the poem in her autobiography, but she did note in one testimony that it was called 'Inukoro' which suggests something about its content: in the testimony where the judge was asking about the scornful terminology the Futeisha used (for emperor, judges, etc.), she explained that they called the police either *burudoggu* (literally, '[watch]dogs of the bourgeoisie') or *inukoro* ('puppies', a variant of 'inu' or 'dog' meaning undercover police or their informers).[126] When she met Pak not long after, however, she was disappointed to find him curt and seemingly uninterested in her. Nevertheless, after that first meeting, she was still very interested because, she said, he had such a powerful presence. According to 'Chung', Pak at that time was unemployed and homeless and Fumiko was amazed that such a shabbily turned out 'homeless dog' could conduct himself almost like 'royalty', but to this 'Chung' responded that this was probably because he was ashamed of being economically dependent on comrades. He added, however, that there were few so 'earnest' in thought and action as Pak.[127] The portrait Fumiko painted of Pak most of the time was one that was meant to emphasize his power and political rectitude, determination and defiance.

Fumiko's account of her 'proposal' to Pak was discussed in Chapter 4 – her asking him first if he was single, next if he was hostile toward all Japanese people, then if he was *only* an independence activist. However, he had his own ideology and his *own task*, according to Fumiko: by the time they met, he had lost interest in a movement that 'only talked and published'; and wanted to 'follow his own path'. Reassured on these three points, she recalled saying at last, 'I have discovered something in you that I've been searching for. I believe I can work with you.'[128] But to this, Pak replied coldly that he was 'no-one of any importance, merely someone who continued to live only because he seemed to be unable to die'. Not long after, however, he apparently decided to find some cheap lodgings to have a base from which to organize politically, and Fumiko responded enthusiastically to his suggestion that she join him.[129] She wrote that he had observed that if the bourgeoisie celebrated their marriages by going on honeymoons, he and Fumiko would mark their 'marriage' by putting out a political publication. Fumiko responded that she had a copy of Kropotkin's *Conquest of Bread*, which they could translate, but Pak pointed out that it had already been done (actually by Kōtoku in 1907). It is interesting that this 'nihilist' would want to translate Kropotkin.

This was the beginning of their political life together. Fumiko therefore added a postscript to her prison memoirs, explaining why they ended abruptly with the promise of a personal and political commitment between herself and Pak. As she had said at the outset, it was meant to be an account only of her past personal-political history (her development into a nihilist); even if Judge Tatematsu had wanted her to, it was not necessary to write about her political involvement with Pak and the Futeisha, or about the treason incident. Near the end of her memoirs she wrote the following:

> My notes end here. I am not at liberty to write here about later events, except about Pak's and my life together as a couple. But it is sufficient for my purposes to have written just this much.
>
> What made me like this? I guess it's not for me to say anything about this. It is enough that I have revealed here the history of half a lifetime. Compassionate readers should understand well enough from this record. I am confident about this.[130]

On one level it is not at all difficult to see what Fumiko had set out to do in this story: she wanted to use her experience as a weapon against those who represented Japan as a harmonious 'family-state' under the paternal protection of a divine emperor and his agents. Also, if readers understood 'what made [her] like this' they might be encouraged to change the society responsible. What her account showed, however, is that however truthful she was about *events* in her life – something that is verified by the testimonies of witnesses – often she interpreted them differently from others.

Fumiko represented Japan as a society that 'warped' its people and forced them to live in an 'unnatural' condition of servitude and inequality. She often described herself as warped, but she expressed no personal sense of shame over this: it was not she who was responsible for it but others. In a broad sense, her target was what I would term the 'authoritarian paternalism' that was very much a part of emperor-system patriarchal-capitalist imperialism. Whether or not she had actually plotted to kill the emperor, her 'treachery' lay both in her statements to judges that the imperial family should be overthrown and in the systematic critique of society she presented in her memoirs, testimonies (including treatises), and poems. Fumiko's critique of society is clear enough in the texts she narrated to and for a judge, but what makes its systematic, many-faceted nature even clearer is comparing and contrasting them with some of the witness interrogation records. In 1925, even while in prison, Fumiko was engaged in a war of words, not just with prison and judicial officials or, more broadly, the state, but still also with her family and others whose representations of her life and character and whose views of reality she opposed. Hopefully, reading her life-story against the accounts of witnesses called before Tatematsu has also served continually to emphasize the fact that he was the immediate audience of Fumiko's and other representations of her life – the central figure in the context of their production, even *their cause*. One cannot lose sight of the fact that this would, in part, determine how such stories were told.

Thus, what Fumiko was saying in the final section of her memoirs was that most of her life she had been exploited by the strong – she had been a victim – but even by 1922 this was no longer the case. Once she had been a creature subject to the will of others, but now she was a creator of her Self and her world. The whole final section of her memoirs is about self-empowerment through nihilism: taking control of her own life and destiny; in short, transcendence.

II

Before turning to the life-construct Fumiko presented in her trial testimonies, it is first necessary to recall that at the end of her memoirs, she wrote of a silent promise to Pak that they would now 'live and die together'. But whether or not they did plan to die together while fulfilling a shared political 'task' remains unclear. There are suggestions in the testimonies of Fumiko and other members of the Futeisha that back in 1922–1923 she had not known all about Pak's terroristic plans and activities. One said that once when he visited Pak to talk about plans to get funds to procure bombs from overseas, Pak had wanted to talk to him outside so that Fumiko would not hear.[131] Fumiko was clearer in her trial testimonies than in her memoirs about the general nature of the pact she apparently made with Pak at the beginning of their relationship. There she emphasized that she had insisted that it be based on mutual respect: he was to forget she was a woman and treat her as a comrade. There is no doubt Fumiko's representation of this ideal personal-political partnership was one that centred upon sexual equality.[132] Equal partners in crime could reasonably be expected to be sentenced equally. It is nevertheless quite possible that Pak had been unaware of her intention to die with him until he was told by the judge what she had been saying. He first tried to protect her. After the judge pointed out that Article 73 carried the death penalty, he had refused to answer further questions until the record of one of Fumiko's testimonies was read out. Pak only said that they had plotted together when it was clear to him that she had already claimed an involvement in a plan to procure bombs through anarchists in Shanghai or Korea – and throw them during an imperial procession for the crown prince in the autumn of 1923. Only then did he change his story.[133] But it is still likely that Fumiko took cues from her interrogators, about what other defendants had said, to exaggerate her own guilt. As we have seen, in 1926 she admitted she had only known about his plans to procure bombs through Kim Choon Han after they had come to nothing, and this was specifically what they were being charged with.

One way in which Fumiko's early testimonies bring clarity to her memoirs is that in the former she summarized the social making of a nihilist more succinctly. Through these testimonies one gets a clearer picture of what she set out to do in the last section of her autobiography, which was to demonstrate her ultimate negation of power. (Not unlike Suga, Fumiko was at pains to present herself as a fully-fledged nihilist of long standing, because to admit that anything had changed substantially after her imprisonment would be to give her adversaries the edge.) There Fumiko indicated that she had arrived at this endpoint through a process of negation: of parents and family, then conventional society, 'socialism', and finally the 'somnolent' masses.[134] It was then that she was asked what nihilism was, and retorted that she had been talking all along about what her nihilism was: a specific sort of negation, total 'annihilation'.

From there Fumiko went on to talk about the survival of the fittest as the universal law of life. Obviously, hers was generally a conflict, not a consensus view of life as inherently based on love, human goodness or social harmony (even if she did sometimes infer that premodern 'primitive communist' society was natural and good). Thus, she stressed that she was not so idealistic as to believe that people would ever live in a condition of real equality and freedom.[135] She then explained that even if she had intended to end her life during an act of throwing a bomb, it was for her own satisfaction: she did not much care whether it started a revolution or not because a new society would simply have new people in power. Asked by Tatematsu how she saw Japan's state-social system, she responded by explaining her three-level theory of power (emperor, state, masses). Unlike Suga, Fumiko expounded her doctrine to the judges at length. She went into more detail about how she saw the world in subsequent testimonies like the twelfth, where she argued against the emperor-system, against law and morality as 'the weapons of the strong' (the ruling class), and against altruism (for egoism).[136] But for her final affirmation of Life, the broad outline of her construction of life was already there in her early testimonies in 1924, which have been referred to throughout. There is no necessity, then, to go any further with a discussion of how she used her perception of socio-political reality as a counter-ideological weapon specifically in her testimonies, so I will close with a quotation from the twelfth testimony where she capped her treachery by doing her best to expose the emperor-system as a grand lie:

> We have been taught that the emperor is a descendant of the gods, and that his right to rule has been bestowed upon him by the gods. . . . We have in our midst someone who is supposed to be a living god, one who is omnipotent and omniscient, an emperor who is supposed to realize the will of the gods. Yet his children are crying because of hunger, suffocating to death in the coal mines, and being crushed to death by factory machines. Why is this so? Because, in truth, the emperor is a mere human being. We wanted to show the people that the emperor is an ordinary human being just like us. So we thought of throwing a bomb at him to show that he too will die like any other human being . . .
>
> The notion that the emperor is sacred and august is a fantasy. The people have been led to believe that the emperor and crown prince represent authorities that are sacred and inviolate. But they are simply vacuous puppets. The concepts of loyalty to the emperor and love of nation are simply rhetorical notions that are being manipulated by the tiny group of the privileged classes to fulfil their own greed and interests.[137]

'To make the emperor bleed!': Fumiko was not the first to express this desire, even if the emperor/family-state/State Shintō system was by now more developed and refined than in Suga's time. Once again, whether or not Fumiko had plotted to prove the emperor was human, it is easy to see why the authorities wanted to be rid of her.

CONCLUSION

While we were able to have a glimpse at the Fumiko of 1922–1923, there are too few texts available from this period for us to get any clear sense of her view of life before her imprisonment. Her writings in the period before her arrest were less radical than we would expect of a nihilist, but were probably deliberately so. The likelihood that the group imposed certain silences on itself make it impossible to state with certainty how Fumiko's arrest and imprisonment affected her total world-view. What is clear, however, is that she did not *moderate* her discursive representations of life when in prison; on the contrary, they became more radical. There are any number of indications that she set herself up in direct antagonism to officialdom, even explicitly to its benevolent pretentions. She once declared to Judge Tatematsu that she would like to be out in the world again sometime, and she knew that *all she had to do was say she had reformed (in order to be forgiven)*. But what she went on to say to the judge was, 'Instead of going down on my knees before power, I'd rather die and remain true to myself!'[138]

At the close of the last chapter I spoke of the many Sugas, all of whom none the less used 'their' lived reality as a political weapon. With her it is possible to see such a continuity from 1902 to 1911. But one can 'know' only one Fumiko – mainly through close interpretation of the texts she produced in prison. Her prison texts cannot be left to speak for themselves about who she was earlier, because of the problem of the time and site of their production. Suga and Fumiko were very different people in some ways, but in others, certainly in the ways they *ultimately* centred life on conflict and struggle, they were very much alike. The one negated ideological constructs of reality with 'anarchism', the other with 'nihilism', and in doing so, they refused to be, or be seen as, social victims. Each *appeared* to be asking for pity about her 'wretched' past, implying at least a defensive self-justification: Fumiko was happy to admit that she was the 'warped', unnatural product of an unnatural society, but also implied in more than one text that that was only before her discovery of nihilism, which through a process of negation finally became her (Zen-ish) 'great affirmation' of life. What comes across most clearly in the late texts of both is their pride in what they had made of themselves.

In the final analysis, the point is not who really won these two wars. What seemed to be most important for each woman was that she not allow the enemy the last 'word'. Ultimately, each of these propagandists by word and deed left behind an important historical legacy, her construction of her life and world. This Fumiko expressed in some of her poems even more succinctly than in her court testimonies, savagely so in the following tanka:

> Bent over,
> watching others from beneath
> my thighs –
> the state of the world I
> need to look at, upside-down.[139]

For her this was a world that made sense only when observed from a 'warped' perspective. In order to look at (and live in) an inverted world, she had first been forced to invert herself, but such a contorted posture could only be temporary. In many ways Fumiko set out to show that with nihilism she had regained her 'natural' posture, which was erect.

Epilogue

'Biographies do not finish with the death of the hero', observed Jean-Michel Raynaud, and the same can be said of the constructions individuals place on their own lives and, in this case, their looming deaths.[1] Their final words, he continued, often go beyond death to suggest something of the 'repercussions', the 'consequences' of the life. This is certainly true of Kaneko Fumiko who went to a great deal of effort to demonstrate to a *judge* the present and future consequences of her life. Kanno Suga probably used her story in a similar way with her official 'father', the prosecutor. Further, when she spoke in her diary and in court of the meaning of her death and life – which would serve to 'revitalize' opposition to the state in the future – she too added 'to a story telling the triumph of death' over an individual, 'a story telling the triumph of an individual over death'.[2] She, like Fumiko, left this autobiographical work to posterity; and she too seemed to want it 'to stand for [her] entire life'. When Suga and Fumiko were *in prison*, life was 'reducible to a [single] meaning', and that meaning was 'struggle'. Yet Raynaud's scepticism about teleological methodology in life-narratives is warranted because we cannot lose sight of the fact that earlier they may not have defined themselves and their lives strictly in such terms. By the time of Suga's final imprisonment, her fight against power had escalated to a point where it could not be other than the (ascribed) *centre* of her life and self.

When Suga and Fumiko engaged in these discursive-political wars, in speaking out about oppression, they obviously sought to empower themselves. In a situation where the full weight of the power of the state was upon them, they threw out a challenge to their opponents and observers that they (too) were the creators of their situations and destinies. If at times they struck out without forethought in frustration at feeling powerless, in trying to wrest the meaning of their lives and deaths from those who believed that only they had the power of life and death over them, Suga and Fumiko laid claim to self-creation and control. While they might never have believed themselves to be really in control of their fates, they were obviously determined not to be seen to be waiting passively for the blow to fall, as if they had nothing to do or say about the matter. In the texts Kanno Suga and Kaneko Fumiko wrote, articulated or acted out, therefore, victims became victors and death meant life. Quite apart from the question of other forms of im-mortality, out of destruction they moulded a *constructive* legacy to others in their political cultures. This legacy contained an admonition to the state, which was that an unequal and oppressive society was sure to give rise to its own negation: people such as Suga and Fumiko themselves. If not quite a 'negation', a society that went so far as to export its abuses of human rights would certainly create its own adversaries, as Fumiko intimated.

Imperial Japan was founded even in late Meiji on a metaphor of paternalism that extended all the way up to a godly father-figure, and while a portion of this divinity was transferred, it was only to the emperor's *own* (obedient) 'children'. Therefore, amongst both Japan's first-class citizens and its 'adopted' children, soon there were those who came to believe in the necessity of 'parricide' or 'deicide'. No longer was the name of the emperor a rallying call only for loyalist radicalism, as it had been in the 1850s and 1860s. In the first and third decades of this century a number of unfilial children dreamed of taking their axes to the base of the pedestal upon which this 'god-the-father' had been placed. One or two did more than dream of it. And the thought of commoners hacking away with axes at the base of this 'holy' monument brings to mind Fumiko's words in the Supreme Court on 26 February 1926:

Judge: Name?
Fumiko: Kaneko Fumiko.
Judge: Age?
Fumiko: According to you officials it's twenty-four, but I myself seem to recollect being twenty-two. But speaking frankly, I don't believe either. Whatever my age, it has no bearing on the life I'm living now anyway.
Judge: Family status?
Fumiko: *Divine* commoner [my emphasis].
Judge: Occupation?
Fumiko: My occupation is the demolition of what now exists.
Judge: Address?
Fumiko: Tokyo Prison.[3]

Pak had preceded Fumiko and answered in similar style, so after her turn came to *perform* for the assembled officials and public audience that included comrades, the judge promptly closed the public gallery in order to have some order in the courtroom. Clearly, for some at least, this was a woman who was magnificent in her 'madness'. Her snide claim to divinity must have really capped the couple's obvious contempt of court. If, as Inga Clendinnen has observed, under the lash adults are made children again,[4] what was made of Fumiko – or of Suga before her – was a daughter who stubbornly remained undutiful.

By the 1920s, the Japanese subjects who were officially defined as treacherous, at least, if not necessarily treasonous, included even those who had the audacity to call for the 'abolition of the monarchy'. The Japan Communist Party did not need to pose a real threat to the physical person of the emperor in order to fall foul of 'peace-keepers' who read this slogan as a direct attack on Japan's *'kokutai'* (national polity or character), or emperor-headed family-state. Communists, too, were unfilial, disloyal, disobedient children. But more than any-thing else, perhaps, what was also a function of the increasingly perva-sive paternalism of the system was the fact that even by the mid-1920s a defendant's state of repentance came to be deemed more worthy of consideration by the prosecution and judiciary. This originated with the Peace Preservation Law and culminated in the institutionalization of *tenkō* in the early 1930s. While some might want to see in this pre-ference for *thought reform* over harsher penalties a 'liberalization' born of 'Taishō Democracy', to my mind it is the example, *par excellence*, of a long-term trend toward greater state authoritarianism. Now, how-ever, the 'lash' was of a different type. Because, all too obviously, many found convincing the patriarchal-nationalist fiction of the fatherly benevolence of (the emperor's) officialdom, it might simply have been a more effective form of *totalitarianism* than institution-alized elsewhere. Not only did the *tenkō* policy prove to be a highly successful weapon against communists in particular; in all likelihood Judge Tatematsu was one of many officials who used the lash in the conviction that these 'un-Japanese' children could thereby be brought back into the nation-state's loving familial embrace.

Both Fumiko and Suga revealed in full measure their intransigence and treachery when face to face with their adversaries. Forgiveness might have been a more realistic possibility for Fumiko, but she too refused to recant and throw herself on the mercy of her paternal 'protectors'. Both women might have been swayed at times by the 'kindnesses' of some of those charged with their protection, but they remained defiant. We can be reasonably sure that Fumiko remained so right until the end, even if we cannot be absolutely certain that her death was by her *own* hand. Only a short time before her death, however, she had declared that neither her life nor her death would be subject to someone else's 'whim' or will. What the prison texts of both Kanno Suga and Kaneko Fumiko reveal, in short, is that ultimately they were determined that both their lives and their deaths would not be *seen* to be largely of someone else's making. Each was happy to admit to being partly the product of her world, but was not resigned to either a fate or a knowledge of herself created by others. Whether in their own estimation Suga and Fumiko really were 'victors over destiny' in the end, they did their best to present themselves in that light. For them not to have done so would have been to accept that victims are only victims, and death is only death – or, rather, 'annihilation'.

Notes

1 TREASON AND TREACHERY, DOCUMENTS AND DISCOURSE

1 Michel Foucault, 'The Life of Infamous Men', in Meaghan Morris and Paul Patton (eds), *Michel Foucault: Power, Truth, Strategy*, Sydney, Feral Publications, 1979, p. 80.
2 I am not suggesting that Foucault did not write elsewhere about regicide, since he began one work with an account of the drawing and quartering of Damien the regicide in 1757 in Paris. Michel Foucault, *Discipline and Punish: The Birth of the Prison*, Harmondsworth, Penguin, 1977, pp. 3 ff.
3 I will henceforth refer to the subjects by their given names. Male historical actors are most often referred to in Japanese sources by their surnames, except in cases where they were known by pen-names, or where using surnames would be confusing. Women, on the other hand, are often referred to by their given names for various reasons including, I would argue, a presumption of familiarity derived from public–private distinctions. The issue is a complex one since it also raises biographical conventions in both Japanese and English, but I ultimately decided to use (legal) given names (hence 'Suga' not 'Sugako'), largely because the similarity of the surnames, Kanno and Kaneko, might prove confusing to readers unfamiliar with the Japanese language.
4 See Setouchi Harumi, 'Kanno Sugako: Koi to Kakumei ni Junjita Meiji no Onna (Bijoden Daikyūwa)' ['Kanno Sugako: the Meiji Woman who Sacrificed Herself for Love and Revolution (Biographies of Beautiful Women)'], *Chūō Kōron*, vol. 80, no. 9 (September 1965), pp. 291–301. One of the first works in English where Suga was discussed in some detail was a biography of Kōtoku. Here, however, she was treated more as a villain than a 'heroine'. F. G. Notehelfer, *Kōtoku Shūsui: Portrait of a Japanese Radical*, Cambridge University Press, 1971, pp. 167–8, 176. More recently, we still find works in Japanese that seem to be mostly interested in the subjects' love-lives, for example, Suzuki Yūko (ed.), *Shisō no Umi e (Kaihō to Kakumei), 21, Josei – Hangyaku to Kakumei to Teikō to*, Tokyo, Shakai Hyōronsha, 1990 (Part Three: 'Hangyaku to Ai to' ['Treason and Love']), pp. 30–52.
5 Foucault, 'Infamous Men', p. 79.

6 On the creation of political martyrs by both the Japanese authorities and their supporters, and opponents, see Robert Jay Lifton, Katō Shūichi and Michael R. Reich, *Six Lives, Six Deaths: Portraits from Modern Japan*, New Haven, Connecticut and London, Yale University Press, 1979, pp. 277 ff.

7 Cited in Notehelfer, p. 185n.

8 Ibid., pp. 188–9.

9 Cf. Kanno, Prison Declaration [to Prosecutors] (3 June 1910), in Shimizu Unosuke (ed.), *Kanno Sugako Zenshū, III*, 3 vols, Kōryūsha, 1984, pp. 198–9; and Supreme Court Pretrial Interrogation [hereafter 'Court Interrogation'], no. 13 (17 October 1910), in ibid., pp. 281–2.

10 Kanno mentioned the five guilty parties more than once in her prison diary, the surviving portion of which covers the period between 18 and 24 January 1911, the last week of her life: 'Shide no Michikusa' ['A Pause on the Way to Death'], in *Zenshū, II*, pp. 245–72. It is somewhat difficult to render its title into English: 'pausing' may imply hesitation but is closer to the sense in Japanese of simply stopping on the way than rather more suggestive possibilities like 'loitering', 'dawdling' or even 'wasting time'. A near-complete translation of the diary can be found in Hane Mikiso (trans., ed.), *Reflections on the Way to the Gallows: Voices of Japanese Rebel Women*, New York, Pantheon, 1988, pp. 58–74.

11 Kanno, Court Interrogation, no. 6 (13 June 1910), in *Zenshū, III*, p. 248. She probably excluded Uchiyama Gudō because he had been sentenced for an explosives violation a year before others were arrested in the (related) treason incident.

12 Cited in Jay Rubin, *Injurious to Public Morals: Writers and the Meiji State*, Seattle and London, University of Washington Press, 1984, p. 160n; Hiraide's views are also discussed in Nakamura Fumio, *Taigyaku Jiken to Chishikijin*, Tokyo, San'ichi Shobō, 1981, pp. 45–6.

13 There is one work in English that deals briefly with this *legal* case: Richard Mitchell's *Janus-faced Justice: Political Criminals in Imperial Japan*, Honolulu, University of Hawaii Press, 1992, pp. 43–5.

14 For information about both the massacre and Pak Yeol's political career, see Michael Weiner, *The Origins of the Korean Community in Japan, 1910–1923*, Manchester, Manchester University Press, 1989.

15 Komatsu Ryūji, 'Hangyaku no Josei, Kaneko Fumiko: "Pak Yeol Jiken" Hashigaki', *Jiyū Shisō*, vol. 6 (July 1961), p. 43; cf. Morinaga Eisaburō, 'Himerareta Saiban: Pak Yeol, Kaneko Fumiko Jiken, I', *Hōritsu Jihō*, vol. 35, no. 3 (March 1963), pp. 58 ff.

16 Mitchell, p. 45.

17 The testimonies of the sixteen Futeisha members are included in *Boku Retsu, Kaneko Fumiko Saiban Kiroku*, Tokyo, Kokushoku Sensensha, 1977.

18 Their defence lawyer, Fuse Tatsuji, remarked on this in *Unmei no Shōrisha: Pak Yeol*, Seiki Shobō, 1946, p. 75.

19 Prosecutors had almost as much freedom to interrogate suspects as the preliminary court judges who, in practice if not by law, were able to continue with interrogations indefinitely in closed rooms. See Kim Il Song, *Pak Yeol*, Tokyo, Gōdō Shuppan, 1974, pp. 172–3.

20 On Nanba Daisuke see Setouchi Harumi, 'Kaneko Fumiko', in Setouchi (ed.), *Jinbutsu Kindai Joseishi, Onna no Isshō, 6, Hangyaku no Onna no Roman*, Tokyo, Kōdansha, 1981, p. 143; on both incidents in Japan, cf. Kim, pp. 226–8; and on the Uiyōldan, Mukuge no Kai (eds), *Chōsen 1930 Nendai Kenkyū*, Tokyo, San'ichi Shobō, 1982, pp. 86–7.

21 Morinaga, p. 60.

22 Cf. Komatsu, loc. cit.; Weiner, p. 152.

23 Shimizu Unosuke (ed.), *Kanno Sugako Zenshū*, Tokyo, Kōryūsha, 1984.

24 Kanno Suga, Diary, in *Zenshū*, II, pp. 245–72.

25 See Rubin, pp. 156–7.

26 For example, Shiota Shōbei and Watanabe Junzō (eds), *Hiroku Taigyaku Jiken, I-II*, Tokyo, Shunjūsha, 1959.

27 *Akai Tsutsuji no Hana: Kaneko Fumiko no Omoide to Kashū*, Kokushoku Sensensha, 1984. The title of this booklet refers to poems about flowers in the prison garden.

28 Hane includes sections of one extract from Fumiko's prison memoirs in his chapter on her in his *Reflections on the Way to the Gallows*, pp. 75–124.

29 Hane Mikiso (trans., ed.), *Reflections*, 'The Road to Nihilism', pp. 75–124; and Jean Inglis (trans.), *Kaneko Fumiko: The Prison Memoirs of a Japanese Woman*, London and New York, M.E. Sharpe, 1991.

30 Kaneko Fumiko, *Nani ga Watashi o Kōsaseta ka*, Tokyo, Chikuma Shobō, 1984, p. 205.

31 On the importance of confession in the prewar and postwar legal systems, cf. Elise Tipton, *The Japanese Police State: The Tokkō in Interwar Japan*, London, Athlone Press, 1990, pp. 35–51; and also on the methods still used to extract confessions today, Igarashi Futaba, 'Forced to Confess', in Gavan McCormack and Sugimoto Yoshio (eds), *Democracy in Contemporary Japan*, Sydney, Hale and Iremonger, 1986, pp. 195–214.

32 Kim, pp. 176–7.

33 Tipton, p. 31.

34 This is still a common practice today, according to Igarashi, p. 205; cf. John O. Haley, 'Sheathing the Sword of Justice in Japan: An Essay on Law Without Sanctions', *Journal of Japanese Studies*, vol. 8, no. 2 (Summer 1982), pp. 266 ff.

35 See Jean Inglis, 'Book Review: "What Made Me Like This?" The Prison Memories of Kaneko Fumiko', *Ampo: Japan–Asia Quarterly Review*, vol. 13, no. 2 (1981), pp. 34–5.

36 Perhaps the Supreme Court judges, for example, were considered too 'lenient' for granting two of Pak Yeol's demands: 1) that since he was in court as a representative of the Korean people, he should be allowed to don a Korean 'crown' and 'royal' (imperial) robes, symbolizing his equality with the judges; 2) that he be allowed to begin the proceedings by accusing Japan of plundering Korea, symbolizing his putting Japan on trial. On his demands, see Kim, pp. 214–15.

2 THE WORK (STRUCTURE, LOGIC, METHOD)

1 Works by Greg Dening, Inga Clendinnen, June Philipp and Rhys Isaac, for example, will be referred to below.

2 Hayden White, 'Interpretation in History', in White, *Tropics of Discourse: Essays in Cultural Criticism*, Baltimore, Maryland, and London, John Hopkins University Press, 1978, pp. 51–80.

3 On liberal-humanist autobiography, see Sidonie Smith, *A Poetics of Women's Autobiography*, Bloomington and Indianapolis, Indiana University Press, 1987; and Sidonie Smith and Julia Watson (eds), *De/Colonizing the Subject: The Politics of Gender in Women's Autobiography*, Minneapolis, University of Minnesota Press, 1992.

4 Hélène Bowen Raddeker, 'The Past Through Telescopic Sights: Reading the Prison-Life-Story of Kaneko Fumiko', *Japan Forum*, vol. 7, no. 2 (Autumn 1995), pp. 155–69; Raddeker, '"Death as Life": Political Metaphor in the Testimonial Prison Literature of Kanno Suga' (forthcoming in *Bulletin of Concerned Asian Scholars*).

5 Elaine Jeffreys, 'What is "Difference" in Feminist Theory and Practice?', *Australian Feminist Studies*, no. 14 (Spring 1991), pp. 3, 10.

6 For example, Joan Wallach Scott, *Gender and the Politics of History*, New York, Columbia University Press, 1988.

7 Sharon Sievers treats Suga as an involuntary martyr by depicting her last days in prison in a way that is suggestive of failure and defeat, even though she concedes that well before her imprisonment Suga had been 'ready to die in battle'. See Sievers, *Flowers in Salt: The Beginnings of Feminist Consciousness in Modern Japan*, Stanford, California, Stanford University Press, 1983, pp. 158–62.

8 Tsurumi Shunsuke and Komatsu Ryūji are among those who emphasize that Kaneko Fumiko was framed. Cf. Tsurumi Shunsuke, 'Kaisetsu', in Kaneko Fumiko, *Nani ga Watashi o Kōsaseta ka*, Tokyo, Chikuma Shobō, 1984, p. 214; Komatsu Ryūji, 'Hangyaku no Josei, Kaneko Fumiko: "Boku Retsu Jiken" Hashigaki', *Jiyū Shisō*, vol. 6 (July 1961), p. 37. Also, on the 'completely trumped up charge' of Kaneko Fumiko's plotting to assassinate the emperor, see Hane Mikiso, 'Introduction', in Jean Inglis (trans.), *Kaneko Fumiko: The Prison Memoirs of a Japanese Woman*, New York and London, M.E. Sharpe, Inc., 1991, p. xv.

9 June Philipp, 'Traditional Historical Narrative and Action-Oriented (or Ethnographic) History', *Historical Studies*, vol. 2 (April 1983), pp. 340, 350.

10 H. D. Harootunian, *Things Seen and Unseen: Discourse and Ideology in Tokugawa Nativism*, Chicago, University of Chicago Press, 1988, p. 3.

11 H. Lawson, *Reflexivity: The Post-modern Predicament*, London, Hutchinson, 1985, p. 10.

12 Paul de Man, 'Task of the Translator', in de Man, *The Resistance to Theory*, Minneapolis, University of Minnesota Press, 1986, pp. 87, 94.

13 Philipp, p. 352.

14 The often-cited phrase, 'confusion of tongues', brings to mind Clifford Geertz, and his warning about the complex nature of analysis of cultural meaning is pertinent. While one might never 'get anywhere near to the bottom' of the interpretative problem at hand, an acceptance of the inevitability of there often being many more layers of meaning than we can possibly suspect is preferable to the over-confident approach to meaning *which has also carried over into translation*. In this work I will often direct my attention to problems of linguistic meaning in such a way as to imply,

like Foucault or de Man, that translation is never true equivalence but rather interpretation or 'reduction'. Cf. C. Geertz, *The Interpretation of Cultures*, New York, Basic Books, 1973, p. 29; Foucault cited in Hayden White, p. 237; de Man, loc. cit.

15 Philipp, p. 350. Cf. Rhys Isaac, *The Transformation of Virginia, 1740–1790*, Chapel Hill, University of North Carolina Press, 1982, p. 325.

16 In Meaghan Morris and Paul Patton (eds), *Michel Foucault: Power, Truth, Strategy*, Sydney, Feral Publications, 1979, p. 79.

17 Ibid., p. 85.

18 Ibid., p. 86.

19 Hane Mikiso, *Reflections on the Way to the Gallows: Rebel Women in Prewar Japan*, New York, Pantheon, 1988, pp. 3, 259.

20 John Crump, *The Origins of Socialist Thought in Japan*, London and Canberra, Croom Helm, 1983, p. 313.

21 While *ken'i* or *kenryoku*, terms the subjects used, could be rendered as either 'power' or 'authority', I prefer the former because neither Suga nor Fumiko would have accepted the latter's implication of legitimacy. On power, authority and legitimacy, see J. G. Merquior, *The Veil and the Mask: Essays on Culture and Ideology*, London, Routledge and Kegan Paul, 1979, pp. 1–38.

22 Ibid. Harootunian is not unlike Foucault in distancing himself from Marxism–Leninism ('diamat') in such a way as to overlook the fact that mechanistic base–superstructure notions and ideology-as-conspiracy assumptions have long been discredited *by Marxists* (not just their liberal-democratic critics). See Harootunian, pp. 1 ff.; and Foucault, 'Truth and Power', in Colin Gordon (ed.), *Power/Knowledge: Selected Interviews and Other Writings 1972–1977 by Michel Foucault*, Brighton, Harvester Press, 1980, pp. 117–18.

23 For a thoughtful discussion of this issue in the context of Japanese historiography, see Herman Ooms, *Tokugawa Ideology: Early Constructs, 1570–1680*, Princeton, New Jersey, Princeton University Press, 1985, pp. 7–9.

24 Andō Shōeki cited in Maruyama Masao, *Studies in the Intellectual History of Tokugawa Japan*, Tokyo, University of Tokyo Press, 1974, p. 261.

25 Ooms, p. 296.

26 On ideological 'masks' versus 'veils', see Merquior, loc. cit.

27 Carol Gluck, *Japan's Modern Myths: Ideology in the Late Meiji Period*, Princeton, New Jersey, Princeton University Press, 1985, p. 78.

28 Jon Halliday, *A Political History of Japanese Capitalism*, New York and London, Monthly Review Press, 1975, p. 41.

29 Ibid., p. 42.

30 Gluck, pp. 281–2.

31 Irokawa Daikichi, *The Culture of the Meiji Period*, Princeton, New Jersey, Princeton University Press, 1985, p. 310.

32 On the Peace Preservation Law of 1925, which allowed for a reduction of penalty if offenders were co-operative, see Richard Mitchell, *Thought Control in Prewar Japan*, Ithaca, New York, and London, Cornell University Press, 1976; on *tenkō*, cf. Mitchell and Patricia Steinhoff, 'Tenkō: Ideology and Social Integration in Prewar Japan', unpublished doctoral thesis, Harvard University, 1969. On one group of communists encouraged to recant while in prison in 1929, the then pro-imperial 'Workers' Faction',

cf. Fukunaga Isao, *Kyōsantōin no Tenkō to Tennōsei*, Tokyo, San-ichi Shobō, 1978, pp. 40–8; and Shisō no Kagaku Kenkyūkai (eds), *Tenkō, I*, Tokyo, Heibonsha, 1978, pp. 147 ff.

33 In August 1926, Judge Tatematsu resigned (after having received a promotion!) apparently in order to avoid disciplinary action over the photo scandal. Morinaga Eisaburō, 'Himerareta Saiban: Pak Yeol, Kaneko Fumiko Jiken, I', *Hōritsu Jihō*, vol. 35, no. 3 (March 1963), p. 60.

34 Inga Clendinnen, *Ambivalent Conquests: Maya and Spaniard in Yucatan, 1517–1570*, Cambridge, Cambridge University Press, 1987, p. 113.

35 Isaac, pp. 344–6.

36 Hane, *Reflections*, p. 258.

37 For an interesting account of the traditional and modern aspects of Meiji hegemonic ideology concerning women, see Sharon H. Nolte and Sally Ann Hastings, 'The Meiji State's Policy Toward Women, 1890–1910', in Gail Lee Bernstein (ed.), *Recreating Japanese Women, 1600–1945*, Berkeley, University of California Press, 1991, pp. 151–74.

38 Ooms, 'Introduction: Beginnings', p. 5.

39 Cf. Jacques Derrida, 'Structure, Sign and Play in the Discourse of the Human Sciences', in Derrida, *Writing and Difference*, London, Routledge, 1990 (Alan Bass, trans., ed.).

40 On teleology in narrative history, see Philipp, p. 34. Leith Morton alludes to this problem when in the conclusion to his biography of the leftist writer, Arishima Takeo, he says, 'This final act of suicide dominates the perspective of virtually all who have written on his life. . . . The compelling need to understand and explain that suicide turns his biography into an examination of cause.' But his warning against reading Arishima's writings 'solely from the perspective of his suicide' looks like an afterthought, given that he begins his biography by raising two central questions to be answered, one being 'Why did the novelist choose to end his life in so dramatic a fashion?' See Leith Morton, *Divided Self: A Biography of Arishima Takeo*, Sydney, Allen and Unwin, 1988, pp. 2, 212.

41 Komatsu (pp. 38 ff.) is simply retells the family history that Fumiko told, problematizing it only when observing that perhaps she was a bit prejudiced against her father. Her account needs to be 'supplemented', he observes, in order to get a 'true' picture – so that we can 'judge' the family. For an extended critique of such approaches, see Bowen Raddeker, 'The Past Through Telescopic Sights', op. cit.

42 Robert Jay Lifton, Katō Shūichi and Michael R. Reich, *Six Lives, Six Deaths: Portraits from Modern Japan*, New Haven, Connecticut, and London, Yale University Press, 1979, p. 14.

43 Jean-Michel Raynaud, 'What's What in Biography', in James Walter (ed.), *Reading Life Histories: Griffith Papers on Biography*, Griffith University, Australia, 1981, p. 93.

44 Ibid.

45 Ooms, p. 5.

46 For example, Itoya Toshio, *Kanno Suga: Heiminsha no Fujin Kakumeika Zō*, Tokyo, Iwanami Shinsho, 1970, pp. 5 ff.; and Sievers, p.140.

47 Suga's left her one-time lover, Arahata, some years before her death, and years after that he was clearly still resentful. None the less, his evaluations of her have too often been uncritically repeated. Cf. F. G. Notehelfer,

Kōtoku Shūsui: Portrait of a Japanese Radical, Cambridge, Cambridge University Press, 1971, p. 167; and Arahata Kanson, *Kanson Jiden*, Tokyo, Ronsōsha, 1961.

48 By '*presenting*' texts I mean a careful consideration of the effects on a text of the conditions of textual production – the text's context or present, its intended audience, etc. On pre*sent*ing and *present*ing, see Greg Dening, 'History as a Symbol Science', in *The Bounty: An Ethnographic History*, Melbourne, University of Melbourne Monograph Series, 1988, pp. 100–2.

49 Lifton *et al.*, p. 289.

3 KANNO SUGA: 'THE UNSWERVING PATH'

1 Kanno 'Sugako', '*Shide no Michikusa*' [Diary] (20 January 1911), in Shimizu Unosuke (ed.), *Kanno Sugako Zenshū, II*, Tokyo, Kōryūsha, 1984, p. 255. This '*hitosuji michi*' (straight road) was clearly meant to indicate a path from which Suga had felt she could not, or would not, deviate. I have therefore preferred 'unswerving' because of its common association with commitment or purpose.

2 While it is common enough to use familiar terms like 'gallows' and 'scaffold' in connection with executions in Japan at this time, in fact Suga and her co-defendants were garrotted.

3 Numanami Masanori, 'Kōtoku Ippa no Keishi Setsuna', in Ichiba Takajirō (hikki), *Numanami Masanori Dan*, cited in Itoya Toshio, *Kanno Suga: Heiminsha no Fujin Kakumeika Zō*, Tokyo, Iwanami Shinsho, 1970, p. 210.

4 Cited in ibid. (account by prison warder, Sugano Josaemon).

5 *Miyako Shinbun* and *Tokyo Asahi Shinbun*, cited in Hane Mikiso, *Reflections on the Way to the Gallows: Rebel Women in Prewar Japan*, New York, Pantheon, 1988, pp. 57–8.

6 On the reactions of Meiji intellectuals to the high treason incident, for example the poet, Ishikawa Takuboku, see Nakamura Fumio, *Taigyaku Jiken to Chishikijin*, Tokyo, San'ichi Shobō, 1981, pp. 44–5.

7 Arahata Kanson, *Kanson Jiden*, Tokyo, Ronsōsha, 1961, p. 220.

8 Kanno, Diary (21 January 1911), in *Zenshū, II*, p. 262.

9 See Kanno, Postcard to Baibunsha (23 January 1911), in *Zenshū, III*, p. 188. The Baibunsha was a literary hackwork (ghostwriting) and translating business venture that Sakai started up in December 1910. It played an important role in helping socialists to survive financially during these 'winter' years of Japanese socialism. Stefano Bellieni, *Notes on the History of the Left-Wing Movement in Meiji Japan*, Napoli, Istituto Orientale di Napoli, 1979, p. 41.

10 Kanno, Diary (23 January 1911), in *Zenshū, II*, pp. 266–7.

11 John Crump reminded me by correspondence that Arahata Kanson erected a stone for Suga in 1971. When he visited Shōshunji he could find no trace of Hide's grave, though there is an unmarked flat stone near a similar (original) one for Suga.

12 Kanno, loc. cit.

13 See Kanno, Sealed Card to Sakai Tameko and Sakai Toshihiko (4 January 1911), in *Zenshū, III*, pp. 176.

14 Letter to Yoshikawa Morikuni (21 January 1911), in ibid., p. 182.
15 [Kanno] 'Yūzukijo', 'Waga Tera' [first published in *Mainichi Denpō*, no. 1618, April 1908], in *Zenshū, II*, pp. 227–9. 'Yūzukijo' was one of the pen-names Suga used as a journalist.
16 Kanno, Diary (23 January 1911), in *Zenshū, II*, p. 266.
17 Cf. ibid., pp. 266–7; and diary entry for 19 January, p. 251.
18 Ibid. (20 January 1911), p. 255.
19 Ibid. (19 January 1991), in *Zenshū, II*, pp. 250–1.
20 See Commentator's notes on Kanno's prison diary in *Zenshū, II*, pp. 274–5.
21 Kanno, loc. cit.
22 On the persecution and martyrdoms or apostasies of European priests (mostly Jesuits) and Japanese laity, mainly after 1614, see George Elison, *Deus Destroyed: The Image of Christianity in Early Modern Japan*, Boston, Massachusetts, Harvard University Press, 1973, Part II, pp. 109 ff.
23 Kanno, Diary (21 January 1911), in *Zenshū, II*, pp. 259–60.
24 Kanno, 'Personal Correspondence', in *Zenshū, III*, pp. 179–80.
25 There has been some debate about whether Ishikawa Sanshirō was already an anarchist in Meiji. However, he seems to have been closer to the 'direct action' faction and, from 1908, was clearly more interested in Kropotkin than Marx: see Ōsawa Masamichi, 'Ishikawa Sanshirō Ron', in Tsurumi Shunsuke (ed.), *Ishikawa Sanshirō Shū*, Tokyo, Chikuma Shobō, 1976, pp. 424–7.
26 In Kanno, Letter to Imamura Rikisaburō (13 January 1911), in *Zenshū, III*, p. 179. She may have sent him three poems as two lines were censored.
27 Shimizu Unosuke, 'Kanno Sugako Shōden: Shōgai to Kōdō' [Biography], in Shimizu (ed.), *Zenshū, III*, p. 305.
28 Sakai Toshihiko in *Heimin Shinbun* (no. 30, 24 February 1907), cited in Sharon Sievers, *Flowers in Salt: The Beginnings of Feminist Consciousness in Modern Japan*, Stanford, California, Stanford University Press, p. 152.
29 See Kanno, Sealed Cards to Tanikawa Takeo, and to Ōsugi Sakae and Hori-Ōsugi Yasuko, both on 21 January 1911, in *Zenshū, III*, pp. 183, 186.
30 On her eternal separation from loved ones, see the same letter to Takeo (ibid.) and a card on the same date to Sakai Tameko, p. 184. The reference to Zōshigaya was in the latter.
31 Kanno, Diary (20 January 1911), in *Zenshū, II*, p. 255.
32 Kanno, Declaration to Prosecutors in Prison [hereafter 'Prison Declaration'] (3 June 1910), in *Zenshū, III*, p. 199.
33 See, for example, Kanno's Prison Declaration of 26 September 1910, in ibid., p. 275.
34 Jay Rubin, *Injurious to Public Morals: Writers and the Meiji State*, Seattle and London, University of Washington Press, 1984, p. 165.
35 Hiraide Shū, *Gyakutō*, cited in Itoya, p. 197.
36 Kanno, Court Interrogation (3 June 1910), in *Zenshū, III*, p. 216.
37 Kanno, Letter to Kōtoku Shūsui (12 May 1910), in ibid., p. 160.
38 Kanno, Letter to Kōtoku Shūsui (16 May 1910), in ibid., p. 162.
39 Cf. [Kanno] 'Yūzukijo', 'Kata Kanroku' [first published in *Murō Shinpō*, no. 581, 18 April 1906], and 'Onna toshite no Kibō [no. 588, 9 May 1906], in *Zenshū, II*, pp. 120, 144.
40 Kanno, Diary (21 January 1911), in *Zenshū, II*, p. 256; and on the 'new shoots', p. 259.

41 See Kanno, Court Interrogation (3 June 1910), in *Zenshū, III*, p. 208.
42 See also [Kanno] 'Sugako', 'Kanson-kun o Okuru' [first published in *Murō Shinpō*, no. 581, 18 April 1906], in *Zenshū, II*, p. 118.
43 Kanno, Court Interrogation, no. 13 (17 October 1910), in *Zenshū, III*, pp. 279–280.
44 Cited in W. R. LaFleur, 'Japan', in Frederick H. Holck (ed.), *Death and Eastern Thought: Understanding Death in Eastern Religions and Philosophies*, Nashville, Tennessee, and New York, Abingdon Press, 1974, p. 245.
45 Kōtoku Shūsui, 'Eleventh Pretrial Hearing Record' (25 July 1910), in Shiota Shōbei and Watanabe Junzō (eds), *Hiroku Taigyaku Jiken, II*, Tokyo, Shunjūsha, 1959, p. 26.
46 Kōtoku's Thirteenth Pretrial Hearing Record (17 October 1910), in ibid., p. 39.
47 Kanno, Diary (23 January 1911), in *Zenshū, II*, p. 269.
48 Ibid.
49 Hiraide, Gyakutō, cited in Itoya, p. 198.
50 Hane, *Reflections*, p. 57; Rubin, p. 165.
51 On death, vengeance and wandering spirits, cf. Lafcadio Hearn, *Kwaidan: Stories and Studies of Strange Things*, Rutland, Vermont, and Tokyo, Tuttle, 1971, pp. 45–9, 53–61; and Robert J. Smith, *Ancestor Worship in Contemporary Japan*, Stanford, California, Stanford University Press, 1974, pp. 41 ff.
52 Kanno, Prison Declaration, no. 1 (2 June 1910), in *Zenshū, III*, pp. 195–6.
53 Ibid.
54 On Yamagata, see R. F. Hackett, 'Political Modernization and the Meiji Genrō', in R. E. Ward (ed.), *Political Development in Modern Japan*, Princeton, New Jersey, Princeton University Press, 1968, pp. 65–97; and for a more critical view, E. H. Norman, 'The Autocratic State', in John Dower (ed.), *Origins of the Modern Japanese State: Selected Writings of E. H. Norman*, New York, Pantheon, 1975, pp. 65–97.
55 Kanno, Court Interrogation (3 June 1910), in *Zenshū, III*, p. 210.
56 On the theme of evil officials around the 'throne' (lord) in Tokugawa peasant tales, see Anne Walthall, *Social Conflict and Popular Culture in Eighteenth-Century Japan*, Tucson, University of Arizona Press, 1986, pp. 178 ff.
57 Kanno, Prison Declaration, no. 1 (2 June 1910), in *Zenshū, III*, p. 198.
58 Kanno, Court Interrogation (3 June 1910), in ibid., p. 209; and for her account of the Red Flag Incident, Court Interrogation, n. 13 (17 October 1910), p. 278.
59 [Kanno] 'Yūzukijo', 'Hiji Deppō' [first published in *Murō Shinpō*, no. 580 (15 April 1906)], in *Zenshū, II*, p. 113.
60 Kanno, Postcard to Kōtoku Shūsui (11 May 1910), in *Zenshū, III*, p. 159.
61 The terms 'pessimism–optimism' have been used to distinguish religious systems on the basis of whether salvation is deemed possible (see Bertrand Russell, *A History of Western Philosophy*, London, Allen and Unwin, 1979, pp. 291, 756). Yet for Nakamura Hajime, optimism about this life or world means that one does not represent it as inherently painful, impure or unreal in opposition to a pure or blessed, true life in the next world. (*Ways of Thinking of Eastern Peoples: India, China, Tibet, Japan*, Honolulu, East–West Center Press, 1964, pp. 361 ff.) The term will be used here in

the second sense, though without necessarily implying anything about belief in an 'other' world.

62 Kanno, Diary (21 January 1911), in *Zenshū, II*, p. 261.
63 Kanno, 'Heiminsha yori' [first published in *Jiyū Shisō* (*Free Thought*), editorial, 10 June 1909], in *Zenshū, II*, p. 242.
64 Kanno, Diary (21 January 1911), in *Zenshū, II*, p. 259.
65 Ibid., p. 256.
66 Ibid., p. 245.
67 Ibid. (22 January 1911), pp. 263–4.
68 Kanno, Letters to Ōsugi Sakae and Hori-Ōsugi Yasuko, and to Sakai Toshihiko (21 January 1911), in *Zenshū, III*, pp. 185–6.
69 Kanno, Diary (20 January 1911), in *Zenshū, II*, p. 253.
70 Ibid., pp. 257–8.
71 Ibid., p. 272.
72 Ibid. (23 January 1911), p. 270.
73 Ibid. (20 January 1911), pp. 255–6.

4 KANEKO FUMIKO: 'THE WILL TO DIE'

1 *Akai Tsutsuji no Hana: Kaneko Fumiko no Omoide to Kashū*, Tokyo, Kokushoku Sensensha, 1984, p. 39.
2 Tokyo *Asahi Shinbun*, 31 July 1926, p. 1 [photocopied newspaper reports included in], *Kaneko Fumiko, Pak Yeol Saiban Kiroku*, Tokyo, Kokushoku Sensensha, 1977, p. 796. [All testimonies referred to in this chapter are from this volume.]
3 Cf. ibid.; Setouchi Harumi, *Yohaku no Haru*, Tokyo, Chūkō Bunko, 1975, p. 66.
4 Facsimile of death certificate in Setouchi, ibid., p. 80.
5 *Asahi Shinbun*, loc. cit.; ibid., pp. 62–3 .
6 Cited in Setouchi, p. 62.
7 *Asahi Shinbun*, loc. cit.
8 See Mochizuki Kei, 'Kaneko Fumiko-san no Shōzō ni tsuite', in *Akai Tsutsuji* (in unnumbered pages in prologue).
9 For a record of the marriage, see copies of the Kaneko entries in the Register of Families, in *Saiban Kiroku*, p. 875.
10 Mochizuki, loc. cit.
11 For such advertisements, see copies of *Kokutō/La Nigra Ondo*, no. 1, July 1922; *Futei Senjin*, nos. 3 and 4, March and June 1923, in *Saiban Kiroku*, pp. 808, 841, 865.
12 On various occasions from the mid-1930s Fuse was disbarred, prosecuted and imprisoned for his radical legal activities. He died of cancer on 13 September 1953. See Fuse Kanji, *Aru Bengoshi no Shōgai: Fuse Tatsuji*, Tokyo, Iwanami Shoten, 1963, pp. 200 ff.
13 Accounts of the exhumation by some present at it are included in Setouchi, p. 339.
14 Richard Mitchell argues that it was usually lower-ranking police personnel who mistreated prisoners, though against express orders. Cf. Elise Tipton, *The Japanese Police State: The Tokkō in Interwar Japan*, London, Athlone Press, 1990, p. 31; Richard Mitchell, *Thought Control in Prewar*

Japan, Ithaca, New York, and London, Cornell University Press, 1976, p. 101.

15 Kurihara Kazuo, 'Hangyakusha Den: Kaneko Fumiko', in *Jiyū Rengō Shinbun*, no. 39 (1 September 1929), reproduced in *Akai Tsutsuji*, p. 60.

16 Cited in Setouchi, pp. 65–6 (date of interview not given but clearly more than forty years later).

17 Fuse Tatsuji, *Unmei no Shōrisha, Pak Yeol*, Tokyo, Seiki Shobō, 1946, pp. 25–7.

18 Cf. Setouchi, pp. 337–8; and *Akai Tsutsuji*, chronology of Fumiko's life (unnumbered pages). The English sources referred to are: Hane, *Reflections*, pp. 79, 259, and 'Introduction', in Jean Inglis (trans.), *Kaneko Fumiko: The Prison Memoirs of a Japanese Woman*, New York and London, M. E. Sharpe, 1991, xv; also Richard Mitchell, *Janus-Faced Justice: Political Criminals in Imperial Japan*, Honolulu, University of Hawaii Press, 1992, p. 45.

19 Kaneko, *Akai Tsutsuji*, p. 11.

20 Cited in Setouchi, pp. 335–6.

21 Kaneko, Tokyo District Court Preliminary Interrogation [hereafter 'Court Interrogation'], no. 3 (22 January 1924), pp. 18–9.

22 Kaneko, Court Interrogation, no. 7 (25 January 1924), p. 25.

23 Cited in Setouchi, p. 329. The full statement, headed '26 February, Late in the Night', in Fumiko's own handwriting, is in *Saiban Kiroku*, pp. 739–48.

24 Cited in Setouchi., p. 320 (in *Saiban Kiroku*, p. 348).

25 See Kim Il Song, *Pak Yeol*, Tokyo, Gōdō Shuppan, 1974, p. 171.

26 Nietzsche and Max Stirner will be discussed in more detail in Chapter 5. Unlike Fumiko, Stirner did expound radical solipsism but, like her, he also spoke of 'annihilating the world': Max Stirner, *The Ego and His Own*, London, Jonathan Cape, 1971 (first published 1845), p. 204.

27 Kaneko, Court Interrogation, no. 2 (17 January 1924), p. 15.

28 Ibid., no. 3 (22 January 1924), pp. 17–18.

29 Nietzsche, *Twilight of the Idols*, Harmondsworth, Penguin, 1968, pp. 129 ff.; *Beyond Good and Evil*, Harmondsworth, Penguin, 1972, p. 64.

30 See Michael Artzibashev, *Sanine*, London, Martin Secker, 1928 (first published in 1914).

31 Kaneko, Letter to Judge Tatematsu, in *Saiban Kiroku*, p. 107.

32 On 7 July that year Tatematsu ruled that he did not have any jurisdiction over matters connected with Article 73 of the Criminal Code; and that it was therefore a matter for the Supreme Court.

33 Artzibashev, p. 247.

34 Cited in Setouchi, pp. 330–1; also in Morinaga Eisaburō, 'Himerareta Saiban: Pak Yeol, Kaneko Fumiko Jiken, 1–2', *Hōritsu Jihō*, vol. 35, nos 3–4 (March and April 1963), Part I, p. 63. There is disagreement about when this untitled and undated statement was made, but Fuse recalled that Fumiko wrote a statement during the preliminaries of the high treason trial (at the end of 1925) for Judge Itakura (who was not appointed to the case until October). Fuse said that this very long statement was written in forty minutes. It appears in Fumiko's (barely legible) handwriting in the Trial Records amongst other records dated the end of October and beginning

of November. Cf. Fuse, pp. 250–1; Kaneko, Untitled and Undated Statement, in *Saiban Kiroku*, pp. 581–9 (this passage, pp. 588–9).
35 Kaneko, Supreme Court Preliminary Interrogation Record, no. 1, cited in Morinaga, loc. cit. [also in *Saiban Kiroku*, dated 17 November 1925, p. 575.]
36 Kaneko, Supreme Court Interrogation Record, no. 1, cited in ibid. [also in *Saiban Kiroku*, dated 26 February 1926, p. 685.]
37 Stirner, 'My Self-Enjoyment' (contrasting the enjoyment of life with the desire/hope for its preservation) in *Ego*, pp. 224 ff.
38 Kaneko, Court Interrogation Record, no. 12 (14 May 1924), p. 62.
39 Kaneko, 'Untitled Statement', cited in Morinaga, loc. cit.
40 See, for example, Hane's *Reflections of the Way to the Gallows*, p. 75, 119 ff.; Mitchell, *Janus-faced Justice*, p. 44.
41 Kaneko, *Akai Tsutsuji*, p. 26.
42 Kaneko, *Nani ga Watashi o Kōsaseta ka*, Tokyo, Chikuma Shobō, 1984, p. 205. Hereafter, references to these memoirs will simply give the surname and page number/s.
43 Kaneko, *Akai Tsutsuji*, pp. 25–6.
44 Ibid.
45 Kaneko, pp. 83–4.
46 Ibid., pp. 84–5.
47 Kaneko, *Akai Tsutsuji*, p. 12.
48 Kaneko, pp. 177–8. On non-registration in Japan today, see Satō Bunmei, *Koseki ga Tsukuru Sabetsu*, Tokyo, Gendai Shokan, 1984, pp. 147 ff.
49 Kaneko, *Akai Tsutsuji*, p. 33.
50 On the massacre see C. Lee and G. De Vos, *Koreans in Japan: Ethnic Conflict and Accommodation*, Berkeley, University of California Press, 1981, pp. 21 ff.; and Richard Mitchell, *The Korean Minority in Japan*, Berkeley, University of California Press, 1967, pp. 38–41.
51 Kaneko, *Akai Tsutsuji*, p. 38.
52 Kaneko, p. 178.
53 Kaneko, Court Interrogation, no. 4 (23 January 1924), p. 20.
54 Kaneko, p. 196.
55 Kaneko, Court Interrogation, no. 2 (22 January 1924), p. 17.
56 Kaneko, Court Interrogation, no. 4 (23 January 1924), p. 20.
57 Kaneko, p. 196.
58 Ibid., pp. 201–2.
59 Cited in Fuse, pp. 253–4.
60 Stirner, pp. 209, 217, 229, 198–9.
61 See Kaneko, Court Interrogation, no. 4 (23 January 1924), p. 20.
62 Cf. Setouchi, p. 324; also Setouchi, 'Kaneko Fumiko', in Setouchi (ed.), *Jinbutsu Kindai Joseishi, Onna no Isshō, 6, Hangyaku no Onna no Roman*, Tokyo, Kōdansha, 1981, p. 144; Kim, p. 214; and Kaneko, Akai Tsutsuji, p. 25.
63 Kaneko, p. 205.
64 Setouchi, *Yohaku no Haru*, pp. 337–8.
65 Kaneko, *Akai Tsutsuji*, p. 9.
66 Ibid., p. 17.
67 Ibid., p. 22.
68 Ibid., p. 25.
69 Ibid., p. 33.

5 COMMENTARY: DISCOURSE ON DEATH AND BEYOND

1 Robert J. Lifton, Katō Shūichi and Michael R. Reich, *Six Lives, Six Deaths: Portraits from Modern Japan*, New Haven, Connecticut, and London, Yale University Press, 1979.
2 Philippe Ariès, *Western Attitudes Toward Death*, Baltimore, Maryland, and London, John Hopkins University Press, 1974, pp. 90–3.
3 Philippe Ariès, *The Hour of Our Death*, New York, Alfred A. Knopf, 1981, pp. 605 ff.
4 Lifton *et al.*, p. 285.
5 Cf. Chan Wing-Tsit, 'The Spirit of Oriental Philosophy', in Charles A. Moore (ed.), *Philosophy East and West*, Princeton, New Jersey, Princeton University Press, 1944, pp. 147 ff.; Lee Jung Young, *Death and Beyond in the Eastern Perspective: A Study Based on the* Bardo Thödol *and the* I Ching, New York, Interface, 1974; P.T. Raju, 'Foreword', in Frederick H. Holck (ed.), *Death and Eastern Thought: Understanding Death in Eastern Religions and Philosophies*, Nashville, Tennesse, and New York, Abingdon Press, 1974; and P.J. Saher, *Eastern Wisdom and Western Thought: A Comparative Study in the Modern Philosophy of Religion*, London, Allen and Unwin, 1969, pp. 241–5.
6 For example, Carl Gustav Jung, 'Psychological Commentary on "The Tibetan Book of the Great Liberation"', in *The Collected Works of C. G. Jung, II: Psychology and Religion, East and West*, Princeton, New Jersey, Princeton University Press, 1969, p. 481.
7 Cf. Nakamura Hajime, *Ways of Thinking of Eastern Peoples: India, China, Tibet, Japan*, East–West Center Press, 1964, pp. 361 ff.; Lifton *et al.*, pp. 22 ff., 284–5; Joseph J. Spae, 'Recent National Trends', in Spae (ed.), *Japanese Religiosity*, Tokyo, Oriens Institute for Religious Research, 1971, p. 227.
8 On the doctrine of *akunin shōki*, see Jan Van Bragt, 'Nishitani on Japanese Religiosity', in Spae (ed.), ibid., p. 277; and Nakamura, ibid., p. 386.
9 William R. LaFleur, *The Karma of Words: Buddhism and the Literary Arts in Medieval Japan*, Berkeley, University of California Press, 1983, pp. 26–59.
10 On uneasy spirits, see Hori Ichirō, *Folk Religion in Japan: Continuity and Change*, Chicago, University of Chicago Press, 1968, pp. 32, 85.
11 Shimizu Unosuke, 'Kanno Sugako Shōden' [Biography], in Shimizu Unosuke (ed.), *Kanno Sugako Zenshū, III*, Tokyo, Kōryūsha, 1984, pp. 299–301.
12 On the Kyōfūkai see Sharon Sievers, *Flowers in Salt: The Beginnings of Feminist Consciousness in Modern Japan*, Stanford, California, Stanford University Press, 1983 (Chapter 5), pp. 87–113.
13 Helen Hardacre, *Kurozumikyō and the New Religions of Japan*, Princeton, New Jersey, Princeton University Press, 1986, p. 4.
14 H. Byron Earhart (ed.), *Religion in the Japanese Experience: Sources and Interpretations*, Belmont, California, Dickenson Publishing, 1974, pp. 251, 131.
15 Murakami Shigeyoshi, *Japanese Religion in the Modern Century*, Tokyo, University of Tokyo Press, 1980, p. 12.
16 Ibid., p. 15.

17 Cited in Irokawa Daikichi, *The Culture of the Meiji Period*, Princeton, New Jersey, Princeton University Press, 1985, p. 193.

18 Jay Rubin, *Injurious to Public Morals: Writers and the Meiji State*, Seattle and London, University of Washington Press, 1984, p. 161. On this tendency amongst Buddhist socialists in the 1930s, see Notto R. Thelle, *Buddhism and Christianity in Japan: From Conflict to Dialogue, 1854–1899*, Honolulu, University of Hawaii Press, 1987, p. 253.

19 Hardacre, p. 7; cf. Murakami, pp. 45, 70.

20 On the close affinities between Pure Land Buddhism and Christianity, cf. Spae, pp. 209–30, and Ninian Smart, 'Western Society and Buddhism', *Journal of Oriental Studies*, vol. 2 (1989), p. 45.

21 Murakami, pp. 14–5.

22 *The Doctrine of Tenrikyō*, Nara, Japan, Tenrikyō Church Headquarters, 1954, pp. 21 ff.

23 Cited in John Crump, *The Origins of Socialist Thought in Japan*, London and Canberra, Croom Helm,1983, p. 310.

24 Janet A. Walker, *The Japanese Novel of the Meiji Period and the Ideal of Individualism*, Princeton, New Jersey, Princeton University Press, 1979, p. 63.

25 Carmen Blacker, *The Japanese Enlightenment: A Study of the Writings of Fukuzawa Yukichi*, Cambridge, Cambridge University Press, 1964, p. 58.

26 Thelle, pp. 196–8.

27 Ihara Saikaku, *Tales of Samurai Honor* (Caryl Ann Callahan, trans.), Tokyo, Monumenta Nipponica (Sophia University), 1981, pp. 73–4.

28 Crump, p. 293. On Meiji Christianity and Christian socialism, see Irwin Scheiner, *Christian Converts and Social Protest in Meiji Japan*, Berkeley, University of California Press, 1970.

29 [Kanno] 'Yūzuki', 'Misohitomoji no Ongakkai Kenmonki' [first published in *Murō Shinpō*, no. 577, 6 April 1906], in *Zenshū, II*, pp. 105–6.

30 Kaneko, *Nani ga Watashi o Kōsaseta ka*, Tokyo, Chikuma Shobō, 1984, pp. 157 ff., 167 (subsequently, only the name and page number/s will be cited for Fumiko's memoirs).

31 See Saitō Otomatsu, 'Witness Interrogation Record' (19 August 1925), in *Kaneko Fumiko, Pak Yeol Saiban Kiroku*, Tokyo, Kokushoku Sensensha, 1977, p. 245.

32 Arahata Kanson's suggestion that Suga drew close to Christianity out of a moral abhorrence for her own 'promiscuity' will be discussed in Part 2.

33 Maruyama Masao, *Studies in the Intellectual History of Tokugawa Japan*, Tokyo, University of Tokyo Press, 1974, p. 263.

34 See Gino K. Piovesana, *Recent Japanese Philosophical Thought, 1862–1962: A Survey*, Tokyo, Enderle Bookstore, 1963, pp. 25–6.

35 Blacker, pp. 58–9.

36 Jean-Pierre Lehmann, *The Roots of Modern Japan*, London, Macmillan, 1982, pp. 250, 257.

37 Earl H. Kinmonth, *The Self-Made Man in Meiji Japanese Thought: from Samurai to Salary Man*, Berkeley, University of California Press, 1981, pp. 100, 111 ff.

38 Piovesana, p. 251.

39 Kinmonth, p. 338.

40 Lewis A. Coser, *Masters of Sociological Thought: Ideas in Historical and Social Context*, New York, Harcourt Brace Jovanovich, Inc., 1977, p. 100.
41 Kanno, '*Shide no Michikusa*' [Diary] (23 January 1911), in *Zenshū, II*, p. 266.
42 Kinmonth, p. 244.
43 Jacques Choron, *Death and Western Thought*, New York and London, Collier-Macmillan, 1963, pp. 209–10.
44 Lucio Colletti, *Marxism and Hegel*, London, New Left Books, 1973, p. 27. Re Hegel's approach to death, see James P. Carse, *Death and Existence: A Conceptual History of Human Mortality*, New York, John Wiley and Sons, 1980, pp. 352 ff.
45 If Fumiko knew of the 'Oriental' Hegelian dialectic, she did not seem to share the interest in it of Japanese philosophers like Nishida Kitarō, founder of the Kyoto School of philosophy, on which see Piovesana, pp. 112–14, 195–6.
46 Interpretations of Nietzsche's 'will to power' differ. Guy Welbon argues that Nietzsche may have been more authentic a Buddhist than Schopenhauer because of his definition of nirvana as a quest for power – not power over this world but rather a cosmic power. Ofelia Schutte points to various ways in which the 'will to power' can be interpreted, but does not refute views of it as oppressive, worldly domination. Schutte, *Beyond Nihilism: Nietzsche Without Masks*, Chicago, University of Chicago Press, 1984 (Chapter 4, 'The Will to Power as Metaphor'), pp. 76–104; Welbon, *The Buddhist Nirvana and its Western Interpreters*, Chicago, University of Chicago Press, 1968, pp. 188 ff.
47 See Piovesana, pp. 60–2.
48 Kinmonth, p. 238
49 Piovesana, pp. 70–3.
50 Friedrich Nietzsche, *Twilight of the Idols*, Harmondsworth, Penguin, 1968, pp. 88–9.
51 Cited in Choron, p. 204.
52 See Kaneko, Untitled Statement in *Saiban Kiroku*, pp. 588–9.
53 For discussion of Schopenhauer's 'pessimism', cf. Bertrand Russell, *A History of Western Philosophy*, London, Allen and Unwin, 1979, pp. 726–7, and Choron, pp. 162, 185; re Schopenhauer on egoism, Choron, p. 180. Concerning Schopenhauer's influence upon Japanese philosophy: Piovesana, pp. 36, 50–1, 75. Also, on the influence of Buddhist notions like ego-annihilation on Schopenhauer, see Welbon, pp. 156–7; and on Zen's double negation, Abe Masao, *Zen and Western Thought*, William R. LaFleur, ed., Honolulu, University of Hawaii Press, 1985, p. 127.
54 Kinmonth, pp. 210 ff.
55 Nancy Andrew, 'The Seitōsha: An Early Japanese Women's Organization, 1911–1916', (Harvard East Asian Research Center) *Papers on Japan*, (1972), pp. 51–2, 63.
56 Kinmonth, p. 236.
57 On authority, idealism and optimism about the future, her special task in life, and worldly success, see Kaneko, pp. 194–6.
58 Thomas A. Stanley, *Ōsugi Sakae, Anarchist in Taishō Japan: The Creativity of the Ego*, Boston, Massachusetts, Harvard University Press, p. 62; and on intellectual leadership of the masses, Ōsawa Masamichi (ed.), *Ōsugi*

Sakae Zenshū, VI, Rōdō Undō Ronshū, Tokyo, Gendai Shichō, 1963, pp. 112 ff.
59 Stanley, loc. cit.
60 Takeuchi Seiichi, *Jiko Chōetsu no Shisō: Kindai Nihon no Nihirizumu*, Tokyo, Perikansha, 1988, pp. 3–4.
61 Max Stirner, *The Ego and His Own*, John Carrol, ed., London, Jonathan Cape, 1971, pp. 226–7.
62 Ibid., pp. 223, 50–3.
63 For Stirner on 'Man' and the 'Unique One', see ibid., pp. 259–61. Re this humanist subject of history, Foucault's debt to Nietzsche is well known, but partly because of Stirner's attack on humanism and essentialism, poststructuralist theorists recently have also 'resurrected' him. See, for example, Jacques Derrida, *Specters of Marx*, New York and London, Routledge, 1994.
64 Paterson argues that Stirner was more a forebear of existentialism than anarchism because existentialists, like Stirner, diagnosed the 'nothingness' of life. Stirner's, however, was a positive nothingness; it was not a terrifying (existentialist) 'emptiness'. Cf. R. W. K. Paterson, *The Nihilistic Egoist: Max Stirner*, London, Oxford University Press, 1971 (Chapters VI and VIII). Also, on existentialist views on life and death, Choron, pp. 222–3.
65 Itō Noe wrote a short piece about the novel about one year after separating from her second husband, Tsuji Jun, who translated Stirner's book. Itō's article was about the sort of hero she respected, and Sanine headed the list for his cool detachment from conventional morality, his independent attitude toward doing just as he liked, his lack of affectation, and also his 'manly indifference' toward the death of a 'young idealist'. Itō Noe, 'Sanin no Taido', in *Itō Noe Zenshū*, vol. 2, pp. 301–4.
66 Ibid., p. 302.
67 Human ugliness, instinctual desires, animalism, and a fascination with death had been common themes in Japanese naturalism in late Meiji. Rubin remarks on official views of such pessimistic 'harmful influences' on Japanese literature and society. See Rubin, pp. 63, 99 ff.
68 Michael Artzibashev, *Sanine*, London, Martin Secker, 1928, p. 180.
69 Ibid., p. 247.
70 Ibid., pp. 45–7.
71 Ibid., pp. 9, 127, 315.
72 Ibid., p. 194.
73 Ibid., pp. 46–7, 68, 118 ff.
74 Ibid., pp. 47, 68, 246, 289.
75 Ibid., p. 314.
76 Ibid., p. 156.
77 Nishitani Keiji (*Religion and Nothingness*, Berkeley, University of California Press, 1982) was interested in parallels between Stirner's 'creative nothingness' and Buddhist nihilism. Bergsonianism in Japan will be discussed in the next chapter.
78 On 'being-*sive*-nothingness' in Zen, ibid., p. 72; Abe, pp. 126–7.
79 Kaneko, pp. 105 ff. The family religion on the maternal side was probably True Pure Land Buddhism, however. See Kaneko Sehi (Fumiko's grandmother), Witness Interrogation Record (13 August 1925), in *Saiban Kiroku*, p. 239.

80 Lifton *et al.*, pp. 22–5, 28.
81 Ibid., pp. 284–5. For Nishitani Keiji too Buddhist pessimism, (other-worldliness and world-negation) was alien to the Japanese: Jan Van Bragt, 'Translator's Introduction', in Nishitani, xxxvi.
82 See Lifton *et al.*, pp. 8–9. Confucianism is said to be a philosophical expression of the biological, familial or ancestral mode.
83 The items Suga wanted left to friends are listed in Kanno, Letter to Sakai Toshihiko (24 January 1911), in *Zenshū, III*, pp. 190–91. Magara, the daughter of Sakai Toshihiko, wrote some fifty years after the event of a formal silk *haori* left her by Suga, which she used to wear in the early 1920s when at times she herself was in the same prison. See Sakai Magara cited in Hane Mikiso, *Reflections on the Way to the Gallows: Rebel Women in Prewar Japan*, New York, Pantheon, 1988, pp. 128–9.
84 Lifton *et al.*, p. 22.
85 The same could probably be said of the murders of Ōsugi Sakae and Itō Noe, who had been ostracized after the famous love quadrangle-'free love' scandal of 1916. On socialist criticisms of their 'free love', see Akiyama Kiyoshi, 'Sei to Jiyū ni tsuite', *Shisō no Kagaku*, no. 123 (November 1971), pp. 26–34.
86 Kaneko, p. 6.
87 Lifton *et al.*, pp. 11–12.
88 Re European Romanticism, for example, Shelley on death as 'oneness with Nature' – see Choron, pp. 156–61. It is interesting that Japanese 'eco-nationalists' of late have represented Japan's environmental crisis as the result of Western influence, since the Japanese have apparently always had a specially harmonious relationship with Nature. See Tessa Morris-Suzuki, 'Concepts of Nature and Technology in Pre-Industrial Japan', *East Asian History*, vol. 1 (June 1991), pp. 81–2.
89 Kaneko, pp. 32 ff. Deguchi Nao, founder of the new religion, Ōmotokyō, had also seen the cities as exploitative of the villages: see Murakami, pp. 70–5, and Hardacre, p. 7.
90 Kaneko, pp. 75–6.
91 See William R. LaFleur, 'Japan' (Chapter VII), in Holck (ed.), pp. 242 ff.
92 LaFleur (ibid., p. 232) refers to a well-known poem by the twelfth-century poet-monk, Saigyō, also about transience and death symbolized by the cry of a cricket.
93 Kaneko Fumiko, *Akai Tsutsuji no Hana: Kaneko Fumiko no Omoide to Kashū*, Tokyo, Kokushoku Sensensha, 1984, pp. 20, 19.
94 In Japan the raven has been a symbol of poignancy, loneliness, sorrow or death, as in some of Bashō's poems: Yuasa Nobuyuki (trans.), *Bashō: The Narrow Road to the Deep North*, Harmondsworth, Penguin, 1966, pp. 26, 58.
95 Lifton *et al.*, p. 27.
96 Greg Dening, *The Bounty: An Ethnographic History*, Melbourne, University of Melbourne Monograph Series, 1988, p. 98.

6 COMMENTARY: MARTYRS, NIHILISTS AND OTHER REBEL HEROES

1 This calls to mind the words of Lord Cromer, once colonial governor of Egypt, for whom Egyptian nationalism was a 'novel idea . . . a plant of

exotic rather than of indigenous growth'. (Cited in Edward W. Said, *Orientalism*, Harmondsworth, Penguin, 1978, p. 39.) As Said observes, his belief that it was an 'unnatural implant' was based on his view of 'Orientals' as 'feudal', unprogressive, childlike and dependent.

2 In syndicalism elsewhere 'direct action' had meant direct *economic* (i.e., not 'political'/parliamentary) action like strikes, industrial sabotage or the General Strike. On 'direct action' in Japan, see John Crump, *The Origins of Socialist Thought in Japan*, London and Canberra, Croom Helm, 1983, pp. 164–7.

3 On Bergsonianism in Japan, see Gino K. Piovesana, *Recent Japanese Philosophical Thought, 1862–1962: A Survey*, Tokyo, Enderle Bookstore, 1963, pp. 74–5, 197 ff.

4 Bertrand Russell, *A History of Western Philosophy*, London, Allen and Unwin, 1979, p. 756.

5 Matsumoto Sannosuke, 'The Idea of Heaven: A Tokugawa Foundation for Natural Rights Theory', in Najita Tetsuo and Irwin Scheiner (eds), *Japanese Thought in the Tokugawa Period, 1600–1868: Methods and Metaphors*, Chicago, University of Chicago Press, 1978, p. 181.

6 Cf. Clifford Geertz, *The Interpretation of Cultures*, New York, Basic Books, pp. 3 ff.; Greg Dening, *The Bounty: An Ethnographic History*, Melbourne, University of Melbourne Monograph Series, 1988, pp. 93–111.

7 Inga Clendinnen, *Ambivalent Conquests; Maya and Spaniard in Yucatan, 1517–1570*, Cambridge: Cambridge University Press, 1987, pp. 131 ff.

8 For extracts from these magazines, see Kōtoku Shūsui Zenshū Iinkai (ed.), *Taigyaku Jiken Arubamu: Kōtoku Shūsui to sono Shūhen*, Tokyo, Meiji Bunken, 1972, pp. 105–9.

9 Stefano Bellieni, *Notes on the History of the Left-wing Movement in Meiji Japan*, Napoli, Istituto Orientale de Napoli, 1979, pp. 20–2.

10 Cf. Arahata cited in Crump, p. 308; Voline, *The Unknown Revolution, 1917–1921*, New York, Free Life Editions, 1974, pp. 103 ff.

11 Ivan Morris, *The Nobility of Failure: Tragic Heroes in the History of Japan*, Harmondsworth, Penguin, 1975, xxi–xxiii, p. 177.

12 Thomas Huber, '"Men of High Purpose" and the Politics of Direct Action, 1862–1864', in Najita Tetsuo and J. Victor Koschmann (eds), *Conflict in Modern Japanese History: The Neglected Tradition*, Princeton, New Jersey, Princeton University Press, 1982, p. 124.

13 Ian Buruma, *A Japanese Mirror: Heroes and Villains of Japanese Culture*, Harmondsworth, Penguin, 1985, p. 189.

14 Ibid., p. 137.

15 Albert M. Craig, *Chōshū in the Meiji Restoration*, Boston, Massachusetts, Harvard University Press, 1961, p. 150.

16 On the reasons for Zen's popularity with samurai, see Suzuki Daisetz, *Zen and Japanese Culture*, New York, Pantheon, 1959, pp. 61 ff. Suzuki's own, rather romanticized account of the Zen–samurai nexus often reveals how violence might come to be justified secularly despite teachings of avoidance of it.

17 See, for example, Michael Polyani and Harry Prosch, *Meaning*, Chicago, University of Chicago Press, 1975, pp. 15 ff.

18 Dōgen, 'Bendōwa', cited in Abe Masao, *Zen and Western Thought*, William R. LaFleur (ed.), Honolulu, University of Hawaii Press 1985, p. 222.

19 Ibid., pp. 58–9.
20 On selflessness and loyalty as central to *the* (singular) 'way of the warrior', see Robert Bellah, *Tokugawa Religion: The Values of Pre-Industrial Japan*, New York, Free Press, pp. 90–8.
21 For a critique of anachronistic and essentialist notions of Shūshigaku neo-Confucianism as the sum total of ideology in Tokugawa, see Herman Ooms, *Tokugawa Ideology: Early Constructs, 1570–1680*, Princeton, New Jersey, Princeton University Press, 1985.
22 Morris, xxi.
23 See ibid., pp. 183, 215.
24 Barbara Smith, 'Itō Noe, Living Love and Anarchy: "Free Love" in Taishō Japan' (unpublished Honours Thesis, Centre for Asian Studies, University of Adelaide), 1991, pp. 37–8.
25 There is much in Takeuchi Seiichi's discussion of Japanese philosophical nihilism that suggests Fumiko's ideas: Takeuchi, *Jiko Chōetsu no Shisō: Kindai Nihon no Nihirizumu*, Tokyo, Perikansha, 1988, pp. 2–3.
26 See E. H. Norman, 'The Restoration', in John Dower (ed.), *Origins of the Modern Japanese State; Selected Writings of E. H. Norman*, New York, Pantheon, 1975, pp. 191–2.
27 Irokawa Daikichi, *The Culture of the Meiji Period*, Princeton, New Jersey, Princeton University Press, 1985, pp. 87–8, 133.
28 Crump, p. 131.
29 Ibid., p. 38; cf. Jay Rubin, *Injurious to Public Morals: Writers and the Meiji State*, Seattle and London, University of Washington Press, 1984, p. 39.
30 Crump, pp. 212–14.
31 Cited in ibid., p. 312.
32 On conservative women's organizations from Meiji to 1945, see Sheldon Garon, 'Women's Groups and the Japanese State: Contending Approaches to Political Integration, 1890–1945', *Journal of Japanese Studies*, vol. 19, no. 1 (Winter 1993), pp. 5–41.
33 See Barbara Alpern Engel, *Mothers and Daughters: Women of the Intelligentsia in Nineteenth Century Russia*, Cambridge, Cambridge University Press, 1983, pp. 4–5.
34 Kanno, Prison Declaration (3 June 1910), in Shimizu Unosuke (ed.), *Kanno Sugako Zenshū, II*, Tokyo, Kōryūsha, 1984, p. 203.
35 Cited in Irokawa, p. 69.
36 Marius B. Jansen, 'The Meiji State: 1868–1912', in J.B. Crowley (ed.), *Modern East Asia: Essays in Interpretation*, New York, Harcourt, Brace and World, 1970, p. 116; cf. Carol Gluck, *Japan's Modern Myths: Ideology in the Meiji Period*, Princeton, New Jersey, Princeton University Press, 1985, pp. 272–3.
37 See Robert J. Lifton, Katō Shūichi and Michael R. Reich, *Six Lives, Six Deaths: Portraits from Modern Japan*, New Haven, Connecticut, Yale University Press, 1979, pp. 155–91.
38 Akiyama Kiyoshi, *Nihiru to Teroru*, Tokyo, Tairyūsha, 1977, p. 252.
39 Even in 1910 the literary critic, Uozumi Setsurō, had argued that naturalism represented an historical alliance of scientific determinism and the ideal of individual freedom – 'against a common enemy, authority'. (Cited in Arima Tatsuo, *The Failure of Freedom: A Portrait of Modern Japanese Intellectuals*, Boston, Massachusetts, Harvard University Press, 1969,

p. 80). Of course, a poet Fumiko particularly admired, Ishikawa Takuboku, responded in his famous essay 'Jidai Heisoku no Genjō' that Japanese naturalists, for all their pretensions, had never really defied authority. Cf. Matsuda Michio, *Gendai Nihon Shisō Taikei, 16: Anakizumu*, Tokyo, Chikuma Shobō, 1963, pp. 45–6.

40 Lifton *et al.*, p. 23.

41 On the mixed reactions of contemporaries to Nogi's suicide, see Gluck, pp. 221–7.

42 See William R. LaFleur, 'Japan', in Frederick H. Holck (ed.), *Death and Eastern Thought: Understanding Death in Eastern Religions and Philosophies*, Nashville, Tennessee and New York, Abingdon Press, 1974, pp. 248–9.

43 Irokawa, pp. 116 ff.

44 Ibid., pp. 161, 254. On peasants creating themselves in the role of the 'perfect warrior', see Anne Walthall, *Social Conflict and Popular Culture in Eighteenth-century Japan*, Tucson, Arizona, The University of Arizona Press, 1986, p. 203.

45 Janet A. Walker, *The Japanese Novel of the Meiji Period and the Ideal of Individualism*, Princeton, New Jersey, Princeton University Press, 1979, p. 6.

46 *Osaka Heimin Shinbun* (20 September 1907), cited in Crump, p. 310.

47 Cited in Setouchi Harumi, *Yohaku no Haru*, Tokyo, Chūkō Bunko, 1975, p. 320 (the original statement is in *Kaneko Fumiko, Pak Yeol Saiban Kiroku*, Kokushoku Sensensha, 1977, p. 348).

48 See Kaneko, Preliminary Court Record, no. 2 (17 January 1924), in ibid., p. 13.

49 Crump, loc. cit.

50 The prewar Marxist, Kawakami Hajime, reported that he had once experienced this 'Great Death' while in the Pure Land sect. It confirmed his ideal of 'absolute unselfishness'. See Lifton *et al.*, pp. 170–1; also on the Great Death, Abe, pp. 165–6.

51 LaFleur, 'Japan', pp. 243–4.

52 Ibid.

53 Norman, loc. cit. For an overview of incidents of political violence (from below) in Japan since early in the Meiji period, see Morikawa Tetsurō, *Ansatsu Hyakunenshi*,Tokyo, Tosho Shuppansha, 1973, pp. 14–81.

54 Even if peasants were happy to appropriate some aspects of samurai action, violence directed at the persons of oppressors (rather than at their property) had not been so common in traditional peasant rebellion. See Stephen Vlastos, *Peasant Protests and Uprisings in Tokugawa Japan*, Berkeley, University of California Press, 1986, pp. 18–20.

55 Lifton *et al.*, p. 27.

56 Irokawa Daikichi seems to ignore Japan's long tradition of peasant rebellion when he argues that in late Tokugawa ordinary village people 'underwent a spiritual revolution and . . . rejected traditional fatalism that led to an acceptance of one's lot in life'. (Irokawa, pp. 180–1.)

57 Joseph J. Spae, 'The Religiosity of "Eschatological Attitudes"', in Spae (ed.), *Japanese Religiosity*, Tokyo, Oriens Institute for Religious Research, 1971, p. 120.

58 Matsuda, pp. 56–7.

59 On Berkman and Vaillant, see Emma Goldman, 'The Psychology of Political Violence', in Alix Kates Shulman (ed.), *Red Emma Speaks: An Emma Goldman Reader*, New York, Schocken Books, 1972, pp. 267–71.
60 Kim Il Song, *Pak Yeol*, Tokyo, Gōdō Shuppan, 1974, pp. 226–7.
61 Wada Kyūtarō was sentenced to life imprisonment, while Muraki Genjirō died in prison during the pretrial. Cf. Akiyama Kiyoshi, *Waga Bōryoku Kō*, Tokyo, San'ichi Shobō, 1977, pp. 34–47; and Eguchi Kan, *Waga Bungaku Hansei Ki*, II, Tokyo, Aoki Shoten, 1968.
62 Irokawa, pp. 138, 168, 181. On the desire of some *shishi* to punish those who had 'offended Heaven', see Huber, p. 110. There are many suggestions of '*tenbatsu*' (visiting 'heavenly' punishment on the evil) also in Walthall's account of Tokugawa peasant protests: cf. Walthall, pp. 173–204.
63 David Plath, 'Where the Family of God is the Family: The Role of the Dead in Japanese Households', extract in H. Byron Earhart (ed.), *Religion in the Japanese Experience: Sources and Interpretations*, California, Dickenson Publishing, 1974, pp. 149–54; and on the significance of '*urami*' (resentment or a grudge) in classical language and culture, cf. Kuno Akira, 'The Structure of "Urami"', *Nichibunken Japan Review* (International Research Center for Japanese Studies), vol. 2 (1991), pp. 117–23.
64 Hori Ichirō, *Folk Religion in Japan: Continuity and Change*, Chicago, University of Chicago Press, 1968, pp. 43, 117 ff.
65 Kaneko Fumiko, *Nani ga Watashi o Kōsaseta ka*, Tokyo, Chikuma Shobō, 1984, p. 85.
66 See Kaneko, Court Interrogation no. 6 (25 January 1924), in *Saiban Kiroku*, p. 23. In this interrogation Judge Tatematsu asked Fumiko about the language she used – the pejorative terminology used by her group not only for the 'Cabinet Ministers or high officials' already mentioned, but also for police, and the emperor and crown prince.
67 Lifton *et al.*, pp. 289, 279.
68 See Nancy Andrew, 'The Seitōsha: An Early Japanese Women's Organization, 1911–1916', *Papers on Japan* (Harvard East Asian Research Center), 1972, p. 52. On the double suicide of the leftist novelist, Arishima Takeo, and a journalist, Hatano Akiko, see Leith Morton, *Divided Self: A Biography of Arishima Takeo*, Sydney, Allen and Unwin, 1988 (Chapter 8, 'Freedom and Death'), pp. 179–211.
69 Kanno, 'Shide no Michikusa' (20 January 1911), in *Zenshū, II*, p. 256.
70 See Kanno, 'Onna toshite no Kibō' [first published in *Murō Shinpō*, no. 588, 9 May 1906], in ibid., pp. 143–5.
71 Lifton *et al.*, p. 289.
72 For such a treatment of (General Nogi's) 'survivor guilt', see Lifton *et al.*, 'The Emperor's Samurai', pp. 29–66.
73 Ooms, p. 288.

7 KANNO SUGA (1902–1911)

1 Two authors who represent information supplied in Suga's 'semi-autobiographical' works as factual are: Kondō Tomie, 'Kanno Suga', in Setouchi Harumi (ed.), *Jinbutsu Kindai Joseishi, Onna no Isshō, 6, Hangyaku no Onna no Roman*, Tokyo, Kōdansha, 1981, pp. 27 ff.; and Sharon

Sievers, *Flowers in Salt: The Beginnings of Feminist Consciousness in Modern Japan*, Stanford, California, Stanford University Press, 1983 (Chapter 7, 'Kanno Suga'), pp. 139–62. Others will be referred to below.

2 Noriko Mizuta Lippit, *Reality and Fiction in Modern Japanese Literature*, New York and London, M. E. Sharpe, 1980, p. 18.

3 Donald Keene, *Modern Japanese Literature*, New York, Grove Press, 1956, pp. 23–6.

4 Noriko Mizuta Lippit and Kyoko Iriye Selden (eds), *Stories by Contemporary Japanese Women Writers*, New York and London, M. E. Sharpe, 1982, ix–xvi.

5 Victoria V. Vernon, *Daughters of the Moon: Wish, Will and Social Constraint in Fiction by Modern Japanese Women*, Berkeley, University of California, Institute of East Asian Studies, 1988, p. 68.

6 Shimizu Unosuke gives precise details about Suga's family history (addresses, etc.), which are clearly derived from local official records. See Shimizu (ed.), *Kanno Sugako Zenshū, III*, Tokyo, Kōryūsha, 1984, pp. 326–37.

7 Kanno, First Criminal Investigation Record (3 June 1910), in ibid., p. 197.

8 Kondō, p. 31.

9 [Kanno] 'Sugako', 'Omokage' [first published in seven parts in *Ōsaka Chōhō*, nos. 23–40, 31 July–9 September 1902], in *Zenshū, II*, Parts II–III, pp. 296–7.

10 Kanno, Criminal Investigation Record, loc cit.; cf. Arahata Kanson, *Kanson Jiden*, Tokyo, Ronsōsha, 1961, p. 126.

11 [Kanno] 'Sugako', 'Omokage', Part I, in *Zenshū, II*, p. 292.

12 Ibid., Part II, p. 295.

13 Ibid., Part VII, p. 302.

14 See [Kanno] 'Sugako', 'Isshūkan' [first published in twenty-two parts in *Ōsaka Chōhō*, nos. 106–31, 29 November–28 December 1902], Part 17 in *Zenshū, I*, pp. 195–6.

15 Setouchi Harumi, *Tōi Koe*, Tokyo, Shinchō Bunko, 1975, p. 14; Itoya Toshio, *Kanno Suga: Heiminsha no Fujin Kakumeika Zō*, Tokyo, Iwanami Shinsho, 1970, pp. 16 ff., 31–2; Kondō, p. 32; Sievers, p. 142.

16 Sievers (p. 221) urges caution about accepting Arahata as a reliable source, so possibly she was not aware that her information in this case (Itoya, ibid.) was based on Arahata's account.

17 Arahata, pp. 125–6.

18 The references to Suga's 'promiscuity' are left unquestioned by Kondō (pp. 34–5). The reason Arahata gave for Suga's despair was that her patron would not permit her to marry. See Setouchi's 'Kanno Sugako: Koi to Kakumei ni Junjita Meiji no Onna (Bijoden Daikyūwa)', *Chūō Kōron*, vol. 80, no. 9 (September 1965), p. 294, on how she had hoped to marry a journalist named Itō Kanezuki, but their engagement was opposed by Udagawa.

19 Arahata, p. 176.

20 On Suga's easy seduction of the innocent Arahata, at least according to his *own* account, see Sievers, p. 221.

21 Jay Rubin, *Injurious to Public Morals: Writers and the Meiji State*, Seattle and London, University of Washington Press, 1984, pp. 37–8.

22 On views of women in Buddhism, see Diana Paul, *Women in Buddhism: Images of the Feminine in Mahāyāna Tradition*, Berkeley, University of California Press, 1979.

23 Cf. Kanno, Court Interrogation (3 June 1910), in *Zenshū, III*, p. 207; [Kanno] 'Yūzuki', 'Tenjōkai [first published in *Michi no Tomo*, December 1904–January 1905], in *Zenshū, II*, pp. 19–29; Shimizu Unosuke, 'Kanno Sugako Shōden – Shōgai to Kōdō' [Biography], in Shimizu (ed.), *Zenshū, III*, p. 302.

24 Sievers, p. 143.

25 On this tendency amongst women in the Moral Reform Society, see Sievers, pp. 95–6.

26 One representative article was [Kanno] 'Yūzuki', 'Komatsumiya-denka no Goitoku' [first published in *Ōsaka Chōhō*, no. 160, 6 March 1903], in *Zenshū, I*, p. 263.

27 Ibid., p. 265.

28 See William Reynolds Braisted (trans. and ed.), *Meiroku Zasshi: Journal of the Japanese Enlightenment*, Cambridge, Massachusetts, Harvard University Press, 1976.

29 See [Kanno] 'Yūzuki-joshi', 'Hakurankai Kogoto' [first published in eight parts in *Ōsaka Chōhō*, nos. 164–71, 11–20 March 1903], Parts V and VI, in *Zenshū, I*, pp. 282–5.

30 On moralistic elitism in the early socialist movement, see Peter Duus and Irwin Scheiner, 'Socialism, Liberalism, Marxism', in Duus (ed.), *The Cambridge History of Japan, Volume 6: The Twentieth Century*, Cambridge, Cambridge University Press, 1988, pp. 663 ff., 672.

31 Sievers, pp. 92–3.

32 [Kanno] 'Yūzuki', 'Shūgyōfu no Butō Kinshi no Undō' [first published in *Ōsaka Chōhō*, no. 186, 8 April 1903], in *Zenshū, I*, p. 379.

33 Itoya, p. 18.

34 Ibid., pp. 29–30.

35 [Kanno] 'Sugako', 'Zekkō' [first published in *Kirisutokyō Sekai*, no. 1050, 8 October 1903], in *Zenshū, III*, pp. 44–50.

36 Suga's literary talent is an area of contention that can, in part, be traced back to Arahata's negative assessment of her writings. Yet Shimizu concurs with Kondō's positive view of 'Zekkō'. For him it has a literary quality that matches works by famous contemporaries like Yosano Akiko. Shimizu nevertheless describes Suga's earliest efforts as only 'competent', or 'immature'. On the other hand, her prison diary he judges a 'masterpiece', a work with 'serenity' and without 'affectation'. Cf. Kondō, pp. 34–5; Arahata cited in Sievers, p. 221; Itoya, p. 17; and Shimizu, Biography, pp. 299–300.

37 On the style of the arguments against war of the Heiminsha, see John Crump, *The Origins of Socialist Thought in Japan*, London and Canberra, Croom Helm, 1983, pp. 44–51.

38 [Kanno] 'Yūzuki-joshi', 'Sensō to Fujin' [first published in *Michi no Tomo*, April 1904], in *Zenshū, II*, pp. 5–8.

39 See Rubin (pp. 55–9) for references to Yosano's ambivalence regarding nationalism. He discusses the jingoistic furore the poem caused, largely because she implied that if the emperor did not fight, then neither should her brother.

40 Kanno, 'Sensō to Fujin', in *Zenshū, II*, p. 7.
41 Kanno, 'Zekkō', in *Zenshū, III*, pp. 47–8.
42 Ibid., pp. 49–50.
43 Letter in English to American anarchist, Albert Johnson, cited in Crump, pp. 291–2.
44 See Kanno, Criminal Investigation Record, loc. cit.; and for another example of the evil geisha-stepmother theme, [Kanno] 'Sugako', 'Ritchi' [first published in *Michi no Tomo*, May Issue, 1903], in *Zenshū, III*, pp. 5–15. 'Ritchi' was the name of a family pet, a dog whose death was caused by the cruel stepmother.
45 [Kanno] 'Yūzuki', 'Tsuyuko' [first published serially in twenty-four parts in *Murō Shinpō*, nos. 529–75, 6 November 1905–30 March 1906], in *Zenshū, III*, Parts III–IV, pp. 87, 90.
46 Ibid., Parts III–IV, pp. 89–90.
47 Ibid., Parts II–III, pp. 84–5.
48 Ibid., Parts XVIII–XIX, pp. 119–20.
49 See Shimizu, Biography, p. 297 (Shimizu mentions the likelihood of Suga's having been raped twice); and [Kanno] 'Oitako', 'Kinenbi' [first published in *Osaka Chōhō*, no. 22, 26 July 1902], in *Zenshū, I*, pp. 80–2.
50 Both the second part of 'Kinenbi' and Part 23 of 'Tsuyuko' (which comes before the heroine is discovered unconscious) are noted in the Collected Works to be not extant and thus not included. One wonders if they fell victim to self-censorship by a concerned editor.
51 Shimizu gives the family's full address in Ōita-ken (in 1895, Suga's fourteenth year). Also, in one article written in 1903, 'Kanno Sugako' wrote of a recent meeting with a woman she had known in Ōita. See [Kanno] 'Sugako', 'Kōgyō Kannai no Kigū' (first published in *Osaka Chōhō*, no. 162, 8 March 1903), in *Zenshū, I*, pp. 267–9.
52 Arahata, p. 126.
53 Itoya, p. 11; Kondō, p. 28.
54 Cf. Arahata, loc. cit.; Setouchi, 'Koi to Kakumei', p. 295; Kondō, pp. 28–9.
55 Kanno Suga, Diary (21 January 1911), in *Zenshū, II*, p. 257.
56 Itoya, loc. cit.
57 Shimizu, Biography, p. 301; Kanno, Second Court Interrogation (5 June 1911), in *Zenshū, III*, p. 222.
58 Cited in Hane, *Reflections*, p. 53. The extract is from 'Fude no Shizuku' [first published in *Murō Shinpō*, no. 535 (24 November 1905)], in *Zenshū, II*, pp. 38–40.
59 Shimizu, Biography, p. 303.
60 Itoya, p. 52.
61 Shimizu, loc. cit.
62 Itoya, p. 60.
63 Shimizu, Biography, p. 302.
64 On '*ryōsai kenbo*', see Kumiko Fujimura-Fanselow, 'The Japanese Ideology of "Good Wives and Wise Mothers": Trends in Contemporary Research', *Gender and History*, vol. 3, no. 3 (Autumn 1991), pp. 345–50. As early as 1875 Meirokusha liberals had argued for equal access to education for women largely because if mothers could be made pure the nation would be pure. See Nakamura Masanao, 'Creating Good Mothers', in Braisted (trans.), *Meiroku Zasshi*, pp. 401–4.

65 Shimizu, loc. cit.
66 [Kanno] 'Yūzuki', 'Yonin no Hahaue' [first published in *Murō Shinpō*, no. 576, 3 April 1906], in *Zenshū, II*, pp. 100–2.
67 Itoya, p. 64.
68 Sievers, p. 144.
69 Kanno, 'Yonin no Hahaue', p. 101.
70 Cf. [Kanno] 'Yūzukijo', 'Kata Kanroku' [first published in *Murō Shinpō*, no. 581, 18 April 1906]; and 'Rōjōki' [first published in *Murō Shinpō*, no. 584, 27 April 1906], in *Zenshū, II*, pp. 119–20, p. 136.
71 [Kanno] 'Yūzukijo', 'Onna toshite no Kibō' [first published in *Murō Shinpō*, no. 588, 9 May 1906], in ibid., pp. 143–5.
72 [Kanno] 'Yūzuki', 'Misohitomoji no Ongakkai Kenmonki' [first published in *Murō Shinpō*, no. 577, 6 April 1906], in ibid., pp. 105–6.
73 Ibid., p. 106.
74 For example, in Kanno, 'Rōjōki', p. 137.
75 [Kanno] 'Yūzukijo', 'Kenka no Joshi ni Gekisu' [first published in *Murō Shinpō*, no. 566, 3 March 1906], in *Zenshū, II*, pp. 69–71. On the wide-spread practice then of selling young girls into prostitution, see Hane Mikiso, *Peasants, Rebels, and Outcastes: The Underside of Modern Japan*, New York, Pantheon, 1982, pp. 172–225.
76 Kanno, ibid., p. 69.
77 On the system of post-publication censorship, see Richard Mitchell, *Censorship in Imperial Japan*, Princeton, New Jersey, Princeton University Press, 1983, pp. 136, 148 ff.
78 Kanno ['Yūzukijo'], 'Hiji Deppō', cited in Sievers, p. 149.
79 Ibid.
80 Cf. [Kanno] 'Sugako', 'Kanson-kun o Okuru' [first published in *Murō Shinpō*, no. 581, 18 April 1906] in *Zenshū, II*, p. 118; also Kanno, 'Kata Kanroku', p. 119.
81 See Kondō, p. 37; [Kanno] 'Yūzuki', 'Kanson-kun ni' [first published in *Murō Shinpō*, no. 579], in *Zenshū, II*, p. 110; also Kanno, 'Kanson-kun o Okuru'.
82 See [Kanno] 'Yūzukijo', 'Sokumenkan ni tsuite' [first published in *Murō Shinpō*, no. 589, 12 May 1906], in *Zenshū, II*, p. 146; cf Itoya, p. 72–4.
83 See Mōri's postscript to Kanno, 'Onna toshite no Kibō', p. 145.
84 Arahata, pp. 126–7.
85 See Sievers, pp. 52–3, 127.
86 [Kanno] 'Yūzuki', 'Danshi Sokumenkan' [first published in *Murō Shinpō*, no. 587, 6 May 1906], in *Zenshū, II*, pp. 139–41.
87 Kanno, '"Sokumenkan" ni tsuite', pp. 145–7.
88 Kanno, Second Court Interrogation (5 June 1910), in *Zenshū, III*, pp. 223.
89 'Kanno Yūzukijo', 'Waga Ningyō' [first published in *Yomiuri Shinbun*, 9 September 1906], in *Zenshū, II*, pp. 165–7.
90 [Kanno] 'Yūzuki', 'Toshi no Hajime ni' [first published in *Murō Shinpō*, no. 664, 1 January 1907], in ibid., pp. 173–4.
91 Kenneth Strong, *Ox Against the Storm. A Biography of Tanaka Shozo: Japan's First Conservationist Pioneer*, British Columbia, University of British Columbia Press, 1977 (Chapters 10–12).
92 For a translation of this essay, see Crump pp. 341–51.

93 On the frustrations of Heiminsha women with socialist men, see Sievers, pp. 114–38.
94 Ibid., pp. 131–2.
95 Ibid., pp. 129–30.
96 Kondō, p. 40; Itoya, p. 95.
97 See [Kanno] 'Sugako', 'Aa, Imōto' [first published in *Mainichi Denpō*, 15 July 1907], in *Zenshū, II*, p. 206.
98 'Kanno Sugako', 'Joshū to Jokō' [first published in *Mainichi Denpō*, no. 1139, 4 January 1907], in ibid., pp. 179–82.
99 On the textile mills see E. Patricia Tsurumi, *Factory Girls: Women in the Thread Mills of Meiji Japan*, Princeton, New Jersey, Princeton University Press, 1990.
100 Kanno Sugako', 'Risō no Fujin' [first published in *Kan'i Seikatsu*, no. 3, 1 January 1907], in *Zenshū, II*, pp. 175–8.
101 See Vera Broido, *Apostles into Terrorists: Women and the Revolutionary Movement in the Russia of Alexander II*, London, Maurice Temple Smith, 1977, pp. 18, 62.
102 [Unsigned], 'Yajima-tōji to Yanaka Mura' [first published in *Mainichi Denpō*, no. 1329, 13 July 1907], in *Zenshū, II*, pp. 205–6.
103 Hane, *Reflections*, pp. 32 ff.
104 See [Kanno] 'Yūjo', 'Shokutaku Kien no Hana' [first published in *Mainichi Denpō*, no. 1328, 12 July 1907], in *Zenshū, II*, pp. 203–4.
105 [Kanno] 'Yūzuki', 'Sugamo no Ichi Yoru' [first published in two parts in *Mainichi Denpō*, nos. 1457 and 1463, 18 and 24 November 1907], in *Zenshū, II*, p. 207.
106 Ibid., p. 208.
107 Ibid., p. 209.
108 For accounts of Suga's involvement in the Red Flag Incident see Kondō, pp. 42–3; and Shimizu, Biography, p. 309.
109 Kondō, p. 44; Sievers, pp. 154 ff.
110 Kanno, Prison Declaration, no. 2 (3 June 1910), in *Zenshū, III*, p. 198; cf. Court Interrogation (of same date), p. 209.
111 Cf. Itoya, p. 137; Shimizu, Biography, p. 310.
112 Itoya, p. 138.
113 See Kanno, Prison Declaration, no. 1 (2 June 1910), in *Zenshū, III*, p. 199.
114 Ishikawa Sanshirō went to jail early in 1910 in connection with *Sekai Fujin*. See Ōsawa Masamichi, 'Ishikawa Sanshirō Ron', in Tsurumi Shunsuke (ed.), *Ishikawa Sanshirō Shū*, Tokyo, Chikuma Shobō, 1976, p. 427.
115 See Notehelfer, pp. 174–5.
116 [Kanno] 'Yūzuki', 'Toraware no Ki' [first published in *Jiyū Shisō*, no. 2, 10 June 1909], in *Zenshū, II*, pp. 238–41.
117 Ibid., p. 239.
118 Ibid.
119 Crump, p. 305; Kanno, Court Interrogation of 3 June 1911, in *Zenshū, III*, p. 208.
120 [Kanno] 'Sugako', 'Heiminsha yori' [first published in *Jiyū Shisō*, no. 2, 10 June 1909], in *Zenshū, II*, pp. 242–4.
121 Uchiyama Gudō was arrested much earlier than the others, but was still one of the twelve hanged.

122 Cited in Notehelfer, p. 174.
123 Letter from Kōtoku to his mother dated 19 September 1909, included in Shiota Shōbei (ed.), *Kōtoku Shūsui no Nikki to Shokan*, Tokyo, Miraisha, 1965, pp. 315–6.
124 Sievers (pp. 121, 219) notes that Kōtoku was unpopular with Heiminsha women some years earlier because he patronized them. She suggests that with them he then had a reputation for being more sexist than other Meiji socialist men.
125 Records of Pretrial Hearing, Sixth Interrogation of Kōtoku Denjirō (6 July 1910), in Shiota Shōbei and Watanabe Junzō (eds), *Hiroku Taigyaku Jiken, II*, Tokyo, Shunjūsha, 1959, p. 19.
126 Cf. Shimizu, Biography, pp. 313–4; Itoya, p. 167.
127 Arahata, pp. 196–201.
128 Shimizu, Biography, pp. 305–6.
129 Kanno, Diary (21 January 1911), in *Zenshū, II*, p. 263.
130 On a Meiji 'Lady Chatterley trial' where one naturalist novelist went on trial for writing about an adulterous affair, see Rubin, pp. 83–93.
131 Kōtoku Shūsui, Jiyū Shisō, no. 1 (25 May 1909), in Asukai Masamichi (ed.), *Kindai Nihon Shisō Taikei, 13: Kōtoku Shūsui Shū*, Tokyo, Chikuma Shobō, 1975, p. 330.
132 On a contemporaneous socialist sex scandal in England, see Christine Collette, 'Socialism and Scandal: the Sexual Politics of the early Labour Movement', *History Workshop*, no. 23 (Spring 1987), pp. 102–11.
133 See Kanno, Prison Declaration, no. 1 (2 June 1910), in *Zenshū, III*, p. 195.
134 Ōsugi cited in Hane, *Reflections*, p. 54. It is ironic that Ōsugi was himself ostracized over a similar anarchist 'free love' incident in 1916.
135 [Kanno] 'Ryūko', 'Chiisaki Kyogi' [first published in *Jiyū Shisō*, no. 1, 25 May 1909], in *Zenshū, III*, pp. 134–5.
136 Hane, *Reflections*, p. 51.
137 See Kanno, Court Interrogation (3 June 1910), in *Zenshū, III*, pp. 207–8.
138 Letter from Kōtoku to Arahata (20 May 1910), in Shiota (ed.), p. 334.
139 Shimizu, Biography, p. 315. See Kōtoku's Sixth Court Interrogation (6 July 1910), in Shiota and Watanabe (eds), II, p. 20.
140 Letter to Furukawa Rikisaku (18 April 1910), in *Zenshū, III*, pp. 156–7.
141 For the argument on their estrangement, cf. Notehelfer, p. 180; Setouchi, 'Koi to Kakumei', pp. 300–1.
142 Kanno, Letters to Kōtoku Shūsui, in *Zenshū, III*, pp. 159–62.
143 See Shiota (ed.), pp. 318, 334.
144 On this, see Notehelfer, pp. 179–83.
145 Mentioned in Kanno, Court Interrogation, no. 2 (5 June 1910), in *Zenshū, III*, pp. 231–2; cf. Itoya Toshio, *Kōtoku Shūsui Kenkyū*, Tokyo, Aoki Shoten, 1967, p. 285.
146 Letter to Furukawa Rikisaku, p. 157.
147 See Arahata cited in Crump, p. 308.
148 Cited in ibid., p. 316.
149 See Kōtoku's Court Interrogation, no. 13 (17 October 1910), in Shiota and Watanabe (eds), pp. 35, 39–40. There are many parallels between the situation, ideas, motives for action, and tactics of the terrorist wing of the Russian populists, Narodnaya Volya (People's Will), and these Japanese 'direct actionists'. See Broido, p. 205.

150 Kanno, Diary (23 January 1911), in *Zenshū, II*, pp. 268–9.
151 *Zenshū, III*, pp. 197–8.
152 Ibid., pp. 202–3.
153 Ibid., pp. 205–8.
154 Barbara Smith, 'Itō Noe, Living Love and Anarchy: "Free Love" in Taishō Japan', Unpublished Honours Thesis, Centre for Asian Studies, University of Adelaide, 1991.
155 *Zenshū, III*, pp. 222–3.
156 See Rubin on Hiraide's works, pp. 162 ff.
157 *Zenshū, III*, pp. 248–50.
158 Ibid., pp. 286–7.
159 See, for example, Kanno, Diary (20 January 1911), in *Zenshū, II*, pp. 252–3.
160 Letter to Tamikawa Takeo (21 January 1911), in *Zenshū, III*, p. 183.
161 Letter to Yoshikawa Morikuni (24 January 1911), in ibid., p. 189.
162 Ibid. It appears to have been from Itoya's biography of Suga (citing Arahata) that Notehelfer gained the mistaken impression that Suga 'sank into a life of prostitution' for several years. If she did lead a so-called 'debauched' life, it was at most only for a few months, and this was while she was a journalist and perhaps Udagawa's lover. There is no suggestion in any works other than Notehelfer's that she was ever a 'prostitute'. Cf. Notehelfer, pp. 166 ff.
163 Kanno, Diary (23 January 1911), in *Zenshū, II*, pp. 268–9.

8 KANEKO FUMIKO (1922–1926)

1 For example, Komatsu Ryūji, 'Hangyaku no Josei, Kaneko Fumiko: "Pak Yeol Jiken" Hashigaki', *Jiyū Shisō*, vol. 6 (July 1961), pp. 37–44; Jean Inglis', 'Book Review: "What Made Me Like This? The Prison Memories of Kaneko Fumiko', *Anpo: Japan–Asia Quarterly Review*, vol. 13, no. 2 (1981), pp. 35 ff.; Hane Mikiso, *Reflections on the Way to the Gallows: Rebel Women in Prewar Japan*, New York, Pantheon, 1988, pp. 75–80.
2 The few available English sources make no use at all of the witness interrogation records: Hane, *Reflections*, pp. 75–124; Introduction to Jean Inglis (trans.), *Kaneko Fumiko: The Prison Memoirs of a Japanese Woman*, New York and London, M.E. Sharpe, 1991, vii–xviii.
3 For Fumiko's rather lengthy account (condemnation) *in court* of her upbringing, see Tokyo District Court Interrogation, no. 2 (17 January 1924), in *Kaneko Fumiko, Pak Yeol Saiban Kiroku*, Tokyo, Kokushoku Sensensha, 1977, pp. 9–15. (Since all interrogations, including those of witnesses, are included in these trial records, all subsequent references will merely give the page number/s.)
4 See Kaneko Fumiko, *Nani ga Watashi o Kōsaseta ka*, Tokyo, Chikuma Shobō, 1984, pp. 5–6. (Hereafter, Fumiko's memoirs will be referred to only by surname and page number/s.)
5 Kaneko, District Court Interrogation, no. 2 (17 January 1924), p. 15.
6 See Matsuda Michio (ed.), *Gendai Nihon Shisō Taikei, 16: Anakizumu*, Tokyo, Chikuma Shobō, 1963, p. 44.
7 Ibid.; cf. John Crump, *The Origins of Socialist Though in Japan*, London and Canberra, Croom Helm, 1983, pp. 278–9.

8 Stephen Large, *Organized Workers and Socialist Politics in Interwar Japan*, Cambridge, Cambridge University Press, 1981, pp. 19, 268.

9 See 'Anarchism in Japan', *Anarchy Magazine*, vol. 1, no. 5, 2nd series (year not given), pp. 5–6.

10 On the Shinjinkai see Henry D. Smith II, *Japan's First Student Radicals*, Boston, Massachusetts, Harvard University Press, 1972, p. 74.

11 Kaneko, Court Interrogation, no. 5 (24 January 1924), p. 21.

12 See the advertisements section in *Kokutō* (also called 'La Nigra Ondo'), no. 2 (10 August 1922), p. 3 (copy in *Saiban Kiroku*, p. 812.)

13 Ōsugi, 'Torotsukii no Kyōdō Sensenron', in Ōsawa Masamichi (ed.), *Ōsugi Sakae Zenshū, VI: Rōdō Undō Ronshū*, Tokyo, Gendai Shichō, 1963, pp. 112 ff.

14 On anarchist printers, see Hagiwara Shintarō, *Nihon Anakizumu Rōdō Undōshi*, Tokyo, Gendai Shichō, 1969, pp. 120 ff.

15 See Ōsugi, 'Sengen–Seishinkai Sōgi', in Osawa (ed.), p. 181.

16 Cf. B.L. Simcock, 'The Anarcho-Syndicalist Thought and Activity of Ōsugi Sakae, 1885–1923', *Papers on Japan* (East Asian Research Center, Harvard University), vol. 5 (1970), pp. 45–7; and Thomas A. Stanley, *Ōsugi Sakae, Anarchist in Taishō Japan: The Creativity of the Ego*, Boston, Massachusetts, Harvard University Press, 1969, p. 141.

17 Cf. George T. Shea, *Leftwing Literature in Japan: A Brief History of the Proletarian Literary Movement*, Tokyo, Hosei University Press, 1964, pp. 140–2, 199–200; and Matsuda, pp. 59–60.

18 See Niiyama, Court Interrogation (27 October 1923), pp. 300–1.

19 Kaneko, Court Interrogation, no. 5 (24 January 1924), p. 21.

20 'Fumiko', 'Omotta Koto, Futatsu–Mittsu' [in *Kokutō*, no. 2 (10 August 1922) p. 1, reprinted in *Saiban Kiroku*, p. 810.

21 C. Lee and G. de Vos, *Koreans in Japan: Ethnic Conflict and Accommodation*, Berkeley, University of California Press, 1981, p. 21.

22 George Totten, *The Social Democratic Movement in Prewar Japan*, New Haven, Connecticut, Yale University Press, 1966, p. 373. On the Japanese government's policy of forced migration of Korean labourers (estimated total of 1,500,000) implemented from 1939, see Tsurumi Shunsuke, *An Intellectual History of Wartime Japan, 1931–1945*, London and Henley, KPI Limited, 1986, p. 56.

23 On the formation of the first Korean nationalist group in Japan in 1920, and the first anarchist group (the Kokutōkai), see Lee and de Vos, p. 68; R. A. Scalapino and C. Lee, *Communism in Korea*, Berkeley, University of California Press, 1972, p. 57; on Korean radical groups in Japan then, cf. Michael Weiner, *The Origins of the Korean Community in Japan, 1910–1923*, Manchester, Manchester University Press, 1989.

24 'Fumiko', 'Eiyō Kenkyūshochō Saeki-hakase ni', in *Kokutō*, no. 2 (10 August 1922) p. 3, in *Saiban Kiroku*, p. 812.

25 Kaneko, loc. cit.

26 For such advertisements, see *Saiban Kiroku*, pp. 813 ff.

27 On the Japanese anarchist practice of '*ryaku*', see John Crump, *Hatta Shūzō and Pure Anarchism in Interwar Japan*, London and New York, Macmillan and St. Martin's Press, 1993, p. 56.

28 Kaneko, Court Interrogation, loc. cit.; and Court Interrogation, no. 1 (25 October 1923), p. 8.

29　For example, in Court Interrogation, no. 6 (25 January 1924), p. 23.
30　See Iwasaki Zenemon, Witness Interrogation Record, no. 1 (20 August 1925), p. 248.
31　Lee and de Vos, p. 22.
32　Cited in ibid., pp. 22–3.
33　Ibid., p. 27.
34　*Futei Senjin*, no. 1 (undated, probably early in November 1922), p. 1, in *Saiban Kiroku*, p. 813.
35　See *Genshakai* [formerly *Futei Senjin*], no. 3 (March 1923), in ibid., p. 834. On the March First Movement, see Frank Baldwin, 'Participatory Anti-Imperialism: The 1919 Independence Movement', *Journal of Korean Studies*, vol. 1 (1979), pp. 123–62.
36　*Futei Senjin*, no. 2 (December 1922), p. 4, and *Genshakai*, no. 4 (June 1923), in *Saiban Kiroku*, pp. 818, 864.
37　'Kaneko Fumi', 'Aru Kaiwa', in *Genshakai*, ibid., p. 863.
38　'Pak Fumiko', 'Iwayuru "Futei Senjin" to wa', in *Futei Senjin*, no. 2 (December 1922), in *Saiban Kiroku*, p. 817.
39　Here I will not attempt to give an overall view of the content of Fumiko's autobiography because it is now available in full English translation by Jean Inglis (cited above).
40　Comrade, Kurihara Kazuo, said Fumiko was born in 1906, in *Jiyū Rengō Shinbun*, no. 39 (1 September 1929), p. 2, in *Saiban Kiroku*, p. 802; for Komatsu (p. 38) it was 1907 (Meiji 38, he said, so really 1905); in Inglis' translation it appears as both 1902 and 1903 (publication details page and page vii of Hane's introduction).
41　See Witness Interrogation Records (10 and 11 August 1925), and copy of Kaneko family register, in *Saiban Kiroku*, pp. 224–5, 229–39, 875.
42　Kaneko, *Akai Tsutsuji*, p. 36.
43　Fumiko's mother's name was therefore given incorrectly as 'Tokuno' in the 1984 Tokyo, Chikuma Shobō edition of her memoirs.
44　Cf. Kaneko 'Kie', Witness Interrogation Record, no. 1 (11 August 1925), p. 228, and Kaneko extract from Register of Families, loc. cit.; also Kaneko, pp. 4, 15.
45　Saeki Fumikazu, Witness Interrogation, no. 1 (10 August 1925), p. 224.
46　Cf. Kaneko 'Kie', p. 230; Saeki, p. 227.
47　See Kaneko, Court Interrogation, no. 6 (25 January 1924), p. 23.
48　Kaneko, pp. 6–7.
49　Kaneko, p. 8; cf. Kaneko 'Kie', loc. cit.
50　Kaneko, ibid.
51　See Saeki, loc. cit.; Kaneko 'Kie', p. 231; and Kaneko Sehi, Witness Interrogation Record (13 August 1925), p. 239.
52　Kaneko, pp. 10–1. Cf. Saeki, loc. cit.
53　Kaneko 'Kie', p. 229.
54　Kaneko, pp. 14–5; Kaneko 'Kie', p. 231.
55　Kaneko, *Akai Tsutsuji*, p. 12.
56　Saeki, p. 227.
57　Kaneko, pp. 114 ff.
58　See Setouchi Harumi, *Yohaku no Haru*, Tokyo, Chūkō Bunko, 1975, pp. 97–8; also Kaneko, p. 12. Inglis gives Takatoshi's name as 'Ken' in

her translation of the memoirs, but both parents referred to him by name in their testimonies.

59 See Kaneko 'Kie', p. 232.
60 Kaneko, pp. 12–3.
61 Ibid., p. 15.
62 See Saeki, pp. 225–6.
63 See Kaneko 'Kie', p. 233.
64 Kaneko, p. 19.
65 Ibid., p. 22. On Nakamura's theft, cf. Kaneko 'Kie', p. 233.
66 Kaneko, p. 23.
67 Ibid., p. 24.
68 Ibid., pp. 24–5; Kaneko 'Kie', loc. cit.
69 Kaneko, pp. 27–9.
70 Liza Dalby, *Geisha*, Berkeley, University of California Press, 1983, pp. 167, 235.
71 Kaneko 'Kie', loc. cit.
72 Kaneko, p. 29.
73 Ibid., pp. 36–7.
74 On the lower incidence of infanticide in villages early this century because now a capital offence (unlike in Tokugawa), see Hane Mikiso, *Peasants, Rebels, and Outcastes: The Underside of Modern Japan*, New York, Pantheon, 1982, p. 209.
75 Cf. Kaneko, p. 38; Kaneko 'Kie', Witness Interrogation Record, no. 2 (12 August 1925), p. 234.
76 For a discussion of the view of nature of one of Japan's 'pure' (not syndicalist) anarchists in Taishō, see John Crump, 'Hatta Shūzō and "Pure Anarchism"', *Japan Foundation Newsletter*, pp. 15–19.
77 Kaneko, pp. 31–6.
78 On the mills in this whole area, Chūbu and Kantō, see Hane, *Peasants, Rebels and Outcastes*, pp. 173 ff.
79 Kaneko, pp. 40–1.
80 See Kaneko 'Kie', pp. 234–5.
81 Kaneko, pp. 41–2. Cf. Kaneko 'Kie', ibid.
82 Copy of register in *Saiban Kiroku*, p. 875.
83 Kaneko, p. 48.
84 Ibid., pp. 47–8. On the means by which Japanese colonists gradually gained control of the land in Korea, see Tsurumi Shunsuke, p. 55.
85 Kaneko, p. 95.
86 Cf. Saeki, p. 226; Kaneko 'Kie', pp. 235–6.
87 Ibid., p. 53.
88 Kaneko, Court Interrogation, no. 3 (22 January 1924), pp. 15–16.
89 Kaneko, pp. 70–3.
90 Ibid., pp. 58–9.
91 Ibid., pp. 91–5.
92 Ibid., pp. 110–1.
93 Cf. Saeki, Witness Interrogation Records (nos. 1 and 2), pp. 226, 243.
94 On endogamous marriage in the villages, see Hane, *Peasants, Rebels and Outcastes*, pp. 69, 82; cf. Robert J. Smith and Ella Lury Wiswell, *The Women of Suye Mura*, Chicago, University of Chicago Press, 1982, pp. 92–3, 151–5.

95 Cf. Kaneko Sehi, p. 240; Saeki (no. 2), loc. cit.
96 Ibid., pp. 127–9.
97 Kaneko, Court Interrogation, no. 2 (17 January 1924), p. 14.
98 Kaneko, pp. 118–19.
99 Ibid., pp. 116, 136–7.
100 Ibid., pp. 138–9.
101 See Kubota Kametarō, Witness Interrogation Record (18 August 1925), pp. 241–2.
102 Cf. Furihata Kazushige, Witness Interrogation Record (25 August 1925), p. 251.
103 Kaneko, p. 145.
104 Kaneko, *Akai Tsutsuji*, pp. 12–3.
105 Cf. Kaneko, pp. 153–5; and Furihata, loc. cit.
106 Kaneko, p. 149.
107 Kaneko, Court Interrogation, no. 3 (22 January 1924), p. 16.
108 Furihata, loc. cit.
109 Cf. Kaneko, pp. 156–7; Furihata, ibid.
110 Cf. Kaneko, pp. 172–4; Saitō Otomatsu, Witness Interrogation Record (19 August 1925), p. 245.
111 Kaneko, pp. 175–6; cf. Suzuki Kanesaburō, Witness Interrogation Record, no. 1 (19 August 1925), pp. 246–7.
112 Kaneko, Court Interrogation, no. 2 (17 January 1924), p. 13.
113 Cf. Kaneko, p. 188; Kaneko, Court Interrogation, no. 3 (22 January 1924), p. 17. Kutsumi herself suggested that she neglected her children, in Hane (trans., ed.), *Reflections*, pp. 154 ff.
114 It is strange that Fumiko obviously retained a respect for Ōsugi Sakae because he and Itō Noe did not register their children, even as 'illegitimate'. See Kondō Kenji, *Ichi Museifushugisha no Kaisō*, Tokyo, Heibonsha, 1965, p. 125.
115 Kaneko, pp. 177–8.
116 Ibid., pp. 178–9.
117 Ibid., p. 180.
118 Cf. ibid., p. 183; and on Ōsugi's attitudes toward intellectuals, see various articles on the subject in Ōsawa (ed.), *Ōsugi Sakae Zenshū, VI*.
119 Kaneko, pp. 184–5.
120 See Kubota Kametarō, p. 242.
121 Iwasaki Zenemon, Witness Interrogation Record (20 August 1925), p. 247.
122 Kaneko, *Akai Tsutsuji*, p. 15.
123 Niiyama Hatsuyo, Court Interrogation (27 October 1923), pp. 300–1. Cf. Kaneko, pp. 192–3. According to Komatsu, Niiyama was mistreated in prison; hence her tuberculosis was aggravated and her kidneys inflamed. (The sources are inconsistent about whether she actually died in prison or was released first.) She died on 27 November 1923 at the age of 21.
124 Kaneko, pp. 194–5.
125 Kaneko's critique of revolution was surely influenced by Ōsugi's critiques of Russian Bolshevik authoritarianism (suppression of the left-wing opposition etc.), on which see Stanley, pp. 138 ff.
126 Kaneko, pp. 193–4. Cf. Kaneko, Court Interrogations, nos 4 and 6 (23 and 25 January 1924), pp. 19, 23.

127 Kaneko, pp. 197–8.
128 Ibid., pp. 201–2.
129 Ibid., pp. 203–4.
130 Ibid., p. 205.
131 See Chung Tae Sung, Court Interrogation, no. 3 (24 November 1923), p. 340.
132 See Kaneko, Court Interrogation, no. 4 (23 January 1924), p. 20.
133 Cf. Pak Yeol, Court Interrogation, no. 16 (2 May 1925), p. 70; and Kaneko, Court Interrogations nos. 13–14 (21 May 1924 and 5 March 1925), pp. 65–6.
134 Kaneko, Court Interrogation, no. 3 (22 January 1924), p. 17.
135 Ibid., p. 18.
136 See Kaneko, Court Interrogation, no. 12 (14 May 1924), pp. 57–62.
137 Hane's translation, *Reflections*, pp. 123–4. (The passage is from her twelfth testimony, ibid.)
138 Kaneko, Court Interrogation, no. 3 (22 January 1924), p. 19.
139 Kaneko, *Akai Tsutsuji*, p. 19.

EPILOGUE

1 Jean-Michel Raynaud, 'What's What in Biography', in James Walter (ed.), *Reading Life Histories: Griffith Papers on Biography*, Queensland, Griffith University, 1981, p. 93.
2 Ibid.
3 Cited in Setouchi Harumi, 'Kaneko Fumiko', in Setouchi (ed.), *Jinbutsu Kindai Joseishi, Onna no Isshō, 6, Hangyaku no Onna no Roman*, Tokyo, Kōdansha, 1981, p. 146.
4 Inga Clendinnen, *Ambivalent Conquests: Maya and Spaniard in Yucatan, 1517–1570*, Cambridge, Cambridge University Press, 1987, p. 116.

Select bibliography of Japanese sources

Akiyama Kiyoshi, *Nihiru to Teroru* [*Nihility and Terror*], Tokyo, Tairyūsha, 1977.
—— 'Sei to Jiyū ni tsuite' ['On Sex and Freedom'], *Shisō no Kagaku*, no. 123 (November 1971), pp. 26–34.
—— *Waga Bōryoku Kō* [*My Studies on Violence*], Tokyo, San'ichi Shobō, 1977.
Arahata Kanson, *Kanson Jiden* [*Kanson's Autobiography*], Tokyo, Ronsōsha, 1961.
Asukai Masamichi (ed.), *Kindai Nihon Shisō Taikei: Kōtoku Shūsui Shū* [*Outline of Modern Japanese Thought: Works of Kōtoku Shūsui*], Tokyo, Chikuma Shobō, 1975.
Eguchi Kan, *Waga Bungaku Hansei Ki, II* [*Record of Half my Life of Literature, Volume II*], Tokyo, Aoki Shoten, 1968.
Fukunaga Isao, *Kyōsantōin no Tenkō to Tennōsei* [*The Tenkō of Japan Communist Party Members and the Emperor-System*], Tokyo, San-ichi Shobō, 1978.
Fuse Kanji, *Aru Bengoshi no Shōgai: Fuse Tatsuji* [*The Life of a Lawyer: Fuse Tatsuji*], Tokyo, Iwanami Shoten, 1963.
Fuse Tatsuji, *Unmei no Shōrisha: Pak Yeol* [*Victor Over Destiny: Pak Yeol*], Tokyo, Seiki Shobō, 1946.
Hagiwara Shintarō, *Nihon Anakizumu Rōdō Undōshi* [*A History of Japan's Anarchist Labour Movement*], Tokyo, Gendai Shichō, 1969.
Itō Noe, 'Sanin no Taido' ['Sanine's Attitudes'], in *Itō Noe Zenshū, II* [*The Collected Works of Itō Noe, Volume 2*], Tokyo, Gakugei Shorin, 1986, pp. 301–4.
Itoya Toshio, *Kanno Suga: Heiminsha no Fujin Kakumeika Zō* [*Kanno Suga: Portrait of a Woman Revolutionary of the Commoners' Society*], Tokyo, Iwanami Shinsho, 1970.
—— *Kōtoku Shūsui Kenkyū* [*Research on Kōtoku Shūsui*], Tokyo, Aoki Shoten,1967.
Kaneko Fumiko, *Akai Tsutsuji no Hana: Kaneko Fumiko no Omoide to Kashū* [*Red Azaleas: Reminiscences of Kaneko Fumiko and her Collected Poetry*], Tokyo, Kokushoku Sensensha [editors and publishers], 1984.
—— *Kaneko Fumiko, Pak Yeol Saiban Kiroku* [*Kaneko Fumiko, Pak Yeol Trial Records*], Tokyo, Kokushoku Sensensha [editors and publishers], 1977 [texts in this collection not by Kaneko are listed under '*Saiban Kiroku*'].

—— 'Aru Kaiwa' ['A Conversation', signed 'Kaneko Fumi', first published in *Genshakai*, no. 4, June 1923], in *Saiban Kiroku*, p. 863.

—— 'Chōsen [illegible text] Kinenbi' ['Anniversary of the Korean . . . ', signed 'Kaneko Fumi', first published in *Genshakai*, no. 3, March 1923], in *Saiban Kiroku*, p. 834.

—— 'Eiyō Kenkyūshochō Saeki-hakase ni' ['To Dr Saeki, Head of the Nutrition Research Centre', signed 'Fumiko', first published in *Kokutō*, no. 2, 10 August 1922], in *Saiban Kiroku*, p. 812.

—— 'Iwayuru "Futei Senjin" to wa' ['So-called "Malcontent Koreans"?', signed 'Pak Fumiko', first published in *Futei Senjin*, no. 2, December 1922], in *Saiban Kiroku*, p. 817.

—— Letter to Judge Tatematsu Kaisei (Morning, 21st [May 1925]), in *Saiban Kiroku*, p. 107.

—— *Nani ga Watashi o Kōsaseta ka* [*What Made Me Like This?*], Tokyo, Chikuma Shobō, 1984.

—— 'Nijūroku Nichi, Yahan' ['26th, Late in the Night', Memo drafted 26 February 1926 and read in the Supreme Court the next day], in *Saiban Kiroku*, pp. 739–48.

—— 'Omotta Koto, Futatsu-Mittsu' ['Two or Three Things I've Thought About', signed 'Fumiko', first published in *Kokutō*, no. 2, 10 August 1922], in *Saiban Kiroku*, p. 810.

—— *Supreme Court Interrogation Records*:
no. 1 (26 February 1926, both Kaneko and Pak questioned), in *Saiban Kiroku*, pp. 673–94.

—— *Tokyo District Court Preliminary Interrogation Records*:
no. 1 (25 October 1923), in *Saiban Kiroku*, p. 8.
no. 2 (17 January 1924), in *Saiban Kiroku*, pp. 9–15.
no. 3 (22 January 1924), in *Saiban Kiroku*, pp. 15–19.
no. 4 (23 January 1924), in *Saiban Kiroku*, pp. 19–20.
no. 5 (24 January 1924), in *Saiban Kiroku*, pp. 21–2.
no. 6 (25 January 1924), in *Saiban Kiroku*, pp. 23–4.
no. 7 (25 January 1924), in *Saiban Kiroku*, pp. 25–8.
no. 12 (14 May 1924), in *Saiban Kiroku*, pp. 57–62.
no. 13 (21 May 1924), in *Saiban Kiroku*, p. 65.
no. 14 (5 March 1925), in *Saiban Kiroku*, pp. 65–6.

—— Untitled and Undated Statement (October/November1925), in *Saiban Kiroku*, pp. 581–9.

—— 'Yabure Shōji kara' ['From the Torn Sliding Door', signed 'Fumiko', first published in *Futei Senjin*, no. 2, December 1922], in *Saiban Kiroku*, p. 818.

—— 'Yabure Shōji kara' [signed 'Fumiko', first published in *Genshakai*, no. 4, June 1923], in *Saiban Kiroku*, p. 864.

Kanno Suga, *Kanno Sugako Zenshū* [*The Collected Works of Kanno Sugako*], 3 Volumes (Shimizu Unosuke, ed.), Tokyo, Kōryūsha, 1984.

—— 'Aa, Imōto' ['Ah, Little Sister', signed 'Sugako', first published in *Mainichi Denpō*, no. 1331, 15 July 1907], in *Zenshū, II*, p. 206.

—— 'Chiisaki Kyogi' ['White Lie/s', general title for five tanka, signed 'Ryūko', first published in *Jiyū Shisō*, no. 1, 25 May 1909], in *Zenshū, III*, pp. 134–5.

272   Select bibliography of Japanese sources

—— 'Danshi no Sokumenkan' ['A Perspective on Men', signed 'Yūzukijo', first published in *Murō Shinpō*, no. 587, 6 May 1906], in *Zenshū*, *II*, pp. 139–41.
—— *Declarations to Prosecutors*:
    no. 1 (2 June 1910), in *Zenshū*, *III*, pp. 195–6.
    [not numbered] (3 June 1910), in *Zenshū*, *III*, pp. 197–205.
    [not numbered] (26 September 1910), in *Zenshū*, *III*, pp. 275–6.
—— 'Fude no Shizuku' ['Ink Drops', signed 'Sugako', first published in *Murō Shinpō*, no. 535, 24 November 1905], in *Zenshū*, *II*, pp. 38–40.
—— 'Hakurankai Kogoto' ['Faults of the Exposition', signed 'Yūzuki-joshi', first published in eight parts in *Ōsaka Chōhō*, nos. 163–71, 11–20 March 1903], in *Zenshū*, *I*, pp. 271–93.
—— 'Heiminsha yori' ['From the Commoners' Society', signed 'Sugako', first published in *Jiyū Shisō*, 10 June 1909], in *Zenshū*, *II*, pp. 242–4.
—— 'Hiji Deppō ['Rebuff', signed 'Yūzukijo', first published in *Murō Shinpō*, no. 580, 15 April 1906], in *Zenshū*, *II*, pp. 111–14.
—— 'Isshūkan' ['One Week', signed 'Sugako', first published in twenty-two parts in *Ōsaka Chōhō*, nos. 106–31, 29 November–28 December 1902], in *Zenshū*, *I*, pp. 154–214.
—— 'Joshū to Jokō' ['Female Prisoners and Female Workers', signed 'Kanno Sugako', first published in *Mainichi Denpō*, no. 1139, 4 January 1907], in *Zenshū*, *II*, pp. 179–82.
—— 'Kanson-kun ni' ['To Kanson', signed 'Yūzukijo', first published in *Murō Shinpō*, no. 579, 12 April 1906], in *Zenshū*, *II*, p. 110.
—— 'Kanson-kun o Okuru' ['Seeing Kanson Off', signed 'Sugako', first published in *Murō Shinpō*, no. 581, 18 April 1906], in *Zenshū*, *II*, pp. 116–18.
—— 'Kata Kanroku' ['Record of Prejudices', signed 'Yūzukijo', first published in *Murō Shinpō*, no. 581, 18 April 1906], in *Zenshū*, *II*, pp. 119–20.
—— 'Kenka no Joshi ni Gekisu' ['Appeal to Women Throughout the Prefecture', signed 'Yūzukijo', first published in *Murō Shinpō*, no. 566, 3 March 1906], in *Zenshū*, *II*, pp. 69–71.
—— 'Kinenbi' ['Days of Remembrance', signed 'Ōitako', first published in *Ōsaka Chōhō*, no. 22, 26 July 1902], in *Zenshū*, *I*, pp. 80–2.
—— 'Kōgyō Kannai no Kigū' ('Chance Meeting in the Industrial Pavilion', signed 'Sugako', first published in *Ōsaka Chōhō*, no. 162, 8 March 1903], in *Zenshū*, *I*, pp. 267–9.
—— 'Komatsumiya-denka no Goitoku' ['To the Memory of His Imperial Highness, Komatsumiya', signed 'Yūzuki-joshi', first published in *Ōsaka Chōhō*, no. 160, 6 March 1903], in *Zenshū*, *I*, pp. 263–6.
—— 'Misohitomoji no Ongakkai Kenmonki' ['Impressions of the Misohitomoji Concert', signed 'Yūzukijo', first published in *Murō Shinpō*, no. 577, 6 April 1906], in *Zenshū*, *II*, pp. 105–6.
—— 'Omokage' ['Memories', signed 'Sugako', first published in seven parts in *Ōsaka Chōhō*, nos. 23–40, 31 July–9 September 1902], in *Zenshū*, *II*, pp. 292–303.
—— 'Onna toshite no Kibō' ['My Desires as a Woman', signed 'Yūzukijo', first published in *Murō Shinpō*, no. 588, 9 May 1906], in *Zenshū*, *II*, pp. 143–5.
—— *Personal Letters to*:
    Furukawa Rikisaku (18 April 1910), in *Zenshū*, *III*, pp. 156–7.

Kōtoku Shūsui (12 May 1910), in *Zenshū, III*, pp. 160–1.
Kōtoku Shūsui (16 May 1910), in *Zenshū, III*, p. 162.
—— *Postcards to:*
Baibunsha (23 January 1911), in *Zenshū, III*, p. 188.
Imamura Rikisaburō (13 January 1911), in *Zenshū, III*, p. 179.
Kōtoku Shūsui (11 May 1910), in *Zenshū, III*, p. 159.
Sakai Tameko (21 January 1911), in *Zenshū, III*, p. 184.
Sakai Toshihiko (21 January 1911), in *Zenshū, III*, p. 185.
Yoshikawa Morikuni (21 January 1911), in *Zenshū, III*, p. 182.
—— *Preliminary Interrogation Records:*
[not numbered] (3 June 1910), in *Zenshū, III*, pp. 205–17.
no. 2 (5 June 1910), in *Zenshū, III*, pp. 221–33.
no. 6 (13 June 1910), in *Zenshū, III*, pp. 246–50.
no. 13 (17 October 1910), in *Zenshū, III*, pp. 276–91.
—— 'Risō no Fujin' ['The Ideal Woman', signed 'Kanno Sugako', first published in *Kan'i Seikatsu*, no. 3, 1 January 1907], in *Zenshū, II*, pp. 175–8.
—— 'Ritchi' [signed 'Sugako', first published in *Michi no Tomo*, May Issue, 1903], in *Zenshū, III*, pp. 5–15.
—— 'Rōjōki' ['Record of a Siege', signed 'Yūzukijo', first published in *Murō Shinpō*, no. 584, 27 April 1906], in *Zenshū, II*, pp. 132–8.
—— *Sealed Cards to:*
Ishikawa Sanshirō (14 January 1911), in *Zenshū, III*, p. 180.
Ōsugi Sakae and Yasuko (21 January 1911), in *Zenshū, III*, pp. 185–6.
Sakai Toshihiko (24 January 1911), in *Zenshū, III*, pp. 190–1.
Sakai Toshihiko and Tameko (4 January 1911), in *Zenshū, III*, pp. 175–6.
Tanikawa Takeo (21 January 1911), in *Zenshū, III*, pp. 182–3.
Yoshikawa Morikuni (24 January 1911), in *Zenshū, III*, p. 189.
—— 'Sensō to Fujin' ['The War and Women', signed 'Yūzuki-joshi', first published in *Michi no Tomo*, April 1904], in *Zenshū, II*, pp. 5–8.
—— 'Shide no Michikusa' ['A Pause on the Way to Death' signed 'Sugako' – Prison Diary, 18-24 January 1911], in *Zenshū, II*, pp. 245–72.
—— 'Shokutaku Kien no Hana' ['Heated Discussion at the Dining Table', signed 'Yūjo', first published in *Mainichi Denpō*, no. 1328, 12 July 1907], in *Zenshū, II*, pp. 203–4.
—— 'Shūgyōfu no Butō Kinshi no Undō' ['The Movement to Prohibit the Dancing of Prostitutes', signed 'Yūzuki-joshi', first published in *Ōsaka Chōhō*, no. 186, 8 April 1903], in *Zenshū, I*, pp. 376–81.
—— 'Sokumenkan ni Tsuite' ['On "A Perspective"', signed 'Yūzukijo', first published in *Murō Shinpō*, no. 589, 12 May 1906], in *Zenshū, II*, pp. 145–7.
—— 'Sugamo no Ichi Yoru' ['An Evening at Sugamo', signed 'Yūzukijo', first published in two parts in *Mainichi Denpō*, nos. 1457 and 1463, 18 and 24 November 1907], in *Zenshū, II*, pp. 207–13.
—— 'Tenjōkai' ['The Celestial World', signed 'Yūzuki-joshi', first published in *Michi no Tomo*, December 1904–January 1905], in *Zenshū, II*, pp. 19–29.
—— 'Toraware no Ki' ['Account of an Imprisonment', signed 'Yūzukijo', first published in *Jiyū Shisō*, no. 2, 10 June 1909], in *Zenshū, II*, pp. 238–41.
—— 'Toshi no Hajime ni' ['At the Beginning of the Year', signed 'Yūzukijo', first published in *Murō Shinpō*, no. 664, 1 January 1907], in *Zenshū, II*, pp. 173–4.

—— 'Tsuyuko' [signed 'Yūzuki', first published serially in twenty-four parts in *Murō Shinpō*, nos. 529–75, 6 November 1905–30 March 1906], in *Zenshū, III*, pp. 83–128.

—— 'Waga Ningyō' ['My Doll', signed 'Kanno Yūzukijo', first published in *Yomiuri Shinbun*, 9 September 1906], in *Zenshū, II*, pp. 165–7.

—— 'Waga Tera' ['Our Temple', signed 'Yūzukijo', first published in *Mainichi Denpō*, no. 1618, April 1908], in *Zenshū, II*, pp. 227–9.

—— 'Yajima-tōji to Yanaka Mura' ['Madam Yajima and Yanaka Village', unsigned, first published in *Mainichi Denpō*, no. 1329, 13 July 1907], in *Zenshū, II*, pp. 205–6.

—— 'Yonin no Hahaue' ['My Four Mothers', signed 'Yūzukijo', first published in *Murō Shinpō*, no. 576, 3 April 1906], in *Zenshū, II*, pp. 100–2.

—— 'Zekkō' ['Severed Relations', signed 'Sugako', first published in *Kirisutokyō Sekai*, no. 1050, 8 October 1903], in *Zenshū, III*, pp. 45–50.

Kim Il Song, *Pak Yeol*, Tokyo, Gōdō Shuppan, 1974.

Komatsu Ryūji, 'Hangyaku no Josei, Kaneko Fumiko: "Pak Yeol Jiken" Hashigaki' ['Treasonous Woman, Kaneko Fumiko: Postscript to the "Pak Yeol Incident"'], *Jiyū Shisō*, vol. 6 (July 1961), pp. 37–44.

Kondō Kenji, *Ichi Museifushugisha no Kaisō* [*Recollections of an Anarchist*], Tokyo, Heibonsha, 1965.

Kondō Tomie, 'Kanno Suga', in Setouchi, Harumi (ed.), *Jinbutsu Kindai Joseishi, Onna no Isshō, 6, Hangyaku no Onna no Roman* [*Figures in Modern Women's History, The Lives of Women, Volume 6: The Romances of Rebellious Women*], Tokyo, Kōdansha, 1981, pp. 21–56.

Kōtoku Shūsui Zenshū Henshū Iinkai (eds), *Taigyaku Jiken Arubamu: Kōtoku Shūsui to sono Shūhen* [*Album of the High Treason Incident: Kōtoku Shūsui and his Environment*], Tokyo, Meiji Bunken, 1972.

Kurihara Kazuo, 'Hangyakusha Den: Kaneko Fumiko' ['Biography of a Rebel: Kaneko Fumiko', first published in *Jiyū Rengō Shinbun*, no. 39, 1 September 1929], reproduced in *Akai Tsutsuji no Hana* [listed under Kaneko Fumiko], pp. 58–60.

Matsuda Michio (ed.), *Gendai Nihon Shisō Taikei, 16: Anakizumu* [*An Outline of Modern Japanese Thought, Volume 16: Anarchism*], Tokyo, Chikuma Shobō, 1963.

Mochizuki Kei, 'Kaneko Fumiko-san no Shōzō ni tsuite' ['About this Portrait of Kaneko Fumiko'], in *Akai Tsutsuji no Hana* [listed under Kaneko Fumiko], 16 June 1972, unnumbered pages.

Morikawa Tetsurō, *Ansatsu Hyakunenshi* [*History of a Century of Assassinations*], Tokyo, Tosho Shuppansha, 1973.

Morinaga Eisaburō, 'Himerareta Saiban: Pak Yeol, Kaneko Fumiko Jiken, 1–2' ['The Closed Trial: Pak Yeol, Kaneko Fumiko Incident, Parts One and Two'], *Hōritsu Jihō*, vol. 35, nos. 3-4 (March and April 1963), pp. 57–63, 60–7.

Mukuge no Kai (eds), *Chōsen 1930 Nendai Kenkyū* [*Research on Korea in the 1930s*], Tokyo, San'ichi Shobō, 1982.

Nakamura Fumio, *Taigyaku Jiken to Chishikijin* [*Intellectuals and the High Treason Incident*], Tokyo, San'ichi Shobō, 1981.

Ōsawa Masamichi, 'Ishikawa Sanshirō Ron' ['On Ishikawa Sanshirō'], in Tsurumi Shunsuke (ed.), *Ishikawa Sanshirō Shū* [*Works of Ishikawa Sanshirō*], Tokyo, Chikuma Shobō, 1976.

Ōsugi Sakae, *Ōsugi Sakae Zenshū, VI, Rōdō Undō Ronshū* [*Collected Works of Ōsugi Sakae, Volume 6: Discourse on the Labour Movement*] (Ōsawa Masamichi, ed.), Tokyo, Gendai Shichō, 1963.

Saiban Kiroku (also listed under Kaneko) –

—— *Futeisha Interrogation Records*:
    Chung Tae Sung, no. 3 (24 November 1923), pp. 336–42.
    Niiyama Hatsuyo (27 October 1923), pp. 300–1.
    Pak Yeol, no. 16 (2 May 1925), pp. 70–1.

—— [Kaneko] Kaiseigen Koseki [Revised Kaneko Family Register], Suwa, East Yamanashi, copies of documents in *Saiban Kiroku*, pp. 871–6.

—— Pak Yeol, 'Torishimari Hōan' ['Control Measures', first published in *Futei Senjin*, no. 1, November 1922], pp. 813–15.

—— *Tokyo Asahi Shinbun* (31 July 1926), p. 1 [excerpt: newspaper report of Kaneko Fumiko's death], p. 796.

—— *Witness Interrogation Records*:
    Furihata Kazushige (25 August 1925), pp. 250–1.
    Iwasaki Zenemon, no. 1 (20 August 1925), pp. 247–8.
    Kaneko Kie [Kikuno], no. 1 (11 August 1925), pp. 228–33.
    Kaneko Kie, no. 2 (12 August 1925), pp. 234–7.
    Kaneko Sehi (13 August 1925), pp. 238–40.
    Kubota Kametarō (18 August 1925), pp. 241–3.
    Saeki Fumikazu, no. 1 (10 August 1925), pp. 224–8.
    Saeki Fumikazu, no. 2 (19 August 1925), pp. 243–4.
    Saitō Otomatsu, no. 1 (19 August 1925), pp. 244–5.
    Suzuki Kanesaburō, no. 1 (19 August 1925), pp. 246–7.

Satō Bunmei, *Koseki ga Tsukuru Sabetsu* [*Discrimination Created by the Family Register*], Tokyo, Gendai Shokan, 1984.

Setouchi Harumi, 'Kaneko Fumiko', in Setouchi Harumi (ed.), *Jinbutsu Kindai Joseishi, Onna no Isshō, 6, Hangyaku no Onna no Roman* [*Figures in Modern Women's History, The Lives of Women, Volume 6: The Romances of Rebellious Women*], Tokyo, Kōdansha, 1981, pp. 141–80.

—— 'Kanno Sugako: Koi to Kakumei ni Junjita Meiji no Onna (Bijoden Daikyūwa)' ['Kanno Sugako: the Meiji Woman who Martyred Herself for Love and Revolution (Biographies of Beautiful Women, No. 9)'], *Chūō Kōron*, vol. 80, no. 9 (September 1965), pp. 291–301.

—— *Tōi Koe* [*Distant Voices*, biography of Kanno], Tokyo, Shinchō Bunko, 1975.

—— *Yohaku no Haru* [*Blank Spring*, biography of Kaneko], Tokyo, Chūkō Bunko, 1975.

Shimizu Unosuke, 'Kanno Sugako Shōden – Shōgai to Kōdō' ['A Short Biography of Kanno Sugako – Her Life and Activities'], in Shimizu Unosuke (ed.), *Kanno Sugako Zenshū, III*, Tokyo, Kōryūsha, 1984, pp. 295–325.

Shiota Shōbei (ed.), *Kōtoku Shūsui no Nikki to Shokan* [*The Diary and Letters of Kōtoku Shūsui*], Tokyo, Miraisha, 1965.

Shiota Shōbei and Watanabe Junzō (eds), *Hiroku Taigyaku Jiken* [*The High Treason Incident, Confidential Documents*], 2 Volumes, Tokyo, Shunjūsha, 1959 –

—— *Preliminary Interrogation Records*:
    Kōtoku Shūsui, no. 6 (6 July 1910), vol. 2, pp. 18–20.
    Kōtoku Shūsui, no. 11 (25 July 1910), vol. 2, pp. 25–8.

Kōtoku Shūsui, no. 13 (17 October 1910), vol. 2, pp. 29–42.

Shisō no Kagaku Kenkyūkai (eds), *Tenkō, 1* [*Ideological Conversion, Volume 1*], Tokyo, Heibonsha, 1978.

Suzuki Yūko (ed.), *Shisō no Umi e (Kaihō to Kakumei), 21, Josei – Hangyaku to Kakumei to Teikō to* [*Into the Sea of Ideas (Liberation and Revolution), Volume 21, Women – Rebellion, Revolution and Resistance*], Tokyo, Shakai Hyōronsha, 1990.

Takeuchi Seiichi, *Jiko Chōetsu no Shisō: Kindai Nihon no Nihirizumu* [*The Idea of Self-Transcendence: Modern Japan's Nihilism*], Tokyo, Perikansha, 1988.

Tsurumi Shunsuke (ed.), *Ishikawa Sanshirō Shū* [*Works of Ishikawa Sanshirō*], Tokyo, Chikuma Shobō, 1976.

—— 'Kaisetsu' ['Afterword'], in Kaneko Fumiko, *Nani ga Watashi o Kōsaseta ka* [*What Made Me Like This?*], Tokyo, Chikuma Shobō, 1984, pp. 207–14.

Index